The Game I'll Never Forget

100 HOCKEY STARS' STORIES

as told to the editors of *Hockey Digest*

**SELECTED BY
CHRIS McDONELL**

FIREFLY BOOKS

A FIREFLY BOOK

Published by Firefly Books Ltd., 2002

Players' stories previously published in the *Hockey Digest*, 1972–2001.

First Printing

National Library of Canada Cataloguing in Publication Data

Main entry under title:
    The game I'll never forget : 100 hockey stars' stories / selected by Chris McDonell.
Includes index.
Stories originally published in the Hockey digest.
ISBN 1-55297-604-1
    1. Hockey players—Anecdotes. 2. National Hockey League—Anecdotes. I. McDonell, Chris
GV848.5.A1G54 2002   796.962'092'2   C2002-901743-2

Publisher Cataloging-in-Publication Data (U.S.)

The game I'll never forget : 100 hockey stars' stories / selected by Chris McDonell.—1st ed.
[224] p. : ill., col. photos. ; cm.
Includes index.
Summary: The stories originally published by The *Hockey Digest* magazine, re-formatted and supplemented with additional statistics, photographs and career highlights.
ISBN 1-55294-604-1 (pbk.)
1. Hockey players—Biography. 2. Hockey players. I. McDonell, Chris. II. Title.
796-962/092/2 B 21   CIP   GV848.5.A1M33 2002

Published in Canada in 2002 by
Firefly Books Ltd.
3680 Victoria Park Avenue
Toronto, Ontario M2H 3K1

Published in the United States in 2002 by
Firefly Books (U.S.) Inc.
P.O. Box 1338, Ellicott Station
Buffalo, New York 14205

The publisher acknowledges the financial support of the Government of Canada through the Book Publishing Industry Development Program for its publishing activities.

Photo Credits

Bruce Bennett Studios
BBS archive photos: 5 (top), 9, 23, 27, 29, 51, 73, 93, 95, 115, 127, 133, 147, 161, 173, 179, 221
Bruce Bennett: front cover, back cover (top), 4, 5 (middle), 11, 21, 31, 33, 37, 43, 47, 55, 59, 61, 67, 69, 71, 75, 77, 85, 91, 101, 111, 117, 118, 119, 125, 131, 135, 139, 143, 145, 149, 153, 159, 163, 165, 169, 171, 183, 185, 187, 189, 191, 193, 197, 199, 203, 207, 209, 211
Melchior DiGiacomo: back cover (bottom), 41, 109, 121, 123, 137, 167, 195, 205, 219
John Giamundo: 13, 176
Robert Laberge: 97
S. Levy: 79
Jim McIsaac: 39
Jo Anne Kalish: 181
UPI telephoto: 107
Brian Winkler: 141

Getty Images (Allsport)
Brian Bahr: 212
Elsa Hasch: 35, 62
Robert Laberge: 5 (bottom), 213

Hockey Hall of Fame
87, 89, 103, 201
Graphic Artists/Hockey Hall of Fame: 17, 19, 57, 99, 157
Imperial Oil-Turofsky/Hockey Hall of Fame: 45, 49, 65, 81, 83, 105, 129, 217
Fred Keenan/Hockey Hall of Fame: 151
Doug MacLellan/Hockey Hall of Fame: 31
Peter Mecca/Hockey Hall of Fame: 25
Frank Prazak/Hockey Hall of Fame: 15, 53, 113, 215

The Toronto Star
Jeff Goode: 7

Cover design by Christine Gilham
Interior design by Christine Gilham and Bob Wilcox

Printed and bound in Canada by Friesen's, Altona, Manitoba

To Sue, Quinn, Tara and Isaac,
who are my greatest loves and support.

TABLE OF CONTENTS

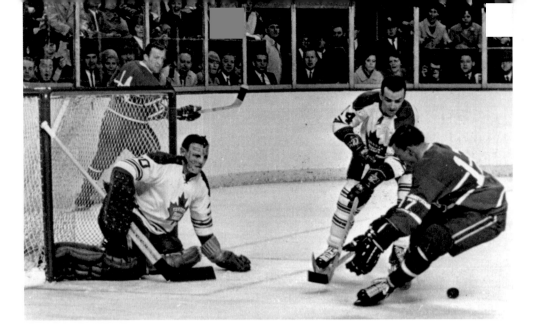

I was hoarse and exhausted but thoroughly exhilarated. Canada had just defeated our archenemy, the Soviet Union, 3–1, in the

round robin preliminaries of the first Canada Cup tournament. My 15-year-old sister Anne, one year my junior, took turns with me waving our big Canadian flag, tied to the end of a hockey stick, as we hung out of our mezzanine seats in Maple Leaf Gardens. The tears welled up in my eyes as my hero Bobby Orr skated out to center ice to accept the award as the game's most valuable player. The crowd in the Gardens (the same folks that had routinely booed Orr whenever he handled the puck as a visiting Boston Bruin) gave the star defenseman his fourth or fifth prolonged standing ovation of the night.

All of the ingredients—the patriotic fervor in the air, the assemblage of, arguably, Canada's most stellar international line-up, Orr's dominance and the end of his career shortly after the tournament ended—enhanced my memories of the night of September 11, 1976. The event has become indelible in my mind rather than receding into the past. It's the game I'll never forget.

Every fan will have similar recollections, but with other players in the spotlight, other teams winning, with the ambience of other eras imbuing their memories with different feelings. But imagine, if you can, what it would mean to actually *play* in such a game. Would the memory be sharper, more personal, more significant? I believe the answer is "Yes," and that the stories in this book support me.

In their own words, these are the accounts of the games that the hockey legends themselves love to recall. *Hockey Digest* started compiling these recollections in the fall of 1972, when Bobby Hull recounted the pressure-filled days leading up to his record-setting 51st goal in 1966. Since then, almost 200 former and current NHL stars and coaches have regaled readers with "The Game I'll Never Forget." Choosing the stories to include in this book sounded like an easy task until it came time to pare the list down to a manageable length. The more significant the game, the greater was its chance for inclusion. And the more important the player is or was to his team and the more esteemed his hockey career has been, the higher priority I gave his blow-by-blow report. Still, there were too many great players with wonderful anecdotes!

Although each man brought his unique perspective to the tale, I decided not to include duplicate accounts of the same game. In the end, I argued successfully for including 100 tales, with a handful from remarkable coaches such as Toe Blake, Punch Imlach and Billy Reay. The mix of stories, as you will discover, includes a wide variety of events and eras. The Stanley Cup playoffs are a perennial source of inspiration, and there are dozens of such stories here, going all the way back to legendary goaltender Tiny Thompson's look at the 1933 Cup finals. While the Cold War contributed to the magnitude of Canada's victory in the 1972 Summit Series and the USA's 1980 Olympic "Miracle on Ice"—mythical events you'll read about here—you will see that international competition still continues to create an intensity that makes for powerful feelings, exciting hockey and vivid memories.

For many players, nothing has duplicated the pride associated with personal milestones, such as a first NHL game. Of course, meaningful goals also abound in these narratives, from finding the back of an NHL net for the first time to potting an important hat trick, a 50th goal of the season or a 500th career goal. The sweet recollections of tallying a multi-goal game, a Stanley Cup–winner or a league record-breaker are also here. Along the way, almost every era of the NHL is touched upon, providing brilliantly colorful snapshots of hockey history. The statistical summary for each game is also provided, adding detail to flesh out the picture. In addition to the words and numbers, great photography augments each story. While choosing the images to accompany the text, I saw more photos that I felt compelled to include. You'll find them interspersed throughout the book.

Some of the games recounted will be familiar to many fans, while some will be unheard or told in a fresh way that makes them new. I'm certain that *The Game I'll Never Forget* will create new memories for every reader. Enjoy.

—*Chris McDonell*

More than 30 years in hockey make it almost impossible for me to single out any game as standing alone in my memory, or

**APRIL 23, 1950
OLYMPIA STADIUM, DETROIT
DETROIT 4, NEW YORK RANGERS 3 (2OT)**

FIRST PERIOD
1. NYR Stanley (Leswick) 11:14 (PP).
2. NYR Leswick (O'Connor, LaPrade) 12:18 (PP).
Penalties: DET Pavelich (holding) 6:12; DET Lindsay (roughing), 8:18; DET Lindsay (slashing) 8:18; NYR LaPrade (roughing) 8:18; DET Pavelich (slashing) 11:27; NYR O'Connor (tripping) 12:42; NYR Slowinski (tripping) 19:14.

SECOND PERIOD
3. DET Babando (Kelly, Couture) 5:09 (PP).
4. DET Abel (Dewsbury) 5:30 (PP).
5. NYR O'Connor (Mickoski) 11:42.
6. McFadden (Peters) 15:57.
Penalty: NYR Stanley (interference) 3:56.

THIRD PERIOD
No scoring.
Penalties: NYR Kyle (hooking), 0:24; DET Dewsbury (holding) 1:33.

FIRST OVERTIME PERIOD
No scoring.
No penalties.

SECOND OVERTIME PERIOD
7. DET Babando (Gee) 8:31.
No penalties.

Goalies: NYR Rayner; DET Lumley
Referee: Bill Chadwick
Linesmen: Hugh McLean, George Hayes

even to recall the details of some of the bigger ones. Still, I guess I could say that among the many memorable games I played with the Detroit Red Wings, the seventh game of the 1950 Stanley Cup finals was one of the highlights. You could certainly call it a game I'll never forget, although you probably could classify at least a half dozen others, if not more, with it. But that game against the New York Rangers belongs right up there not just because of the way it went but the circumstances surrounding it.

We had a powerful, well-balanced team at Detroit in 1949. We had been coming on for several seasons after falling off during World War II, although we hadn't won the Stanley Cup since 1943. We finished first in 1949, and were to do so for the next six seasons, quite a record in a league containing such powerful teams as the Montreal Canadiens and Toronto Maple Leafs. But in 1949 we couldn't win the Cup, losing to Toronto four straight in the finals.

The next year, 1949–50, we got another shot at the Cup and this time we weren't going to miss. We'd finished first again under coach Tommy Ivan and had some fine players. All I have to do is mention the names Gordie Howe, George Gee, Marcel Pronovost and Ted Lindsay. Harry Lumley was our goalie. Our first round opponent was Toronto, which had won three straight Stanley Cups. We'd lost 11 games in a row to them in the playoffs.

For a couple of days, it didn't look as if this time it would be different. They beat us 5–0 in the opening game, but what was even more serious was that Howe was severely injured. Howe collided with Ted Kennedy of the Leafs in the third period and suffered a fractured nose and skull. Surgery was required to save his life. So we were without Howe, our top goal scorer, the rest of the way.

Ivan put Doc Couture in at right wing with Ted Lindsay and me and he did a fine job. We came back to win the second game against the Leafs and then took them all the way to the seventh game. We beat them in that one 1–0 on an overtime goal by Leo Reise to go into the finals against the Rangers, who had beaten the Canadiens in five games.

We beat the Rangers 4–1 the first game of the finals on our ice. Then the series shifted to Toronto, which was "home ice" for the Rangers because Madison Square Garden in New York was occupied by a circus. We split the two games there, then the Rangers beat us the fourth game in Detroit. The fifth game was in Detroit again and we tied the Rangers 1–1 with less than two minutes left, on a goal by Lindsay. But they beat us in a couple of minutes of overtime on a goal by Bones Raleigh to take a 3–2 lead in the series.

It looked like the Rangers had the edge, two games to play and needing only one win, but we beat them the sixth game. I was fortunate enough to get the winning goal midway in the third period. I found myself in front of Chuck Rayner, the Ranger goalie, and got off a wrist shot. Somehow he stopped it and I was knocked to my knees at the same moment the puck hit him. But the rebound came back to me and I was able to get the stick on it and put the puck past him.

So the series was even, 3–3, and it all came down to the seventh game, the one I'll never forget, April 23, 1950, at the Olympia. The Rangers got off to a good start, scoring twice before we were able to get one in the net. And they still had a 3–2 lead in the middle period. We were working hard, and kept pressing them. Finally, we got a break. Jim McFadden beat Allan Stanley, the Ranger defenseman, to the puck in the Ranger zone near the boards and got off a wide angle shot that skipped past Rayner to tie the game 3–3. The score stayed that way to the end of regulation time. Now it was "sudden death" in overtime but it took a lot longer in coming than most people expected.

We had by far the better chances. We were carrying the attack to the Rangers in the first overtime but either couldn't get the puck past Rayner or couldn't put it on net. Our best chance might have come when Nick

We'd lost 11 games in a row to Toronto in the playoffs...it didn't look as if this time would be different.

Mickoski pulled Rayner out of the net with a fine deke but then hit the post and the puck went the wrong way.

We went eight minutes into the second overtime before the break came. Ivan sent out Gee to take a face-off against Buddy O'Connor, to the left of the Ranger net. The other forwards out there with Gee were Pete Babando and Couture. Gee told Babando to move directly behind him. He'd try to get the puck to him.

That's the way it happened. Gee beat O'Connor to the draw and whipped the puck back to Babando. Rayner, of course, had moved over to the near corner of the net at the face-off. He was still there when Babando got the shot off, but he couldn't see it because Stanley was blocking his view. It went for the far side.

At the last split second, Rayner kicked out his left pad, but the puck went over it into the far corner of the net. Babando's goal had won the Stanley Cup, but you had to admire the way the Rangers had fought us. I remember walking into their dressing room later and saying, "Don't you guys know when to quit?"

—*As told to George Vass*

Winner of the Hart Trophy (1949) and Hall of Fame member **Sid "Boot Nose" Abel** was a four-time NHL All-Star. He centered Detroit's "Production Line" between Gordie Howe and Ted Lindsay for six seasons, captaining the Wings to Stanley Cup victories in 1950 and 1952. He coached Chicago before returning to Detroit, where he served as coach and general manager.

DAVE ANDREYCHUK

If I had to pick just one game that sticks out in my mind from my NHL career, it would have to be the night we were

FEBRUARY 6, 1986
BOSTON GARDEN, BOSTON
BUFFALO 8, BOSTON 6

FIRST PERIOD
1. BUF Foligno (Smith) 0:37.
2. BUF Andreychuk (Ramsey) 7:37.
3. BUF Andreychuk (Housley, Cyr) 14:30.
4. BOS Burridge (Middleton, Pederson) 15:14 (SH).
5. BOS Pederson (Burridge) 16:54 (PP).
Penalties: BUF Dykstra (holding) 4:35; BOS Campbell (tripping) 10:27; BUF Tucker (hooking) 11:27; BOS Simmer (roughing) 13:07; BUF Ruff (roughing) 13:07; BOS Crowder (slashing) 13:37; BUF Smith (roughing) 16:01; BUF Seiling (delay of game) 19:08.

SECOND PERIOD
6. BUF Andreychuk (Cyr, Housley) 4:40 (PP).
7. BOS Simmer (Crowder, Linseman) 6:11.
8. BUF Andreychuk (Tucker) 7:54.
9. BOS Pederson (Burridge) 10:57.
10. BUF Lacombe (Tucker, Andreychuk) 13:38 (PP).
11. BUF Andreychuk (Lacombe, Tucker) 17:15.
Penalties: BOS Campbell (high-sticking/fighting) 3:55; BUF Hamel (fighting) 3:55; BOS Sleigher (high-sticking) 10:22; BUF Dykstra (high-sticking) 10:22; BOS Thelven (holding) 12:46; BUF Hajt (holding) 14:19.

THIRD PERIOD
12. BOS O'Connell (Pederson) 2:03.
13. BOS Middleton (Bourque, Pederson) 14:45.
14. BUF Cyr (Foligno, Hamel) 15:55.
Penalties: BUF Lacombe (holding) 2:35; BUF Perreault (tripping) 6:11.

SHOTS ON GOAL:

BUF	7	10	4	**21**
BOS	14	18	14	**46**

Goalies: BOS Keans, Riggin; BUF Barrasso
Referee: Bryan Lewis
Linesmen: Bob Hodges, Randy Mitton

playing in Boston and I wound up scoring five goals. We ended up beating the Bruins 8–6 that night. The game was played in February of 1986, and since it did happen a while ago, I don't exactly remember everything that went on that night. I do remember I only had seven shots on goal that game, but it seemed everything I touched went in. I wish nights like that came a bit more often for me.

Although it wasn't a playoff game, it was important for us because it was a divisional game. And because of the rivalry between the Sabres and the Bruins we always seem to get up for them no matter where we we're playing. I can't go into any exact details of how I scored all my goals, but I do remember I scored all of them in the first two periods. I also remember I didn't get off to a great start that game; I had a breakaway on my first shot, but I didn't score. I did score two goals in the first period though, and then I added three more in the second.

A couple of my goals were scored on the power play. I was near the front of the net and was just banging away and they eventually went in. At the time, I was on the Sabres' fourth line, and my linemates that night were John Tucker and Norm Lacombe. Because we were mostly a checking line, we weren't really playing that much in that game. We were just getting spotted and seeing a little bit of action on the power play.

Even though I was playing on the fourth line, overall I was having a decent season, and I scored 36 goals that year. As for the big game, my line really didn't do anything differently that night. It just happened that I was in the right place at the right time, and I ended up scoring five goals.

The last time I got five goals in one game was back in junior when I was playing for the Oshawa Generals. I really like playing in Boston, though. They have the same type of rink as ours—small and about the same size as ours in Buffalo. We go in there a lot every year, and because of that we almost feel like we're playing at home. And Boston's fans are always into the game, so that gets you into the game fairly quickly. Players like it when fans are into a game and are yelling, even if they're cheering for the other team.

On the ice, nobody was really trying to do anything special to get me the puck that night, but most of the guys on our bench were telling me just to keep shooting and they'll keep going in. After the game, we went out and celebrated as a team. It was pretty rare for us to go out in Boston because we usually don't end up staying overnight, but we did spend the night there on this trip.

To tell you the truth, I don't really think about that game much these days. You just have to put something like that behind you because every night is a different game, but Channel 7 from Buffalo did end up sending me a video of all the goals I scored that night. It's got to be pretty dusty, though, because I haven't pulled it out for a while.

I don't really talk about that game much, and there aren't too many guys left with our team now that were with the club back then,

but once in a while when we're playing in Boston it's brought up. Some guy in our dressing room will tell everybody that I once scored five goals in this rink and then tell me I should try to do it again that night. Because I did score five goals and we won, I'll always remember that game. And if I'm lucky, it will happen again sometime.

—As told to Sam Laskaris

Traded by Buffalo to Toronto in February 1993, **Dave Andreychuk** also played for New Jersey, Boston and Colorado before returning to Buffalo as a free agent in the summer of 2000. Although never a fleet skater, Andreychuk is tough to move in front of the net and has a deft touch around the net. He scored his 500th career NHL goal on March 15, 1997 while with the Devils.

DAVE BABYCH

GAME 5, 1994
STANLEY CUP FINALS

Game 5 of the 1994 Stanley Cup finals was about as strange as it gets. We were trailing 3–1 in the series, and

APRIL 23, 1994
MADISON SQUARE GARDEN, NEW YORK
VANCOUVER 6, NEW YORK RANGERS 3

FIRST PERIOD
No scoring.
Penalties: VAN Hunter (elbowing) 0:49; VAN Momesso (slashing, fighting) 10:06; VAN Ronning (roughing) 10:06; NYR Beukeboom (instigation, fighting, game misconduct) 10:06; NYR Wells (high-sticking) 10:06; NYR Matteau (roughing) 10:06; VAN Hunter (roughing) 13:20; NYR Wells (roughing) 13:20; VAN Ronning (holding) 17:20; NYR Larmer (holding) 17:20; NYR Nemchinov (elbowing) 19:32.

SECOND PERIOD
1. VAN Brown (Ronning, Antoski) 8:10.
Penalties: VAN Courtnall (elbowing) 10:13; NYR Messier (hooking) 18:19.

THIRD PERIOD
2. VAN Courtnall (LaFayette, Hedican) 0:26.
3. VAN Bure (Craven) 2:48.
4. NYR Lidster (Kovalev) 3:27.
5. NYR Larmer (Matteau, Nemchinov) 6:20.
6. NYR Messier (Anderson, Graves) 9:02.
7. VAN Babych (Bure) 9:31.
8. VAN Courtnall (LaFayette, Lumme) 12:20.
9. VAN Bure (Ronning, Hedican) 13:04.
Penalty: NYR Kocur (slashing) 18:41.

SHOTS ON GOAL:

VAN	12	8	17	**37**
NYR	10	13	15	**38**

Goalies: VAN McLean; NYR Richter
Referee: Andy Van Hellemond
Linesmen: Randy Mitton, Ray Scapinello

in Game 5 we went from a seemingly insurmountable three-goal lead to a tie score within just a few minutes. We were playing the New York Rangers, and Madison Square Garden became a deafening zoo when they tied the score. They were only one goal away from winning the Stanley Cup and had all the momentum. But then I scored the goal to send us ahead and quiet the crowd. That was something I'll never forget.

Just getting to the finals was an accomplishment. We were down 3–1 to the Calgary Flames in the first round series, but we came back to win. We captured each of the last three games in overtime, with Pavel Bure providing the heroics by scoring the winning goal in double overtime of the seventh and final game.

After winning two more series, we found ourselves in the finals. We won the first game in overtime on a goal by Greg Adams, but the Rangers came back to take the next three. What's worse, they won Games 3 and 4 at our place.

Going back, we sensed that New York was ready for a big celebration; the Rangers wanted to win the Stanley Cup. We were in top form that night, going out to a 3–0 lead. Up to that point, we were probably playing our best game of the series. We had to—our backs were against the wall.

Then, in the third period, the Rangers came back. They scored one goal and then another. Mark Messier followed by notching the game-tying goal. He was coming down the right wing; he took a wrist shot sort of back against the grain; and it deflected off my leg or the top of my skate or something and went past our goalie, Kirk McLean.

Usually, you're not aware of the crowd during a game; you only hear a muffled noise when you're on the ice. But when you blow a 3–0 lead, everything comes back. It became obvious to the Rangers fans that their team was gaining the momentum. That was probably the loudest crowd I've ever heard.

Chicago Stadium got really loud, and there will probably never be another place like it, but Madison Square Garden was rocking. It was like a zoo in there. I guess they thought they were on their way to winning the Stanley Cup.

With the game tied 3–3, it might have seemed easy to just let ourselves fold. But this was the playoffs, and our adrenaline was pumping at 100 mph. As soon as one guy would hang his head or feel sorry for himself, there was positive talk on the bench.

On the next shift, Pavel got the puck and was dangling with it like he always does. During an average game, you have to be really calculating when you want to take a chance as a defenseman. But it's the defense's job to follow up on a rush—maybe not down to the goal line, however. But that's what

Reading the play and waiting for the pass, my eyes got huge; I could see the whole thing developing.

happened. Pavel carried the puck down the right side. He stopped up, saw me coming in wide open, and passed it to me. Reading the play and waiting for the pass, my eyes got huge; I could see the whole thing developing.

Their goalie, Mike Richter, was caught out of position. I went for the short side. He couldn't get across quickly enough, and my shot flew into the net. The thing I'll always remember is how quiet it got in the building. The silence was almost eerie.

We scored two more times and won the game. The victory gave us some life, and we went back to Vancouver and took Game 6. Then we dropped Game 7 in a real battle.

I've had some other memorable games. In 1986, I was traded to the Hartford Whalers from the Winnipeg Jets, and we barely made

the playoffs. Then we beat the Quebec Nordiques in the first round. In the second round, we took the Montreal Canadiens to Game 7. We were trailing 2–1 with about three minutes left when I took a slap shot from just inside the blue line that deflected off Patrick Roy's glove and went into the net. We were thinking that maybe it was our year to beat the Canadiens, but we eventually lost in overtime.

And then last year, I played in my 1,000th game. They really put on a big production. Before the game against Hartford, there was a ceremony and a highlight film. All I expected was a handshake and a "thanks for coming." But it was great. My whole family was there on the ice with me. It was really unexpected.

—*As told to Chuck O'Donnell*

Late in his memorable game, **Dave Babych** (44) puts the puck behind Ranger goalie Mike Richter. Babych, a former Winnipeg Jet and Hartford Whaler before joining Vancouver in the summer of 1991, was traded to Philadelphia in March 1998. He concluded his 19-year NHL career the following season as a Los Angeles King.

RALPH BACKSTROM

GAME 1, 1969
STANLEY CUP SEMIFINALS

During my 12 years with the Montreal Canadiens, I was on six Stanley Cup winners and I enjoyed each championship

APRIL 10, 1969
MONTREAL FORUM, MONTREAL
MONTREAL 3, BOSTON 2 (OT)

FIRST PERIOD
1. BOS Sanderson (Westfall, Shack) 13:28.
Penalties: BOS Westfall (tripping), 1:04; BOS Sather (fighting) 1:57; BOS Sanderson (fighting) 1:57; MON Cournoyer (fighting) 1:57; MON Duff (fighting) 1:57; MON Harris (elbowing) 6:47; BOS Orr (slashing) 6:47; MON Backstrom (interference) 10:54; MON Backstrom (hooking) 16:08; BOS Sanderson (kneeing) 18:17; MON Redmond (slashing) 18:46.

SECOND PERIOD
2. BOS Sanderson (Green) 15:53 (SH).
Penalties: BOS Sanderson (slashing) 13:18; Orr (tripping) 14:45; MON Savard (delay of game) 17:18.

THIRD PERIOD
3. MON Ferguson (Beliveau, Savard) 13:28 (PP).
4. MON Beliveau (Savard, Laperriere) 19:04.
Penalties: BOS Green (interference) 2:07; BOS D. Smith (tripping) 7:10; BOS Shack (elbowing) 13:11; MON Richard (high-sticking) 15:21.

FIRST OVERTIME PERIOD
5. MON Backstrom, (Savard) 0:42.
No penalties.

SHOTS ON GOAL:

MON	11	14	9	1	**35**
BOS	9	9	5	0	**23**

Goalies: MON Worsley; BOS Cheevers
Referee: Bruce Hood
Linesmen: Bob Myers, Pat Shetler

more than the one before. Every sip out of the Cup was sweeter than the last.

I've been playing professional hockey 19 years and I have just as much love for the game, just as much desire to play as I ever did. It never has become a chore for me to get out on the ice, just a means of making a living. I've always enjoyed it.

It has been a demanding game. When I was with the Canadiens, a lot was expected of us. Finishing first wasn't enough. The season was a disappointment unless we won the Cup. Anything short of that made it a long summer. No excuses were accepted.

I had some good years with the Canadiens. You know what a great team they were when I came up as a rookie in 1958–59. That season, we won the Cup for the fourth straight year and I was honored by being chosen rookie of the year in the NHL, getting the Calder Memorial Trophy. The next year we won our fifth straight Cup.

I didn't always get all the ice time I wanted, and sometimes it was a battle to keep my job. Two of the other centers were Jean Beliveau and Henri Richard and every year the Canadiens brought up some young kids who were hungry to stick. It was a situation that kept you on your toes.

There were many great moments during those dozen seasons but one in particular stands out for me. It came in the 1969 Stanley Cup semifinals against the Boston Bruins. By that time, the league had expanded from the Original Six teams to 12, and had split into two six-team divisions. All the "old teams" were still in one division, the East, and were clearly superior to the six newer teams in the West. We finished first in the East, but the Boston Bruins gave us a run for the title.

The Bruins were the "coming" team in the league. Phil Esposito and Bobby Orr were moving into their prime seasons and the Bruins played a rugged, rough game that was earning them quite a reputation. The season before, in 1967–68, we swept them in four

games during the semifinals but this time they figured to be much more confident and mature. The playoffs at the time were set up so that the quarter and semifinals were played among the teams in one division, with the winners of the East playing the champions of the West for the Cup in the finals. Because of that, the finals were considered anticlimactic, the East Division teams being so much stronger than those in the West. The real showdown was to come in the East Division semifinals.

We opened the playoffs against the New York Rangers and took four straight. The Bruins, meanwhile, handled Toronto similarly, and there was a lot of comment about the Bruins having intimidated the Maple Leafs. Some people predicted the Bruins would slow us down with their rough play. Even some of the Bruin players were overconfident. Orr and others were quoted as predicting they'd take us four straight. We didn't have much to say.

The semifinals opened in Montreal [April 10, 1969], and that's the game I'll never forget. Claude Ruel was coaching the Canadiens and he gave me my assignment, to check Esposito and stay on top of him all night. "Don't even worry about the puck," Ruel told me. "Just keep Esposito off the scoresheet. I don't care if you don't get a shot all night. Just don't let that big guy out of your reach."

I followed Esposito around all night. It was quite an assignment because he was strong and hard to move off the puck. He'd scored 49 goals during the regular season and he and Orr made a formidable combination. But I did my job and he didn't get much in the way of scoring chances. Meanwhile, though, the game wasn't going well for us. Derek Sanderson scored a goal for Boston late in the first period and another with about four minutes left in the second period. We were firing a lot of shots at goalie Gerry Cheevers, but nothing was getting past him. When I say "we" were getting shots, I don't include myself. I didn't shoot at all. My job was to keep Esposito from scoring and I concentrated on that.

Boston took a 2–0 lead past the midpoint of the third period and the situation was

looking bleak for us. The Bruins were concentrating on keeping the shutout for Cheevers and winning the opening game on Forum ice, which would have been a big lift for them. Even when John Ferguson finally scored our first goal with about seven minutes to play, it still looked like we were out of luck. And as the game went into the final minute, there was little chance we'd pull it out, trailing 2–1.

Coach Ruel pulled goalie Gump Worsley to put a sixth attacker on the ice. That maneuver results in a tying goal maybe one time in 10. This must have been the 10th time, because Beliveau slipped a shot in behind Cheevers at 19:04 to tie the game and send it into overtime.

I was on the ice when we opened the overtime period. I hadn't taken a shot all night, too busy shadowing Esposito to concern myself with offense. I can't remember exactly how I got the puck. I think Orr lost it at the Boston blue line. He backed up and I moved in on him. I shot from just inside the blue line as Orr went down to try to block it. The puck went into the net over Cheevers' right shoulder.

That goal won the game 3–2 at just 42 seconds of overtime. And it was the first shot I'd taken all night! There's a game I'll always remember. The goal got us off to a winning start in a good semifinal series, which we won in six games over Boston, three of the games going into overtime. Beating Boston in the semifinals really meant the Cup for us because the finals against St. Louis were anticlimactic as expected. We took the Blues four straight.

—As told to George Vass

Ralph Backstrom, the NHL's rookie of the year in 1958–59, won six Stanley Cup rings as a member of the Montreal Canadiens. He had his best offensive season in 1961–62, when he tallied 27 goals and 38 assists, despite playing a checking role. The Canadiens traded Backstrom to Los Angeles in January 1971. He joined Chicago late in the 1972–73 season for one last run at the Cup before jumping to the WHA. Backstrom retired in 1977.

ANDY BATHGATE

It was a match made in hockey heaven: The 1963–64 Toronto Maple Leafs wanted to shake up their roster for a late-season

APRIL 25, 1964
MAPLE LEAF GARDENS, TORONTO
TORONTO 4, DETROIT 0

FIRST PERIOD
1. TOR Bathgate (unassisted) 3:04.
Penalties: TOR Horton (holding the puck) 5:05; DET Joyal (holding) 6:34; TOR Harris (elbowing) 8:51; DET Gadsby (cross-checking) 8:51.

SECOND PERIOD
No scoring.
Penalties: TOR Harris (cross-checking) 4:00; DET MacMillan (tripping) 15:29.

THIRD PERIOD
2. TOR Keon (Harris) 4:26.
3. TOR Kelly (Stanley, Mahovlich) 5:53.
4. TOR Armstrong (Mahovlich) 15:26.
Penalties: DET Pronovost (interference) 11:41; TOR Horton (tripping) 15:36; TOR Brewer (charging) 18:44.

SHOTS ON GOAL:

TOR	13	10	14	**37**
DET	8	12	13	**33**

Goalies: TOR Bower; DET Sawchuk
Referee: John Ashley
Linesmen: Neil Armstrong, George Hayes

run at the Stanley Cup and I had been in the league for years and was still looking to win my first championship. I knew the second New York Rangers management told me I was on my way to Toronto that I had a great chance to finally win that big, silver chalice.

The Rangers had struggled for many of my years in New York, and even when we put together a good run, we always lacked that little something to put us over the hump. Now, I was joining a talented team that had won the past two Stanley Cups. If I allowed myself to really dream I could almost taste the champagne. But I was snapped back to reality by the knowledge that was a long, long road ahead.

When I joined the Maple Leafs in February, they were mired in a deep slump. They had trouble scoring and were dangerously close to falling behind the Rangers into fifth place—and out of playoff contention. The Leafs had even lost to the last-place Boston Bruins in mid-January, 11–0.

I pulled on that big white leaf, laced up my skates, and fit in right away with my new teammates. We finished the last few weeks of the season strong, losing just once in our final nine games. Finishing third, we faced the daunting task of having to play the first-place Montreal Canadiens in the opening round of the playoffs.

We beat the Habs in seven games, but it was a war. Not high-tech rockets and bombs, but hand-to-hand combat and trench warfare. Luckily, our best players responded to the pressure with some brilliant play. Big Frank Mahovlich had five points in our win in Game 4, and Johnny Bower made 38 saves and Dave Keon scored all three goals—one short-handed, one at even strength, and one into an empty net—in Game 7. While we were slugging it out with the great Canadiens, the fourth-place Detroit Red Wings were staging their own war against the Chicago Blackhawks. The Red Wings dangled on the edge of elimination, three

games to two, before riding Gordie Howe's milk-bottle shoulders to victories in Games 6 and 7.

That set up a classic matchup. This was Original Six hockey at its best: No helmets, no advertising all over the boards and ice, no aluminum sticks, no holds barred. The main bouts were Mahovlich versus Howe and Bower versus Terry Sawchuk. On the undercard, there was Keon vs. Alex Delvecchio and Red Kelly vs. Norm Ullman. We had Allan Stanley, Tim Horton, Carl Brewer and Bob Baun on defense. They had Marcel Pronovost, Bill Gadsby, Doug Barkley and Junior Langlois. The teams nodded at each other and came out battling.

Early in the series, the teams were mirror images of each other. In each of the first three games, the winning goal was scored in dramatic fashion. We took Game 1 on Bob Pulford's goal with two seconds remaining in the first overtime. Detroit rebounded, winning Game 2 at 7:52 of overtime on Larry Jeffrey's goal, and took control of the series when Delvecchio deflected Howe's shot past Bower for the tie-breaker with 17 seconds remaining in Game 3.

If there was a difference in the teams, I think the Red Wings seemed a little more fresh. The series was hanging in the balance as the teams headed into the third period of Game 4, but I scored and Mahovlich scored to give us a 4–2 victory and knot the series at 2–2.

Sawchuk didn't give us much in Game 5, stopping 33 shots as the Red Wings regained control of the series. We had a savior of our own in Game 6, Bob Baun, who in one of the greatest displays of heroism I've ever seen, scored in overtime to even the series. Here's the unbelievable part: After the finals were over, Baun went for X-rays and discovered he had been playing on an ankle that had been fractured by a slap shot earlier in the series. I'll never understand how he could have played in such pain.

Game 7 was everything I dreamed it would be: It was pressure-packed, it was fast-paced, it was intense, it was the game I'll never forget.

I was lucky enough to get the Leafs out to a fast start. I put us ahead 1–0, thanks to a fortunate bounce. The Red Wings were attacking when the puck went out to their point. Langlois tried to pinch in, keep the puck in, and keep the flurry going. But as he wound up, I tipped the puck by him and kept going. I came pouring in on Sawchuk. In those moments, I wasn't thinking about the significance of the game or whether someone was on my tail or even how my wife and kids were doing. With nothing but my next move in my mind, I cradled the puck and whipped it over Sawchuk's shoulder. Goal. 1–0 Leafs.

It stayed that way through the second period. As the tension mounted, we defended our goal with our sticks, legs, bodies—even crossed fingers. In the third period, we broke through again, and again, and again. Keon, Kelly and George Armstrong scored and we coasted home with a 4–0 victory.

Finally, I knew what it was like to win the Stanley Cup, to hold it skyward, cradle it like a baby and hug it like a loved one.

—*As told to Chuck O'Donnell*

Andy Bathgate, shown above scoring the Stanley Cup–winning goal for Toronto in 1964, had his most glorious seasons with the New York Rangers. He won the Hart Trophy in 1958–59 when he scored a career-best 40 goals and 88 points. Bobby Hull narrowly defeated him for the 1961–62 scoring crown with more goals, although they both had 84 points. Traded to Detroit in May 1965, Bathgate also played for Pittsburgh before retiring.

It is a very difficult task to select one game out of the many I played during 18 seasons in the National Hockey League, especially

APRIL 24, 1969
BOSTON GARDEN, BOSTON
MONTREAL 2, BOSTON 1 (2OT)

FIRST PERIOD
1. BOS Murphy (P. Esposito) 2:29.
Penalties: BOS Awrey (elbowing) 3:42; MON Savard (holding) 4:49; BOS D. Smith (elbowing) 5:21; BOS Shack (charging) 12:30; MON Ferguson (fighting) 12:49; BOS Awrey (fighting) 12:49.

SECOND PERIOD
No scoring.
Penalties: MON Savard (tripping) 3:54; MON Richard (charging) 8:11; BOS Sanderson (elbowing) 8:11; MON Ferguson (charging) 9:21; MON (bench, served by Grenier) 9:57.

THIRD PERIOD
2. MON Savard (Beliveau) 1:10 (PP).
Penalties: BOS Awrey (cross-checking) 1:05; BOS Hodge (tripping) 1:50; MON Harper (tripping) 13:42.

FIRST OVERTIME PERIOD
No scoring.
Penalty: MON Ferguson (holding) 10:19.

SECOND OVERTIME PERIOD
3. MON Beliveau (Provost) 11:28.
No penalties.

SHOTS ON GOAL:

MON	18	8	10	8	3	**47**
BOS	6	22	7	11	5	**51**

Goalies: MON Vachon; BOS Cheevers
Referee: Art Skov
Linesmen: Matt Pavelich, Neil Armstrong

because we won so many championships with the Montreal Canadiens. When I think for a while about it, there are three games that I remember even more than most of the big ones. And there were so many.

The first one was the second time I came up to the Canadiens from Quebec, in 1952. I had an amateur trial the year before and had scored my first NHL goal. But I did not sign with the Canadiens.

In December 1952, I again came to the Canadiens for a three-game trial from Quebec. A large group of fans from Quebec came to the Montreal Forum to be with me. The first game was against the New York Rangers. Charlie Rayner was the goalie for them that night. I scored three goals, my first hat trick in the NHL, and the fans from Quebec went wild. So that's one game I will not forget.

Another game was the one against Minnesota on February 11, 1971, in which I scored the 500th goal of my career. I went into that game with 497 goals and I scored No. 498, No. 499 and No. 500 all in one night. Sometimes you wait five games to score one goal when you are trying for a certain figure, but I got them all three in one game. You could pick either one of these as the game I'll never forget without going wrong, but there's another one that stands out just as much.

That game was in the Stanley Cup playoffs of 1969—the sixth game of the second round against the Boston Bruins on Thursday, April 24, 1969 in the Boston Garden. Boston had a very good team that year. Phil Esposito, Derek Sanderson, Johnny Bucyk and all the rest had played well. The Bruins finished just three points behind us in second place during the regular season. They went on to beat Toronto in four games in the first round and we beat the New York Rangers four straight, too. So everybody thought we were evenly matched teams in the semifinal.

I was injured during the last weeks of the regular season and missed six games. It was cartilage damage under the ribs and very painful. It was an unfortunate time to have an injury because I was not as sharp as I could have been going into the playoffs. Yet I was ready to play and the series against Boston went pretty much as expected through the first five games, each team taking advantage of the home ice. We won the first two games in Montreal, Boston won the next two on its ice, then we took the fifth game in the Forum.

The sixth game went back to Boston on April 24 and the Bruins were still very much in the series, having the advantage of their home ice in this one. A seventh game would not have surprised me. Anything could happen in that one.

Boston was very much "up" for this sixth game. They tried to blitz us but at first it didn't work. Then, Phil Esposito, who had played very well, checked Terry Harper, who was trying to freeze the puck behind our net. The puck squirted away from Harper and rolled out to the front of the net. Ron Murphy of Boston was there and he beat our goaltender, Rogie Vachon. It was 2:29 of the first period.

We were moving well and we got more shots on their goaltender, Gerry Cheevers, in the first period than Boston did on Vachon. In the second period the Bruins outshot us. They came on and on—and you know what that crowd is like in Boston, screaming at them—but they could not put the puck past Vachon. He was making very good saves.

After two periods it was still 1–0 in favor of Boston, a real Stanley Cup game, good, tight-checking, taking the good percentage shots. Good play all around. A minute after the third period opened, I won a draw at Cheevers' right. I had good control of the puck and I passed back to Serge Savard at the right point. He made a strong shot, low, right on the ice, and it beat Cheevers to tie the game 1–1 at 1:10. When the third period ended, the game was still tied 1–1. We went into overtime again for the third time in the series. We had won the first two games in Montreal in overtime.

The first overtime was scoreless. Boston

They came on and on—and you know what that crowd is like in Boston, screaming at them—but they could not put the puck past Vachon.

had a power-play chance when John Ferguson drew a minor penalty midway through, but they could not take advantage of it. Midway in the second overtime, I felt coach Claude Ruel tap me on the shoulder and I went out on the ice again. A minute later, Boston had the puck in its own zone. Defenseman Don Awrey juggled the puck along the boards and our Claude Provost picked it up on his stick as he lost it. The puck was on the right boards and I swung across in front of the net as Provost got it. He passed it right on my stick, on the forehand.

I took a high wrist shot into the upper corner of the net past Cheevers.

It was 11:29 of the second overtime period. We had won the game 2–1. It was the first time in all the years I had played in the Stanley Cup playoffs that I had ever scored an overtime goal. We beat St. Louis in four games for the Cup. Yes, you could choose that as the game I'll never forget, and you would not be wrong.

—As told to George Vass

Jean Beliveau pulls away from Toronto's Tim Horton with the strength and determination that made him the consummate Canadiens captain for 10 years. He won the Art Ross Trophy, the Hart Trophy twice, the Conn Smythe Trophy, 10 Stanley Cup rings and was named to an All-Star Team 10 times, Beliveau retired after the 1970–71 campaign shortly after hoisting the Stanley Cup for the last time.

Nobody ever has to wonder about the game I'll never forget, it being almost self-evident. Once in a while, a few odd

NOVEMBER 7, 1968
THE SPECTRUM, PHILADELPHIA
ST. LOUIS 8, PHILADELPHIA 0

FIRST PERIOD
1. STL Berenson (McDonald, Picard) 16:42.
Penalties: STL Picard (cross-checking) 3:27; STL Picard (slashing) 6:57; STL Crisp (slashing) 13:20; PHI Gendron (slashing) 13:20.

SECOND PERIOD
2. STL Berenson (unassisted) 10:26.
3. STL Berenson (Henry, Picard) 14:42.
4. STL Berenson (Henry) 15:14.
5. STL Berenson (McCreary) 19:35.
No penalties.

THIRD PERIOD
6. STL Crisp (Sabourin) 3:46.
7. STL Henry (McDonald, Berenson) 9:50.
8. STL Berenson (unassisted) 14:04.
No penalties.

SHOTS ON GOAL:

STL	7	11	12	**30**
PHI	7	9	10	**26**

Goalies: STL Plante; PHI Favell
Referee: Bill Friday
Linesmen: Neil Armstrong, W. Norris

hockey players or newspapermen remind me of it so it keeps my memory even fresher than it might be otherwise.

Most people, I guess, probably know right away what game I'm talking about. I scored six goals in for the St. Louis Blues on November 7, 1968, at Philadelphia. It was such an extraordinary game for me that even now I wonder how it could have happened. Even if I say so myself, I'm proud of one aspect of it. No one could ever say "six goals, but"—meaning that none of the goals were tainted. None of them were on rebounds or deflections, but they were all what you would call good goals.

I was having trouble scoring goals at the time. They just weren't going in. I remember when I scored the first one that night, thinking to myself, "It's about time—I guess I can still score the odd goal now and then." But that was just the start, although I had no way of knowing it.

Another thing, it took me a long time to get to that six-goal night. I played my first big league game with the Montreal Canadiens in 1962 and I spent the next years shuttling between them and their farm clubs until they traded me to the New York Rangers in 1966. I didn't get much more ice time with the Rangers either. One season, I played 30 games for the Rangers without scoring a goal. It was frustrating. Frankly, I don't know how I persevered. I felt right on the edge of quitting several times. It was hard on my family. We had to move 40 times in six-and-a-half years.

When the 1967–68 season started, I was still sitting on the Ranger bench and wondering about my future. I thought again about quitting. I wasn't fulfilling myself in hockey. I even thought about going back to school and eventually teaching at a university. Early that season [November 29, 1967], the Rangers traded me to the Blues and I finally found myself on a team that needed me, that gave me the ice time every

hockey player wants to have. Scotty Bowman, who was coaching the Blues at the time, gave me the chance to prove I could play.

Scotty showed he had confidence in me to play full time. I was able to respond to it. Instead of being inhibited about making a mistake and being pulled off the ice, I was able to play my game. I guess you could say that being traded to St. Louis was the turning point of my career. The rest of that season [1967–68] was a good one for me. I scored my share of points [22 goals, 29 assists] and got some attention, not that I was looking for it. In fact, I can get along without it. But I felt I was playing better, although when I look at myself I always say I should be shooting better, checking better.

That was St. Louis' first season in the league and it turned out to be a good one. We finished third in the division but went to the finals in the Stanley Cup, which we lost to Montreal. For the first time, when I went to camp the next fall, I felt I had a job. But I started out slowly that season. I got the odd goal here and there but I was in a bit of a drought in early November and I was beginning to wonder if I could still score.

Then came that night in Philadelphia against the Flyers. They had Doug Favell in goal. It didn't start out better than the games before. We couldn't do anything with Favell for a time and Jacques Plante, who was in goal for us, turned aside the Flyers on several scoring chances. Late in the period I got a breakaway. There was only one man, defenseman Ed Van Impe, between me and the goal and I got around him and wheeled in on Favell. I swerved to the right, pulling Favell out, put the puck on my backhand and lifted it into the net.

That goal probably felt the best of the lot because it had been so long in coming. In the middle of the second period, I got another breakaway and put the second goal past Favell. The third one came even faster, just five minutes later. I was coming across the blue line and I decided to let go with a slap shot. It hit the post and ricocheted past Favell into the net. I went right after that puck, almost without slowing down. I

I went right after that puck... skidded into the goal and grabbed it. It was my first hat trick ever.

skidded into the goal and grabbed it. It was my first hat trick ever and I wanted the puck to save it for a memento.

Three goals! A good night's work. But less than a minute later I got No. 4. This time Camille Henry hit me with a pass. I was almost wide open and I put it past Favell with a wrist shot.

I got No. 5 with less than a minute left in the second period. I think it was another slap shot, like the third goal. Five goals and I was surprised to hear even the Flyer fans cheering me. I had scored five goals but I didn't know I was just one away from the record [six goals scored by Detroit's Syd Howe in 1944]. I was told that after the game.

I got No. 6 late in the third period on another breakaway. I think that was the last goal of the game. Scotty was ready to send me out for a few more turns but I was getting tired. I didn't want to miss a check and maybe cost Jacques his shutout. As it was, we won 8–0.

One of the unusual things about it was that all the goals were scored with the teams evenhanded; there wasn't one power-play goal. Two or three of the goals were on breakaways, two were on slap shots. But none of them was what some people would call tainted. They were all "honest" goals and that makes that night even more satisfying to me.

—*As told to George Vass*

The 1968–69 season, which included his remarkable six-goal game, proved **Red Berenson's** career best. "The Red Baron" tallied 35 goals and 47 assists, good for an eighth-place tie with Jean Beliveau in league scoring. Berenson captained the St. Louis Blues in both 1970–71 and 1977–78 before beginning a long and successful coaching career.

HECTOR TOE BLAKE

GAME 1, 1956
STANLEY CUP FINALS

You remember your first year as a coach because, so often, you don't know what to expect or how the team will play for you.

MARCH 31, 1956
MONTREAL FORUM, MONTREAL
MONTREAL 6, DETROIT 4

FIRST PERIOD
1. DET Delvecchio (Reibel, Howe) 8:17 (PP).
Penalties: MON Beliveau (high-sticking) 2:13; DET Lindsay (high-sticking) 2:13; MON Turner (high-sticking) 3:21; DET Dineen (roughing) 3:21; MON M. Richard (high-sticking) 4:44; DET Howe (hooking) 5:45; MON M. Richard (high-sticking) 8:02; DET Dineen (interference) 13:18; MON M. Richard (hooking) 14:32; DET Ullman (charging) 15:35.

SECOND PERIOD
2. MON Beliveau (Olmstead) 3:00 (PP).
3. DET Dineen (Ullman, Bucyk) 3:45.
4. MON H. Richard (M. Richard, Moore) 6:40.
5. DET Lindsay (Howe) 8:11.
6. DET Delvecchio (Howe, Ferguson) 11:20 (PP).
Penalties: DET Prystai (kneeing) 1:10; MON Johnson (cross-checking) 11:13; DET Hollingworth (roughing) 16:29; MON Johnson (roughing) 16:29.

THIRD PERIOD
7. MON LeClair (Curry, Harvey) 5:20.
8. MON Geoffrion (Talbot) 6:20.
9. MON Beliveau (Geoffrion, Olmstead) 7:31.
10. MON Provost (LeClair, Curry) 10:49.
No penalties.

Goalies: MON Plante; DET Hall
Referee: Jack Mehlenbacher
Linesmen: Bill Morrison, George Hayes

It's one thing to be a player for the Montreal Canadiens, but it's another to be their coach. I played for them 13 years and I coached them 13 years. There were Stanley Cups as a player and there were Stanley Cups as a coach, eight of them. So many games, so many moments.

If I sat down and thought about everything, I guess I could tell many stories. There would be many highlights, many big moments. But I know I got a helluva thrill my first year as a coach, in the first game of the 1956 Stanley Cup finals. That is a game I remember!

When I first became coach, I was worried. Not about whether we had good players. Not that. We had so many: Rocket Richard, Jean Beliveau, Doug Harvey, Bernie Geoffrion, Tom Johnson, Dickie Moore, Bert Olmstead, Jacques Plante, Butch Bouchard, Henri Richard, those were some of them. No, what you think about is that it might be tough to coach players you once had as teammates. You think about that and it makes you nervous. You know, with a club like that, you should win. So much talent, so much potential, it can't be wasted. It's a big test for a coach, a big pressure.

In those days, Detroit was the toughest club in the league for us to beat. They had Gordie Howe, Ted Lindsay, Alex Delvecchio, Red Kelly, Marcel Pronovost, Glenn Hall and many other good players. For seven straight years before I became Montreal coach, the Red Wings finished in first place in the regular season. They defeated Montreal in the Stanley Cup finals the two years before I took over, with the series going seven games each time.

We always had trouble with Detroit and the boys were disappointed with what had happened the previous two years. You could see that right from training camp in 1955. They worked very hard. They knew they could win if they didn't beat themselves. They all went out of their way to help me,

knowing what was expected of me in my first year as coach. Rocket was very good that way. So were Butch Bouchard and Kenny Mosdell.

I felt that if we finished anywhere but first, I wouldn't have done a good job. But you never know in hockey. Everything doesn't always go right. They played in the season as well as I could have expected, maybe better. We won 45 games and lost only 15 [in a 70-game season] and finished with 100 points. Detroit was second, 24 points behind us.

What a power play we had! Harvey and Geoffrion were on the points, Rocket Richard, Beliveau and Olmstead up front. Sometimes we scored two or three goals on a power play, which you could do at that time. After the season, they changed the rule because of that, letting the man come out of the penalty box after a team scored a goal.

We played the New York Rangers in the first round of the playoffs and beat them in five games. Detroit beat Toronto. So it was our club against Detroit again. Nobody had to tell us they'd be tough again.

The first game of the finals was in Montreal. There was a lot of feeling between the two clubs and it showed in the first period. There were brawls and stick swinging and the referee, Jack Mehlenbacher handed out penalties. Detroit scored the only goal in the first period. I think Delvecchio got one past our goalie, Plante, in the middle of the period. We couldn't score on Hall, not that we were pressuring him that much. We were being outplayed.

The second period was much worse. Beliveau tied the game, 1–1, with a goal for us early, but Detroit then scored three of the next four goals. I know Henri Richard got our other goal that period, but Detroit came out of it with a 4–2 lead.

Maybe I said a few things to our guys between the second and third periods. I thought they could do better than be behind after two periods, in their own rink. You have to win on your own ice. I figured maybe our third line could get us started. It worked. Floyd Curry, John LeClair and Claude Provost bailed us out.

That tied the game and the fans went wild. It took five minutes to clear the ice.

LeClair's goal was the one that got us started, about five minutes into the third period. That made it 4–3 and we were just a goal down. I can still see the next goal, about a minute later, by Geoffrion. He wheeled around and put a backhander past Hall that the goalie didn't see. That tied the game and the fans went wild. It took five minutes to clear the ice.

We still weren't in the clear, not against the explosive Detroit team. But we were aroused and kept up the pressure. We were checking them now and Plante wasn't having to stop too many shots. We got one more goal to give us room. There was a scramble around the Detroit net and Provost banged in a loose puck to give us a 6–4 lead.

We were able to hang on to that lead and win that opening game. We went on to take the finals in five games, and that was the start of five straight years of winning the Stanley Cup. A lot of people ask me which team was the greatest. I couldn't tell you. It was pretty much the same for those five years, with a few changes on the third line. But I can tell you this, though: That first game of the finals in my first year as coach was a game I'll never forget. When we came from behind like that, it was the start of those great seasons. If we'd lost that game, who knows what would have happened?

—As told to George Vass

Toe Blake began a legendary coaching career in 1955, leading Montreal to five consecutive Stanley Cup victories. He retired after coaching the club to an eighth Cup win in 1967–68. Blake, however, made his first mark with the Habs as a player. A five-time All-Star, Blake won the Art Ross, the Hart and the Lady Byng trophies in a career that spanned from 1934–35 to 1947–48.

It has been almost nine years now since the USA Olympic hockey team played the Soviets at the 1980 Games in Lake Placid,

New York. I've played in a lot of big games, but that game is definitely one I'll never forget.

We weren't expected to have much of an impact at the Olympics. I thought that a medal would have been nice, but we didn't expect even that. We had lost to the Soviets 10–3 in Madison Square Garden before the Olympics officially began, and we saw the best team in the world that night. So we went to Lake Placid just wanting to play well and make the fans proud of their team.

When we played Sweden in the first game, and Bill Baker scored to tie it 2–2 in the last minute, I don't think any of us felt that it was the turning point. But from then on, everyone on the team started to realize that we tied a better team. We had gained confidence, which caused us to jell as a unit.

Even before the game against the Soviets, we had great fan support, and everything seemed to be going our way. The excitement in Lake Placid got us geared up for the game. There had been so many big thrills already, like beating the Czechs and tying Sweden, two teams considered among the best in the world. But beating the Soviets didn't seem possible. All we could do was try.

We weren't really worried about the game. We just wanted to play as hard as we could. At times we thought we could win the silver and maybe even the gold because after the first few games, we were on a roll. But then we would look at the Soviets and think about beating them. Here was a team that the Canadian Olympic team couldn't beat and the NHL All-Stars couldn't beat—it didn't seem likely that we'd have a chance. The Soviets had won the Challenge Cup in 1979, and they were world champions. After beating some good teams, our confidence was up, but the Soviets figured to be too much of a match. We really just hoped to keep it close. We would have to make some big plays to stay in the game. But if our goalie Jimmy Craig was great, as he had been throughout

the Olympics, we thought we'd be OK.

We definitely were ready for the game. Coach Herb Brooks got us into excellent shape before the Olympics. It was a tough, long tour, but we were physically ready. His strategies were excellent, and he kept us under control. He said we didn't have to go out of our way to create something against them, but we had to force mistakes and capitalize on them. And we did exactly that. We got some breaks at opportune times and took it from there.

The specifics of the game haven't stayed with me as much as just winning it has. I remember Mark Johnson getting that big goal with one second left in the first period. We were tied after one, and the guys really felt we could win it. We were down 3–2 after two periods, but we still felt that we had a real chance. We had to keep at them and not make any mistakes. Johnson scored again, then Mike Eruzione got that goal that everyone remembers.

No personal moments stick out other than the last 10 seconds, seeing the excitement in the arena and everyone on the ice making sure we held on. And Jimmy raising up his arms. The atmosphere the fans had created, the whole environment was just such an uplifting feeling.

Then came the celebrations. I'm only 170 pounds, so I didn't want to get under all those big guys jumping on top of each other into a pile. I was circling and hugging teammates, and I knew exactly what is meant by the thrill of victory. The Soviet players were astounded at what had happened. In their faces, I could see the true agony of defeat. But when we shook hands, some of them said we played a great game and deserved to beat them.

I can't remember what I did after the game, except going out for a bite to eat. This was the biggest win we could have had, but we couldn't go too crazy. We had to be prepared for Finland two days later to decide the gold medal. We were down after two periods in that game, but we all felt we'd come back. We got a couple goals in the third period, and then the fans started chanting, "U-S-A, U-S-A." We had relied on the fans' support throughout the Olympics. They

---

FEBRUARY 22, 1980
LAKE PLACID NY
USA 4, SOVIET UNION 3

FIRST PERIOD
1. SOV Krutov (Kasatonov) 9:12.
2. USA Schneider (Pavelich) 14:03.
3. SOV Makarov (A. Golkov) 17:34.
4. USA Johnson (Christian, Silk) 19:59.
Penalty: SOV Mikhailov 3:25.

SECOND PERIOD
5. SOV Maltsev (Krutov) 2:18 (PP).
Penalties: USA Harrington 0:58; USA Craig 9:50; SOV Lebedev 17:08; USA Morrow 17:08.

THIRD PERIOD
6. USA Johnson (Silk) 8:39.
7. USA Eruzione (Pavelich, Harrington) 10:00.
Penalty: SOV Krutov 16:47.

SHOTS ON GOAL:

USA	8	2	6	**16**
SOV	18	12	9	**39**

Goalies: USA Craig; SOV Tretiak, Myshkin
Referee: Karl-Gustav Kaisla

The Soviet players were astounded at what had happened. In their faces, I could see the true agony of defeat.

always pulled us back up when we started getting down on ourselves.

I'm sure we could beat the Finns again in the same situation. But beating the Soviets was what we had all dreamed of. If we played them another 20 times, we might not have won again.

After we beat Finland, champagne was waiting for us in the locker room. Then we had the medals ceremony, and Mike Eruzione called all of us up with him on the medal stand. I remember the togetherness of the team. I've played on many teams on which the players developed strong bonds. The 1979 University of Minnesota team that won the NCAA Tournament was special to me. But the camaraderie on that 1980 Olympic team was one of the major reasons we won the gold medal.

A lot has happened since those Olympics. I don't look back on it often, but I do keep the gold medal at home, and I take it out for signings and promotions. In 1987, the members of the team got together. I went out with Mike Eruzione, Mike Ramsey, Phil Verchota, Bill Baker, Mark Johnson and Steve Janaszak. We like to reminisce about some of the things that happened throughout that year. There's a family feeling among us when we see each other.

Of course, I see some of the guys in the NHL. Many of us are playing, and others could have played but didn't get a chance. But I've been lucky. Hockey has given me some great memories.

——*As told to Barry Wilner*

Over 16 seasons with the Minnesota North Stars/Dallas Stars franchise, **Neal Broten** established team records for longevity, assists and points (the latter since broken). He helped New Jersey win the 1995 Stanley Cup but returned to Dallas to conclude his NHL career in 1996–97. Broten and his Olympic teammates lit the torch to open the 2002 Winter Olympics.

JOHNNY BUCYK

I've been playing hockey a long time, longer than I thought possible when I played my first NHL game for the Detroit

MARCH 16, 1971
DETROIT OLYMPIA, DETROIT
BOSTON 11, DETROIT 4

FIRST PERIOD
1. BOS McKenzie (Stanfield) 3:24.
2. BOS Bucyk (R. Smith) 9:49.
No penalties.

SECOND PERIOD
3. DET Libett (Berenson, Ecclestone) 1:03.
4. BOS Carleton (Walton, Green) 6:41.
5. DET Howe (Collins) 7:51 (PP).
6. BOS Stanfield (Bucyk, Esposito) 11:39 (PP).
7. DET Charron (unassisted) 16:13.
8. BOS R. Smith (Cashman, Esposito) 17:24.
Penalties: DET Robitaille (hooking) 3:38; BOS Esposito (holding) 7:47; DET Brown (tripping) 10:21; BOS Orr (holding) 17:55.

THIRD PERIOD
9. BOS R. Smith (unassisted) 1:10.
10. DET Redmond (Collins, Robitaille) 2:42.
11. BOS Westfall (Orr) 3:23.
12. BOS Esposito (unassisted) 4:15.
13. BOS Carleton (Walton, Westfall) 13:18.
14. BOS Bucyk (Stanfield, Green) 16:52.
15. BOS Hodge (Esposito, Green) 19:01.
Penalties: BOS Westfall (elbowing) 8:30; DET Luce (roughing) 8:30.

SHOTS ON GOAL:

BOS	17	16	15	**48**
DET	11	11	12	**34**

Goalies: BOS Cheevers; DET Edwards
Refereee: Bruce Hood
Linesmen: W. Norris, G. Ashley

Red Wings more than 20 years ago. I've been lucky in many ways, lucky that injuries didn't cut short my career, and fortunate to have played on some great teams.

Perhaps the luckiest thing that ever happened to me was being traded by the Red Wings to the Boston Bruins in 1957. There have been good years and bad years in Boston, but I've never been sorry that I was traded to the Bruins. For a time there, in the 1960s, we were down there on the bottom but slowly things began to improve, especially after Bobby Orr and Derek Sanderson arrived on the scene in 1966 and we made the big trade with Chicago in 1967 in which we got Phil Esposito, Ken Hedge and Freddie Stanfield.

Nothing, of course, can top winning the Stanley Cup, which we did in 1970 and 1972. Each time after we won the final game, I skated around the rink with the Stanley Cup and each time it was among the greatest moments of my entire life.

I've had other great thrills in hockey. A couple of the highlights came in the 1970–71 season, which was like a dream for me because everything went my way. I was on a line with Stanfield at center and Johnny McKenzie on right wing and we just fit together perfectly. We not only were together on the ice but spent a lot of time with each other off. We'd help each other, criticize each other, work out things together.

The previous season, I'd scored 31 goals and before the 1970–71 season started, I thought I could reasonably hope for 38 this time. That was the goal I set myself. But the goals and the assists kept piling up, the team was winning, and by February I began to realize that I might score 50 goals and get 100 points. Of course, the whole team was going well at that time, which made it easier for me in a way. Still, people kept asking me, talking to me, about 100 points and 50 goals and that made it a little tougher. You don't want to think too much about something

like that because it might result in a mental block.

But by mid-March I was up to 99 points, so it was a sure thing, barring injury. We played at Vancouver on March 13, 1971, and I had quite a few friends at the game because my home was in British Columbia. I thought it would be something extra if I got that 100th point with friends there to see me do it. I tried not to think about it, but you can't help it.

It was a tight checking game at first but a Canuck got a penalty and I was on the ice for the power play. It didn't take long for us to score and I got the goal. I was in a mass of players in the slot when Esposito passed the puck to me. I faked a defenseman, who went down, then shot. It was a low shot and I don't think the goalie, Charlie Hodge, saw it until after it went in.

For an instant, I could hardly believe it. I'd scored my 100th point, something only four players ever had done before up to that time. What made it even more satisfying was that there were about 50 friends and relatives on hand to see me do it.

Four days later, I went into Detroit with 49 goals for the season and looking for my 50th. I was 35 years old at that time and I'd never dreamed before that I'd ever have a chance at 50 goals. Only four players, Esposito, Bobby Hull, Boom Boom Geoffrion and Rocket Richard, had ever scored 50 goals or more in a season. I was at an age at which most players are trying to hang on and I was having my best season. But age never bothered me because I stayed in good shape, kept my weight down and was lucky enough to be healthy.

I remember that 50th goal because it was certainly one of the greatest moments of my career. Stanfield and I got a two-on-one breakaway into the Red Wing zone. I was carrying the puck and passed it to Stanfield near the blue line. A Detroit defenseman checked me to the ice but I bounced right up and kept going.

Stanfield went in on the Red Wing goal and I yelled at him to give me a drop pass. He left the puck for me just before a defenseman took him out. I must have been about 20 feet

> The goals and the assists kept piling up, the team was winning, and by February I began to realize that I might score 50 goals and get 100 points.

from the net when I took a shot. The Detroit goalie, Roy Edwards, got his stick on the puck but knocked the rebound right out in front.

I was still going and I got the end of my stick on the puck and flipped it up just as Edwards went down to try for the save. The puck went over him into the net for my 50th goal. I skated into the net right after it. I wanted that puck for a souvenir. I finished the season with 51 goals and 65 assists for 116 points.

It was a great season until the Stanley Cup finals, which we lost to Montreal. But those two games in which I got my 100th point and my 50th goals were among the highlights of my career. I was grateful to get the opportunity to achieve those marks.

—*As told to George Vass*

Johnny Bucyk served as the *de facto* captain of the Boston Bruins for more than a decade. After 23 NHL seasons, 21 of them in Beantown, "The Chief" retired in 1978, third in all-time games played, sixth in scoring history with 556 goals and 1,369 points. The Bruins retired his No. 9 and he entered the Hockey Hall of Fame in 1981.

New York City was the biggest city in the world in the 1930s and '40s, but it wasn't big enough for both the New York Rangers

MARCH 27, 1938
MADISON SQUARE GARDEN, NEW YORK
NY AMERICANS 3, NY RANGERS 2 (4OT)

FIRST PERIOD
No scoring.
No penalties.

SECOND PERIOD
1. NYR Shibicky (M. Colville, Keeling) 6:27.
2. NYR Hextall (Watson) 7:31.
Penalties: NYR Pratt 16:48; NYA Carr 16:48.

THIRD PERIOD
3. NYA Carr (Beattie) 4:36.
4. NYA Stewart (Callagher, Wiseman) 10:38.
No penalties.

FIRST OVERTIME PERIOD
No scoring.
No penalties.

SECOND OVERTIME PERIOD
No scoring.
Penalties: NYR Shibicky 5:07; NYA Beattie 5:07.

THIRD OVERTIME PERIOD
No scoring.
No penalties.

FOURTH OVETIME PERIOD
5. NYA Carr (Jerwa, Chapman) 0:40.
No penalties.

Goalies: NYA Robertson; NYR Kerr
Referees: Bert McCaffrey, Ag Smith

and New York Americans. The two teams were too close for comfort. We shared Madison Square Garden for years, and it created a real friction between the teams. It made us natural rivals—bitter rivals.

The two teams really hated each other. We would play regular-season games with such intensity that you would think they were the seventh game of the Stanley Cup Finals. If we passed each other on the streets, we would just look away. The Rangers had their watering holes, and we had ours—and we made sure they weren't anywhere near each other.

The press labeled us the "Bowery Boys." They tagged us with a blue-collar identity—I guess it all stemmed from the team's original owner, "Big Bill" Dwyer, who did some time for bootlegging. Meanwhile, the Rangers were known as the white-collar team, probably in the mold of regal Lester Patrick, their longtime coach and general manager. On the ice, they were known for their fancy, whirling passing. Their fans wore designer dresses and dinner jackets to games.

I originally came up with the Rangers in 1933, but was traded to the Americans the next season. I spent seven seasons with the Americans before being traded to the Toronto Maple Leafs, and while playing in New York I saw a lot of bad blood spilled on the ice between the Americans and Rangers.

The games would turn into wars. Every game was really physical. There were a lot of fights and a lot of pushing and shoving. You had to watch your back because there was probably someone behind you ready to put a knife in it, so to speak. Sometimes we'd go after Phil Watson, who would do a lot of needling—I guess today you'd call it "trash talking"—during the game. In return, they'd try to knock Sweeney Schriner or Lorne Anderson or some of our other good players off their games.

The crowds would be mixed. Some would be rooting for the Americans, others for the Rangers. When we played each other, you couldn't get near Madison Square Garden. And inside, it would get so loud that you couldn't hear yourself think The records show that the Rangers almost always won. We would battle them tooth and nail, but they just had younger, stronger and better players. So you understand why we had extra incentive to beat them when we faced them in the 1938 playoffs.

That season had been one of our best. We finished tied for second in the Canadian Division. [Imagine that, a team called the Americans in the Canadian Division.] The Rangers, who had lost in the finals the year before, finished second in the American Division, with the second-highest points total in the league behind the Boston Bruins. Sweeney Schriner and Nels Stewart put together great seasons for us. Schriner had 38 points and Stewart 36. Both finished in the top 10 in the league. We also had a rookie goalie named Earl Robertson who played every game for us that year, posting six shutouts and a 2.31 goals-against average. More importantly, Robertson was an established Rangers nemesis. One year earlier, Robertson had been an emergency call-up for the Detroit Red Wings. With just a few NHL games under his belt, he posted two shutouts and led Detroit to a four-games-to-one victory over the Rangers in the Stanley Cup Finals.

Robertson played wonderfully in the first game of the series against the Rangers, leading us to a 2–1 overtime win. Johnny Sorrell, a tall, thin winger we acquired from Detroit earlier in the season, scored the game-winner.

The Rangers recovered to win Game 2, setting the stage for a third and final game—the game I'll never forget. Game 3 began on March 27, 1938. The Rangers took a 2–0 lead but we weren't despondent. We rallied and knotted the game in the third period. The game turned into one of the longest in Garden history, with more twists and turns than a paperback murder mystery. It also was a test of our physical and mental conditioning. We played through three overtimes without determining a winner.

In the fourth overtime, I was on the verge of exhaustion. I had played a lot during the

The game turned into one of the longest in Garden history, with more twists and turns than a paperback murder mystery.

game and had probably lost 10 pounds. The game started on Saturday night, but by now it was 1:15 a.m. Sunday. One shift, I was on the ice against Lynn Patrick. The puck was in their zone and Patrick was lagging behind, waiting for someone to get him the puck quickly and catch me out of position. But instead of getting a fast break on me, I intercepted the puck. My first instinct was just to shoot it toward the net, and that's what I did.

My shot beat Rangers goalie Davey Kerr, giving us the win and the series. We were too exhausted to even celebrate the victory. By the time we got dressed it was past 2 a.m., and we just headed back and went to sleep.

We were eliminated in the next round by the Chicago Blackhawks. The Americans would be forced to fold during World War II because of financial woes, and I'd go on to win two Stanley Cups with the Maple Leafs. I enjoyed my best years in Toronto, finishing in the top five in league scoring twice. I also was named a first-team NHL All-Star twice. But I never scored a more meaningful or satisfying goal in my career.

That goal would have been memorable no matter who I scored it against, but because I scored it against the Rangers—our bitter rivals—it was the goal, and the game, I'll always remember.

—*As told to Chuck O'Donnell*

Lorne Carr played right wing on the New York Americans top line with center Art Chapman and winger Sweeney Schriner. The cash-strapped Amerks sold him to Toronto in October 1941, and the club folded after one more season. As a Leaf, Carr earned two Stanley Cup rings and two First All-Star Team berths before retiring after the 1945–46 campaign.

DINO CICCARELLI

GAME 3, 1994
STANLEY CUP SEMIFINALS

There was a time when my only goal was to play in an NHL game and score an NHL goal. That was when I was in junior,

JANUARY 8, 1994
GREAT WESTERN FORUM, INGLEWOOD CA
DETROIT 6, LOS ANGELES 3

FIRST PERIOD
1. DET Probert (Kennedy, McCarty) 11:14.
2. LA Rychel (Conacher, Robitaille) 18:13.
Penalties: DET Kruppke (roughing) 8:18; LA Granato (charging, unsportsmanlike conduct) 19:30.

SECOND PERIOD
3. LA Robitaille (Sydor, McEachern) 5:20.
4. DET Kozlov (Fedorov, Ciccarelli) 6:18.
5. DET Kennedy (McCarty, Probert) 7:50.
6. LA Robitaille (Blake, Sandstrom) 13:54 (PP).
7. DET Coffey (unassisted) 18:23.
Penalties: LA Granato (high-sticking) 10:55; DET McCarty (boarding) 13:34.

THIRD PERIOD
8. DET Ciccarelli (Kozlov, Fedorov) 4:20.
9. DET Primeau (Yzerman, Chiasson) 7:08 (SH).
Penalties: DET Carkner (high-sticking) 5:59; DET McCarty (fighting) 15:28; LA Crowe (fighting) 15:28; DET Primeau (roughing, slashing) 16:37; LA Kurri (slashing) 16:37.

SHOTS ON GOAL:

DET	17	16	11	**44**
LA	8	14	10	**32**

Goalies: DET Cheveldae; LA Hrudey
Referee: Don Koharski
Linesmen: Ryan Bozak, Mark Wheeler

playing for the London Knights of the Ontario Hockey League. I broke my right leg sliding into the boards in a freak accident. The road back was long, and there were many times when I wanted to pack up my skates and go back home to Sarnia, Ontario. The rehabilitation process was grueling, and despite my efforts, improvement came very slowly. I realized that a lot of players don't ever recover from a broken leg.

After about a year of therapy, my leg began to improve. A year-and-a-half after the accident, I was back on the ice. I had been an OHL Second All-Star Team selection before the injury, scoring 72 goals in my first year in the league, and soon I was back to that level. However, my future was bleak.

No NHL team wanted to take a chance on this skinny kid with a bad leg. I wasn't even selected in the entry draft. After getting passed over by every team, I was just happy to sign a free-agent contract with the Minnesota North Stars in 1979.

Sometimes I forget about that whole battle just to make it to the NHL. But there were two nights in particular when I reflected on how far I had come: when I scored my 500th goal, and when my Detroit Red Wings beat the Chicago Blackhawks in double overtime in last season's Western Conference finals.

On a personal level, the night I scored goal No. 500 is the game I will never forget. Throughout my career, I always considered myself a goal scorer first. I felt that I could help a team in a lot of ways, but it was no secret that scoring goals was what I did best.

All those goals over all those years began to build up. I remember eclipsing 200, then 300, then 400. Before I knew it, I was closing in on 500. When it got down to the end, I was stuck on 499 after a few cracks at 500 at home. We finally went on the road. I wanted to fly my father out to San Jose, but there was a snowstorm back in Detroit and he couldn't get a flight out. As it turned out, I didn't score.

The next night, we played in Los Angeles and my father was able to get a flight out and be at the Forum for the game. It's a good thing, too—that's where I scored No. 500.

It was January 8, 1994, and Kelly Hrudey was in goal for the Kings. We beat them 6–3. I hit the post about three or four times. For a while it seemed like it wasn't meant to be. When you're on the verge of a milestone like that, you just want to get it done and get it over with. When it finally happened, I was relieved. It was great that my dad was able to be there when it happened. When you look at the history of hockey and how few players have reached the 500-goal mark—guys like Mike Bossy, Wayne Gretzky and Gordie Howe—it really is a special achievement.

But hockey is a team game, and all achievements can't be measured simply in goals, assists and points. Sure, individual milestones are nice, but what do they mean if your team isn't winning? That's why our double-overtime victory over the Blackhawks last year in Game 3 was such a special game. Teamwise, it's the game I'll never forget.

In games like that, when it goes into overtime and so much is riding on the next goal, you really tend to become nervous. You might be surprised that guys who have been around as long as I have would still get nervous, but that's just the nature of the game. Teams become tentative in overtime playoff games—they tighten up. You certainly don't want to give any opportunities to the other team, and you have to become very selective about the chances that you take.

They say that the majority of big games are won by fluke goals. Well, I don't know if you could call Vladimir Konstantinov's game-winning goal at 10:35 of the second overtime a fluke, but it sure wasn't pretty. Effective, but not pretty. I'll never forget being on the ice when his wrist shot from the blue line went in to give us a 4–3 victory in the game and a 3–0 advantage in the series. It seemed like a harmless shot—I guess it just got away from Chicago goalie Eddie Belfour.

At any rate, we eventually won the series

My future was bleak. No NHL team wanted to take a chance on this skinny kid with a bad leg.

Dino Ciccarelli had an auspicious NHL debut, notching 14 goals and 21 playoff points as a rookie during Minnesota's surprising 1981 run at the Stanley Cup. After several seasons with Washington and four with Detroit, Ciccarelli spent three seasons in the Sunshine State. He retired after the 1998–99 season with 608 goals and 1,200 career points.

in five games. We continued into the finals against the Devils, and we lost that series in four games. Hopefully, one day I can say a Stanley Cup victory is the game I'll never forget.

—*As told to Chuck O'Donnell*

JOHN CULLEN

OCTOBER 7, 1988

It's easy to pick the game I'll never forget. It was my first NHL game in 1988. I was playing for Pittsburgh then, and our first

OCTOBER 7, 1988
CAPITAL CENTER, LANDOVER MD
PITTSBURGH 6, WASHINGTON 4

FIRST PERIOD
1. WAS Gartner (Hunter, Corriveau) 1:01.
2. PIT Quinn (Cunneyworth) 4:18.
3. WAS Courtnall (Gustafsson, Miller) 11:23.
Penalties: PIT Dykstra (cross-checking) 7:01; WAS Hunter (unsportsmanlike conduct) 7:31; PIT Coffey (holding) 16:40; WAS Stevens (high-sticking) 17:21.

SECOND PERIOD
4. PIT Bourque (Hannan, Brown) 1:23.
5. PIT Zalapski (Brown, Lemieux) 5:50 (PP).
6. WAS Ridley (Christian, Courtnall) 17:01 (PP).
Penalties: PIT Hillier (hooking) 2:13; WAS Pivonka (hooking) 5:03; PIT Lemieux (interference) 8:23; WAS Gartner (cross-checking) 12:49; WAS Stevens (roughing) 12:49; PIT Dykstra (cross-checking) 12:49; PIT Quinn (high-sticking double minor) 13:30; PIT Frawley (misconduct) 13:30; WAS Hunter (high-sticking double minor) 13:30; WAS Corriveau (misconduct) 13:30; PIT Siren (hooking) 14:54; PIT Lemieux (slashing) 15:19; PIT Stevens (high-sticking) 15:19; WAS Gould (roughing) 17:40.

THIRD PERIOD
7. WAS Christian (Ridley, Courtnall) 6:00.
8. PIT Cunneyworth (Quinn, Frawley) 9:10.
9. PIT Cunneyworth (Frawley) 14:34.
10. PIT Coffey (Hannan, Cullen) 16:26.
Penalties: WAS Hatcher (slashing) 0:49; WAS Gartner (hooking) 6:38.

SHOTS ON GOAL:

PIT	6	8	8	**22**
WAS	17	12	6	**35**

Goalies: PIT Young; WAS Malarchuk
Referee: Dave Newell
Linesmen: Gord Broseker, Bryan Murphy

game that season was in Washington. I'll always remember this game because of what I had gone through to get to the NHL.

I played hockey for four years at Boston University but was never selected in the NHL draft. Of course, I was disappointed at not being drafted, but I just took it as one of those "life" things. Things happen in life and you just have to deal with them and keep going on.

The year after I finished school, I went to play for Flint in the International Hockey League. I had a really amazing year there. I scored 157 points and was selected the most valuable player in the league. After that, I signed on with Pittsburgh as a free agent.

I had been dreaming about playing in the NHL probably since I was about 10 years old. Both my father Barry and uncle Brian had played in the NHL and I wanted to make it there as well. Because I wasn't drafted, though, I didn't really think I'd get a chance to play in the NHL. But after that great season I had in the minors, I really started believing I could play.

I went to Pittsburgh's training camp and we had about 10 exhibition games. I played fairly well and they gave me a pretty good indication I'd be with the team for the year. But the days leading up to that first regular season game were still pretty nerve-wracking. A lot of the guys on my team told me just to relax. They had been through the same thing before and told me not to worry and to just go out, play the game and do my best.

When we got to the rink in Washington, I remember sitting in the stands before the game. Paul Coffey was on my team then and he told me he always sat in the stands before games. I started doing that as well. I don't do it all the time now, but every once in a while I'll go and sit up in the stands. I talked to Coffey for a while before we went to the dressing room to get ready. I remember looking around the rink and thinking, "This is where I'm going to play my first NHL game." I had a lot of butterflies in my stomach and Paul was talking to me, trying to calm me down.

When the game started, I still had the butterflies. All players are nervous in their first game, though. And it took me a while to get going. I couldn't really believe I was playing in the NHL with guys like Paul and Mario Lemieux. Mario and Wayne Gretzky are simply the best hockey players from this era.

I think my linemates that game were Phil Bourque and Kevin Stevens. We were playing on the third line. We didn't start the game and it was a couple minutes into the game before we got our first shift. When I was sitting on the bench at times during the game, I was thinking, "I've reached my goal." I wanted to play in the NHL and I was actually playing my first game.

The crowd was just great. There were about 18,000 people there. I had never played in front of so many people before. Plus, it was a divisional game and that made things even more intense. As far as goals go, I don't remember too many of them. I know we won 6–4, but it's been so long to remember a lot of details. But I do remember I got my first ever point in the NHL that night.

I got an assist on a goal that Coffey scored. Because he's such an amazing player and has done so much for the game, I'll never forget that first point. It was late in the third period and I was carrying the puck in the Washington zone. Then I passed it over to Coffey. He just took a slap shot and it went into the net, beating Clint Malarchuk, who was playing goal for the Capitals. I didn't keep the puck though. I'm not big on things like that.

After the game I phoned my dad and told him things went well. And he told me how happy he was for me. He knew what I had been through and how hard I had worked to get to the NHL.

—As told to Sam Laskaris

John Cullen was awarded the 1999 Bill Masterton Trophy for his courageous and successful battle against cancer during the 1997–98 season. Cullen briefly returned to his team, the Tampa Bay Lightning, for four games in 1998–99 before announcing his retirement and move into coaching. His father Barry and two uncles, Brian and Ray, also had NHL careers.

HULL OF A GOAL

It was an epic game marred by controversy. Dominik Hasek backstopped Buffalo to the 1999 Stanley Cup finals. Dallas' Eddie "The Eagle" Belfour, while playing behind a stronger team, had just as strong a playoff. Belfour posted his third shutout of the 1999 postseason in Game 5, blanking the Sabres 2–0. The two stalwart netminders turned Game 6 into a marathon as the Sabres valiantly tried to extend the Stars to a seventh game.

The match went into a third overtime period locked at a single goal apiece. Finally, at 54:51 of overtime, the Stars got the break that lifted them to victory. Brett Hull, seeking a Cup ring to augment his outstanding career, hammered home his own rebound past Hasek into the Sabre net. Controversy ensued when replays showed Hull's foot in the crease as he scored. A rule at the time (instituted in 1991 and changed two days after Hull's goal) dictated that a goal would be disallowed should there be an attacking player in the crease. The referees, later backed by the league, ruled that Hull had maintained possession of the puck while entering the crease, allowing him to be there, and the goal stood. Hull and the Stars celebrated the club's first Cup win.

—*Chris McDonell*

JUNE 19, 1999
MARINE MIDLAND ARENA, BUFFALO
DALLAS 2, BUFFALO 1 (3OT)

VINCENT DAMPHOUSSE

1991 NHL ALL-STAR GAME

> # The 1991 NHL All-Star Game proved to be more than anything I had expected. It was my first time playing in the All-Star Game

in this league, and what a wonderful experience it was. It's definitely a game I'll never forget.

The whole weekend was exciting. We arrived in Chicago on Friday and introduced ourselves to all the other players. There were so many members of the media there, and I talked to some of the Toronto guys, but as it turned out most of my interviews were after the game.

On Friday night, we had the All-Star competitions. I was in the relay. We had to go around cones and make passes. That was interesting because we had a lot of people watching us. The following afternoon was time for the game. Even before the game started, there was plenty of excitement. Chicago is one of the loudest rinks around, but this day was really something, especially with the Persian Gulf war going on. People were waving flags, and everybody was screaming. I was standing right beside Mark Messier, and we were talking, but I couldn't understand what he was saying. It was so loud it was scary.

It seemed to go on and on. We were waiting about 45 minutes on the ice before the game started. They were doing all the introductions and ceremonies, and I was pretty nervous. We were just standing there forever. But after that was done, I calmed down a bit, and everything turned out to be all right.

On my first shift, I was still a bit nervous. I was playing on a line with Steve Yzerman and Adam Oates, and because it was my first All-Star Game, my goal was simple: I didn't want to look out of place. But things turned out way better than I had expected. I didn't think I'd be the star of the stars and score four goals, but that's what happened. Only Wayne Gretzky and Mario Lemieux had scored four goals in an All-Star Game before; it's quite the honor being mentioned in the same breath as those two.

It also was quite an honor being named the most valuable player of the game and winning a car. I didn't think of winning the MVP award until my third goal. There were so many other guys who also had played well, but after my third goal, I started pressing hard trying to make things happen.

I scored my fourth goal on a breakaway on Andy Moog. My first goal was against Patrick Roy in the first period, and then I scored three times in the third period against Moog. After my fourth goal, I knew I was going to be the MVP; the guys on our bench were asking me what color car I wanted.

Even after the game, things were pretty hectic. We had to go to a dinner at a museum, and there was no rest there as everybody wanted to talk about the game. There were about 4,000 people there.

It was a great game for me, and I'll be able

to watch it whenever I want because a lot of people taped it for me back in Toronto. I got one of the tapes from a friend of mine. It's in the drawer right now, but I'll take it out when I have kids and show it to them. As for my teammates, they were happy for me. They had all watched the game on TV. It was awhile, though, before we got back to Toronto.

When I rejoined the team, we were on a road trip. About a week later, we came back to play at home for the first time. We were playing Minnesota, but I was really upset I wasn't able to play in that game because I was suspended. In the final road game before that [in Chicago], I got a game misconduct for high-sticking. It was my second such infraction of the year, so I was auto-

matically suspended for one game. There was nothing I could do; I was cooked. But because of the way I played at the All-Star Game, I was looking forward to playing in Toronto. I wanted to get right back in there.

The All-Star Game turned out to be good not only for me but for our team as well. Toronto had a bad year, so it was good that we at least had something that put us in the spotlight for a while.

While growing up, you never really think about playing in the NHL All-Star Game; you just dream about playing in the NHL. But once you're there, then the All-Star Game is something you shoot for. Hopefully, I'll get to play in a couple more games during my career. I'm sure if I go there in the future, people will

The Toronto Maple Leafs traded **Vincent Damphousse** to Edmonton in 1991 and a year later he joined the Montreal Canadiens. Damphousse won a Stanley Cup ring with the Habs in 1993 and became team captain in 1996–97. He moved to the San Jose Sharks in March 1999, where he remains an elite scorer.

remember I scored four goals in my first game, so I'll have a lot of pressure to do just the same. It will be tough because I'll probably be thinking about my first All-Star Game also. I knew it was my day. I'll never forget it.

—*As told to Sam Laskaris*

When you play as long as I have, you end up playing in many memorable games. I have competed in a couple of great playoff

series, I've had a bunch of hat tricks, I had a four-goal game against the Chicago Blackhawks and I've managed to reach a few personal milestones along the way. But I would guess that of all the big games in my career, the last game I played in Hartford is the game I'll never forget.

It had been pretty strange to be a Whaler the past few years. Paul Coffey asked to be traded. Brendan Shanahan asked to be traded. There were always new faces coming into the line-up, and that's always hard to adjust to. Off the ice, there was a lot of instability. No one knew when or if we were going to move. No one knew where we were going to move to. There were always these rumors swirling around, and the players never knew what was going on. It was really a weird time in my career.

Despite the distractions, we managed to concentrate on playing and winning games. Right up until the last week of the season, we were in the hunt for a playoff spot. But then we lost to the New York Islanders in the second to last game of the season on Long Island, and we were eliminated from any hopes of postseason play.

Because of that loss, we went into the last game at the Civic Center feeling a little sheepish. We felt we had let the fans down. They had supported us so tremendously over the years. Even when there was a season ticket drive under way to try and keep the team in Hartford, our fans came through. They got the season ticket total up to about 9,000 by the end of the year, but that still wasn't enough to keep us in Connecticut. We had no idea how the fans were going to react in that last game against the Tampa Bay Lightning. No one could have blamed them for being mad because the team was moving or because we didn't make the playoffs. We were embarrassed at ourselves.

The fans, however, came out and made it such a special night. You could feel the emotion in the building that night right from the start of the game. People came with signs and really showed off their loyalty for the team.

It was a good game, even though neither team really had anything to play for. I entered the game with 18 goals, and everyone on the team knew I would get a bonus if I reached the 20-goal mark. I got my 19th early in the game. Andrew Cassels got the puck behind their net. He's a great playmaker, and he doesn't need much room to make a play. I've always been a believer that good centers make good wings, and he really worked well with me and Geoff Sanderson on the wings last year. Anyway, he made a blind pass to me in front of the net, and I just popped it in from the slot.

As the game went on, the spirit in the building was increasing. It got really loud when they played our theme song, "Brass Bonanza," over and over before the beginning of each period. I found myself trying to savor the game as it wore on. I would stand at the gate as the guys came on to the ice for the start of the period and whack them with my stick just because of the importance of this last game. During the third period, I was running on pure emotion. I must have played at least 15 minutes in that period. My teammates were trying to get me that 20th goal and that bonus.

We had taken a 2–1 lead, and I was on the ice for the last minute. By this point, I had become totally exhausted. In that last minute, I took a shot from just outside the Tampa Bay blue line, and it hit the inside of the post. It looked like it was going to squeak in, but out of nowhere came one of the Lightning's defensemen, Roman Hamrlik, stopping the puck before it had a chance to go over the line. They stopped the game to go upstairs and review it, but I already knew it wasn't going to be a goal. Sure enough, they ruled that it never crossed the goal line, and we got ready for one last face-off. By this time there were about six seconds left. The fans really let everything out. They were so loud and so demonstrative, it was amazing.

We didn't really have anything planned for after the game, so we went over and congratulated our goalie like any other

---

APRIL 13, 1997
HARTFORD CIVIC CENTER, HARTFORD
HARTFORD 2, TAMPA BAY 1

FIRST PERIOD
1. HAR Wesley (Rice, Kron) 2:30.
Penalties: HAR Burke (roughing) 7:48; HAR Cassels (slashing) 19:12; TB Burr (roughing, misconduct) 20:00; HAR Muzzatti (roughing, misconduct) 20:00.

SECOND PERIOD
No scoring.
Penalties: TB Poeschek (double minor high-sticking) 4:37; TB Wiemer (holding) 11:38.

THIRD PERIOD
2. HAR Dineen (Sanderson, Cassels) 0:24.
3. TB Ciccarelli (Gratton, Zamuner) 2:50.
No penalties.

SHOTS ON GOAL:

HAR	13	10	16	**39**
TB	8	9	6	**23**

Goalies: HAR Burke; TB Tabaracci
Referee: Scott Zelkin
Linesmen: Kevin Collins, Brian Murphy

> As the game went on, the spirit in the building was increasing. It got really loud when they played our theme song, "Brass Bonanza."

contest and let things happen naturally. The team ended up staying together in a circle, and then we eventually went around the rink, waving and saying our goodbyes to the crowd. Some of the guys were handing their sticks and helmets and other equipment to the fans in the stands in acknowledgment of their loyalty over the years.

As the team's captain, I felt I had to say something. I got on the microphone in the arena and thanked the fans for their support over the years. I also thanked them for supporting our charities. It was a hard speech to make because it was a very touching moment.

The fans had been so loyal through the years, even though they didn't always have a lot to cheer about. Hartford was really a great place to play hockey. You had thousands of loyal fans, who would also respect your privacy off the ice. Those fans suffered through so much: a bunch of ownership changes and indecision and bad trades and new regimes coming through. I think they saw that the situation was starting to change during that last season. There seemed to be a glimmer of hope. This team had accumulated a lot of good young players. We had begun to make some good trades, and the team was really planning for the future for a change. The fans might have had something to really be excited about. I think we were beginning to resemble a team on the rise. But unfortunately for those fans, now we're a team on the rise in North Carolina.

—*As told to Chuck O'Donnell*

Kevin Dineen's father Bill won two Stanley Cup rings with Detroit in the 1950s and his brothers Gord and Peter both played in the NHL. Dineen, the Hartford/Carolina franchise career penalty-minute leader, signed as a free agent with Ottawa for the 1999–2000 season. The Columbus Blue Jackets, seeking veteran savvy and grit for their inaugural campaign, drafted Dineen in the summer of 2000.

GAME 7, 1974
STANLEY CUP SEMIFINALS

You play 14 years in the National Hockey League and you have a lot of memories, especially when you've played on two

THE SPECTRUM, PHILADELPHIA
PHILADELPHIA 4, NEW YORK RANGERS 3

FIRST PERIOD
1. NYR Fairbairn (Park, Tkaczuk) 13:43.
2. PHI MacLeish (Clarke, Barber) 14:40 (PP).
Penalties: NYR Park (slashing) 2:23; PHI Barber (slashing) 3:41; NYR Fairbairn (elbowing) 7:01; PHI MacLeish (elbowing) 7:01; PHI Barber (holding) 8:52; NYR Rolfe (fighting) 11:55; PHI Schultz (fighting) 11:55; NYR Tkaczuk (elbowing) 14:05; PHI Wolet (slashing) 15:39; NYR Stemkowski (tripping) 18:37.

SECOND PERIOD
3. PHI Kindrachuk (unassisted) 2:27.
4. PHI Dornhoefer (MacLeish) 11:26.
Penalty: PHI Van Impe (holding) 6:29.

THIRD PERIOD
5. NYR Vickers (Tkaczuk, Fairbairn) 8:49.
6. PHI Dornhoefer (Lonsberry, MacLeish) 9:01.
7. NYR Stemkowski (Vickers, Seiling) 14:34.
Penalties: NYR Stemkowski (roughing) 2:16; PHI Saleski (roughing) 2:16; PHI Clarke (hooking) 3:59; PHI Saleski (tripping) 12:31; NYR (too many men, served by Hadfield) 19:09.

SHOTS ON GOAL:

PHI	18	19	9	**46**
NYR	9	10	15	**34**

Goalies: PHI Parent; NYR Giacomin
Referee: Art Skov
Linesmen: Matt Pavelich, John D'Amico

Stanley Cup-winning teams as I did with the Philadelphia Flyers in 1974 and 1975.

It took a while for me to stick in the NHL, which was pretty hard for a young fellow to break into in the days before expansion when there were only six teams. I spent parts of three seasons with the Boston Bruins in those days, though I never really stuck until I was drafted from Boston by the Flyers when they first started in 1967.

I remember my first game-winning NHL goal, with the Bruins in 1964. I was playing on a line with Murray Oliver and Johnny Bucyk and we were in Toronto. What makes me remember that goal is the fact I just missed an easy shot before I scored it. Then, on a much tougher chance, I scored the goal, the first of the game. Guess what? We won 11–0.

Being drafted by the Flyers was the real break of my career. The season before, I'd been playing with Hershey in the American Hockey League and wondering if I'd ever stick in the NHL. But the Flyers came along and I began to get some ice time and feel I'd won a job.

I can't say I was ever a big goal scorer, though one year I did score 30 goals. But I wasn't a natural. If I aimed a shot, it didn't go there. I could take 10 shots during practice and only one would go where I aimed it. What I did well was park myself near the crease and stand my ground. I probably did that better than anything else. Of course, some goalies would give you the stick and others would try to pull your feet out from under you, but that just made you want to go back and work twice as hard.

That was my style, that and going in the corners and mixing it up. You paid the price, of course, in injuries. You'd never miss a game if you went out on the ice and didn't go near anybody. But that's no accomplishment. Hockey is a game of hit and be hit. You get hit in front of the net, sure, but you get rewarded, too. You take a lot of sticks in the ribs, but it's worth it when your team scores a goal. Not that goal-scoring is everything. Sure,

everybody enjoys scoring goals but the main thing is to win as many games as you can. Goal scorers get the credit, but hockey people know the value of guys who work the corners and check and play good defense. I always liked to think that's what I was valued for.

I guess I paid a price for that. Hardly a season went by that I didn't have one or two injuries, some serious, like two broken legs, a broken ankle, fractured cheekbone, and elbow problems that required operations. I must have had 15 serious injuries over the years.

The one I remember most is a shoulder separation because it kept me out of the Stanley Cup clinching game against Boston the first time we won in 1974. I got hurt in the third game of the finals when Don Marcotte threw a hip check into me while I was diving for a loose puck. At the time, I didn't even know who hit me, what had happened. So I had to sit and watch that sixth game when we beat the Bruins in the Spectrum. All the same, it was quite a feeling being on a winner for the first time. No matter what's happened during the year, what you've done as an individual, if your team wins the Stanley Cup, you've had a good season regardless.

Up to that year [1974], we hadn't had too many highlights with the Flyers. I remember one game before that, the fifth game of the quarterfinals against Minnesota in 1973 when I scored the winning goal in overtime. Everybody is in a daze after a game like that. I don't even know how I scored. I just remember getting the puck at center ice and fortunately it stayed with me until I was able to get off a backhand that got past the goalie.

Of all the games I played, though, I'd have to say the most memorable for me personally might have been the seventh game of the 1974 semifinals. We met the New York Rangers before we played Boston and won the Cup. I don't think there could have been two better matched teams than in that series. The Rangers had a good club, and though we won the first two games, they came right back. We went the route, to the seventh game in the Spectrum.

We were counting on the home ice advantage, but you never know. It had been

> You get hit in front of the net, sure, but you get rewarded, too. You take a lot of sticks in the ribs, but it's worth it when your team scores a goal.

a rough series and we were an awfully tired hockey club. But so were the Rangers. We thought we wanted it more than they did, but I suppose every team has that feeling.

Bernie Parent was in the nets for us and Eddie Giacomin for the Rangers, just like they had been for the whole series. The Rangers got the first break, Bill Fairbairn scoring a goal for them. That seemed to wake us up. We got a power play goal about a minute later and two more goals in the next 15 minutes of play. I think Rick MacLeish scored the tying goal, then Orest Kindrachuk put us ahead 2–1. I got our third goal, getting a stick on a rebound and flipping it past Giacomin.

That 3–1 lead looked pretty good going into the third period, but the Rangers got a goal midway through and with half a period left, a one-goal lead didn't look like much. But right after the face-off, Ross Lonsberry gave me the puck from behind the net. I was able to get off a shot from 15 feet out that beat Giacomin to make it 4–2. That proved the game-winner, though the Rangers got one more goal to cut our final margin to 4–3.

The strange thing about it was it was the first time all year I had scored two goals. I'd had only 11 all season. That win put us into the finals and even though I wasn't able to play in the game that clinched the Cup, I was able to feel I'd helped. Fortunately, the next year I was able to play all the way through and enjoy that great feeling of being on a Cup winner for the second time.

—As told to George Vass

Gary Dornhoefer had his best offensive season in 1972–73, when he scored 30 goals and 49 assists. An abrasive right winger, he endeared himself to Philadelphia fans for his tenacious work in front of opposition nets. Retiring after the 1977–78 campaign, he has become known to a new generation as a TV broadcaster and analyst, first with *Hockey Night in Canada* and then with Philadelphia's home broadcasting team.

KEN DRYDEN

**GAME 3, 1976
STANLEY CUP FINALS**

Something that I have thought about from time to time is that there are very, very few saves that I can remember. Over all of the

years I've played, I can remember only five or six specific saves. That's all. Instead I remember games, and I can remember goals. I retain a sort of feeling of winning and losing games, feelings that come from those wins and losses. And I can remember an awful lot of goals that have been scored. I can tell you scores of games long afterwards and goals that were scored, but the rest is mostly gone.

When I think about my most memorable games, I would choose three. One of them would be the final game of the Stanley Cup playoffs against the Blackhawks in 1971, a game we won 3–2 in Chicago Stadium. Another game would be the eighth game in Moscow in 1972, when we defeated the Russians to take the series against them after being shocked by their skill in the beginning. But the game that is the most memorable is Game 3 of the 1976 Stanley Cup finals against the Philadelphia Flyers. It wasn't made memorable for me so much by the outcome, or anything that took place during the game itself, but by the general atmosphere.

I think the part that made that game, and even that Stanley Cup series, so different was that we had gone two years without winning the Cup while the Flyers had won it, that we had won the first two games of that series at Montreal and that it was almost required for Philadelphia to win this game if it was to retain hopes of another Cup. All these factors combined to heighten the emotions leading up to the game itself.

The Flyers management pulled out all the stops and put on an extravaganza. What I mean by "extravaganza" is the atmosphere they built up before the game was to start. They turned the lights down, put the spotlights on and brought in Kate Smith to sing "God Bless America." It was a very special start to a game. All these parts of the extravaganza were to be expected, except whether Kate would be there or not. Nobody knew, but all of the other elements alone were enough to get everyone

excited. Then, at the last moment, the Flyers public address announcer said, "Now, Kate Smith will sing 'God Bless America'" and the place just went crazy.

Everyone, including the players, got very excited. Usually after the anthem is sung, most of the players start skating around the net until the referee blows the whistle, then tap the goalie on the pads and line up for the start of the game. This time, when Kate finished singing everybody just took off. Everybody was so hyped that they were all skating around like Keith Magnuson of the Blackhawks skates when he comes out on the ice for the start of a period. Then, when the players came back to me, instead of the usual perfunctory taps on the pads, they whacked me hard. I needed the pads to save my legs from the sticks. Everybody was more pumped up for this game than for any that I can recall. Perhaps the extravaganza had the opposite effect of what Flyers management intended, though it certainly excited their

**MAY 13, 1976
THE SPECTRUM, PHILADELPHIA
MONTREAL 3, PHILADELPHIA 2**

FIRST PERIOD
1. MON Shutt (Lafleur) 3:17 (PP).
2. PHI Leach (Clarke, Goodenough) 8:40 (PP).
3. PHI Leach (unassisted) 18:14.
Penalties: PHI Barber (elbowing) 1:52; MON Risebrough (high-sticking) 8:02; MON Gainey (elbowing) 9:18; PHI Bridgman (hooking) 15:45; PHI Dornhoefer (elbowing) 19:59.

SECOND PERIOD
4. MON Shutt (Lafleur, Mahovlich) 1:09 (PP).
Penalties: MON Nyrop (interference) 2:38; PHI McIlhargey (tripping) 5:47; MON Robinson (roughing) 9:57; MON Gainey (roughing) 9:57; PHI McIlhargey (roughing) 9:57; PHI Kelly (roughing) 9:57.

THIRD PERIOD
5. MON Bouchard (Wilson) 9:16.
No penalties.

SHOTS ON GOAL:

MON	5	13	7	**25**
PHI	9	6	7	**22**

Goalies: MON Dryden; PHI Stephenson
Referee: Wally Harris
Linesmen: John D'Amico, Matt Pavelich

players. But it also pumped up ours.

As for the game itself, it was like the rest of the series—a very tough battle. Looking back, people will think that since we won that final series in four games, it was easy. But they couldn't be more wrong. The Flyers played well, and they were a good team. We just played better, and that year we were an outstanding team.

I don't believe there were many outstanding ones for me in that game because my defense protected me so well. I do recall the key moments. We scored first and then Reggie Leach scored twice for the Flyers before we tied the game in the second period. Leach, of course, had a remarkable playoff record that year, scoring 19 goals in 16 games. He played on a line with center Bobby Clarke and left wing Bill Barber.

Our tactics included wearing down Clarke by double-shifting men against him throughout the series. Clarke clearly was the key player for the Flyers, and though it was impossible to keep him or Barber and Leach from scoring some goals, at least you could limit their opportunities.

Our players did an extremely good job of controlling the pace of the game and of keeping the Flyers' scoring chances to a minimum. The game was still tied 2–2 midway in the third period when we scored the winning goal. Rick Chartraw had the Flyers' Dave Schultz tied up in front of Wayne Stephenson, the goaltender, when Pierre Bouchard fired a 45-foot shot. Stephenson undoubtedly was screened and never saw the puck go into the net. We won the game 3–2, and two nights later defeated the Flyers again to sweep the finals in four games.

The sweep made it seem that the series had been easy, but it really wasn't. We had to sip our champagne sitting down.

—*As told to George Vass*

Ken Dryden concluded a relatively brief but spectacular career in 1979, when he earned his sixth Stanley Cup ring. The five-time Vezina Trophy winner and First All-Star Team member made a brilliant debut in the 1971 playoffs, winning the Conn Smythe Trophy and then winning rookie-of-the-year honors the following season. After publishing numerous acclaimed books, Dryden became president of the Toronto Maple Leafs in 1997.

Different players have different places they remember, places they have good games on the road. I had some good nights in

**APRIL 22, 1962
CHICAGO STADIUM, CHICAGO
TORONTO 2, CHICAGO 1**

FIRST PERIOD
No scoring.
Penalties: CHI Evans (holding) 2:57; CHI Hull (boarding) 6:08; TOR Pulford (high-sticking) 12:09.

SECOND PERIOD
No scoring.
Penalties: CHI Fleming (tripping) 5:19; CHI Nesterenko (high-sticking) 7:42; TOR Baun (holding) 11:46; CHI St. Laurent (holding) 18:07.

THIRD PERIOD
1. CHI Hull (Balfour, Hay) 8:56.
2. TOR Nevin (Baun, Mahovlich) 10:29.
3. TOR Duff (Horton, Armstrong) 14:14 (PP).
Penalties: TOR Horton (tripping) 4:30; CHI Nesterenko (hooking) 13:27; TOR Horton (tripping) 19:02.

SHOTS ON GOAL:

TOR	4	8	8	**20**
CHI	13	14	8	**35**

Goalies: TOR Simmons; CHI Hall
Referee: Frank Udvari
Linesmen: Neil Armstrong, Matt Pavelich

Detroit when I was playing for the Toronto Maple Leafs and the Montreal Canadiens, but I had some of my best in Chicago.

In the late 1950s and the 1960s, Chicago Stadium was always an exciting place to play. They had some great teams in Chicago after I first started in the National Hockey League with the Leafs in 1955–56. Stan Mikita was coming on the scene, Bobby Hull and Glenn Hall—they had some great, entertaining hockey players. We always knew we had our hands full because the Chicago Blackhawks were an explosive team.

Hockey in those days was pretty rough, always very competitive, which added to the excitement. We played each other 14 times a season [in the then six-team NHL] and feelings built up a little more and carried over more than they do today when teams play each other less often. The Leafs were a team that was coming on in the late '50s and early '60s after Punch Imlach took over in 1959. Detroit and Montreal had had things pretty much their own way in Stanley Cup play during the '50s, but you had a feeling things were changing, that Toronto and Chicago were improving.

The team, when Imlach took over at Toronto in '59, was mostly young guys—Bob Pulford, George Armstrong, myself—then he got Bert Olmstead from the Canadiens. He got Allan Stanley, Johnny Bower, a few young guys to work in with the veterans and we just kind of picked it up. Even in 1959–60, though we got beat out in the playoffs in the finals against the Canadiens, and the next year, too, when we lost out in the semifinals, we had a feeling the team was there.

We felt that we were one of the good teams anyway, we were in the group that could win the Stanley Cup. In 1960–61, Montreal finished with 92 points and we chased them all year, finishing with 90. We lost out in the playoffs, and Chicago won the Cup that year, but we knew we had the right blend to do it. The next year, we finished second again to the Canadiens in the regular season, but went into the playoffs feeling good about our chances.

We put the New York Rangers out in the semifinals while Chicago was beating Montreal. Chicago had won the Cup the year before—they were never to do it again—and I guess you'd have to say that gave them an advantage in the finals against us. If you've won before, it's a little advantage, it's the edge you have. You know you can do it because you have.

We weren't quite healthy going into the series. Olmstead had been out with a broken shoulder for more than a month. I'd been hurt, too, and had missed 19 games, but I was coming around. Chicago had a reputation as a rough team. They'd slowed Montreal down with heavy checking, and some people figured they'd do the same to us. That was a challenge to our pride.

We won the first two games in Toronto, even if it cost us. Pulford tore the ligaments in his shoulder the first game of the series, and had to play hurting. When we went into Chicago for the third and fourth games we were a bit handicapped, and Chicago won both games. What's more, our goalie, Bower, was hurt in the fourth game and had to be replaced by Don Simmons, who hadn't played in more than two months.

Fortunately, when the series went back to Toronto for the fifth game, we got a break right at the beginning. Pulford scored a goal just 17 seconds into the game, and that took the wind out of Chicago's sails. We went on from there to win 8–4, and Pully, bad shoulder and all, had a hat trick.

Our win didn't convince everybody, because it had been in our own rink. Sure, we had a 3–2 edge in the series, but people were saying, wait until they go back to Chicago for the sixth game. That's the game I'll never forget, the sixth game in the Stadium.

It was one of the most exciting, emotional and best-played games I was ever involved in. The Chicago crowd at that time was unbelievable, the noise they made. It seemed like everybody brought something special to throw on the ice. Anytime a Chicago player made a solid body check or scored a goal, the crowd noise was deafening and seemed like it would never end. Chicago wanted to carry the series back to Toronto and we wanted to end it right there, to win the Cup. It was a tough, well-skated, hard-hitting game. Nobody was giving anything away. And Simmons, as rusty as he'd been going into the series, played great goal, matching Hall save for save.

It wasn't until the midway point of the third period that a goal was scored, by Bobby Hull. I was responsible for the goal that Hull got. I went back to take the puck from Simmons and I misplayed it and it went in front of the net. Hull drove it in to make it 1–0.

The crowd went mad. They threw so much stuff on the ice that it took about 15 minutes to clean it up. Sometimes the home crowd excitement of the game works to the advantage of the other team. The delay gave us a chance to recuperate, to rally, to get our composure back.

Just a few seconds after the puck was finally dropped again, Bobby Nevin scored to tie the game up 1–1. It went like that for

another three or four minutes until Eric Nesterenko of Chicago drew a holding penalty. It must have been near the 14-minute mark. I remember looking up at the clock and I'm pretty sure it said 14:41 when the winning goal was scored.

The play started with Dave Keon winning a face-off and getting the puck back to defenseman Tim Horton. Horton gave it to Armstrong, who gave it back to him in our zone. Horton gave it a rush, and saw me breaking for the net. I must have been about 20 feet from the goal. The pass was slightly behind me, but I swung around and put a shot on the net. It went in past Hall to give us the 2–1 lead that stood up.

That was the first time I'd played on a Stanley Cup winner—Toronto hadn't won it for 11 years—and I'd scored the winning goal. There are some other great games I remember, but that one really stands out.

—*As told to George Vass*

Dick Duff, above, wheels around in front of the New York Rangers net. Duff was a major contributor to Toronto's Stanley Cup victories in 1962 and 1963 before being dealt to New York in February 1964. Traded to Montreal in December 1964, he helped the Habs win the Cup in 1966, 1968 and 1969. Duff also played for Los Angeles and Buffalo before retiring in the 1971–72 season.

RON DUGUAY

**GAME 6, 1979
CAMPBELL CONFERENCE FINALS**

New York Rangers fans are on their feet, howling and screaming as loudly as they can. Madison Square Garden—its girders

---

MAY 8, 1979

MADISON SQUARE GARDEN, NEW YORK
NY RANGERS 2, NY ISLANDERS 1

FIRST PERIOD
1. NYI Bossy (Trottier, Persson) 8:54 (PP).
Penalties: NYI Lorimer (cross-checking) 3:59; NYR Murdoch (cross-checking) 7:47; NYI Hart (interference) 10:24; NYR Esposito (interference) 10:24; NYI Gillies (roughing) 15:50; NYR Dave Maloney (hooking) 15:50.

SECOND PERIOD
2. NYR Murdoch (Marois) 5:03.
3. NYR Greschner (Don Maloney, Esposito) 8:45 (PP).
Penalties: NYI Lorimer (holding) 7:33; NYI Persson (roughing) 11:56; NYR DeBlois (roughing) 11:56.

THIRD PERIOD
No scoring.
No penalties.

SHOTS ON GOAL:

NYR	9	9	9	**27**
NYI	10	9	3	**22**

Goalies: NYR Davidson; NYI Resch
Referee: Wally Harris
Linesmen: Leon Stickle, Ray Scapinello

---

and walls and roof—reverberate from the deafening roar. The tension and excitement in the air is almost tangible. The Islanders are warming up at one end and we're in the other, almost like two heavyweights about to answer the bell.

Under my jersey, I feel goose bumps forming and my heart rate rising. I look into the stands as the fans bellow: "Let's go Rangers! Let's go Rangers! Let's go Rangers!" Over and over. Again and again. Louder and louder. It's sheer pandemonium.

The buildup for Game 6 of the 1979 Campbell Conference final—the game I'll never forget—was intense. It was almost as intense as the Rangers-Islanders rivalry on the ice. There was a big misconception about the "Battle for New York." People would write that the teams hated each other. It wasn't hatred. It was just an extremely high level of competition. Did we want to beat them? You bet. Did we hate them? No.

How couldn't you respect the players on that team? In net, they had Billy Smith, one of the best playoff goalies of all time. On defense, Denis Potvin was flawless. Up front, Bryan Trottier was one of the most complete players I ever saw. He and Mike Bossy—one of the best natural goal scorers ever to step foot on NHL ice—were a lethal combination. Besides its stars, the Islanders had some great character players: Clark Gillies, Bob Bourne, Bobby Nystrom and Stefan Persson. To top it off, they were coached by a consummate professional: Al Arbour.

We went into that series as the underdogs. Phil Esposito led us that year with 42 goals. Anders Hedberg [78 points] and Ulf Nilsson [66 points] flourished in their first season with the Rangers. We had a lot of guys come up with solid campaigns, including Ron Greschner, Pat Hickey, Dave Maloney and Carol Vadnais. I myself managed 27 goals and 36 assists that season, playing primarily on a checking line with Walt Tkaczuk at center and Steve Vickers on the left wing.

We opened the playoffs with the Los Angeles Kings and dispatched them in two games. We roared past the Philadelphia Flyers in five games, and three highly unlikely things became clear: A rookie named Don Maloney was playing like a veteran on a line with Espo and Don Murdoch, a guy named Bobby Sheehan, who hadn't played one game with us during the regular season, was scoring some timely goals, and John "J.D." Davidson was hot in goal.

Our coach, Fred Shero, saw that we were peaking. In order to keep us going, he began to install a defense-first system. When we were on the ice, it was almost like Shero was our conscience, that little voice in the back of our minds saying, "Stay high...don't get caught up ice...stay with your man...You win with defense, boys."

Despite our choking defense, most observers believed the Islanders were going to send us straight to the golf course. We won

Each second seemed to last an hour as we held on to the lead.

With dashing good looks, **Ron Duguay** became one of New York City's more visible celebrities. He tallied 40 goals in 1981–82 but hit his highest point totals as a Detroit Red Wing (38 goals, 51 assists) in 1984–85. After a short stint with Pittsburgh, Duguay returned to the Rangers in January 1987. Traded to Los Angeles just over a year later, he finished his NHL career in the spring of 1989.

Game 1, but Potvin scored in overtime to give the Islanders a 4–3 victory in Game 2. We won Game 3, but again the Islanders rebounded to win the subsequent game in overtime, 3–2, on a goal by Nystrom. Then we won Game 5 on a goal by Hedberg, giving us the chance to return to the Garden and wrap up the series.

That contest wasn't a mere game, it was an event. The entire city was affixed to the series. Going into the game, between the goose bumps and the butterflies, I was a mess. The Islanders came out fast and owned the first period. Despite the barrage, J.D. was brilliant. He allowed just one goal, by Bossy.

We came back in the second period. Murdoch tied the game, defenseman Ron Greschner gave us a 2–1 lead. From there, we went back on the defensive. We clung and clutched, tripped and tugged and did whatever we could to keep Trottier, Bossy and Co. from scoring. Each second seemed to last an hour as we held on to the lead. But the final buzzer sounded and we had eliminated our arch rivals.

In the chaotic seconds after the game ended, two images are etched into my mind: First, how the whole team skated out to J.D. and hugged him. J.D. was the center and the soul of our team. Second, I remember the image of Potvin, slumped against the boards, utterly drained. The look of pain and fatigue on his face said more about the series than words ever could.

Fans took to the streets of New York. Around the Garden, they stopped traffic with their raucous celebration. In Brooklyn and Queens, they ran outside, blew their horns, and banged pots and pans. In the Bronx, the fans continued to carry on into the wee hours of the morning.

We continued to surge in the Stanley Cup finals, winning the first game in Montreal. We took a lead early in Game 2, but the mighty Canadiens came to life and went on to beat us in six games.

After the season, we were treated as if we had won the Stanley Cup. The city threw a big rally for us at City Hall. We couldn't go anywhere without people stopping us and shaking our hands, offering their congratulations, and wishing us luck for the next year. We didn't just win the battle of New York when we beat the Islanders, we won the admiration of an entire city.

—As told to Chuck O'Donnell

I had been up with the New York Americans for a handful of games in 1939–40 when we went in to play the

MARCH 17, 1940
MAPLE LEAF GARDENS, TORONTO
NEW YORK AMERICANS 5, TORONTO 2

FIRST PERIOD
1. NYA Carr (Chapman, Anderson) 3:06.
2. TOR Drillon (Apps, Davidson) 4:38.
No penalties.

SECOND PERIOD
3. NYA Smith (Sorrell, Egan) 3:32.
4. NYA Egan (Anderson, Gagnon) 17:04.
Penalty: NYA Egan.

THIRD PERIOD
5. TOR Drillon (Apps, McDonald) 11:16.
6. NYA Egan (unassisted) 13:08.
7. NYA Egan (Sorrell) 14:51.
Penalties: NYA Shore (major); TOR Davidson (major); TOR McDonald (major); NYA Conacher (major); NYA Egan.

Goalies: NYA Robertson; TOR Broda
Referees: Bill Stewart, Bill Chadwick

Toronto Maple Leafs on St. Patrick's Day. Being Irish, and still trying to comprehend that I was finally an NHL player, it was a really big game for me. Fortunately, the luck of the Irish was on my side that day.

I was lucky, first of all, because my coach, Red Dutton, was giving me a lot of playing time that night. We had been eliminated from the playoff race and were playing out the string that year. In a seven-team league, we finished sixth. We were short in talent, but we had some good nicknames. We had guys like "Cowboy" Anderson, "Buzz" Bell, Charlie "the Bomber" Conacher, Johnny "the Black Cat" Gagnon, and "Busher" Jackson. Other guys you won't find on any All-Star roster included Wilfrid Field, Art Chapman and Earl Robertson. We were a really close-knit team.

Dutton had given me a chance earlier in the season. I was beaten for a goal, though, and Dutton sent me down to our farm team in Springfield, Massachusetts, the very next day. I guess he figured that since we weren't going anywhere anyway, he might as well give me a lot of ice time that night in Toronto.

When I stepped on the ice, it was like I had found the pot of gold at the end of the rainbow. I became the second defenseman to score a hat trick in an NHL game, despite the fact that Turk Broda—a future Hall of Famer—was in net.

The first goal came while the teams were skating four-on-four. There had been some big fights, and we must have played four-on-four for about eight minutes. At one point, they sent all four men into our zone, and we trapped them. I took off on a breakaway, and they had no chance of catching me. I came in on Broda, and I saw I had a six-inch hole on the right side of the net, so I slid a backhander low on the ice that he couldn't stop.

The second goal, for some reason, I don't remember much. I took a pass and let a really good shot go from about 35 feet away. It went just over Broda's pads. But the third goal I remember, because it was very lucky. I was at the red line on the right side, and I just shot the thing. I don't know if it deflected off someone or what, but it ended up hitting Broda right in the neck. It trickled down his back and went in.

I knew that it was my night after that one went in. The only defenseman up to that point to score a hat trick was the great Hap Day. That was the most memorable game of my career for the next 10 years. But as lucky as I was to get a hat trick as a rookie, I was unlucky in my bid to win a Stanley Cup with the New York Rangers.

In 1950, we limped into the playoffs and drew the Montreal Canadiens in the first round. Somehow, we suddenly got hot and eliminated Montreal in five games. That sent us into the finals against the Detroit Red Wings. We had momentum, but we weren't able to play any of our games at Madison Square Garden. The circus had come to town as it did every year, forcing us to play on the road.

Because of that, we had to play the games that would have been home games in Toronto. Thanks to a couple of overtime goats by Don "Bones" Raleigh, we took a 3–2 lead in the series. We then took a lead in Game 6 but couldn't hold it. The Red Wings, who played the final four games at home, won to force a Game 7.

Again in Game 7, we took the lead, a two-goal lead. Chuck Rayner was playing fantastic for us in net, and rookie Pentti Lund came out of nowhere and led everyone in playoff scoring that year. Allan Stanley, Tony Leswick, Edgar Laprade, Buddy O'Connor, and Nick Mickoski were just a few of the other guys playing great. And when we took a 2–0 lead, it looked like they would be rewarded for their great play with a Stanley Cup ring.

But the Red Wings, led by future Hall of Famers like Ted Lindsay, Harry Lumley and Sid Abel, weren't about to quit. Despite playing without Gordie Howe, who suffered terrible head injuries in the previous series when he crashed into the boards, Detroit held on. The Wings scored twice on a power play when Stanley was called for an

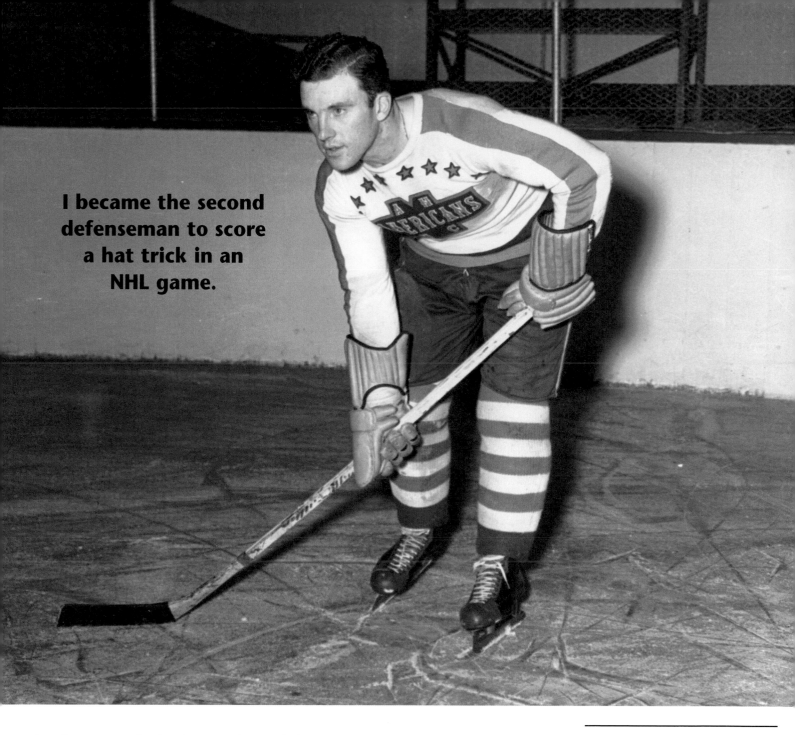

I became the second
defenseman to score
a hat trick in an
NHL game.

interference penalty in the second period, and we went into overtime tied 3–3.

In the first overtime, we carried a lot of the play. O'Connor hit the post once. And another time, I came down on a two-on-one with Jack Gordon, and when I passed it over to him as we came down, he hit the post. The teams kept slugging it out as the game went into the second overtime, but both teams were getting tired. And to make matters worse, the ice was becoming softer and softer. There was no such thing as a Zamboni back then. That made it harder to skate.

Midway through the second overtime, the Red Wings won the face-off and got the puck

to Pete Babando. Babando, who had fresh legs because he had hardly played during the game, got off a shot. It went through a maze of legs and found its way through Rayner. After 88 minutes and 31 seconds of play, the game was finally over.

That loss was really hard to take. We were such a Cinderella team, and to get that close and lose was a bitter pill to swallow. But I guess everybody's luck eventually runs out.

—*As told to Chuck O'Donnell*

Pat "Boxcar" Egan was a hard-hitting defenseman who made his 1939–40 NHL debut with the New York Americans. He made the 1942 Second All-Star Team, leading the league in penalties, just before the franchise folded. After a stint in the army, Egan played 23 games for Detroit before being traded to Boston in January 1944. After five-and-a-half seasons with the Bruins, Egan joined the New York Rangers for two campaigns, concluding his NHL career in the spring of 1951.

It's awful tough to pick out one game out of so many hundred that you've played in and say that's the one I'll never forget.

MAY 11, 1972
MADISON SQUARE GARDEN, NEW YORK
BOSTON 3, NEW YORK RANGERS 0

FIRST PERIOD
1. BOS Orr (Hodge, Bucyk) 11:18 (PP).
Penalties: BOS McKenzie (slashing) 2:32; NYR Irvine (slashing) 5:44; BOS Hodge (tripping) 7:07; NYR Tkaczuk (hooking) 10:25; BOS Hodge (high-sticking, fighting) 13:06; NYR Hadfield (high-sticking, fighting) 13:06; BOS Cashman (charging) 14:46; BOS Orr (misconduct) 14:46; NYR Doak (high-sticking) 14:46.

SECOND PERIOD
No scoring.
Penalties: BOS Vadnais (holding) 3:45; NYR Hadfield (roughing) 3:45; BOS Sanderson (kneeing, fighting) 4:33; BOS Marcotte (boarding) 4:33; NYR Gilbert (fighting) 4:33; NYR Carr (tripping) 9:16; BOS Cashman (high-sticking) 12:05; NYR Doak (high-sticking) 12:05; BOS Cashman (fighting) 16:01; NYR Tkaczuk (fighting) 16:01.

THIRD PERIOD
2. BOS Cashman (Esposito, Orr) 5:10 (PP).
3. BOS Cashman (Hodge, Esposito) 18:11.
Penalties: NYR Rolfe (holding) 3:20; BOS D. Smith (tripping) 10:36.

SHOTS ON GOAL:

BOS	9	11	13	**33**
NYR	8	9	10	**27**

Goalies: BOS Cheevers; NYR Villemure
Referee: Art Skov
Linesmen: Matt Pavelich, Neil Armstrong

There's the one I scored my 59th goal in to beat Bobby Hull's record of 58, or the one in which I got number 76. Then there's the first time I was on a Stanley Cup winner, when we beat the St. Louis Blues in 1970 to take it all. You'll never forget the first time you drink out of that cup. And you can never get that feeling back, although it's still sweet every time you win something like that.

But we figured to beat St. Louis in that 1970 series—it would have been a great upset if we hadn't. That was only the third year of expansion and the way the league was aligned at the time, all the power was in the Eastern Division. We'd beaten two tougher teams, New York and Chicago, in the playoffs before we defeated St. Louis. The Blues did give us a fight in the fourth game of the finals. We had to go into overtime before we beat them to win the Cup. But we probably would have beaten them in five games even if they'd won the fourth. It wasn't the kind of finals we had in 1972. That was much tougher. And there's a game to remember: Game 6 of the Stanley Cup finals on May 11, 1972, in New York.

You know the strong feelings between the Bruins and the Rangers. A lot of it went back to when we beat them in the opening round of the 1970 playoffs. And it was still strong two years later, when we played them in the final round. We won three of the first four games of the series and then lost the fifth game on our home ice. Later on we could laugh about it, although it didn't seem funny at the time. When we were playing the fifth game, the champagne was ready. Everybody assumed we'd beat the Rangers on our ice and take the Cup in Boston.

It didn't work that way, though. Bobby Rousseau scored a couple of goals for the Rangers, and they beat us 3–2 to take the series back to New York for Game 6. They had to cancel the reception at City Hall in Boston, which had already been planned for the next day. All the instructions on how the

Stanley Cup was to be presented had to be put on ice.

Well, we could wait—but not too long. Just two days. When we took the ice in Madison Square Garden on May 11, we were confident. The Garden fans greeted us in their usual complimentary way, but we'd heard all that before. They couldn't be any rougher than in 1971, when they'd hung up signs like "Pigface McKenzie."

The Rangers started Gilles Villemure in goal. Gerry Cheevers worked for us. They both were good, but Cheevers wasn't going to be beaten this time out. He was all around the cage, but he didn't have to work as hard as Villemure. We put the pressure on the Rangers.

Bobby Orr got the first goal for us, around the middle of the first period. He'd gone into the game with his knee heavily taped. It had been bothering him quite a while—he had surgery on it later—but you could hardly tell from the way he played. He made some kind of move around Bruce MacGregor and put a wrist shot past Villemure from about 30 feet out to give us a 1–0 lead early in the first period.

That goal had to stand up the rest of that period and right through the second. Early in the third we were leading 1–0, but it was still anybody's game when we had a face-off near Villemure. I squared off with Walt Tkaczuk, the strong Rangers center. Rangers coach Emile Francis tried to send out Pete Stemkowski in place of Tkaczuk, whom I'd been beating, but the referee waved him back to the bench. While they were arguing, I skated over to Orr and told him I'd try to get the puck back to him.

I beat Tkaczuk on the drop and laid the puck right on Orr's stick. He shot from the point, and Wayne Cashman got in front of the net and deflected the shot past Villemure to give us a 2–0 lead.

We weren't home free yet. You couldn't be sure, with the Rangers pressing like they were and about 14 minutes to play. But with just a couple of minutes left in the game, we broke their backs when I got a semi-breakaway. I spotted Kenny Hodge and passed the puck to him. He got it over to Cashman, who dumped one between Villemure's legs.

We could wait—but not too long. Just two days. When we took the ice in Madison Square Garden, we were confident.

That made it 3–0 with less than two minutes to play, and for the first time I was sure we'd win. We did, 3–0.

After the final buzzer, NHL president Clarence Campbell presented Johnny Bucyk, our captain, with the Cup, and we got off the ice in a hurry. Those Rangers fans had pretty good aim, and they were zeroing in on us.

It was our second Cup in three years. Not many players get a chance to be on one winner, let alone two. To beat the Rangers twice on their own ice was something special, too. There wasn't any champagne that night. We had to settle for beer, but it tasted just as good.

Any time you win, it's sweet.

—*As told to George Vass*

In 1968–69, **Phil Esposito** tallied 126 points, becoming the first NHL player to top 100. "Espo" also became the first to lead the league in scoring in five consecutive seasons. His 76 goals in 1970–71 remained a record for 11 years. Traded to the New York Rangers in 1975, Esposito hung up his skates in 1981. He has served as general manager of the Rangers and Tampa Bay.

When you've played as many games in goal as I have there are a lot of them that are special. You might remember them for

APRIL 5, 1970
CHICAGO STADIUM, CHICAGO
CHICAGO 10, MONTREAL 2

FIRST PERIOD
1. MON Cournoyer (Beliveau, Laperriere) 9:12 (PP).
2. CHI Pappin (Magnuson) 15:49 (PP).
3. CHI Martin (Mohns, Pinder) 17:42 (PP).
Penalties: MON Laperriere (high-sticking) 3:18; CHI Koroll (high-sticking) 3:18; CHI Jarrett (tripping) 8:35; MON Harris (holding) 14:47; MON Lemaire (tripping) 17:18; MON Ferguson (roughing) 18:56; CHI Magnuson (roughing) 18:56.

SECOND PERIOD
4. CHI B. Hull (Maki) 1:24.
5. MON Beliveau (Cournoyer, Gauthier) 3:27.
Penalty: MON Mahovlich (elbowing) 12:08.

THIRD PERIOD
6. CHI Martin (Pinder, Magnuson) 7:15.
7. CHI Martin (Koroll, Mohns) 10:44.
8. CHI Nesterenko (B. Hull, Mohns) 12:27 (EN).
9. CHI Koroll (Mikita, D. Hull) 13:57 (EN).
10. CHI B. Hull (Maki, Magnuson) 14:44 (EN).
11. CHI D. Hull (unassisted) 17:08 (EN).
12. CHI Pinder (Pappin) 19:57 (EN).
Penalty: CHI Martin (tripping) 7:52.

SHOTS ON GOAL:

CHI	12	13	13	**38**
MON	9	16	12	**37**

Goalies: CHI Esposito; MON Vachon
Referee: Art Skov
Linesmen: Neil Armstrong, Bob Myers

any number of things, like being crucial during the regular season, or being in Stanley Cup play, or even if the score was something unusual like 0–0 or even 8–7, like that one 1973 playoff game we had against Montreal.

The trouble is I don't remember details of most games even if they meant something extra to me. As an example, there was one game my first year in Chicago that was really crucial, a game we won in the stretch against Detroit. I know we won it 1–0, but I'm not even sure who scored the goal for us, though I think it might have been Pit Martin. But speaking about my first year with Chicago reminds me of the last game of the regular season; one that really was something extraordinary. It was a game against Montreal, the club I first came up to the NHL with, and it was just as important for them as for us.

That whole season [1969–70] was something special—both for the Blackhawks and me personally. The season before the Blackhawks had finished last in the division though they had some great players, guys who really could put the puck in the net, like Bobby Hull, Stan Mikita, Martin, Kenny Wharram and a lot of others. I got a brief shot with the Canadiens the year the Hawks were having their problems and I didn't do too badly. But the Canadiens really didn't have any plans for me so they left me unprotected in the draft and the Hawks picked me up. So when I joined the Hawks in the fall of 1969 we both had something to prove. The Hawks had to show they were one of the better clubs in the league and I wanted to prove I was a big league goalie.

I was fortunate. Coach Billy Reay gave me a good shot at the job and the guys played well in front of me. But we had our problems early in the season. We had a lot of rookie players, like Keith Magnuson and Cliff Koroll among others, and it took a while for the club to jell. We were in last place at mid-season, but then we began to put some streaks together. Getting defenseman Bill White from Los Angeles in a deal was a big

help. White was a fine experienced defenseman and it was hard to understand why Los Angeles traded him away. But it was a great break for us because he solidified our defense. From the time we got him, we really started moving up the ladder.

You may remember that's the season we had 15 shutouts. You won't find a better indication of how well the guys played in front of me. They really worked hard and if the guys in front of him play like that it picks up the goaltender. You're always thinking, "Don't ease up...you don't want to let the guys down." Those shutouts were really team efforts and I can't take credit for them by myself.

With a defense like that and the goal-scoring we had, we'd suddenly jelled into a good team. We kept winning and moving up until we were in a battle for first place with Boston. It went right down to the last day of the season [April 5, 1970, Chicago Stadium]. We were tied for first place with Boston on points but we had more victories. So even if we both won that day, we'd finish first. Boston was playing Toronto while we were playing Montreal.

The game was just as important for Montreal, which was battling New York for fourth place and a playoff spot. It was unthinkable for the Canadiens to be out of the playoffs. They hadn't missed them for 22 years. But they needed a victory, a tie, or at least five goals to beat out the Rangers for fourth place. You can see that a lot was at stake. What added to the game was that we'd beaten the Canadiens, 4–1, the night before at Montreal, and to beat them twice in a back-to-back weekend series would really be something special—especially for me, who'd been with them the year before.

The game started out the way most Canadiens games go. You try to check them tight and look for the break. You can't give them anything because they've always got the skating going for them. They got the first goal. I think it was midway in the first period. Like I said, I don't remember many details of games, but it seems to me that Yvan Cournoyer scored on a shot on which I was screened. That hurt, but it didn't get us down. That season we'd often fallen behind 1–0 or

2–0 and come back. We'd been doing it all season and had the confidence we could do it again. But it took a lot of work and Rogie Vachon, who was in goal for the Canadiens, was playing great. He made some good saves before we tied the game later in the first period, Jim Pappin scoring. That gave us a lift and we went on from there. Before the first period was over, Martin scored a power-play goal and we took a 2–1 lead into the second period. Like I said, I don't remember too many details. But I do recall that Martin scored three goals and we led the Canadiens, 5–2, in the middle of the final period.

There must have been eight minutes left in the game when the Canadiens coach, Claude Ruel, realized our 5–2 lead was too much to overcome the way things were going. He decided to forget about winning and concentrate on getting at least five goals. If the Canadiens lost, they'd finish in a tie with New York for fourth on the basis of wins, ties and losses, but could get into the playoffs if they had more goals scored. And they needed five. Ruel began to pull Vachon off the ice every time the Canadiens got control of the puck so that he could put another forward on. It was a gamble, and it didn't work.

I had to make some stops, but I wasn't really tested that much. Every time Vachon skated off, we got control of the puck and scored. We got five goals into the empty net in short order. I never saw a wilder game. The fans went crazy, and there were more than 20,000 of them in the Stadium. It was like a turkey shoot and they really enjoyed it. We beat the Canadiens, 10–2, and knocked them out of the playoffs, as well as finishing first ourselves. I can't think of a more satisfying game. We'd gone from last place one year to first the next, and capped it off on the final day of the season by beating Montreal, which was personally satisfying to me. I've been in a few wild scenes since, but never one that was crazier or happier than that one, including the game. The fans were just wild, screaming "We're No. 1! We're No. 1!" even after some of the players carried Reay to center ice, then rushed down to the locker room to celebrate.

I've had a lot of other games I ought to remember more about. But I don't. I forget the details. But this one, while I don't remember everything, sticks out for me. It was the combination of things: clinching first place, knocking the Canadiens out of the playoffs and the wildness of the game that made it memorable for me. Most games I can't remember, but this one I won't forget.

—*As told to George Vass*

Tony Esposito, shown making a save against Montreal's Yvan Cournoyer, played his first 13 NHL games for the Canadiens in 1968–69. Claimed by Chicago in the postseason, he established the modern day goaltending record with 15 shutouts in 1969–70, winning his first of three Vezina Trophies, the Calder Trophy and the first of five All-Star Team berths. Esposito retired in 1984 and entered the Hall of Fame in 1988, the same year the Hawks retired his No. 35.

Doug Wickenheiser fought cancer like he fought opposing defensemen for the puck in the corner—battling courageously with

MAY 12, 1986
ST. LOUIS ARENA, ST. LOUIS
ST. LOUIS 6, CALGARY 5 (OT)

FIRST PERIOD
No scoring.
Penalties: CAL Johnson (roughing) 3:54; STL Nattress (tripping) 5:30; CAL Eaves (slashing) 6:10; CAL Johnson (roughing) 9:02; STL Sutter (roughing) 9:02; CAL Sheehy (roughing) 10:19; STL Bourgeois (roughing) 10:19; STL Pavese (holding) 13:23; CAL Peplinski (fighting) 13:23; STL Ramage (fighting) 13:23; CAL McDonald (interference) 14:45; CAL Sheehy (charging) 16:00; STL Nattress (roughing) 16:00; STL Sutter (slashing) 19:20; CAL McDonald (high-sticking) 20:00; STL Gilmour (high-sticking, roughing) 20:00; CAL Otto (fighting, misconduct) 20:00; STL Bourgeois (fighting, misconduct) 20:00.

SECOND PERIOD
1. CAL Quinn (McDonald, Reinhart) 0:20 (PP).
2. CAL Quinn (Reinhart) 1:57 (PP).
3. STL Ronning (Ramage, Hunter) 5:58 (PP).
4. CAL Peplinski (Bozek, Hunter) 9:19.
5. CAL Tonelli (Quinn) 14:44 (PP).
Penalties: STL Norwood (roughing) 0:50; CAL Eaves (hooking) 5:02; STL Pavese (roughing) 6:51; STL Norwood (slashing) 14:41; STL Ramage (misconduct) 14:44; CAL MacInnis (hooking) 18:49.

THIRD PERIOD
6. STL Wickenheiser (unassisted) 5:00 (PP).
7. CAL Mullen (Peplinski) 7:04.
8. STL Sutter (Paslawski, Gilmour) 8:08.
9. STL Paslawski (Sutter, Gilmour) 15:49.
10. STL Paslawski (unassisted) 18:52.
Penalties: CAL Quinn (cross-checking) 4:11; CAL MacInnis (cross-checking) 4:55.

FIRST OVERTIME PERIOD
11. STL Wickenheiser (Hunter, Federko) 8:00.
No penalties.

SHOTS ON GOAL:

STL	5	7	19	4	**35**
CAL	9	18	10	5	**42**

Goalies: STL Wamsley; CAL Vernon
Referee: Kerry Fraser
Linesmen: Swede Knox, Ray Scapinello

all his might. And when Wickenheiser finally lost that five-year battle early this year, many of the guys he had played with in St. Louis went to his funeral to grieve the loss of a fine player and a great father and husband.

It was a very sad time, a time to reflect on what "the Wick" had meant to us. It was a time to reflect on the great things he had done with his life. And as a few of us former Blues reminisced about the Wick, we began talking about his goal that made the "Monday Night Miracle" possible.

Most of the guys that day said the Monday Night Miracle was their proudest moment with the St. Louis Blues. You could hear the emotion in their voice rise as they reminisced about the night that our blue-collar team—exhorted by our throngs of die-hard fans—showed that if it pulled together and worked hard, it could overcome the odds. It didn't matter that the Calgary Flames—our foes in the 1986 Campbell Conference finals—were superior to us in almost every phase of the game. It didn't matter that we were trailing by three goals with less than 12 minutes between us and elimination. We had to win this game—the game I'll never forget.

The Monday Night Miracle was the capper on a short series of little miracles during the 1986 playoffs. Heading into the playoffs, no one had illusions of us going very far. We limped into the postseason after finishing third in the Norris Division behind the Chicago Blackhawks and Minnesota North Stars. We had finished just three games over .500.

Injuries really hurt us that season. The leader of our team, forward Brian Sutter, was limited to just 44 games. Another key forward, right winger Greg Paslawski, played just 56 games. And Wick, who was a very strong skater and played both ends of the ice well, played in just 36 regular-season games.

The other thing that held us back was a lack of talent. We didn't have a big budget like they have now. Harry Ornest bought the franchise in the early 1980s after it almost

collapsed. As the debt mounted, the authorities padlocked the doors to the Checkerdome, and the franchise was in such disarray that it didn't participate in the 1983 entry draft. While Ornest saved the franchise, he kept the payroll low, so there was no room for mega-salaried superstars. We didn't always have extra players. We basically had 20 guys that played all the time. If we had an injury, we just had to live with it most of the time. Things were so bad, I played most of the season on two lines. I was on the first line with tough Mark Hunter and Kevin LaVallee. Then, I also played on the third line with Wick. With all that ice time, I finished the season with 102 points.

You could sense the team was starting to jell at the end of the season. But even with the team hitting its stride, no one thought we were going to get very far in the postseason. Even when we pulled off a minor upset in the Norris Division semifinals, beating the North Stars in the final game of a best-of-five series, not much was made of it.

In the second round, we had to go the distance again, this time seven games to beat the upstart Toronto Maple Leafs. It took a LaVallee goal in the final game of the best-of-seven series to knock the Leafs out.

All of a sudden, it's the middle of May—the flowers are blooming, the weather is warmer—and we're still playing, gearing up to play the Flames in the Campbell Conference finals. We were on a roll, and we rolled into Calgary and won the opening game, 5–2. Calgary stormed back and won Games 2, 3 and 5.

Despite knowing we were facing elimination, we didn't play well for the first two periods of Game 6. I can remember sitting in the locker room before the third period when coach Jacques Demers began to address the team. "You guys have had a great playoff," Demers said. "Here you are in Game 6. No one expected you to be here. Let's just go out and whatever happens, happens. If we don't come back and don't win, it's no big deal. But hey, let's keep going. Let's go down fighting." Then Demers began to talk about Barclay Plager, a former Blues player and coach, who was battling cancer. "Let's win it for Barc," Demers exalted.

It seemed as though the Flames had dodged the bullet. The next second, however, the rebound dribbled to Wick, and he pushed it into the open net.

Sutter's rebound goal off a shot by Paslawski launched the comeback, cutting the deficit to 5–3 with 11:52 to go. Paslawski—who scored 10 goals in the playoffs that year—scored yet again, this time with 4:11 remaining to cut it to 5–4.

Pazzer wasn't done. Mike Vernon, Calgary's rookie goalie, made a fatal mistake that allowed us to tie the game with 1:08 remaining. He was caught out of the net by Paslawski and he never expected Pazzer to lift his stick, steal the puck, come around the net, and stuff it in.

Then Wick made the miracle complete in overtime. I had stolen the puck from defenseman Paul Reinhart and gave it to Hunter. He moved in with Wick on a two-on-one. The crowd rose to its feet, sensing this could be the game-winner. When Vernon stopped Hunter, there was a second there where it seemed as though the Flames had dodged the bullet. The next second, however, the rebound dribbled to Wick, and he pushed it into the open net.

We would eventually lose, 2–1, in Game 7, but I'll never forget how the team poured off the bench and gathered around Wick after he scored that goal. I'll never forget how proud we were to be Blues and that big smile across Wick's face. That's how I'll always remember him.

—*As told to Chuck O'Donnell*

Bernie Federko joined the league's top 10 scoring list three times. He set St. Louis franchise records that still stand for seasons (13), games (927), career assists (721) and points (1,073). Federko has been a broadcaster for the Blues since he retired in 1990. His sweater No. 24 was officially retired on March 16, 1991.

I know there have been some great rivalries in the history of hockey, but I can't imagine a more heated, emotional

APRIL 8, 1971
BOSTON GARDEN, BOSTON
MONTREAL 7, BOSTON 5

FIRST PERIOD
1. MON Cournoyer (Beliveau) 3:32.
2. BOS Orr (Stanfield, McKenzie) 4:34.
3. BOS Green (Hodge, Esposito) 5:43.
Penalties: BOS Green (minor, misconduct) 7:27; BOS Awrey (major) 7:27; MON Tardif (major) 7:27; MON Roberto 8:14.

SECOND PERIOD
4. BOS McKenzie (Orr, Stanfield) 2:49 (PP).
5. BOS Cashman (Esposito, Orr) 6:31.
6. BOS Sanderson (Orr, Westfall) 8:41.
7. MON Richard (unassisted) 15:33.
Penalties: MON Harper 1:06; MON Larose 7:42; BOS Awrey 7:42; BOS Orr 9:59; MON Roberto 15:33; BOS Sanderson 15:33; BOS (bench) 15:33; BON Bailey (misconduct) 20:00.

THIRD PERIOD
8. MON Beliveau (Cournoyer, Ferguson) 2:58 (PP).
9. MON Beliveau (Ferguson, Cournoyer) 4:22.
10. MON Lemaire (unassisted) 9:59.
11. MON Ferguson (Beliveau) 15:23.
12. MON F. Mahovlich (Roberto) 18:40.
Penalties: BOS Esposito 2:07; MON F. Mahovlich 8:34; BOS Cashman 8:34; MON Beliveau 19:14; BOS Sanderson 19:14; MON Harper 19:47.

SHOTS ON GOAL:

MON	12	11	14	**37**
BOS	14	12	10	**36**

Goalies: MON Dryden; BOS Johnston
Referee: Art Skov
Linesmen: John D'Amico, Ron Ego

one than the one my Montreal Canadiens had with the Boston Bruins in the 1960s and '70s. When they saw us take the ice in our blue, white and red jerseys, their hearts raced, their teeth gnashed and their fists clenched. We had the same reaction at the very sight of Bruins black and gold.

The rivalry brought out the best in the players. We shot and hit harder, passed better, skated faster, and played with more passion than ever before. The only thing better was when we would meet in the playoffs. The play became even fiercer, if that's possible.

The 1971 playoffs were one of the early classics of the rivalry. The Bruins were big, bad and immensely talented. With Bobby Orr as the catalyst, the defending Stanley Cup champions had put on one of the greatest offensive explosions that side of the Edmonton Oilers of the 1980s. Strapping center Phil Esposito led the league that season with a then-record 152 points, defenseman Orr was second with 139; winger Johnny Bucyk was third and Ken Hodge was fourth. Tough left-winger Wayne Cashman was seventh in the NHL with 79 points, John McKenzie was right behind him with 77, and Fred Stanfield tied for ninth in the league with 76 points.

When they weren't busy scoring one of their then-record 399 goals—122 more than any other club that season—the Bruins could play defense. Derek Sanderson and Eddie Westfall were very effective checkers and Dallas Smith, Ted Green and Don Awrey were solid backliners. When all that failed and an opponent actually got off a shot, Gerry Cheevers and Eddie Johnston were like stone walls in front of the net.

Comparatively, that was not a vintage season for us. In fact, it was a transition year. It was Jean Beliveau's last year and Guy Lapointe's and Peter Mahovlich's first full seasons. Henri Richard's great career was winding down and Serge Savard and Jacques

Lemaire were just coming into their own. Guys like lightning-fast winger Yvan Cournoyer and defensemen J.C. Tremblay and Jacques Laperriere formed the backbone of the club. Several changes during the season breathed life into the team. Al MacNeil took over as coach for Claude Ruel early in the season. The addition of Frank Mahovlich, Peter's brother, gave us some much-needed offensive spark down the stretch. The decision to call up a young goalie named Ken Dryden from our Nova Scotian farm team and give him the starting job would soon prove to be a fantastic idea.

In 1971, we entered the playoffs as the underdogs for a change. We were paired with the Bruins in the first round. That they had finished 24 points ahead of us in the East Division made them the overwhelming favorites. After the Bruins won Game 1, 3–1, it seemed like they were going to prove everyone right. They took a 5–1 lead late in the second period in Game 2 and everybody figured it was lights out for the Canadiens. Orr was flying, Espo had set up shop in our crease, and Cheevers could have stopped a grain of rice with a thimble. I guess you could say there was a Boston Garden party on tap.

Cournoyer had opened the scoring, but Orr and Green scored in the first period to give Boston a 2–1 lead. McKenzie, Cashman and Sanderson added second-period goals. When Richard scored to pull us to within 5–2 late in the second period, no one on the Bruins bench batted an eyelash.

We retreated to the locker room between the second and third periods. You might imagine a rah-rah speech or some dramatic pep talk from MacNeil, considering a loss would have been devastating to our chances of winning the series, but there wasn't. I think it was at that point we tapped into the Montreal Canadiens tradition. We were a team that did not panic. We were confident. You respected the other team but you were confident enough to know you had to win the game. You were expected to win when you were a Canadien. We took the ice for the third period with that thought in mind.

Beliveau scored early in the third period,

> **When they saw us take the ice in our blue, white and red jerseys, their hearts raced, their teeth gnashed and their fists clenched.**

and it was a game once more. He scored again, and the Bruins began to panic. Lemaire tied the game. We were coming on strong. Then I scored to give us the lead. I don't remember anything about the goal. I didn't even see it go in. I got hit and couldn't follow the puck. I only knew it went in when the light went on.

My goal was extra sweet because my job when we played Boston was to check Orr. Usually the left wing checks the right wing, but my duty was to go in deep and check him and come out of the zone with him so he couldn't handle the puck. Nowhere in the game plan was I supposed to score. But with the goal, the tide had turned. Frank Mahovlich added an insurance goal and we had stormed back from nowhere to win the

game, the game I'll never forget, 7–5.

By no means did it mean we had control of the series. In one of the most bitter battles I can remember, we beat them in seven games, winning the final game in Boston, 4–2. We beat the Minnesota North Stars to advance to the Stanley Cup finals. In the finals, we lost the first two games to Chicago, but rallied to beat the Blackhawks in seven.

When I look back, I don't think we would have been sipping out of that great, big silver cup had we not rallied to beat the Bruins in Game 2 of that opening round.

—*As told to Chuck O'Donnell*

In only eight NHL seasons, **John Ferguson** collected five Stanley Cup rings. An aggressive checker and willing fighter, he played an enforcer's role while still contributing important goals. After retiring in 1971, he served as assistant coach to Team Canada in the 1972 Summit Series. Ferguson coached and managed the New York Rangers and the Winnipeg Jets. He led the scouting department of the Ottawa Senators before taking on the same job for the San Jose Sharks.

RAY FERRARO

Players and teams often play their best when no one gives them a chance to win. That's how it was in 1993 when I was

MAY 14, 1993
CIVIC ARENA, PITTSBURGH
NEW YORK ISLANDERS 4, PITTSBURGH 3
(OT)

FIRST PERIOD
No scoring.
Penalties: NYI Dalgarno (roughing) 0:06; PIT Stevens (holding) 0:06; PIT Tocchet (elbowing) 5:25; NYI Vaske (interference) 7:45; NYI Kasparaitis (cross-checking) 9:56; PIT Mullen (high-sticking) 9:56; NYI Thomas (charging) 18:00.

SECOND PERIOD
1. PIT U. Samuelsson (Lemieux, K. Samuelsson) 7:59.
2. NYI Thomas (Hogue) 18:28.
Penalties: PIT Tippett (holding the stick) 2:32; NYI Malakhov (interference) 5:46.

THIRD PERIOD
3. NYI Volek (Ferraro, Fitzgerald) 6:10.
4. NYI Hogue (Malakhov, Healy) 9:09.
5. PIT Francis (Murphy) 16:13.
6. PIT Tocchet (Francis, Murphy) 19:00.
Penalties: NYI Pilon (unsportsmanlike conduct) 7:50; PIT Tocchet (unsportsmanlike conduct) 7:50; NYI Krupp (slashing) 15:35; PIT Lemieux (slashing) 15:35.

FIRST OVERTIME PERIOD
7. NYI Volek (Ferraro, Vaske) 5:16.
No penalties.

SHOTS ON GOAL:

NYI	7	4	6	3	**20**
PIT	19	7	16	3	**45**

Goalies: NYI Healy; PIT Barrasso
Referee: Andy Van Hellemond
Linesmen: Ray Scapinello, Swede Knox

playing for the New York Islanders against the Pittsburgh Penguins in the Patrick Division final.

We were heavy underdogs the whole series. Nobody—I mean nobody—thought we could beat the Penguins, who were two-time defending Stanley Cup champions. We'd barely finished over .500 in the regular season, and came into the playoffs as the 13th team of the 16 that made the playoffs.

In the first round, we'd upset the Washington Capitals four games to two. I scored the game-winning goal in overtime of Game 3, and the game-winner in double overtime of Game 4. I also scored four goals in Game 5. People figured our luck was about to run out.

By the time we advanced to play Pittsburgh, we were a little beaten up. Even at full strength, we would have been underdogs against the Penguins, but we were playing the series without forwards Pierre Turgeon, Travis Green and Pat Flatley. Still, we were hoping we could surprise a few people. We'd won twice in Pittsburgh during the regular season that year and had played them tough in just about every game.

In the first game of the playoff series, there was an early indication that things might go right. We took two penalties in the first minute of the first game, so we were down five-on-three. Not only did we kill off the two-man disadvantage, but as I came out of the penalty box, the puck jumped over defenseman Larry Murphy's stick. I got a breakaway and went in and scored. We ended up winning the first game 3–2. Winning in Pittsburgh really helped our confidence. The series turned into a real war, but we managed to push it to a seventh game in Pittsburgh that, once again, no one gave us much chance of winning.

We played solidly right from the start of Game 7. We took a 1–0 lead late in the second period, then David Volek scored about five minutes into the third period. David and I

came in two-on-two, I dropped the puck to him and he beat Penguins goalie Tom Barrasso. David hadn't been playing much, but with the injury to Flatley he was put into the line-up. I really hadn't played with him at all that season, but the lines became a mishmash because of all the injuries.

With about four minutes left in the game, we had a 3–1 lead. Then our Uwe Krupp and Pittsburgh's Mario Lemieux took roughing minors. We thought—or should I say, I thought—that it was good for us, that maybe we'd be able to sneak through the last few minutes of the game with Mario off the ice. But Pittsburgh ended up scoring twice. Ron Francis scored on a deflection to force the game into sudden-death overtime.

Waiting for overtime to start, our locker room was filled with emotion. Players were saying, "I can't believe we let this one get away—we were so close." Yet the feeling that won out was: If we were told before the series we would be given one shot to beat Pittsburgh, would we take that? Of course we would.

Francis had a great chance about two minutes into overtime. He took a slapshot that forced Glenn Healy to make a great glove save. Healy was great all series, but especially in Game 7. A few minutes later, Pens defenseman Ulf Samuelsson got caught pinching up. That created a two-on-one for me and David Volek. I'd scored a lot of goals in the playoffs to that point, and I thought more of shooting at that instance because I felt so confident. But Kjell Samuelsson was the guy back for them, and he came closer to me and really took that shot away. I made a little flip pass to my right to David, who took it in stride and one-timed it past Tom Barrasso, high to the glove side.

We piled on top of one another in the corner. When I started to skate out of the pile, the arena was so deafly quiet that I could hear Glenn Healy skating down from the other end screaming. I'll never forget the shocked looks on the Penguins' faces—nor the jubilation on ours.

It was bedlam in the locker room, but we didn't have long to celebrate. We had a plane to catch in two hours to go play Montreal in

The arena was so deafly quiet that I could hear Glenn Healy skating down from the other end screaming. I'll never forget the shocked looks on the Penguins' faces—nor the jubilation on ours.

the Wales Conference finals. We eventually lost to the Canadiens, four games to two. They went on to beat the Los Angeles Kings and win the Stanley Cup.

There are other games that stick out in my mind. In my second game in the league, while playing for the Hartford Whalers, I had a goal and three assists. That was a thrill. Another time, while playing for the Islanders, we were in Detroit. About an hour

before the game, I got called out into the hallway. Coach Al Arbour and a reporter told me I had just been named to play in the All-Star Game. That really got me pumped up— I went out and had four goals and an assist.

Those games were memorable, but our series-clinching overtime victory over the Penguins in 1993 was simply unforgettable.

—*As told to Chuck O'Donnell*

Ray Ferraro broke into the NHL with the Hartford Whalers during the 1984–85 season. Traded to the New York Islanders in November 1990, he had his most productive offensive season in 1991–92 with 40 goals and 40 assists. Dealt to Los Angeles in March 1996, he signed with the Atlanta Thrashers as a free agent in August 1999. The St. Louis Blues acquired the veteran goal scorer at the March 2002 trade deadline.

It might be a better idea to rewrite the title of this to "The Games I'll Never Forget," simply because the one I like so much is so

**MAY 9, 1992
CIVIC ARENA, PITTSBURGH
PITTSBURGH 5, NEW YORK RANGERS 4
(OT)**

FIRST PERIOD
1. NYR Gilhen (unassisted) 4:56.
2. NYR Amonte (Gartner) 13:04.
3. PIT Needham (Loney, Callander) 13:28.
Penalties: NYR Beukeboom (high-sticking) 1:49; NYR King (slashing) 7:01; NYR Leetch (hooking) 15:12; PIT Francis (elbowing) 16:04.

SECOND PERIOD
4. NYR Messier (Leetch, Gartner) 10:49 (PP).
5. PIT Francis (Stevens, Stanton) 19:54 (PP).
Penalties: NYR Kocur (holding) 3:19; PIT Tocchet (slashing) 9:51; PIT Errey (holding) 10:15; NYR Erixon holding) 18:27.

THIRD PERIOD
6. NYR Messier (Amonte, Beukeboom) 0:46.
7. PIT Francis (Hrdina, Stevens) 10:27.
8. PIT Loney (Jagr, Murphy) 11:52.
Penalties: PIT Roberts (cross-checking, game misconduct) 5:19; NYR Beukeboom (charging) 15:26; PIT Stevens 15:26.

FIRST OVERTIME PERIOD
9. PIT Francis (Murphy, Stevens) 2:47 (PP).
Penalty: NYR Beukeboom (holding) 1:17.

SHOTS ON GOAL:

NYR	13	8	9	0	**30**
PIT	6	13	13	4	**36**

Goalies: NYR Richter, Vanbiesbrouck; PIT Barrasso
Referee: Rob Shick
Linesmen: Kevin Collins, Gerard Gauthier

closely intertwined with at least two others. They all came together in the end to be part of Pittsburgh's second straight Stanley Cup.

We had entered the playoffs as defending champion, but plenty of doubt had surrounded our club. There was the death of our 1991 coach, Bob Johnson; there were trades; there was the disappointing finish and questions about whether we had the goods to repeat. Certainly our first four games in the opening round against Washington created plenty of skeptics. We went down three games to one and had to play Game 5—and 7 if we made it that far—at the Capital Center.

But we had already overcome a lot. Bob Johnson was like a father to us, but we made the adjustment to Scotty Bowman. We overcame the sale of the team. The sign of a good hockey club is how it handles adversity, and we handled it pretty well—beating Washington in three straight games to reach the Patrick Division finals. Now we were up against the Rangers, who had finished first overall in the league.

The series opened at Madison Square Garden, and we surprised the Rangers with a 4–2 win. I played well. I had an assist and the final goal and took most of the important face-offs for us. Everything seemed to be falling into place for us again in Game 2, until Mario Lemieux was slashed by Adam Graves and right after that Joey Mullen went down with a damaged knee. We blew a lead and lost the game, then returned home and lost Game 3. That brings me to my most memorable game.

No question, we were in a hole. Not only were we down two games to one, but we were desperate. If we lose Game 4, we're trailing the Rangers three games to one, with the series returning to New York, and we knew that Mario and Joey were gone for the duration. Plus two other key guys, Rick Tocchet and Kjell Samuelsson were still out with injuries.

I thought I did well in Game 3. I led all players with nine shots on goal and had two goals and an assist, but we still lost in overtime. Going into Game 4, I knew I had to do a lot more. I made a point of thinking I had to hang higher in our own end and think more offensively all over the ice. My game never was speed and skating. I just try to anticipate and figure out the shortest way from A to B.

We didn't start very well. The Rangers went up 2–0, but we trimmed it to 2–1. Then it was 3–1 for them. In the last minute of the second period, we had a power play, and with six seconds left in the period, I got a rebound of a Kevin Stevens shot. I was standing right in front of the net and had no trouble putting it in.

Unfortunately, Mark Messier got one for the Rangers in the first minute of the third, and we were down by two again. As if that wasn't bad enough, we got hit with a five-minute major against a team whose power play had been dynamite.

Somehow, we survived the five minutes and kept them off the scoreboard. But we were still down by two with only 10 minutes left in the third period. Our club wasn't disheartened, but we knew we were in a crucial situation.

I've often said that the one thing about luck is, it's going to change. In my case, I had had a lot of opportunities against Washington and I missed them. Guys I was setting up were missing opportunities. But all of a sudden my luck changed. I had the puck just outside their blue line and decided to wind up and put the puck on the net. I'd like to lie and tell you that I shot a rocket, but that wasn't the case. For some reason, Richter seemed handcuffed by the shot. The puck hit his glove, bounced off, and wound up behind him and, finally, in the net.

Now we smelled blood. Less than two minutes later, Troy Loney rapped Jaromir Jagr's pass into the net, and we were all tied up. Rangers coach Roger Neilson yanked Richter, and John Vanbiesbrouck finished the game in the Rangers net.

Into overtime we went, and when Jeff Beukeboom got penalized for holding Jaromir Jagr, that really put us in a good spot.

I managed to get my stick on it, and all I knew was that the puck went behind me. Then I heard the crowd roar, and Kevin Stevens absolutely tackled me.

Ironically, when we lined up for the face-off in the Rangers end, Scotty Bowman originally wanted me to play the point. I told him I'd rather be up front. As a centerman, I'd rather work down low on the power play. "Fine," he said. "You go up, and Phil [Bourque] will work the point."

We managed to get the puck in deep, and it wound up behind the net in the right corner. Messier tried to skate out with it, but Larry Murphy pinched in and got the puck away from him. That was the big play. I went to the net as Murph swiped at the puck. I managed to get my stick on it, and all I knew was that the puck went behind me. Then I heard the crowd roar, and Kevin Stevens absolutely tackled me.

How about that! I had my first Stanley Cup sudden-death goal and my first playoff

hat trick. But the biggest thing was that the goal got us a very important win.

We didn't look back after that, and we won the next two games to clinch the Patrick Division championship—all without Mario and Joey. Then we swept Boston in four— Mario returned for Game 2—and then knocked out the Blackhawks in four as well.

It wouldn't be fair to history if I didn't also mention Game 4 of the finals in Chicago. After all, there aren't many guys who can claim they played on two straight Stanley Cup winners, and there aren't many who can say they scored the game-winning goal in the Cup-winning game. But you can look it up. We beat Chicago 6–5 in the finale, and for the sixth goal it says, "Francis (McEachern, Paek), 7:59."

—*As told to Stan Fischler*

Ron Francis broke into the NHL with Hartford in 1981–82. After almost a decade of productive work for the also-ran Whalers, Francis was dealt to the up-and-coming Pittsburgh Penguins. He promptly helped the Pens win consecutive Stanley Cups. Francis has won the Lady Byng Trophy twice and the Frank Selke Trophy. He signed with Carolina (the transplanted Whalers) in July 1998. Francis, still one of the league's top playmakers, holds the franchise records for games, goals, assists and points.

RAY'S TRIUMPH

While the Stanley Cup finals always produce emotional moments, Ray Bourque added one of the most poignant memories in recent years when he hoisted the Cup in 2001. The 1979–80 rookie of the year, Bourque requested a trade after almost 21 seasons with the Boston Bruins. Eighteen times an All-Star, five times the Norris Trophy winner as top defenseman and the highest scoring rearguard in NHL history, Bourque joined Colorado for a Cup run on March 6, 2000. That season ended earlier than he wished, but Bourque and his Avalanche teammates were on a mission in 2000–2001.

All was going according to plan and Colorado plowed through the playoffs until their star center Peter Forsberg's season ended suddenly. Forsberg had his spleen removed in emergency surgery. The Avalanche fell behind 3–2 in games to the New Jersey Devils, the defending Cup champions. Relying heavily on goalie Patrick Roy, though, Colorado rallied to win Games 6 and 7.

Joe Sakic, Colorado's classy captain, accepted the Stanley Cup from NHL Commissioner Gary Bettman but immediately handed it to Bourque, allowing his teammate the honor of raising the hallowed mug first. Bourque's tears of jubilation were shared by most. He announced his retirement several weeks later.

—*Chris McDonell*

JUNE 9, 2001
PEPSI CENTER, DENVER
COLORADO 3, NEW JERSEY 1

As an 18-year-old rookie defenseman in the NHL, you look for little things to help improve your confidence. A nice pass here,

FEBRUARY 16, 1947
CHICAGO STADIUM, CHICAGO
CHICAGO 3, DETROIT 2

FIRST PERIOD
1. CHI Kaleta (Brown, Gadsby) 4:06 (SH).
2. CHI M. Bentley (D. Bentley, Brown) 16:15 (PP).
Penalties: CHI Gee (elbowing) 0:58; DET Horek (high-sticking) 0:58; CHI Mariucci (elbowing) 3:02; DET Howe (slashing) 14:51; DET Lumley (high-sticking, served by Bruneteau) 16:04; CHI Gee (high-sticking) 16:04; CHI Brown (holding) 16:44.

SECOND PERIOD
3. DET Lindsay (Abel, R. Conacher) 12:49.
Penalties: CHI D. Bentley (high-sticking) 3:54; DET Lindsay (high-sticking) 3:54; CHI Mariucci (charging); CHI Gadsby (tripping).

THIRD PERIOD
4. DET Reise (unassisted) 0:47.
5. CHI Gadsby (D. Bentley, M. Bentley) 19:58.
Penalties: CHI Mariucci (fighting) 16:14; CHI Brown (fighting) 16:14; CHI Kaleta (fighting) 16:14; J. Jackson (fighting) 16:14; DET McCaig (fighting) 16:14; Taylor (fighting) 16:14; DET Horeck (fighting) 16:14.

Goalies: CHI Francis; DET Lumley
Referee: King Clancy
Linesmen: Ed Mepham, Jim Primeau

a blocked shot there. Just making the routine plays helped to tell you that you belonged with the big boys. In my first year with the Chicago Blackhawks, 1946–47, I got the biggest confidence booster of them all. I was chosen to play with the great Bentley brothers on a three-on-three situation in a game against the Detroit Red Wings. On that shift, I scored the game-winning goal with two seconds remaining.

It was a big win, especially considering we didn't win many games that year. There were only six teams in the league, and five of them finished ahead of us. We won just 19 of our 60 games, allowing 81 more goals than any other team. On the other hand, the Red Wings were one of the up-and-coming teams in the league. They had some good forwards like Sid Abel and Ted Lindsay. They had a pair of absolutely brilliant defensemen in Bill Quackenbush and Black Jack Stewart. In goal, they had Harry Lumley. And, oh yeah, they also had this rookie named Gordie Howe. He scored just seven goals that year but, over time, he would become a pretty good goal scorer.

Even though we were struggling, we fought every game—sometimes literally. Our game with the Red Wings turned out to be a real fight-filled contest. It was building up until we had the main event between Stewart and Johnny Mariucci. They were both tough, nasty defensemen. When they dropped the gloves, everyone just stopped and watched. Those guys must have gone at it for two or three minutes before they were separated. In those days, there was only one penalty box, so they resumed fighting while they were in there.

Between the Stewart-Mariucci fight and others, we ended up having a three-on-three situation. The score was 2–2, and there were only a few minutes remaining in the game. Of course, coach Johnny Gottselig was going to use Max and Doug Bentley. They were the stars of our team. Max won the scoring title that year with 72 points, and Doug finished sixth with 55 points. A third linemate, Bill Mosienko, who completed our "Pony Line," finished ninth in the league with 52 points.

But Gottselig needed another player, preferably a defenseman, out there with the Bentleys. He called them over to the bench and said, "Who do you want out there with you?" They pointed to me and said, "Give us the kid. Give us Bill."

I was in the middle of a pretty good rookie year. I finished with eight goals and 10 assists. Those were pretty good numbers for a defenseman back then. Defensemen didn't go rushing down the ice with the puck like they do now. Back then, it was defense first, and then maybe you thought about helping out on the attack.

Although it made me feel good that the Bentleys picked me, it also made me nervous. For one thing, it was a three-on-three. There wasn't much room for error. All you had to do was get behind your man by a half-step, and the game was over. I was also nervous because I grew up a big fan of Max and Doug. While I was playing junior hockey, I would watch them on *Hockey Night in Canada* or listen to Foster Hewitt broadcast their games on the radio. Now, all of a sudden, I was playing with these guys. It was a real thrill.

Max was a magician with the puck. He could really cut and turn on his skates, and he made some great passes. Doug was more of a goal scorer. He had a really strong, accurate shot. They were a great complement to each other. I handled the puck pretty well, and I could pass it, so I guess that's why they picked me.

So Max, Doug and I took the ice. My plan was just to get them the puck and let them go with it, and it worked. They took it into the zone and passed it around and finally set up for a shot out in front. I shot the puck right into the side of the net—Lumley didn't have much of a chance to stop it—giving us a 3–2 lead. I looked up at the scoreboard after and saw there was two seconds left. I couldn't believe it. My teammates mobbed me after the game. We were happy we had beaten the Red Wings because the game was so bitterly fought. It was a rewarding victory.

In those days, there was only one penalty box, so they resumed fighting while they were in there.

I went on and played in 1,248 regular-season games over 20 seasons and another 67 playoff games, but that was the one game I'll never forget. Getting to play in that situation and scoring that goal gave me a lot of confidence at a time when I needed it. It showed me that I could play with the best of them. In some ways, I attribute my long career to that goal. After all, I'm still looking back on it as if it were yesterday.

—As told to Chuck O'Donnell

Bill Gadsby captained the Chicago Blackhawks in 1952–53 and 1953–54, when he earned his first two of seven All-Star Team nominations. Traded to New York in November 1954, he helped anchor the Rangers' blue line through the 1960–61 season while finishing runner-up for the Norris Trophy three times. Gadsby played five seasons for the Red Wings, retiring after the 1965–66 campaign. He entered the Hall of Fame in 1970.

BOB GAINEY

When we were having our good years with the Montreal Canadiens, winning Stanley Cups, a lot of people asked me if I was

MAY 19, 1979
MADISON SQUARE GARDEN, NEW YORK
MONTREAL 4, NEW YORK RANGERS 3 (OT)

FIRST PERIOD
1. NYR Hickey (Dave Maloney, Sheehan) 1:19.
2. MON Houle (Gainey) 2:39.
3. NYR Murdoch (Esposito, Hickey) 17:03.
Penalties: MON Chartraw (interference) 3:34; NYR Don Maloney (slashing) 3:34; MON Chartraw (elbowing) 5:49; MON Lupien (tripping) 10:13; MON Chartraw (slashing) 11:06; NYR Esposito (slashing) 11:06; NYR Johnstone (slashing) 13:54.

SECOND PERIOD
4. MON Lambert (Houle) 16:05.
Penalties: NYR Dave Maloney (hooking) 1:18; MON Lemaire (tripping) 2:15; NYR McEwan (holding) 7:41.

THIRD PERIOD
5. NYR Esposito (Don Maloney, Dave Maloney) 4:26.
6. MON Gainey (unassisted) 6:27.
Penalty: NYR Greschner (tripping) 7:58.

FIRST OVERTIME PERIOD
7. MON Savard (Lafleur, Shutt) 7:25.
No penalties.

SHOTS ON GOAL:

MON	11	15	11	5	**42**
NYR	9	4	7	1	**21**

Goalies: MON Dryden; NYR Davidson
Referee: Andy Van Hellemond

happy with being an "unsung hero." The answer is, I was always happy to be on a winner. Sure, if the players on the Canadiens were ranked in terms of publicity, maybe I was 12th, 13th, or even lower—but to tell the truth, so many people called me underrated that maybe I was overrated.

None of that ever bothered me. I always knew what my role was with the Canadiens, and as long as I fulfilled it, I felt satisfied that I was doing a good job. You've got to score goals to win in this league, but it's just as important to have players going the other way, which is what I've been doing ever since I started playing hockey. The Canadiens always have had the goal scorers since I've been with them, people such as Guy Lafleur, Jacques Lemaire, Steve Shutt and a lot of others. But they also had their defensive players, and when we had our best years, the defensive play was just as much of a factor as the goal-scoring, if not more.

I was a little disappointed, maybe concerned, when the Canadiens drafted me in 1973. It was hard for a rookie to get much opportunity to play on the Canadiens, especially with me not being known for my goal-scoring, but then I figured the Canadiens wouldn't have wasted a No. 1 draft choice on me if they didn't think I had NHL potential. That reassured me.

I spent part of my first season in the minors, but most of it with the Canadiens, and I dressed for every game, though I didn't get much ice time. My second year, I was on a regular line with Lemaire and Yvan Cournoyer, two veterans who helped me a great deal. Over the next couple of years, our team fell into place, with Ken Dryden coming back to play goal after taking a year off, and Guy Lafleur breaking through as the best player in the league. Larry Robinson came along, as did Mario Tremblay, Doug Jarvis and some others.

By my third year, I knew I could play in this league. I didn't have to sit on the bench and worry. What gave me confidence was

our 1975 Stanley Cup playoff series against the Buffalo Sabres. We didn't win the Cup that year, but I thought I had a good series. The next year, we started winning that series of four Stanley Cups in a row. There were a lot of outstanding games to remember, such as the one in which we won our first Cup.

I can't say I recall too many games in which my goals were the difference, though there were some. I just never have been a goal scorer. It's hard to explain why. I could always skate well enough to get into position to score goals, and I shoot the puck well enough. But I've never let my offensive play take anything away from my defensive positioning, and that has made a difference.

I'm aware that the club has a right to expect a few goals from me. And I know how much I can produce. I know when I've played a good game. That's when I've done my job checking and I've had a few chances and the guys I'm playing against haven't had any.

Of course, it's good to know other people appreciate the way you play, even if it doesn't show up in goals scored. I've been lucky enough to win the Frank Selke Trophy several times and it has been a great satisfaction to me. But the greatest satisfactions of my career have been first making the NHL as a regular player and then winning those Stanley Cups.

Then comes the Conn Smythe Trophy, which I was awarded after our fourth Stanley Cup, in 1979. The award really surprised me because it almost always goes to an offensive standout. I did have my best Stanley Cup playoffs that year in terms of scoring, however, with six goals and 10 assists. Maybe that had something to do with winning the trophy, because it showed I could be an all-around player.

One game in particular sticks out for me from that playoff: The fourth game of the finals against the New York Rangers in Madison Square Garden. We had won two of the first three games of the series, but New York could have got back into contention by winning the fourth game on its own ice, making it 2–2. It was a pivotal game. It was probably the best game of the set, tightly played, and with the Rangers fired up in front of their own fans. I think New York took a 2–1 lead out of the first period, and we didn't tie the game until Yvon Lambert got a goal late in the second period to make it 2–2.

Early in the third period, Phil Esposito scored to put the Rangers ahead 3–2. A couple of minutes later I scored the tying goal, and the way the play developed is what makes it stick out in my mind. David Maloney had the puck for the Rangers in their end, and I threw a body check into him. The check jarred the puck loose, and I got my stick on it and got away a shot.

The Rangers goalie, John Davidson, was screened, and the puck went into the net to tie the game 3–3, which is the way it went into overtime. Serge Savard scored the winning goal after about seven minutes of overtime to give us a 3–1 lead in games in the series, and we won the next game to make it four Stanley Cups in a row.

That was a key goal for me in a key game, because if the Rangers had won it would have tied the finals at two apiece. Savard's goal was probably the turning point of the series, but mine—by tying the game—had made it possible by sending the game into overtime. That game has to rank among my most memorable, though there were a lot of them during the many fine seasons we had with the Canadiens.

—As told to George Vass

Bob Gainey was a member of five Stanley Cup winners with the Montreal Canadiens. He won four Selke Trophies as the league's top defensive forward, a league record. Gainey retired in 1989 and entered the Hall of Fame in 1993. Named coach of the Minnesota North Stars in 1990, he became general manager in 1996 when the team transferred to Dallas. The transplanted Stars won the 1999 Stanley Cup.

One thing you learn quickly in this game is that it doesn't take long to go from goat to hero—or in the other direction.

APRIL 27, 1975
MEMORIAL AUDITORIUM, BUFFALO
BUFFALO 6, MONTREAL 5 (OT)

FIRST PERIOD
1. MON Lapointe (unassisted) 0:32 (PP).
2. BUF Martin (Stanfield, Perreault) 5:12 (PP).
3. BUF Robert (Perreault) 11:22.
4. BUF Dudley (Lorentz, McNab) 18:07.
5. MON Lafleur (Lemaire) 18:29.
Penalties: BUF Martin (high-sticking) 0:20; MON Richard (holding) 3:47; BUF Carriere (interference) 8:22; MON Shutt (hooking) 15:46.

SECOND PERIOD
6. MON Lapointe (Mahovlich, Awrey) 6:44 (SH).
7. MON Cournoyer (Mahovlich, Lemaire) 10:57 (PP).
8. BUF Perreault (Martin) 18:15.
Penalties: MON Lafleur (hooking) 5:05; BUF Schoenfeld (hooking) 9:35; BUF (bench, served by McNab) 9:35; BUF Martin (holding) 13:07; BUF Hajt (hooking) 15:20.

THIRD PERIOD
9. BUF Lorentz (McNab, Stanfield) 4:20.
10. MON Lemaire (Cournoyer) 19:36.
Penalty: MON Gainey (tripping) 9:28.

FIRST OVERTIME PERIOD
11. BUF Gare (Ramsay) 4:42.
Penalty: MON Gainey (tripping) 1:50.

SHOTS ON GOAL:

BUF	16	12	12	3	**43**
MON	12	13	4	2	**31**

Goalies: BUF Crozier, Desjardins; MON Dryden
Referee: Bruce Hood
Linesmen: John D'Amico, Ron Finn

I learned that in my first year in the National Hockey League with the Buffalo Sabres. It sort of helps you stay on an even keel, which is what you have to do if you play hockey. You can't let success go to your head or let things get you down if everything doesn't always go your way.

My third year in the league [1976–77] is a good example of what I mean. The year before, I'd scored 50 goals—everything was going my way. Then came a back problem just before the third season. It nagged me all through the season. I missed something like 45 games and I scored only 11 goals. But that season, as frustrating as it was, did me some good. It brought me back down to earth, reminded me that you have to work harder when things go against you. Setbacks help build success. You learn something from adversity. The back injury mentally prepared me to handle any kind of physical trouble that came up after that.

I'd been very fortunate up to that time. I never had been hurt in hockey, at least not enough to keep me out of more than a game or so. The year my back acted up taught me that things don't go great forever. You remember that as well as the games in which everything goes well, so well that you never forget them.

There are probably three games that really stick out for me. One of those was my first game in the NHL in 1974. I got my first NHL goal 18 seconds into the game, against the Boston Bruins. You dream of doing something like that when you're a kid: playing in an NHL game, scoring a goal right away.

Another game I remember is the final regular season game in 1975–76. I had 47 goals going in, then got a hat trick to score 50 for the season. But the game that really comes to mind first is the first Stanley Cup semifinal game against the Montreal Canadiens in my rookie season. That was the goat-to-hero game for me and it happened just like that.

I was fortunate in that in my rookie season coach Floyd Smith teamed me up on a line with Don Luce and Craig Ramsay. We fit in well together, which is something you have to have if a line is to click. And we hit it off right from the start. We had a good season and we beat the Chicago Blackhawks in the quarterfinals of the Stanley Cup in five games, winning all three on our ice.

I scored the first goal in two of our wins and had another goal against Chicago, so I felt pretty confident going against the Canadiens. Still, just playing Montreal is a thrill and you always wonder how well you will do. You hope for the best. The series against Montreal started in our rink, Memorial Auditorium, and we had a pretty good idea of how we'd have to play them. You had to stay on them, force the play. You had to take it to them and disrupt their great attack. Especially, we had to win on our ice because it's just that much harder to win in the Montreal Forum.

Our system had been working against the Canadiens during the regular season. In five games, we didn't lose to them once, winning four and tying the other. But this was Stanley Cup play. You go into a game like that thinking, for sure, it's going to be low scoring, but this one wasn't. I don't think there was a minute gone when Montreal scored the first goal. But we came right back and the first period ended with us leading, 3–2.

The second period was more of the same, a lot of shots on goal. The Canadiens tied the game 4–4, and both goalies were under almost steady pressure. Ken Dryden was playing for the Canadiens. Denis Desjardins had started for us but suffered a knee injury in the first minute and Roger Crozier had come in. When you're tied with the Canadiens after two periods in a Stanley Cup game, naturally you're not discouraged. But you don't like to see that many goals scored against you and I think we were determined to tighten up our defense that last period, to wait for a break and not gamble.

Well, we did get lucky—or good. We scored the first goal in the third period. I think Jim Lorentz scored it and it came early. So we were ahead, 5–4, with some 15 minutes to play. The thing to do was avoid making mistakes in our end and to play a smart checking style, stay on top of them, not let them get any good shots.

It hit my stick and went up over the top of Crozier's shoulder into the net to tie the game 5–5, with 24 seconds left. I felt like a real goat.

It worked, up to a point. I think they only got four shots on goal against us that third period, after getting a dozen or so in each of the first two periods. We seemed to be slowing them down, and we were hanging on to that goal lead. With about a minute to go, I went out with Luce and Ramsay for what we hoped would be our final shift of the game. It was our job to kill off the last minute and protect that 5–4 lead.

As it was, the puck came down to our end of the ice. Jacques Lemaire of the Canadiens shot the puck out from the corner. It hit my stick and went up over the top of Crozier's shoulder into the net to tie the game 5–5, with 24 seconds left. I felt like a real goat. We'd had the game almost won and now we went into overtime. I felt like it was all my fault.

You try to shake that off and concentrate on doing the job. After all, the game wasn't lost. We had the overtime. Something like four minutes into the overtime there was a face-off in our zone. Ramsay won the draw and set up a three-on-two break with Donnie and me. I went down and scored the winning goal against Dryden and then went sliding into the boards.

Like I said, it was goat-to-hero, just like that, and that's the game I'll never forget. We went on to eventually beat out the Canadiens in the series but lost to the Philadelphia Flyers in the finals. That's the game that comes to mind, though, the one I'll never forget.

—*As told to George Vass*

Danny Gare remains one of the most popular players in Buffalo Sabres history. Twice a 50-goal scorer, his 56 goals in 1979–80 tied for the league lead. He captained the Sabres from the start of the 1977–78 season until his surprising trade to Detroit in December 1981. Gare signed as a free agent with Edmonton for the 1986–87 campaign but retired mid-season, missing his last chance at a Stanley Cup ring.

I've had a lot of memorable moments over the last 15 years. But if I had to pick out just one game that sticks out in my mind,

APRIL 7, 1985
CAPITAL CENTRE, LANDOVER MD
WASHINGTON 7, PITTSBURGH 3

FIRST PERIOD
1. WAS Carpenter (Gartner, McEwen) 1:42 (PP).
2. WAS Hatcher (Gould, Christian) 6:07 (SH).
3. WAS Murphy (Christian, Laughlin) 8:44.
Penalties: PIT Rissling (holding) 1:25; WAS Franceschetti (holding) 4:56.

SECOND PERIOD
4. WAS Gartner (Franceschetti) 4:36.
5. PIT Young (Shedden, Bullard) 7:19 (PP).
6. WAS Gustafsson (unassisted) 9:49 (SH).
7. WAS Gartner (Gustafsson, Franceschetti) 14:05.
8. PIT Lemieux (Babych, Young) 16:08.
Penalties: WAS McEwen (tripping) 5:39; WAS Gould (slashing, fighting, misconduct) 9:46; WAS Stevens (roughing, misconduct) 9:46; WAS Jarvis (game misconduct) 9:46; PIT Weir (roughing, misconduct) 9:46; PIT Hannan (fighting, misconduct) 9:46; WAS (bench minor) 14:05.

THIRD PERIOD
9. WAS Stevens (Gartner, Murphy) 15:42 (PP).
10. PIT Babych (Lamoureux, Weir) 17:25.
Penalties: WAS Adams (elbowing) 13:49; PIT Geale (charging) 13:49; PIT (bench minor) 13:49.

SHOTS ON GOAL:

WAS	18	13	21	**52**
PIT	12	8	6	**26**

Goalies: WAS Jensen; PIT Herron
Referee: Terry Gregson
Linesmen: Dan McCourt, Mark Pare

it would be the final game of the 1984–85 regular season. I was playing for the Washington Capitals at the time, and we were playing Pittsburgh in Washington. I had 48 goals and 98 points heading into that final game, going for a double milestone—scoring my 50th goal and 100th point.

I remember getting my 49th goal early in the second period, my 100th point. I had already got an assist in the first couple minutes of the game. After that, I just needed one more goal. I got that late in the second period.

I was going down the ice on a two-on-one with my linemate Bengt Gustafsson. He dished the puck over to me and I was there just reaching into the crease. I deflected the puck in for my 50th goal of the season. It was the first and only time I've scored 50 goals in the NHL. It was a thrill at the time. I also got another assist after that, so I ended up with 102 points.

Heading into that season, I don't know if you could say those were goals I set—to get 50 goals and 100 points. They're more lofty milestones than you hope to accomplish during the course of a season. But, by that last game, I had attained something close to that level, and it was just that little bit extra that I needed. So I was a bit nervous heading into the last game, wondering whether I was going to get a shot at that 50-goal mark or not.

My teammates knew what I was trying to accomplish that night. Before the game, in the dressing room I remember Bengt Gustafsson said to me, "Get open. I'm going to try and get you the puck all night."

I usually played with a lot of different left-wingers in Washington, so I don't even remember who else was on our line for that particular game. The game didn't have any affect on the regular-season standings, whether we won or lost, either for us or Pittsburgh. So it was one of those games that you sometimes see in the last couple of games of a season. We were just playing out the regular season and getting ready for the

playoffs. I remember, though, we won the game 7–3. And the most important thing is always winning the game.

I certainly wanted to get 50 goals, so I was obviously going to try to do all I could do to facilitate that. Getting a goal early in the game made things a lot closer and a lot more attainable. When you get that goal, you know you only need one more shot in order to hit the 50-mark.

I mentioned earlier that Bengt said he was going to try and give me the puck a lot that night. And he did. I could have had three or four goals that night. He gave me the puck quite a bit and I ended up with four points. So I was in the action a lot and our coach, Bryan Murray, put me on the ice quite a bit as well.

I collected both pucks that night, for the 50th goal and 100th point. They're both around the house somewhere. I've also got a nice picture of the 50th goal. Somebody snapped a photo and I got a copy about three weeks later. Like the pucks, it's stashed away in a box somewhere. We've been moving quite a bit the last couple of years, so we haven't been able to get everything out of the boxes.

I don't think that game is something I'll remember more, say, 20 or 30 years from now. It's just one moment that I remember, one of those dozen or so things that stick out in your mind. I remember my teammates came streaming over the boards after I scored my 50th goal. We ended up getting a two-minute penalty for having too many men on the ice. I didn't have to serve the penalty, though.

After the game, I had my son Josh down in the dressing room with me. He was about one-and-a-half or two years old at the time. We got a couple pictures of him holding the puck I scored my 50th with. That was kind of fun, being able to share it with him. We made the playoffs that year so it was a good way to end the regular season. We went into the playoffs on a high. Like I said before, I've had a lot of great moments in my career. And that game is definitely one that sticks out for me.

—As told to Sam Laskaris

He dished the puck over to me and I was there just reaching into the crease. I deflected the puck in for my 50th goal of the season.

Mike Gartner used his great speed and quick shot to amass Hall of Fame numbers: 708 goals and 627 assists. Gartner's consistency—17 30-goal seasons (15 of them in a row)—also put him into the record books. Traded by Washington to Minnesota in March 1989, he also played for the New York Rangers, Toronto and Phoenix before retiring in 1998 to work for the NHL Players' Association.

BERNIE GEOFFRION

FEBRUARY 19, 1955

It was a big accomplishment to score 50 goals, becoming the first man to do it after Rocket Richard, but that wasn't my biggest

thrill in hockey. It is the night that I scored five goals, in the game I'll never forget.

The Montreal Canadiens were having a tough time in February 1955. In those years, it was always either Detroit or Montreal that finished first and won the Stanley Cup. But we Canadiens were going badly. The New York Rangers came to town for a game and they were not a good team. At the time, it was always the Rangers down on the bottom with Boston. Our players met privately to talk things over. We had a good meeting and decided to pull things together, to see if we couldn't make a move up in the standings.

When we came out on the ice, we showed the Rangers we were ready. Gump Worsley was in goal for them that night. Poor Gump. He had a tough time with the Rangers, always facing 50 to 55 shots on goal, and this was another of those games. Bert Olmstead got the first goal for us early. I got the next one, with Jean Beliveau and Rocket Richard helping to set me up on a 15-footer. We got another goal that period and the Rangers got one too, so we were leading 3–1.

In the second period, we just about ran the Rangers off the ice with four more goals. I got a pair of them. After so many years, I couldn't tell you exactly how the goals were scored—not all of them. I do remember getting my second goal on another 15-footer just two minutes into the second period. We got two more goals before I scored my third one for the hat trick.

I deked Gump on that third one. I came in on him and he made the first move, leaving an opening on the short side and I put it past him. When you get a hat trick, you are happy, you jump in the air, you go after the puck and pick it up and that's what I did. But I was thinking to myself, "I might as well go for the bundle. I'll never have a better chance. Three goals already and a full period to go."

I didn't need the full period, not even a minute of it. The second period ended with two Rangers in the penalty box, so we had a power play going with a two-man advantage when the third period started.

At the time, we had a great power play with Doug Harvey, Beliveau, Rocket Richard, Olmstead and myself. I think we scored maybe one-fourth of our goals on the power play. The league still had the old rule that even if you scored a power play goal, the team with a man in the penalty box didn't get him back. They changed the rule the next year because our power play was scoring so much.

I was starting to feel sorry for Gump. He was a great goalie—I played against him in junior too—but if you get 50 to 55 shots at you every game like he did all those years with the Rangers, I think some of the pucks have to go in.

It didn't take long for me to get my fourth goal. We made two rushes and on the second

---

FEBRUARY 19, 1955
MONTREAL FORUM, MONTREAL
MONTREAL 10, NEW YORK RANGERS 2

FIRST PERIOD
1. MON Olmstead (Beliveau, Harvey) 2:11 (PP).
2. MON Geoffrion (Beliveau, Richard) 2:37 (PP).
3. MON Mackey (Richard, Harvey) 5:58.
4. NYR Gadsby (Bathgate, Popeil) 8:27.
Penalties: NYR Ezinicki (interference) 0:43; MON Curry (interference) 8:54; NYR Christal (tripping) 11:24; NYR Irwin (holding) 12:27; MON Richard (tripping) 15:14.

SECOND PERIOD
5. MON Geoffrion (Harvey) 2:55.
6. MON Marshall (Moor, St. Laurent) 4:55.
7. MON Leclair (Talbot, Moore) 18:16.
8. MON Geoffrion (Beliveau, Richard) 19:01.
Penalties: MON Curry (misconduct) 12:43; NYR Fontinato (charging) 18:42; NYR Irwin (tripping) 19:19.

THIRD PERIOD
9. MON Geoffrion (Harvey, Olmstead) 0:41 (PP).
10. MON Geoffrion (Harvey, Olmstead) 0:55 (PP).
11. MON Johnson (Beliveau, Geoffrion) 14:05.
12. NYR Popeil (Bathgate) 18:48.
Penalties: NYR Gadsby (slashing) 7:43; MON Beliveau (slashing) 7:43; NYR Howell (interference) 12:03; MON Richard (high-sticking) 12:42; NYR Guidolin (slashing) 13:21; MON Curry (interference) 15:44.

Goalies: MON Plante; NYR Worsley
Referee: S. Morrison
Linesmen: Doug Davies, Bill Roberts

I said to myself, "I might as well go for the bundle. I'll never have a better chance. Three goals already and a full period to go."

one, Harvey laid the puck on my stick and I beat Gump with a slap shot. I was thinking, four goals, that's pretty good, and maybe I'll get five. But I didn't know it would be so soon.

One of the Ranger penalties ended but they were still short a man when we faced off after the goal. We won the draw and moved the puck around pretty good. Gump didn't get much help and I scored my fifth goal just 13 seconds later.

Getting that fifth one was the biggest thrill I ever had. I just danced around and grabbed the puck and even went up to Gump and said, "This is very nice of you, Gump." I can't tell you what he said to me because I don't think it's very proper to write about, but he was kind of unhappy.

I suppose he'd have been even more unhappy if I'd scored a sixth goal on him

and I almost did. Late in the third period, I got a perfect chance to score. Gump flopped for the puck but couldn't control it. He was stretched out on the ice and the puck was right on my stick. All I had to do was lift it over him into the net. I shot it wide, though, or I would have had six.

But five goals was a big enough thrill. And after that game, the team started to roll again. We won five or six games in a row and finished second behind Detroit. Those five goals also meant the scoring championship for me that season. I finished with 75 points [38 goals, 37 assists] and won by just one point. You can see why that's the game I'll never forget.

—*As told to George Vass*

Bernie Geoffrion buries one of his 393 career NHL goals behind Chicago goaltender Glenn Hall, above. "Boom Boom" introduced the slap shot to hockey, forever changing the game. Geoffrion won the 1952 Calder Trophy and two scoring championships, in 1955 and 1961, earning the Hart Trophy in the latter season. Geoffrion retired in 1964 but returned to the NHL in 1966 for two more seasons with the New York Rangers.

ED GIACOMIN

One of the finest memories of my hockey career is of the reception the fans gave me in Madison Square Garden a few days after

---

APRIL 13, 1972
MONTREAL FORUM, MONTREAL
NEW YORK RANGERS 3, MONTREAL 2

FIRST PERIOD
1. NYR Fairbairn (Tkaczuk) 9:31.
2. MON Cournoyer (Richard) 11:32.
Penalties: NYR Tkaczuk (tripping) 19:30.

SECOND PERIOD
3. NYR Fairbairn (Carr) 9:33.
4. MON Lemaire (Lafleur, Tardif) 14:48.
Penalties: NYR Park (tripping) 17:06.

THIRD PERIOD
5. NYR Tkaczuk (Fairbairn, Seiling) 0:29.
Penalties: MON Lafleur (hooking) 1:51; NYR Seiling (holding) 8:23; MON Larose (hooking, misconduct) 11:55; MON P. Mahlovich (hooking) 15:19; MON P. Mahlovich (roughing) 18:23; NYR Park (roughing) 18:23; NYR Park (roughing) 18:23; NYR Neilson (holding) 18:42

SHOTS ON GOAL:

NYR	9	10	16	**35**
MON	11	5	9	**25**

Goalies: NYR Giacomin; MON Dryden
Referee: John Ashley
Linesmen: Claude Bechard, Bob Kilger

---

the New York Rangers sent me to the Detroit Red Wings in 1975. I tried not to be bitter about the Rangers letting me go to Detroit like that. But it was difficult. I was shocked and hurt. I had done everything I could to help the Rangers for 11 years. I would have preferred to retire if they didn't want me, to go out gracefully as a Ranger. Instead, they let me go on waivers to Detroit.

If it hadn't been for the fans it might have taken me a lot longer to get over the hurt than it did. The fans were the ones who gave me a lift just two days after I changed uniforms. My first game in goal for Detroit was against the Rangers in Madison Square Garden.

We won the game 6–4, but that wasn't what made it memorable for me. It was the Ranger fans yelling, "Eddie!… Eddie!… Eddie!" when the crowd stood up before the game for the national anthem. The reception I got was amazing, just unbelievable. I couldn't hear "The Star Spangled Banner," I was shaking so. I thought I might faint. There were tears in my eyes. I felt like blessing those people.

There are many other games, of course, that stand out for me in my career. It's naturally hard to choose one that means more to me than five or six others, or maybe even more, that I recall well. One I can remember in particular, though, came in the 1972 Stanley Cup playoffs. That year we made it all the way to the finals, though we lost to Boston. But the game I remember was in the opening round in which we beat the Montreal Canadiens. The Canadiens were the team to beat that year, as they always were. They were the defending Stanley Cup champions. But they had had some problems in 1972 and finished third in the East Division, behind the first place Boston Bruins and us. We had one of our best seasons at New York but went into the playoffs without center Jean Ratelle, one of our top players. I'm convinced we could have won the Cup that year if Jean had not been hurt late in the season and missed the first two rounds of the playoffs. He played in the finals against

Boston, but he still wasn't himself.

We had to play the Canadiens in the first round without Jean but we played well defensively and we were able to turn off their scoring. I never had better defensive play in front of me than I did in that series.

The series opened in New York and we won the first two games. The turning point came when we were able to win one of the two games at Montreal to give us a 2–1 edge in the series. The Canadiens won the fifth game, at New York, but we still had two more opportunities so that didn't dishearten us.

The sixth game, at Montreal, is the one I remember best. It certainly was one of the high spots of my career. You don't beat the Canadiens too often on their home ice, especially not when the stakes are as high as they were in that game. They faced elimination from the playoffs and were as keyed up as usual in front of that home crowd. They really came out on the attack in the first period. I had to make some saves, but I also got some good support from the guys in front of me. Brad Park and Dale Rolfe on defense were outstanding. We put a rookie, Gene Carr, on Yvan Cournoyer, a winger who could really fly, and Gene did a good job of checking him.

We fought them even in the first period, which was an accomplishment in itself on the Forum ice. Bill Fairbairn scored a goal for us, but the lead didn't last long, Cournoyer scoring a couple of minutes later, so we came out of the first period tied 1–1.

The second period was more of the same, the Canadiens getting a lot of the action, but we were able to play them even. We moved ahead again, 2–1, on another goal by Fairbairn, who played a great two-way game, midway in the period. The Canadiens again tied it within minutes, Jacques Lemaire scoring this time.

So we went into the third period tied 2–2. But we got a break right at the start of the period. Walt Tkaczuk scored for us with less than a minute gone to put us ahead. You know that a one-goal lead against the Canadiens, especially in the Forum, especially in a game that's so important, doesn't mean much. You can't let up a moment against them. They kept coming right to the end.

> **I had to throw myself across the crease. It was just a dive, a lunge, but somehow I got in front of the puck.**

I remember one save in particular, one of the best saves I ever made. It was on Frank Mahovlich, the big left wing. He was set up perfectly in front of the net. He couldn't have been more than a stride or two from the crease when he shot. I'd been hugging the left goalpost, looking for a shot from the short side. But Mahovlich found an open net on the other side. I had to throw myself across the crease. It was just a dive, a lunge, but somehow I got in front of the puck.

That was a tough save, but it wasn't the last one of the game. Down a goal with a minute to play, the Canadiens pulled their goalie, Ken Dryden, and put an extra attacker on the ice. But our guys played great in front of me and we held them to win, 3–2, and eliminate the Canadiens from the playoffs.

I guess a lot of people who saw that game in particular or on television will recall what I did when the game ended. I just flung myself down on the ice on my back and kicked my legs in the air. I was just so happy that I had to do something to show how good I felt. I was just so thrilled I had to go down in the ice and roll around, kicking and yelling. Beating the Canadiens after all those years, in a big game and making that save on Mahovlich gave me a great feeling. I just had to show how happy I was. It was my most memorable playoff game.

I wish we could have gone on to win the Stanley Cup. We did beat Chicago in four games in the next round, but then lost to Boston in the finals. Yet I'll never forget that game in Montreal.

—As told to George Vass

One of the last NHL goalies to don a mask, **Ed Giacomin** was a courageous and effective goaltender. He holds the New York Rangers record with 49 career shutouts and his retired sweater No. 1 hangs from the rafters of Madison Square Garden. A five-time NHL All-Star, Giacomin entered the Hall of Fame in 1987.

It wasn't until after I was traded from the Los Angeles Kings to the New York Islanders late in the 1979–80 season that I

APRIL 22, 1976
GREAT WESTERN FORUM, INGLEWOOD
LOS ANGELES 4, BOSTON 3 (OT)

FIRST PERIOD
No scoring.
Penalties: BOS Doak 4:03; LA Murphy 4:29; BOS Park (major) 14:42; BOS Forbes (major) 14:42; LA Kozak (major) 14:42; LA DeMarco (major) 14:42.

SECOND PERIOD
1. LA Williams (unassisted) 0:21.
2. BOS Schmautz (Sheppard, Cashman) 1:00.
3. BOS Edestrand (Park, Sheppard) 16:14.
4. BOS Sheppard (Schmautz, Cashman) 19:45.
Penalty: BOS Milbury 8:49.

THIRD PERIOD
5. LA Corrigan (Dionne, Hutchinson) 10:50.
6. LA Corrigan (Murphy) 17:48.
Penalties: LA Wilson 6:11; BOS Ratelle 7:49.

FIRST OVERTIME PERIOD
7. LA Goring (Nevin, Murdoch) 18:28.
Penalty: LA Komadoski 6:06.

SHOTS ON GOAL:

LA	6	8	12	10	**36**
BOS	7	8	9	3	**27**

Goalies: LA Vachon; BOS Cheevers
Referee: Ron Wicks
Linesmen: John D'Amico, Ray Scapinello

was able to enjoy the ultimate thrill of every hockey player, to be part of a Stanley Cup winning team. But as great a feeling as it was to be on a Stanley Cup winner in 1980, there's another high spot in my career that I am not likely to forget, and that came with the Kings. That was during the Stanley Cup quarterfinal against the Boston Bruins in 1976.

The game I'll never forget with the Kings is an easy choice for me, though I played about 10 seasons at Los Angeles. When I first came up to the Kings in 1969, they were only in their third year in the National Hockey League, trying to build a respectable team and a following of fans. It was a long process and there were always setbacks. We'd get to a point at which we would be doing fairly well, then would slip again. There were a lot of player changes, but I was fortunate enough to stick with the club after the first couple of years and do fairly well.

A couple of years, I had injuries and they set me back, but you figure those are part of the game and do your best to overcome them. The same with the club. We had our problems at first trying to keep up with the better clubs, but began to make headway when Bob Pulford took over as coach in 1972. The next three seasons we got into the playoffs.

As the club improved, the fans began to turn out and hockey got going in Los Angeles. I think L.A. has some great fans and they supported us well. Still, no one took us seriously when it came to playoff time. We kept making player changes, trying to improve the team, but it never quite worked out for us.

The 1975–76 season was one of our better ones. We finished second in the Norris Division with 85 points and we had some goal-scoring ability, particularly since we'd added Marcel Dionne. In goal, we had Rogie Vachon, who was playing as well as anybody in the league.

We went into the preliminary round of the playoffs against Atlanta and got great goaltending from Vachon. We won 2–1 and 1–0 to sweep that series. That took us into the quarterfinal round against the Boston Bruins. No one figured we'd win that one. Boston had 113 points during the season against our 85 and all the experts figured the Bruins would sweep us. At the time they still had Phil Esposito, Bobby Orr, Johnny Bucyk and a lot of other good players, as well as Gerry Cheevers in goal. It was a good club.

We didn't know if we could win, but we felt we could give a pretty good account of ourselves. The series opened in Boston and the first game was pretty one-sided [4–0] as they beat us. We weren't too discouraged, figuring if we could get a split and take a win back to Los Angeles we'd do well.

That's the way it happened. Vachon was just tremendous in the second game at Boston and we held down the Bruins' big guns to end regulation time tied 2–2. Just a few seconds into overtime, I got a break and found myself in front of the Boston net. I was fortunate enough to score the first playoff goal of my career [in my 12th game] and win the game at 27 seconds of overtime.

The series went to Los Angeles, where we split the next two games, then the fifth game was in Boston, where we were routed 7–1. The sixth game, the game that is most in my mind, was in Los Angeles and we had to win it to even the series at 3–3. By this time the L.A. fans were really aroused because we'd been able to extend Boston that far. The Forum was packed and we were given a standing ovation before the game started.

With the fans behind us the way they were, giving us ovations before and during the game, going crazy every time we had a threat going, we got a tremendous lift. The first period was a standoff, nobody scoring, both Vachon and Cheevers making some fine stops. And when Tommy Williams scored the first goal for us just seconds into the second period, the fans went wild screaming. But the Bruins came right back with a goal by Bobby Schmautz, then got two more.

Going into the third period, it looked bad, with Boston leading, 3–1. We were on the brink of elimination. It wasn't until past the midway point of the final period that we were able to get another one past Cheevers. Mike Corrigan scored to cut their lead to 3–2.

My teammates mobbed me and carried me off the ice as the 15,000 screaming fans gave us another standing ovation.

Then, with just a couple of minutes left, he scored again to tie the game, 3–3.

We went into overtime and Vachon was tremendous. Even a Boston power play early on failed and, meanwhile, we were dominating the play. I think Boston, an older club, was getting a little tired. Then, just past the 18-minute mark of the overtime, Bob Murdoch, one of our defensemen, got a pass off to Bob Nevin, whose pass gave me a break into the Boston zone.

Nobody was between me and Cheevers. I must have been about 30 feet out when I took a slap shot. The puck got past him into the upper corner of the net. We'd won the game, 4–3. It was like heaven. The crowd went wild. My teammates mobbed me and carried me off the ice as the 15,000 screaming fans gave us another standing ovation.

We lost the seventh game in Boston, and that was a blow. No matter how hard we tried, or whom we played, during my years at Los Angeles we were never able to get past the quarterfinal. We won two games in overtime, one in Boston, one in L.A. It was a tremendous series and I'm sure Boston would gladly admit that we gave them all they could handle.

For me, that sixth game overtime goal at that point in my career was a tremendous thrill—as was the one in the second game. In fact, now that I think about it, it was kind of odd. I scored two goals in that series, and each won a game in overtime.

—*As told to George Vass*

Butch Goring was a consistent goal scorer for the Los Angeles Kings, as well as one of the cleanest players in the game. Goring won the Lady Byng Trophy after compiling 37 goals, 36 assists and only two penalty minutes in 1977–78. Traded in March 1980, Goring has been credited with being the essential new ingredient that catapulted the New York Islanders to four consecutive Stanley Cup victories.

DIRK GRAHAM

I've got a lot of fond memories of playing in the NHL, so it's kind of tough picking just one game that I'll never forget. Of

MAY 22, 1992
NORTHLANDS COLISEUM, EDMONTON
CHICAGO 5, EDMONTON 1

FIRST PERIOD
1. CHI R. Brown (Smith, Chelios) 9:35.
Penalties: EDM Klima (elbowing) 4:41; CHI Hudson (cross-checking) 11:04; CHI Sutter (hooking) 14:34.

SECOND PERIOD
2. CHI Roenick (Kravchuk, Larmer) 4:59 (PP).
3. CHI Noonan (R. Brown, Sutter) 7:35 (PP).
4. CHI Hudson (Kravchuk, Graham) 8:46.
5. CHI Noonan (R. Brown) 10:37.
Penalties: EDM Nicholls (elbowing major) 3:44; EDM MacIver (cross-checking) 4:48; EDM Manson (elbowing) 11:14; CHI Grimson (10-minute misconduct) 19:56.

THIRD PERIOD
6. EDM Buchberger (Gelinas, Richardson) 1:23.
Penalties: CHI Smith (holding) 2:38; EDM Buchberger (slashing) 4:15; EDM Manson (boarding) 8:57; CHI Marchment (hooking) 14:15; CHI Marchment (tripping) 19:11.

SHOTS ON GOAL:

CHI	10	15	6	**31**
EDM	8	7	6	**21**

Goalies: CHI Belfour; EDM Ranford
Referee: Andy Van Hellemond
Linesmen: Gord Broseker, Kevin Collins

course, every player remembers his first game in the NHL; my first game was when I was playing with Minnesota. But the game I probably will never forget came with Chicago.

In 1992, we made it to the Stanley Cup finals—but I don't want to talk about any of those games because Pittsburgh swept us in four straight games. The game I'll remember is the one that got us into the finals. We beat Edmonton 5–1 in the fourth game of the Campbell Conference finals. By winning that game, we set a league record of 11 straight playoff wins. Pittsburgh ended up tying the record that same year when the Penguins beat us in the finals, but it was still quite an accomplishment for our team to do it.

Even though we were leading the series 3–0, that fourth game, which was played in Edmonton, was a pretty big one for us. I considered it a big one for myself because that was as far as I had gone with any team in the playoffs in the NHL.

Prior to the game, there was a lot of talk about our winning streak. When you get into those types of situations, I think the media is most concerned about it. It gives them something to talk about. As players, of course we were aware of the streak, but we were too involved in each game to actually worry about it or talk about it on an ongoing basis.

Going into the final game in Edmonton, we tried not to talk about the streak. We looked at it more from the point that we had to take care of the Oilers. We didn't want them to win that game and let them back into the series. That was first and foremost on our minds.

With all the Stanley Cups the Oilers have won, teams from Edmonton have a rich history. Of course, by the time we played them in '92, Wayne Gretzky was gone to Los Angeles, and Mark Messier had left Edmonton for New York. But the Oilers still had a lot of talented players: Joe Murphy, Bernie Nicholls, Kevin Lowe, Craig Muni,

Craig MacTavish. All these guys knew what it took to win. We had to make sure we didn't give them anything. It was a matter of not giving them any life because we knew what they were capable of doing.

After the game, though, we sort of sat back in the dressing room and talked about how we had won 11 straight. Even though we were playing in Edmonton, their fans weren't booing us. Edmonton fans are very knowledgeable, and even though the Oilers didn't win a game in the series, they were playing some really good hockey. It's just that our team was on a roll and playing a bit better. Even though their team lost, the fans were appreciative of the effort from both teams. To me, it didn't really matter where we were playing. Sure, it would have been great if that game was in Chicago, because our fans are some of the best around. It would have been nice to win in front of them, but sometimes you can't pick where you want to play.

We played a really solid game. It was the style of game we were accustomed to— typical Blackhawks hockey. I don't remember too much about most of the goals, but one that does stick out in my mind came in the second period. I remember it because I got an assist on it.

Mike Hudson scored the goal for us. I went into Edmonton's zone with the puck and then dropped it back to the blue line to Igor Kravchuk. He made a really nice pass across to Hudson, who went in and chipped the puck over Bill Ranford in the Edmonton net. It wasn't that big of a goal because we were already ahead by three goals. By that point the game had already been pretty much decided.

After the game, they gave us the Campbell Conference trophy. The presentation wasn't on the ice, though. It was just under the stands. John Ziegler, who was the president of the league then, presented me, the captain, with the trophy. Chris Chelios and Steve Larmer were also in on the presentation. It felt very nice to be able to represent the Blackhawks and accept that trophy. It was a big thrill because of what the team had just accomplished—making it to

> We had to make sure we didn't give them anything. It was a matter of not giving them any life because we knew what they were capable of doing.

the Stanley Cup finals—and also because we had won our 11th straight game.

In the dressing room, we were celebrating a bit, but we knew we still had a lot of hard work ahead of us. We had to start thinking about the next series. Pittsburgh clinched a spot in the finals the night after we did.

Obviously, it was disappointing to lose in the finals. Even though we had a great year, you always want to go that extra step and win it all. I learned a lot from that finals series. You try to learn from your negatives and make them into positives. I realized how hard you have to work in order to win.

Everybody wants to play for the Stanley Cup during their career. Because we lost, though, I can't say any of those games were the highlight of my career. You have to look at things from the losing and the winning side. And we lost that series. So the one game that means the most to me is that Game 4 series clincher against Edmonton in 1992. Winning 11 straight—that was really something. I don't think I'll forget that.

—As told to Sam Laskaris

Dirk Graham broke into the NHL with the Minnesota North Stars in 1983–84 but was traded to Chicago in January 1988. He posted his best offensive season in 1988–89 with 33 goals and 45 assists, but Graham brought more than scoring to the Hawks. Named captain midway through the 1988–89 campaign, he wore Chicago's "C" because of his strong leadership skills until his retirement in 1995.

I was sitting at home in December 1952, just enjoying a few days off during the holidays with my family in Saskatchewan,

DECEMBER 27, 1952
MONTREAL FORUM, MONTREAL
DETROIT 2, MONTREAL 2

FIRST PERIOD
1. DET Skov (Leswick) 3:00.
Penalties: MON Deslauriers (hooking) 5:53; MON Meger (tripping) 6:41; DET Pronovost (holding) 9:20.

SECOND PERIOD
2. MON Harvey (Curry) 3:33.
3. MON Geoffrion (Meger, Deslauriers) 6:20.
4. DET Sinclair (Bonin, Delvecchio) 15:32.
Penalties: MON Mosdell (hooking major) 10:51; DET Lindsay (misconduct) 14:12; DET Leswick (slashing) 17:30.

THIRD PERIOD
No scoring.
No penalties.

Goalies: DET Hall; MON McNeil
Referee: Red Storey
Linesmen: Jim Primeau, Doug Davies

sipping eggnog and wrapping gifts, when I got the biggest Christmas present of my life.

The phone rang. It was for me. I recognized the voice on the other end of the line. It was my coach from the Western Hockey League's Edmonton Flyers. "Pack your stuff and catch the next plane in Saskatoon," he said. "You're going to Montreal. Your equipment will be on the plane. Good luck."

When I hung up the phone I was speechless. Slowly it sunk in: I was going to join the Detroit Red Wings and play my first NHL game. I kissed my friends and family goodbye and I was off to live out my lifelong dream.

Growing up, I dreamed of playing in the NHL, dreamed of standing my ground as Milt Schmidt or the Bentley brothers came down the ice at me, dreamed of flashing a leg pad or getting the paddle on a Maurice Richard ripper. Although this was going to be my first regular-season game with the Red Wings, I wasn't a strange face to them. I had been at preseason camp with them a few times and had been called up to work with the team during the playoffs.

For coach Tommy Ivan's defending Stanley Cup champs, Mr. Hockey, Gordie Howe, was in his goal-scoring, playmaking, elbow-throwing prime. On the left wing, you had Ted Lindsay, whose talent for putting the puck in the net was matched only by his talent for getting in opponents' faces and under their skin. At center, the smooth, classy Alex Delvecchio made everything go. Those three stars combined to produce 97 goals and 128 assists during the 1952–53 season. With the likes of Red Kelly and Marcel Pronovost back on defense, the forwards didn't have to worry about it if they got caught up ice from time to time. And of course there was Terry Sawchuk in net. Sawchuk, who was nursing an injury, was probably the best goalie in the world at the time, thanks to his enormous competitiveness and quick reflexes.

Sawchuk was the reason the Red Wings traded another future Hall of Famer, Harry Lumley, a few years earlier and why I had spent four seasons in the minors waiting to get a chance in the big leagues. I wasn't in the minors any more, even though my equipment apparently was. Whether they had forgotten to send my gear from Edmonton or it got lost en route, I arrived at the Montreal Forum without as much as my skates.

Even though Red Wings trainer Lefty Wilson was good enough to lend me his equipment, there's nothing worse than using someone else's stuff. The biggest problem was the skates. Luckily, they fit OK, but the problem was that I was used to very sharp blades and not only were they not that sharp, but there was no place to sharpen them. The teams didn't take a sharpener with them on the road in those days. We managed to touch them up a bit, but they just didn't feel right. I was going to have to make do with what I had.

I put the equipment crisis behind me and began my pregame routine I had developed in the minors. Before each game, I would work myself up so much that I would have to throw up. It wasn't that I threw up out of nervousness—although there were a bunch of butterflies floating around in my stomach as I sat in the Forum locker room. It was more from building myself up for the game. It was like this excitement and anticipation building inside of me that had to get out.

The guys didn't realize this was part of my routine. So as everyone was getting dressed and taping their sticks, I ran into the bathroom and got sick. I'm sure it was loud enough for all the players to hear. When I came out, I was white as a ghost. They all got a little laugh out of that. But when the puck was dropped, the laughing stopped and each man put on his game face.

Here I was, in the vaunted Montreal Forum, facing some of the best players ever. I was staring at those big, piercing eyes of Richard. I was watching Elmer Lach put on moves. I was flinching as Bernie "Boom Boom" Geoffrion wound up and let go with his patented slap shot. It was like a childhood daydream come to life.

I forced myself to settle down, realizing how important this game was for my career. I

Before each game, I would work myself up so much that I would have to throw up.

wanted to make the best impression I could because I had no idea if I would ever get the call again. There were only six teams in the league and only six goalies in the world, and there was a long line of guys looking to take their place. For all I knew, I could have been on a plane back to Edmonton or Saskatoon or Newfoundland or Omaha, or wherever they wanted to send me, the very next day.

About the only thing I remember specifically about the game I'll never forget is that I played well. If you ask me about specific plays or if I made any acrobatic saves, I must admit my memory isn't that good. I don't remember any of those minute details. If it were today, someone would have the game on tape. Nowadays, it seems like every game is saved on videotape for

posterity's sake, and I would just have to watch it to jog my memory. But about the only thing I took away from that game was a feeling that I played well.

I must have played well, because we tied the Canadiens—who went on to win the Stanley Cup that year—2–2. There was further proof that I must have played well; the Red Wings played me in five more games that season. I went 4–1–1 with a 1.67 goals-against average.

Within a few seasons, I had earned one of those six goaltending jobs and held it for nearly two decades. Over the years, I spent a lot more Christmases away from home. But most of the time, I didn't seem to mind.

—*As told to Chuck O'Donnell*

Beginning with the 1955–56 season, when he won the Calder Trophy, **Glenn Hall** played 502 consecutive regular season games, 552 including playoff matches. His remarkable record was split between Detroit and Chicago, where he was traded in the summer of 1957. "Mr. Goalie" helped the Blackhawks win the 1961 Stanley Cup. Named an All-Star 11 times, Hall also won three Vezina Trophies and the 1968 Conn Smythe Trophy while toiling for the St. Louis Blues.

It doesn't seem like it is getting close to 20 years since I played in a game I'll never really forget, but you can't argue with the

MARCH 13, 1954
DETROIT OLYMPIA, DETROIT
NEW YORK RANGERS 5, DETROIT 2

FIRST PERIOD
1. NYR Mickoski (Kullman, Raleigh) 7:47.
2. NYR Henry (M. Bentley, Howell) 9:19.
3. DET Dineen (Howe, Lindsay) 13:15 (PP).
4. DET Howe (Wilson) 19:01 (PP).
Penalties: DET Pavelich (high-sticking) 8:15; NYR Evans (interference) 12:28; DET Skov (hooking) 15:57; NYR Evans (elbowing) 18:11.

SECOND PERIOD
5. NYR Henry (Howell) 13:19 (PP).
Penalties: DET Goldham (high-sticking) 6:58; NYR Prentice (tripping) 8:29; NYR Irwin (holding) 9:58; DET Goldham (holding) 12:47; DET Irwin (hooking) 16:01.

THIRD PERIOD
6. NYR Henry (M. Bentley, Prentice) 12:25 (PP).
7. NYR Henry (M. Bentley, Howell) 12:58 (PP).
Penalties: DET Howe (high-sticking) 11:58; NYR Howell (holding) 13:37.

Goalies: NYR Bower; DET Sawchuk
Referee: Bill Chadwick
Linesmen: George Hayes, Douglas Young

calendar. I can tell you the date exactly, which shows how much it must have meant to me. The game was on March 13, 1954, in Detroit when I was in my first year with the New York Rangers.

When I went to the Rangers training camp in the fall of 1953, I was more hopeful than sure that I could make the team as a rookie. I was fresh off the Quebec Citadels, the Junior A hockey team in my home town of Quebec City, and I wasn't the most impressive-looking hockey player you ever saw. The book says I am five-foot-ten, so we'll say it's so. It also says I weighed 150 in my younger days. Maybe I did, maybe I didn't when I first came up. Anyway, I was afraid my size might keep me out of the National Hockey League. But I must have impressed Ranger coach Frank Boucher with my skating and shooting, if not my size, because when the 1953–54 season started I was with the club.

"I'm going to take you with us, but I'm not going to dress you for games for a while," Boucher told me. "I'm going to take you around with us and maybe give you a spot here and there." My first NHL game came more quickly than Coach Boucher expected. In the first game of the season, Dean Prentice suffered a shoulder separation. So the next game, in Chicago against the Blackhawks, Boucher dressed me.

I started out well. That first game, I scored my first NHL goal. You never forget that one. I beat Al Rollins, the Chicago goalie, and although I got 278 more NHL goals before I retired after the 1969–70 season, the first one gave me as big a thrill as any.

After that Chicago game, I started playing regularly and scoring pretty good, too. A lot of people wondered how a little guy like me could keep from getting banged up by the other guys, but I kept an eye out for them and could usually give them the slip. I guess everybody was sort of surprised the way I was scoring. Going into the middle of March, I had 20 goals, which was far more than the

Rangers had figured I could get as a rookie. We were going pretty fair as a team, too, with a chance to get in a playoff spot when we went to Detroit March 13, 1954, with four games left in the season.

In those days, the Red Wings were the powerhouse of the league, with guys like Gordie Howe, Sid Abel, Ted Lindsay and Red Kelly. They had Terry Sawchuk as their goalie, and there was never a better one. Detroit was on its way to its sixth straight Prince of Wales Trophy that night. So you can see what kind of a team it was. Sawchuk looked like he was a cinch for the Vezina Trophy. He was two or three goals ahead of Toronto's Harry Lumley going into that game. It also looked like he'd beat out Lumley for the First All-Star team.

Nick Mickoski scored the first goal of the game early in the first period to put us ahead 1–0. A minute or so later, while Detroit's Marty Pavelich was serving a penalty, I tipped a shot past Sawchuk for my 21st goal of the season to give us a 2–0 lead.

We couldn't hang on to that edge. Detroit scored a couple of goals later in the first period to tie the game 2–2. The game stayed tied for the first half of the second period but we got another break. Bob Goldham of the Red Wings tripped one of our guys and got a penalty. I was right in front of the net when Harry Howell hit me with a pass. I flipped the puck past Sawchuk again for my second goal of the game, both on power plays. That gave us a 3–2 lead.

I would have been happy with two goals but I got another chance in the third period. Gordie Howe got called for high-sticking so we had another power-play opportunity. In those days, the penalty was for the full two minutes, even if the team that had the power play scored. They didn't let the guy out of the penalty box after the other team scored, no matter how many goals they got. I don't even remember just how I got my third goal of the game on that power play. But I beat Sawchuk to get the hat trick and I can tell you I was feeling pretty good.

We still had the power play going, so we went up the ice again. I had the puck and came in on Sawchuk. I faked him and he

People wondered how a little guy like me could keep from getting banged up by the other guys, but I kept an eye out for them and could usually give them the slip.

sprawled in front of the net but instead of shooting I carried it behind. Then I looked and noticed that his stick was smack against the ice at just the right angle. So I shot the puck against his stick and it caromed back in the opposite direction into the net for my fourth goal. And all power-play goals!

That four-goal night won the Calder Trophy for me as rookie of the year. It also knocked Sawchuk out of all the honors he practically had in his pocket. I ran into him a week or so later.

"You little French baboon," he said to me, "You cost me plenty." I guess I cost him a couple of thousand dollars because Lumley beat him out for both the Vezina and the first All-Star team on the strength of my four goals that night.

Funny thing is, I might have scored another. There was still time left on the penalty on Howe when I scored the fourth one. When I got back to the bench after scoring the fourth, Muzz Patrick, who had replaced Boucher as our coach, yelled at me. "Hey! Get back out there and get another." But I got off the ice.

"I can't even skate, I'm shaking so much," I told Patrick.

Four goals—all on power plays—and Sawchuk never let me forget about that night. Whenever I'd see him he'd say, "You little French squirt. I keep you in business. If it wasn't for me, you wouldn't be in the league."

—*As told to George Vass*

Although only five-feet, nine-inches and about 150 pounds, **Camille "The Eel" Henry** takes Toronto strongman Tim Horton, above, into the boards. Henry won the 1954 Calder Trophy but he returned to the minor leagues the following season. Back with the Rangers in 1956–57, he had his career-best season in 1962–63, with 37 goals and 23 assists. Henry played the last quarter of the 1964–65 campaign for Chicago. After a brief retirement, he returned to New York in 1967–68 and later played part of two seasons for St. Louis.

I've had some very memorable games in my three years with the Flyers, some in regular-season games, a lot of them in the

OCTOBER 9, 1986
THE SPECTRUM, PHILADELPHIA
PHILADELPHIA 2, EDMONTON 1

FIRST PERIOD
1. EDM Kurri (Huddy, Coffey) 2:08 (PP).
Penalties: PHI Tocchet (hooking) 1:34; EDM Coffey (holding) 10:44; PHI Sutter (interference) 12:54; EDM Messier (hooking) 14:47; EDM Huddy (tripping) 18:25.

SECOND PERIOD
No scoring.
Penalties: EDM Tikkanen (hooking) 2:10; PHI Stanley (hooking) 13:09; EDM Anderson (roughing) 14:09; PHI Carson (double minor roughing) 14:09; EDM McSorley (fighting) 16:40; PHI Stanley (fighting, instigating) 16:40; EDM Anderson (roughing) 18:37; EDM Lowe (holding) 18:47.

THIRD PERIOD
2. PHI Sutter (Tocchet, Crossman) 9:20.
3. PHI Zezel (Marsh) 14:24.
Penalty: EDM Krushelnyski (holding) 3:41.

SHOTS ON GOAL:

PHI	8	12	10	**30**
EDM	11	6	5	**22**

Goalies: PHI Hextall; EDM Fuhr
Referee: Denis Morel
Linesmen: Gord Broseker, Dan McCourt

playoffs. People tend to talk about the ones when I scored goals, but probably the first game I played in the NHL was the one I'll never forget.

The two times I scored goals were just moments. I was thrilled by those moments, but they're only parts of the games. For the first one, a goal against Boston, I remember the puck was dumped in a few seconds earlier, and the fans at the Spectrum were yelling for me to shoot. We were ahead by two goals, but I didn't have an angle on the net, so I couldn't shoot it accurately.

The second time I got a chance, [Gord] Kluzak dumped it to my left, and I was able to get to the puck right away. I just tried to get as much height and power on it as possible. It goes pretty far when you use a goalie's stick. I got it just inside the post.

My teammates came over the boards and they were so excited. That's what was such a big thrill, the way they responded. Although it was a highlight of my career, they could have said, "Big deal." But they were all screaming around me, and I remember being in the middle of the pile thinking, "What did we do, win the Stanley Cup?"

On my second goal, the magnitude of the game overshadowed my scoring. It was the fifth game of our playoff series against Washington last year, at the Cap Center. We were picked to lose to Washington and, naturally, we all felt we could win. There was a lot of pressure, with the series tied 2–2. I tried to play it down when I scored and not let it disrupt the team. We were shorthanded, and if they get a quick one, who knows? It was 7–5 when I scored, and it took a bit of pressure off all of us.

I always said I wouldn't risk hurting the team in any way, which meant if we were even-strength with a one-goal lead, I wasn't going to try scoring unless I was pressured into shooting it by someone. When I have to put the puck down the ice, I might as well go for the net. But as great as the goals were,

that first game is the one to remember.

In training camp, I felt they would give me a shot and it was up to me to prove that I could play. I don't know if they felt I was ready, but I knew I was committed to play right then in the NHL. I'd had my success in the minors, felt I had grown as a goalie and was mature enough for the NHL. We went to the finals in the AHL that year, and I'd been in the minors for two years.

The Flyers had Bobby Froese there, and Chico [Resch]. It was tough to come in with two veterans there. Mike Keenan and the coaches made it clear they were going to give me a couple of games and see how it went. When Mike started me against Edmonton in the opener, I was pretty sure I would have got at least one more game, or two, if things had not gone well in the first game. I think any full decision probably was up in the air until I played 10 games.

Mike told me the morning of the game that I was starting. He called me and Bobby and Chico into the room and told all three of us I was playing against the Oilers. He said to Bobby that he wanted to see what I could do, and that this was as good a time to give me a shot as any. Obviously, I was surprised. With a guy of Bobby Froese's stature, it was a surprise. But what the heck, if I'm going to get a start, why not start the first night?

I was happy and nervous. I remember standing in the Philly airport waiting for my wife—who was coming in the night before the game—when the Oilers came off the plane. It was a little intimidating to see them filing off—Wayne Gretzky, Mark Messier, Grant Fuhr. They didn't know me from a hole in the ground.

The fans always have been great to me in Philly. I still get emotional when we come out on the ice for the games. They rock the Spectrum, and it makes me feel like playing. That first night, though, I didn't pay much attention to the crowd because I was concentrating so much on the game. I was extremely nervous; I'll be the first to admit. Who wouldn't be? You're out there against one of the greatest teams of all time, and playing your first NHL game to boot. Then they scored on their first shot—Jari Kurri got it. It wasn't

Gretzky came in twice on me, once really late in the game, and I stopped him. Esa Tikkanen came out of the penalty box and I made a pad save on a breakaway.

really my fault, but still, your first shot....

Then it turned around. We took charge of the game, got into the flow, and shut them down. I said to myself, "Just play hard. That's all you can do." I remember Gretzky came in twice on me, once really late in the game, and I stopped him. Esa Tikkanen came out of the penalty box and I made a pad save on a breakaway.

I was busy at the end. Peter Zezel scored for us with six minutes or so to go, putting in a rebound that hit a defenseman's skate. I looked up at the clock, saw six minutes were left, and thought, "This could be a long six minutes." It was well worth the work.

Mike would always come over and shake the goalie's hand when you won. All he said was, "Great game." I think he expected a lot of me.

It was a touchy situation with Bobby Froese, and I tried not to put him in a bad position. I'm there trying to do the job, and so is he. I'm not trying to take his job, but to do my best. I think he understood that. It worked out well for both of us. He got to go to the Rangers and play, and I stayed and played in Philly.

—*As told to Barry Wilner*

Rookie Philadelphia Flyer netminder **Ron Hextall** made the 1986–87 First All-Star Team and won the Vezina Trophy and Conn Smythe Trophy. An amazing puckhandler, Hextall scored against Boston on December 8, 1987, and against Washington in the 1989 playoffs. Traded to Quebec in 1992, he joined the New York Islanders a year later before returning to Philadelphia for six more seasons, retiring in 1999.

NOVEMBER 8, 1959

It's 45 minutes after our final game of the 1959–60 season. I'm sitting in the locker room in Chicago Stadium, with tears

NOVEMBER 8, 1959
BOSTON GARDEN, BOSTON
BOSTON 5, CHICAGO 3

FIRST PERIOD
1. BOS Leach (Labine) 5:20.
2. BOS Horvath (Bucyk) 9:06.
Penalties: CHI Hay (hooking) 1:20; BOS Armstrong (holding) 9:56; BOS Gendron (holding) 13:46; BOS Boivin (holding) 16:30; CHI Vasko (tripping) 18:23.

SECOND PERIOD
3. CHI Maloney (Mikita) 3:39.
4. BOS Horvath (Mohns, Stasiuk) 14:20.
Penalty: BOS Armstrong (interference) 6:20.

THIRD PERIOD
5. BOS Mackell (Burns, Mohns) 2:21.
6. CHI Hull (Vasko, Pilote) 6:11.
7. CHI Sloan (unassisted) 7:50.
8. BOS Stasiuk (McKenney, Horvath) 12:18.
Penalties: BOS Toppazzini (interference) 4:00; CHI Arbour (throwing stick; penalty shot awarded to Leach) 6:30; BOS Lumley (interference, served by Mickoski) 8:31; CHI Hay (interference) 10:42; BOS Gendron (boarding) 13:19; CHI Pilote (high-sticking) 14:08; BOS Mackell (high-sticking) 14:08; CHI Hull (misconduct) 17:50; CHI Mikita (misconduct) 17:50.

Goalies: BOS Lumley; CHI Hall
Referee: Dalton MacArthur
Linesmen: Bob Barry, Jock Patterson

streaming down my Bruins jersey. I had just lost the scoring title to Blackhawks star Bobby Hull by one point.

The game had been sheer frustration. Early in the game, I went to a local hospital to have my jaw looked at after getting hit with a deflected puck. It turned out there was a crack there and I wouldn't have a solid meal for eight weeks, but eventually I came back to play that night.

When I got back, the Blackhawks sicked their checking line on me every time I stepped on the ice. Eric Nesterenko, Ron Murphy and Glen Skov grabbed me, pushed me, tackled me and did anything they could get away with to keep me from scoring. They tried everything to make sure Hull won that scoring title.

It worked. My only shot rang off both goalposts and ricocheted out, refusing to go in. Hull finished with 81 points. I had 80. After the game, I was so distraught, I was in tears. How many guys get a chance to win a scoring title during the Original Six? How could I come so close without winning it? Over the course of the 68 games I played, couldn't I have scored just one more goal? I couldn't believe what had happened to me.

Bobby came in to console me. He hugged me and said, "I know they did a number on you, kid." But it wasn't Hull's fault I didn't win. It wasn't Nesterenko, Murphy or Skov. Heck, it wasn't even goalie Glenn Hall's fault. Sitting there crying, my mind went back to our game against Chicago on November 8 that season. I realized that I had the scoring title taken from me early that season; I had been robbed of one precious goal that would have given me the title. The events that unfolded that game—the game I'll never forget—were the true reason I had lost the scoring title.

The 1959–60 season was probably my best. It was the third season I was centering a line with Vic Stasiuk on one wing and Johnny Bucyk on the other. Together, we were the "Uke Line," since we all had some Ukrainian blood in us. We were really clicking that season. We had great chemistry. Vic and Johnny were big guys and could really dig the puck out of the corners and get it to the net. We would know right where the other guys were going to be, and we could get our shots off before the goalies knew it.

We didn't have a great team that year—in fact, we missed the playoffs—but playing with those guys was a real thrill. I had a point in a team-record 22 straight games, a mark that still stands. Vic finished ninth in league scoring with 68 points. Bucyk finished with 52 points, but he would have done a lot better had he not missed 14 games with an injury.

I was already off to a quick start to the season when Chicago pulled into town for that November game. Before I knew it, I found myself with a clear breakaway in against Hall. I began thinking about what I was going to do with the puck. Go high? Low? Left? Right? Forehand? Backhand? Fast? Slow?

I was getting closer and closer when I looked down and saw there was no puck there anymore. Out of nowhere, a stick had come sliding along the ice from behind me. Blackhawks defenseman Al Arbour, a lifelong friend of mine, had thrown his stick in desperation and knocked the puck into the corner.

The whistle blew, play stopped and I got ready to take a penalty shot. I was thinking, "This is fine, so I had my breakaway broken up, I'll just score on the penalty shot. No big deal." But there was some confusion. The referee, Dalton MacArthur, was delaying, talking with other officials. He didn't know the rule and allowed the Blackhawks to pick the shooter. We should have picked the shooter: Me.

I was irate. I wouldn't leave center ice. I wanted to take that penalty shot so badly. Everyone on our team was arguing. They had to drag me off the ice so play could continue.

I know I would have scored if I had taken that penalty shot. I would have wound Hall up in a knot. I would have had him going out one way and I would have been going

The Blackhawks sicked their checking line on me every time I stepped on the ice. [They] grabbed me, pushed me, tackled me and did anything they could get away with to keep me from scoring.

the other. I know his weakness. I played with him in Edmonton in the old Western Hockey League. I would have gone between his legs. He always opened his legs. That was one way to beat the guy. He was a tremendous goalie, but he knows that I knew that's how you could beat him. And if he closed his legs, I would have gone another way. In that situation, he would have been at my mercy. I would have scored.

But no matter how we protested, MacArthur wouldn't let me have that penalty shot. The Blackhawks selected Larry Leach to take the shot. Leach, who didn't know Hall's weakness, failed.

We eventually won the game, 5–3, but I was still steaming. I knew they had taken a goal from me. What I didn't know was that it

would cost me a scoring title. Hull finished with 39 goals and 42 assists. I finished with 39 goals and 41 assists. Not only was I one goal away from finishing atop the goal-scoring leaders chart alone, but it cost me a share of the points lead.

Winning a scoring title would have meant a little extra money in my pocket the next season. I would have had better bargaining position going in to negotiate my next contract. But winning that scoring title wasn't about the money. Being second doesn't mean anything. If I come in second in anything, I don't want to talk about it. If I can't win, I don't want to be bothered. No one remembers who finishes second.

—As told to Chuck O'Donnell

Bronco Horvath broke into the NHL with the New York Rangers in 1955–56. Dealt to Montreal in November 1956, he went to the minors until Boston claimed him in the 1957 intra-league draft. Horvath notched 30 goals and 36 assists in 1957–58 and narrowly lost the 1960 scoring title. Brief turns for Chicago, New York and Toronto precipitated his return to the minors in 1963. Horvath appeared in 14 games for Minnesota in 1967–68 and he hung up his skates two seasons later.

There have been two games that gave me a bigger thrill than any others and it's a funny thing neither one of them meant

MARCH 3, 1959
DETROIT OLYMPIA, DETROIT
DETROIT 2, BOSTON 2

FIRST PERIOD
1. DET Pronovost (Wilson, Burton) 11:01.
2. DET Delvecchio (Howe, Kelly) 18:21.
Penalty: BOS Mohns 3:33.

SECOND PERIOD
3. BOS Horvath (Bucyk, Armstrong) 7:18.
Penalties: BOS Boivin 6:36; DET Godfrey 8:56; DET Howe 10:56.

THIRD PERIOD
4. BOS Bucyk (Stasiuk, Armstrong) 2:14.
Penalty: DET Grogan 4:45.

Goalies: DET Sawchuk; BOS Lumley
Referee: Red Storey
Linesmen: George Hayes, Bill Morrison

anything in the league standings or was a Stanley Cup game. Sure, I've had a lot of great thrills in hockey, the latest winning the World Hockey Association playoffs with the Houston Aeros and being able to realize my dream of playing with my sons, Marty and Mark. Before that, we had some Stanley Cup winners with the Detroit Red Wings and I scored goals that gave me a special satisfaction. But that was playing for money and a pro is expected to do well, which is not quite the same thing as the two games I'm thinking about as the ones I'll never forget.

One of those games was played on February 17, 1971 and eventually led to my return as a player after retiring from the Red Wings. My wife Colleen and I were chairmen of the March of Dimes in Detroit that year and somebody came up with the idea of having a "game" between the Red Wings and the Junior A Red Wings, for which Marty and Mark played at the time. I lined up with the Junior Red Wings.

Marty, Mark and I were on one line and my youngest son Murray and my brother Vic were on defense. About 16,000 people turned out for the game and gave us about a 15-minute standing ovation. That was the time I thought to myself, "Wouldn't it be nice if this was for real and I could play on a team with my sons?" That stayed in my mind, although I never believed it could happen until it really did in 1973, when we all signed with the Aeros.

We had a nice game, which ended as a 6–6 tie, not that it makes much difference. The chief thing was that the game was for a good cause, the kids got to play against some of their idols on the Red Wings and I got a chance to play with all the family members. I do remember a couple of things about the game. Mark scored the first goal and then he fed me a super pass, one that takes a little thinking even when you become a pro. He saw me open moving toward the net but there was somebody between us. He passed

the puck off the boards and it came to me perfectly. I knew what he was going to do because he had watched a lot of hockey and had picked up quite a bit just as a spectator. That's one of the great advantages today's kids have. They can learn an awful lot by sitting in the stands or on the bench if they're students of the game. Thank heavens, my boys Marty and Mark and even the little one, Murray, study the game thoroughly, which is a satisfaction to me.

As I said, that game was just for fun but, more importantly, it raised quite a bit of money for the March of Dimes. It also was the start of my thinking about playing on a team with my boys, so it's natural that I'd never forget it. The other game I recall was played on March 3, 1959, against the Boston Bruins. Some good friends got together that season and gave me a "night" at the Olympia. Getting recognition from the fans is always a great thing but to think they went out of their way to give me a night—well, that was fantastic.

I guess it would have been a fine thing if I'd been able to do something spectacular on the ice that night but I couldn't. The first period, I caught a knee to knee hit and I had to go to the trainer. In order to finish the game I had to have a shot to "freeze" the knee and stop the pain. That's something I don't ordinarily approve of doing but this was a special night. They had the special presentations at the first intermission and among the gifts I was given was a station wagon. The car was all wrapped in cellophane when they wheeled it out on the ice and I couldn't see who was in it. Then they pulled the cellophane off and my Mom and Dad were in the car. It knocked me over. I couldn't believe it. Their being there was the farthest thing from my mind. They had never before seen me play a league game, though I'd been in the NHL 15 seasons. The only time they'd come to Detroit was in 1950 when I had been badly hurt. The only other time they'd seen me play with the Red Wings was when we trained in my home town of Saskatoon.

A lot of old friends and former teammates, including Ted Lindsay, had come to the

> **They pulled the cellophane off and my Mom and Dad were in the car. It knocked me over. I couldn't believe it. Their being there was the farthest thing from my mind.**

game and naturally I was called on to speak. I went on to thank a lot of people by name, not so much for the gifts as for the fact they'd helped me in hockey, because hockey is my life. One of the gifts I remember getting was a toy bruin from Fern Flaman, captain of the Bruins at the time. Another was a diamond ring from my teammates. It was a great night, even if I didn't do much of anything on the ice and the game ended in a 2–2 tie.

As I said, it might sound funny, but those two games are the ones I remember best, not that winning big games and scoring hat tricks doesn't mean a great deal. They do. But above all, it has been my family and the love and appreciation of the fans for what I've done on the ice that have been most important to me. Those are the kind of things that you truly appreciate and give you a lasting great feeling.

——*As told to George Vass*

A six-time NHL scoring leader, six-time Hart Trophy winner, 21 times an All-Star, **Gordie Howe** spent most of his 26 NHL seasons and six WHA campaigns as a living legend. Howe retired from the Detroit Red Wings in 1971 but resumed his professional career in the WHA to play with his sons Mark and Marty. Howe rejoined the NHL with the Hartford Whalers in 1979–80, tallying 15 goals and 26 assists before retiring at age 52.

KELLY HRUDEY

Without question, the seven-period overtime game against Washington in the 1987 playoffs is the game I'll never forget.

APRIL 18, 1987
CAPITAL CENTER, LANDOVER MD
NY ISLANDERS 3, WASHINGTON 2 (4OT)

FIRST PERIOD
1. WAS Gartner (Adams, Stevens) 19:12.
Penalties: NYI Konroyd (hooking) 7:36; NYI Kerr (elbowing) 19:51; WAS Gould (holding) 19:51.

SECOND PERIOD
2. NYI Flatley (Konroyd, Trottier) 11:35.
3. WAS Martin (Adams, Murphy) 18:45.
Penalties: NYI Boyd (slashing) 3:55; WAS Blum (cross-checking), NYI Gilbert (high-sticking) 6:04; WAS Kastelic (high-sticking) 6:04; NYI Trottier (holding) 14:58.

THIRD PERIOD
4. NYI Trottier (Kerr, Konroyd) 14:37.
Penalties: WAS Martin (holding) 1:31; NYI Diduck (high-sticking) 10:21; NYI Franceschetti (high-sticking) 10:21; NYI Sutter (high-sticking) 19:06; WAS Jensen (high-sticking) 19:06.

FIRST OVERTIME PERIOD
No scoring.
No penalties.

SECOND OVERTIME PERIOD
No scoring.
Penalties: NYI Kerr (slashing) 8:46; WAS Stevens (high-sticking) 8:46; WAS Duchesne (cross-checking) 10:49; NYI Flatley (high-sticking) 10:49; WAS Adams (misconduct) 16:47.

THIRD OVERTIME PERIOD
No scoring.
No penalties.

FOURTH OVERTIME PERIOD
5. NYI LaFontaine (Dineen, Leiter) 8:47.
No penalties.

SHOTS ON GOAL:

NYI	5	5	11	11	9	11	5	**57**
WAS	15	10	11	11	17	10	1	**75**

Goalies: NYI Hrudey; WAS Mason
Referee: Andy Van Hellemond
Linesmen: John D'Amico, Ron Finn

Going into the game, we were confident. We had just won two big games in a row after being down 3–1 in the series. The Islanders have a history of coming back, and we felt we could do it again.

Anytime we play Washington, we have to be ready, especially early in the game. They always come out flying in the first period and, mainly, in the first 10 minutes. In that game, we wanted to weather the storm early and get out of the first period without falling behind. We went 19 minutes without being scored against and felt that we were accomplishing what we wanted. Although Washington's Mike Gartner scored a goal in the last minute of the first period, we got out of the first period in decent shape.

Between periods, as I sat in the dressing room, I sensed excitement. We were still in the game and were playing with great emotion. They came out flying again in the second period, but we held them off. Patrick Flatley scored a goal for us to make the score 1–1. Then Grant Martin scored late in the second period for a 2–1 lead for Washington.

That goal put the fans in a frenzy. I could sense that the fans thought that the goal had lifted them over the top, that it had wrapped up the game. They were getting ready to celebrate. And it was a tough goal to come back from. The Capitals had the lead and a good defensive team, and they had great fan support in their home rink. But we worked our tails off, and Bryan Trottier scored with a backhander to tie the score.

I hoped we would win it in regulation and save ourselves from a long night. We had some good chances too, but Bob Mason made some great saves. Both teams hit the post with less than five minutes to go. There was a scramble in front of our net, and Washington's Dave Christian whacked at the puck. It seemed like time slowed down while the puck was in the air. It rolled slowly on end toward the net, hit the outside of the post and went into the corner. Then it seemed like play

sped up again. I had felt that sensation before, but never in a seventh game of a series.

When we got through regulation time, after the big goal we'd scored, we were really excited. I looked around the locker room and saw more enthusiasm than I saw all season.

I remembered another overtime game against Washington the year before when they swept us. We had lost 2–1 in the second overtime and I kept thinking about how hard they came out and how badly they wanted the goal then. They did it again, of course, and they had about 10 shots in the first 10 minutes of the first overtime. They were good shots, too.

Then we took over the play. Mason made two big saves on shots that could have ended it. At one whistle, I sensed both teams and both goalies had a rhythm. I felt invincible— so "on" and so aware of what was happening. The anticipation was there. I got the feeling that the game would go on all night, the way Mason and I were playing.

Nobody wanted to jinx the team, so nothing was said in the locker room. I never thought of it as a historic game. I didn't even notice when they flashed the news on the scoreboard that it was the fourth-longest game in league history.

I never got really tired, but my feet hurt. I wear tight skates, and after a normal game, they hurt, but this was beyond that, beyond being sore. I took my skates off immediately after the game and my toes cramped up.

I stayed with the same superstitions, performed the same routine I normally do between periods. As a goalie, I am a little removed from the other players on the team; everyone is trying to do his own thing. At the intermissions, we became more positive in the dressing room. After the third period, I thought we were the most confident we'd ever been, but then we kept surpassing that level. I thought, "This is as high as we can be," but it wasn't the case. We seemed to be more prepared each overtime.

I was amazed at the pace of the game and how hard all the guys were working, even through the second and third overtimes. It would seem a guy was exhausted and could barely lumber back to the bench, but when his next shift was on, he would pounce over

I thought, "This is as high as we can be," but it wasn't the case.

the boards and give it all he had again.

I could sense more than anything that the fans were thoroughly enjoying the game. Give them a lot of credit, they didn't leave despite the late hour. After that game, I felt differently about the Washington fans; they were part of history. In regulation time they were as hostile as any fans at a visiting rink, but as the game progressed, they became hockey fans rather than just Capitals fans.

When Patty LaFontaine finally scored, there was no buildup. That's how those goals often are scored. I remember Gordie Dineen circling the net. I didn't realize how big a play it would be, but I remember him shooting, with Dale Henry in front creating havoc. Then Patty turned around and shot without even looking.

Then the red light was on. My first reaction was disbelief. I thought, "No, this game can't end, we've been playing this long. There must be a penalty or a man in the crease." But then I realized it was over, and I remember jumping without any energy and Randy Boyd coming to hug me and knocking me over.

I don't look back at it very often, but that game has brought me some notoriety. I've been in the league five years, but wherever I go, the people I meet mention that game. When I went back to Canada for the Canada Cup, people always mentioned that game. I thoroughly enjoyed it but hope I never go through another game like it unless I'm on the winning side again.

—As told to Barry Wilner

Kelly Hrudey broke into the NHL with the New York Islanders in 1983–84. He left Long Island in February 1989, traded to the Los Angeles Kings. Hrudey backstopped the Kings to the 1993 Stanley Cup finals but the Montreal Canadiens prevailed. A free agent in the summer of 1996, Hrudey signed with San Jose. He spent two seasons with the Sharks before moving into a broadcasting career with *Hockey Night in Canada*.

When I scored my 50th goal of the season on March 2, 1966, I thought the pressure was off me. The goal came in the 57th

---

MARCH 12, 1966
CHICAGO STADIUM, CHICAGO
CHICAGO 4, NEW YORK RANGERS 2

FIRST PERIOD
No scoring.
Penalty: CHI Stapleton (hooking) 9:10.

SECOND PERIOD
1. NYR Marshall (Hicke) 2:50 (PP).
2. NYR Hicke (Ingarfield, Seiling) 13:08.
Penalties: CHI Wharram (holding) 0:57; CHI Mikita (high-sticking) 7:23; NYR Fleming (high-sticking) 7:23; NYR Howell (holding) 9:26.

THIRD PERIOD
3. CHI Maki (Hull, Pilote) 2:57.
4. CHI Hull (Angotti, Hay) 5:34 (PP).
5. CHI Maki (Mohns, Esposito) 7:25.
6. CHI Mohns (Esposito, Pilote) 18:41.
Penalties: NYR Howell (slashing) 4:05; CHI Angotti (holding) 7:53; NYR Brown (interference) 12:36.

SHOTS ON GOAL:

CHI	13	11	9	**33**
NYR	10	12	6	**28**

Goalies: CHI Hall; NYR Maniago
Referee: John Ashley
Linesmen: Neil Armstrong, Matt Pavelich

---

game of the season and with 13 games left to play, I wasn't too concerned about getting No. 51.

I'm always enthused when I score a goal—it's something you never lose no matter how many you score. You always get a thrill out of seeing the puck go into the net, whether you've scored 600 goals in your career or 25. Each one is a thrill in itself.

I'd scored 50 goals four years before, in 1962, to become the third National Hockey League player to reach that level, after Rocket Richard and Boom Boom Geoffrion of the Montreal Canadiens. But that year, I didn't get my 50th goal until the last game of the season, so I didn't have much of a chance to break the 50-goal record. This time, though, in 1966, everybody naturally was wondering when I'd get No. 51.

After I got No. 50, the radio, newspapers, magazines and television were full of stories about when I would set a new record. The headlines were asking, "When will Hull get his 51st goal?" I wasn't too concerned at first. I never worry too much about records, and besides, I figured that with 13 games left I wouldn't feel like I was under much pressure. I could play my normal game and the goal would come. I remember saying after scoring goal No. 50, "That takes the monkey off my back." It did, too, because I can't remember being more enthused about a goal than I was about that one. I'd been a little tense and frustrated for a while before I got it and I guess I'd taken it out on my family at times. So it was a great relief to get No. 50 and I expected that I'd get No. 51 to set a new record the next game.

But I was shut out the next game and so were the Blackhawks. The next game, the same thing happened. It was almost unbelievable, a team with great scorers such as Stan Mikita, Kenny Wharram, Doug Mohns and a lot of other good shooters being shut out two games in a row like that. The pressure was beginning to get on my nerves.

I got to be snappish. One day, my wife started speaking and I turned on her. "Don't talk to me," I said.

Unbelievably, the Hawks were shut out for the third game in a row. I think the whole team might have been reacting to the pressure. I couldn't get a goal. Mikita couldn't get a goal. Nobody could get good wood on the puck. I was dissatisfied with my hockey stick. A few weeks before, I asked the manufacturer to send me new sticks with an extra curve in the blade. For some reason, the sticks were delayed. Finally, just before the next game, on March 12 in Chicago against the New York Rangers, I got a batch of the new-style sticks. I tested them in the warm-up. But they weren't right. I just wasn't shooting well with them.

When the game started, it wasn't any better. I got my chances in the first two periods but the goalie, Cesare Maniago, had no trouble handling the shots I got on goal. Most of the time, I couldn't get enough wood on the puck or put it on target. It looked like I would be shut out again for the fourth game in a row, although at least the team finally scored a goal.

Early in the third period came a break. My teammate, Lou Angotti, outfought Reggie Fleming of the Rangers for the puck in our defensive zone. I was already moving when Louie got the puck and he kicked it over to me with his skate. I took the pass on the curved blade of my stick and headed for the Ranger goal, going all out. I could see Eric Nesterenko at my right and he cut in front of Maniago, who came out to cut down the angle.

Just as I crossed the blue line, I cut loose with a slap shot. I put everything into it and I got solid wood on the puck this time. Nesterenko not only helped screen the shot but also lifted the blade of Maniago's stick and the puck went under it into the net. That was No. 51, a new record.

That goal meant a great deal, not only because it set a record and because of the pressure leading up to it, but more than anything, because of the reaction of the fans. When the red light went on to signal the goal, the crowd just exploded. They littered the ice with hats, confetti, scorecards,

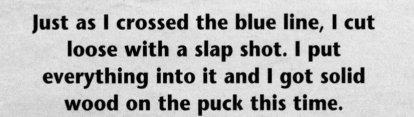

Just as I crossed the blue line, I cut loose with a slap shot. I put everything into it and I got solid wood on the puck this time.

newspaper, hot dog wrappers, anything they could lay their hands on. I can't even describe the feeling that I get when a crowd gives me an ovation like that.

I remember picking up one of the sillier hats and placing it on my head at a jaunty angle. That drew another roar from the crowd as I skated toward the east end of the ice toward where my wife, Joanne, was sitting. I owed her a kiss after the way I'd acted all week. I had been pretty hard to live with during the frustration of the previous

three games. She told me later that when I scored the goal she cried, the first time she had ever done that over a goal.

I was doubly glad to have scored that goal on home ice for the Chicago fans who had been so good to me for so many years.

—As told to George Vass

The most explosive player of his generation, **Bobby Hull** joined the Chicago Blackhawks in 1957–58. He won his first scoring championship two years later with 39 goals and 42 assists. "The Golden Jet" concluded the 1965–66 season with a league-record 54 goals, a mark he bettered with 58 goals in 1968–69. He stunned the hockey world by joining the WHA in 1972, returning to the NHL for a brief star turn in 1979–80. He is the father of Brett Hull, who emerged as a superstar in the 1990s.

Every kid practicing alone in a deserted rink or on a pond on some frozen winter morning shares the fantasy of playing in

MAY 18, 1971
CHICAGO STADIUM, CHICAGO
MONTREAL 3, CHICAGO 2

FIRST PERIOD
1. CHI D. Hull (Koroll, B. Hull) 19:12 (PP).
Penalties: MON Harper (holding) 1:22; MON Lemaire (roughing) 4:09; CHI Magnuson (roughing) 4:09; CHI D. Hull (tripping) 7:55; MON Houle (holding) 17:35.

SECOND PERIOD
2. CHI O'Shea (Martin) 7:33.
3. MON Lemaire (Laperriere) 14:18.
4. MON Richard (Lemaire) 18:20.
Penalties: CHI Magnuson (tripping) 1:49; MON P. Mahovlich (roughing) 3:20; CHI Nesterenko (roughing) 3:20; CHI (bench, too many men on ice, served by Angotti) 4:14; CHI Magnuson (charging) 12:32; MON Tremblay (hooking) 13:07; CHI Jarrett (holding) 17:54; MON Ferguson (holding) 18:11.

THIRD PERIOD
5. MON Richard (Houle, Lapointe) 2:34.
Penalties: MON Harper (hooking) 5:32; MON P. Mahovlich (hooking) 7:37.

SHOTS ON GOAL:

MON	6	9	10	**25**
CHI	12	9	12	**33**

Goalies: MON Dryden; CHI Esposito
Referee: John Ashley
Linesmen: Matt Pavelich, John D'Amico

Game 7 of the Stanley Cup finals. Alone with his thoughts, the roar of the crowd washes over him. The pressure of the moment rides on his shoulders. In his little world, he's swooping in on net, using his best move, twisting the goalie into a pretzel, rifling the puck between the posts and whipping the home town crowd into a frenzy. The gleaming chalice is now his to claim.

Seconds after the puck crossed the goal line, I realized the dream I dreamt as a kid—a dream I still dreamed as a man—was coming true. I had let a shot go from the slot area and it somehow found its way past Montreal Canadiens goalie Ken Dryden. The scoreboard read: Blackhawks 1, Canadiens 0. When Danny O'shea scored in the second period, we had a two-goal lead. The Chicago Stadium crowd was loving every second of it. We were surging, skating hard and playing smart. It was Game 7 of the Stanley Cup finals and we were rising to the occasion. We were like a championship boxer with the opponent on the ropes—we wanted to move in for the kill. All we had to do was keep the pressure on the Habs and the Cup was ours. The dream was ours.

Win or lose, we knew that was the final game of a grueling season. That year, we switched from the East Division to the West and finished 20 points ahead of the second-place St. Louis Blues. Our roster was a strong mix of talent and character. The leader in both areas was my brother, Bobby Hull. He finished fifth in the league in scoring with 96 points and third with 44 goals. Stan Mikita was also among the best players in the league, finishing with 72 points. Our defense—featuring Bill White, Keith Magnuson and Pat Stapleton—was ferocious. Led by goaltender Tony Esposito we allowed the second-fewest goals [184] in the league that year.

I played on a line with Pit Martin and Jim Pappin. Someone figured out that the first initials of Martin, Pappin and Hull spell out MPH—and instantly we had a nickname. We were proof that chemistry is more than a cliche—it is crucial to the success of a line. Jim was a great playmaking right wing. He was the smartest guy I ever played with, the cerebral leader of the line. Pit brought speed and good forechecking. He also knew how to finish when he had a chance to score. My forte was shooting. These guys gave me a lot of chances. Offensively, the 1970–71 season turned out to be my best. I finished with 40 goals; Jim and Pit had 22 apiece.

Entering the playoffs, we were seeded first in the West. We swept the Philadelphia Flyers in the first round of the playoffs, and edged the New York Rangers in seven games to earn the right to play the Canadiens in the finals.

The Canadiens were loaded. Yvan Cournoyer [37 goals], Peter Mahovlich [35], Frank Mahovlich [31], Jacques Lemaire [28], Jean Beliveau [25] and Henri Richard [12] gave them plenty of firepower, and defensemen Serge Savard, Guy Lapointe, Jacques Laperriere and J.C. Tremblay ended up in the Hall of Fame. The key to the Canadiens, however, may have been Dryden, the rookie. He came out of nowhere that year to become the fabled "hot goalie" by helping the Habs beat the Boston Bruins and the Minnesota North Stars en route to the finals.

From the start, the Blackhawks and Canadiens were very evenly matched. Jim Pappin scored in overtime to give us a Game 1 victory and Lou Angotti scored twice as we took Game 2, 5–3. The Canadiens' luck changed when the series moved to the Montreal Forum. Frank Mahovlich scored twice as the Habs won Game 3, and Cournoyer scored two goals for the Habs in a 5–2 Game 4 victory to even the series.

I scored a power-play goal in the first period of Game 5 and, coupled with Esposito's 31 saves, it turned out to be the game-winner in a 2–0 victory. The Canadiens, however, had the knack for knowing how to win and they won Game 6, with the key goal coming shorthanded from Peter Mahovlich.

It was a warm spring day in Chicago for Game 7—the game I'll never forget. We came out hot. I scored in the last minute of the first period and O'Shea scored in the eighth

The Chicago Stadium crowd was loving every second of it. We were surging, skating hard and playing smart.

minute of the second period to make it 2–0. Dreams of sipping from the Cup began to dance in our heads.

We came inches away from icing the game. On the power play, Pit had set up my brother for one of his patented slap shots. Bobby shot it so hard that when it hit the crossbar, it nearly ricocheted out of the zone. So Lemaire gets control of the puck and skates it to center. It was such a warm day there was a slight fog, like a mist, hanging in the air. Lemaire lofts the puck toward Tony, but Tony can't pick it up because of the mist. Finally, Tony sees it at the last second, but it's too late. The puck ends up going in. Richard adds another about four minutes later. We go into the dressing room for the second intermission tied 2–2. The dream was

ending. A nightmare was unfolding.

Richard gave the Canadiens a 3–2 lead at the 2:34 mark of the third period. We had a few chances to even the score when we got two power plays, but Richard was terrific on the penalty kills. We tried everything we could. We tried every way we knew how to get the equalizer. It never came.

As the final seconds ticked away, I felt the dream die slowly and painfully. The little kid in me never stopped dreaming the dream. Even today, he's in there, hands raised, waving to the crowd, watching the Cup pass from teammate to teammate, from Martin to Pappin to White to Esposito. The kid in me still dreams it—even though the man never got to live it.

—*As told to Chuck O'Donnell*

Dennis Hull, seen above battling Montreal's Larry Robinson for the puck, skated out of the shadow of his superstar brother Bobby to forge his own respectable NHL career. Possessing a slap shot that rivaled his sibling's, Hull scored 303 NHL goals before retiring in 1978. He had his best offensive season in 1972–73, after helping Team Canada beat the Soviet Union in the famed Summit Series, with a 39-goal, 51-assist campaign.

WORLD CUP TRIUMPH

When the USA won Olympic gold in 1960 and 1980, it entered competition as an underdog. But by 1996, the Americans had as many proven NHL stars on their roster as any other nation. The World Cup of Hockey, the successor to the Canada Cup tournaments, offered the USA a shot at international hockey supremacy—a shot the Americans didn't miss.

Team USA advanced confidently through the World Cup semifinals to meet archrival Canada in a best-of-three final. After splitting the first two games, the teams met for the rubber match in Montreal, Canada's hockey heartland. The powerhouse Canadian squad dominated most of the game but Team USA netminder (and tournament MVP) Mike Richter made spectacular save after save. Shortly after Canada moved into a 2–1 lead at 12:50 of the third period, the tide finally turned. American snipers Brett Hull and Tony Amonte found the net 43 seconds apart to put their country ahead 3–2 with less than four minutes to play. The Americans potted two more goals against the shocked Canadians before Team USA jubilantly hoisted the World Cup.

—*Chris McDonell*

SEPTEMBER 14, 1996
MOLSON CENTRE, MONTREAL
USA 5, CANADA 2

No one really thought we had a chance at Toronto for the Stanley Cup in 1967. The whole season was either down or

APRIL 15, 1967
CHICAGO STADIUM, CHICAGO
TORONTO 4, CHICAGO 2

FIRST PERIOD
1. TOR Walton (Stemkowski, Pappin) 6:16.
2. CHI Angotti (Pilote) 9:31.
3. CHI B. Hull (Hay, Jarrett) 11:01.
4. TOR Mahovlich (Keon, Walton) 14:14 (PP).
Penalties: TOR Horton (interference) 2:36; CHI D. Hull (hooking) 5:05; TOR Stemkowski (high-sticking) 9:09; CHI Van Impe (high-sticking) 9:09; CHI Hodge (hooking) 11:41; CHI Hay (hooking) 13:24; TOR Pulford (holding), 15:48; TOR Pulford (roughing) 19:28; CHI Nesterenko (roughing) 19:28.

SECOND PERIOD
No scoring.
Penalties: TOR Stanley (charging) 3:19; CHI Wharram (slashing) 5:32; TOR Pappin (holding) 7:10; TOR Pappin (high-sticking) 13:12; CHI D. Hull (holding) 17:03.

THIRD PERIOD
5. TOR Stemkowski (Pulford, Pappin) 2:11.
6. TOR Pappin (Pulford, Horton) 17:14.
Penalties: TOR Stemkowski (tripping) 4:23; TOR Stemkowski (tripping) 10:13; CHI Angotti (slashing) 13:54; TOR Pulford (high-sticking) 19:28; CHI Mikita (high-sticking) 19:28.

SHOTS ON GOAL:
TOR	7	9	15	**31**
CHI	12	15	22	**49**

Goalies: TOR Bower, Sawchuk; CHI DeJordy
Referee: John Ashley
Linesmen: Neil Armstrong, Pat Shetton

up, and sometimes it seemed mostly down with the Maple Leafs.

There was a stretch of 10 games from mid-January to mid-February when we never won once. We slid down to fifth place and winning the Stanley Cup was no longer the question—just getting a chance to get in the playoffs by finishing fourth seemed problem enough.

To make matters worse, at the height of the slump, I ended up in the hospital. Stayed there two weeks, but luckily by the time I got out the Leafs had straightened out and were making a run for third, which is where they finished.

A lot of the talk was that the Chicago Blackhawks would win the Stanley Cup. They had finished a mile in front of everybody else during the regular season. Others liked the Montreal Canadiens, who had come in second, 17 points behind Chicago. Not too many people were talking about us, and you couldn't blame them. We hadn't come on strong until the end of the season.

That 1966–67 season was the last one before expansion so there were still just six teams in the league and two rounds of the playoffs, best-of-seven in each. The third-place team played the first-place team, which put us up against Chicago in the opening round. Well, a lot of people thought Chicago had the best team they had ever had that year, with Bobby Hull, Stan Mikita, Ken Wharram, Doug Mohns, Pierre Pilote, Glenn Hall and quite a few other good ones. But we had some good ones, too, in Frank Mahovlich, Larry Hillman, Tim Horton, Johnny Bower, Bob Pulford, Pete Stemkowski and Jim Pappin, to mention a few.

Even when we lost the first game in Chicago 5–2, I had a feeling we would come out all right. As good as Chicago was, we stayed right with them. George Armstrong got hurt but we put Brian Conacher in his right-wing spot and he played the greatest hockey of his life. We came back after losing the first one and after four games we were even with Chicago.

The fifth game was in Chicago on Saturday afternoon, April 15, 1967. This is always the big one, because if you lose it the other team has two chances left to beat you.

I had a tough decision to make before the game—and during it too. Our goalie, Terry Sawchuk, had played the first four games and he had taken a lot of shots and bumps from the Hawks. He needed a rest and asked if he could sit this one out. I agreed and started Johnny Bower, who hadn't played much.

Bower was nervous and shaky right from the start. He missed a shot and it went in. Then he missed a couple more, one hitting the post, the other just missing the net. I could see he was having trouble and I called him over to the bench. "What's the matter?" I asked him. "You look shaky."

"I don't feel too good," he admitted. "My stomach's jumping."

"You want to come out of there now?" I asked, thinking I'd send Sawchuk in right there.

"No, let me finish the period," he said, and Sawchuk said the same thing, that he'd rather go in at the start of the second period. Bower stayed in and finished the first period, with the score tied 2–2.

When the second period started, I had Sawchuk in goal. Sawchuk hadn't been on the ice two minutes when Bobby Hull swung around to his left and let go with one of his bombs, from maybe 15 to 20 feet out. It caught Terry right under the neck and the way he went down, for a moment, it looked like he had been killed. He lay flat on the ice for at least a minute, out cold.

Our trainer, Bob Haggert, ran out to him and then came back to me. "Terry told me to tell you he's all right," said Haggert.

"That's the best news I've had in a long time," I said in relief. Sawchuk got up, picked up his stick and from then on it was him against the Chicago team. They kept coming at him all period and even more so in the third period when they put 22 shots on goal without scoring.

I remember Mohns coming across the whole front of the net, just he and Terry alone, and Sawchuk stayed with him all the way for the best save of the game. They couldn't get one past Sawchuk and we scored

TORONTO MAPLE LEAFS

THE PRICE OF SUCCESS IS HARD WORK

Bobby Hull let go with one of his bombs. It caught Terry Sawchuk right under the neck and the way he went down, for a moment, it looked like he had been killed.

a couple, one by Stemkowski and the other by Pappin, and won the game 4–2.

Later on, Haggert told me that when he had asked Sawchuk whether he thought he was all right just after he had taken the shot from Hull, Terry snapped, "I stopped the damn shot, didn't I?!"

That was the turning point of the series. It turned it around and gave us the edge we needed. We won the next game to take the first round and then went into the finals and beat Montreal for the Stanley Cup.

Any time you want to talk about superstitions, I can bring up one. The whole playoffs that year we never won a game on a Thursday and never lost one on any other day. We lost four Thursday games in a row and won all the rest. "The Game I'll Never Forget" was that Saturday one, though, the afternoon Sawchuk beat the Chicago team although Bobby Hull knocked him cold.

—*As told to George Vass*

Stressing a defense-first style, **Punch Imlach** had a knack for bringing in veteran players and getting the most from them. As both coach and general manager, he guided the Leafs to Stanley Cup wins in 1962, 1963, 1964 and 1967 but was fired after the team was swept in the Stanley Cup quarterfinals. Hired by the 1970 Buffalo expansion team, Imlach managed the Sabres until 1978 and rejoined the Leafs from 1979 to 1981.

CRAIG JANNEY

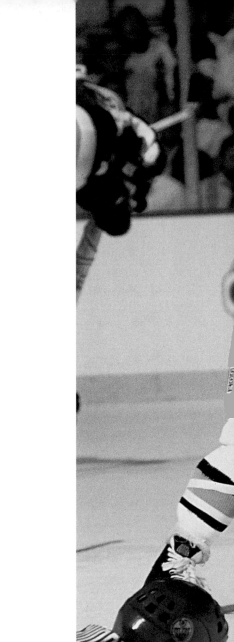

GAME 7, 1988
WALES CONFERENCE FINALS

The one game that stands out in my mind took place during my first year in the league, 1988, when I was with the Boston

MAY 14, 1988
BOSTON GARDEN, BOSTON
BOSTON 6, NEW JERSEY 2

FIRST PERIOD
1. BOS Janney (Bourque, Kluzak) 8:59 (PP).
2. BOS Lemay (Thelven, Wesley) 11:59.
Penalties: BOS Plett (hooking) 5:33; NJ Johnson (hooking) 8:09; BOS Sweeney (high-sticking) 9:41; NJ Daneyko (high-sticking) 18:49; BOS Neely (roughing) 19:16.

SECOND PERIOD
3. BOS Middleton (Bourque) 2:57.
4. NJ MacLean (Sulliman) 15:28.
Penalties: NJ Daneyko (roughing) 3:56; NJ Broten (cross-checking) 7:55; NJ Broten (roughing) 10:15; BOS Plett (interference) 17:32.

THIRD PERIOD
5. NJ Muller (Broten, MacLean) 3:41.
6. BOS Janney (unassisted) 12:05.
7. BOS Neely (Kasper, Burridge) 13:19.
8. BOS Linseman (Middleton) 19:36 (SH).
Penalties: NJ MacLean (holding) 15:38; BOS Bourque (high-sticking) 18:56.

SHOTS ON GOAL:

BOS	9	12	10	**31**
NJ	8	3	8	**19**

Goalies: BOS Lemelin; NJ Burke
Referee: Don Koharski
Linesmen: Kevin Collins, Ron Finn

Bruins. It was Game 7 of the Wales Conference finals. We were playing the New Jersey Devils, with a berth against the Edmonton Oilers in the Stanley Cup finals at stake.

Bobby Joyce and I had joined the Bruins late in the 1987–88 season; it was after the Olympics, Bobby coming from the Canadian team and me from the United States squad. We each played in 15 regular-season games with the Bruins, then got thrown right into the playoffs.

We finished the regular season 44–30–6—second in the Adams Division, nine points behind Montreal—then we beat the Buffalo Sabres in six games and the Canadiens in seven in the opening two rounds of the playoffs. The Devils were 38–36–6 and in fourth place in the Patrick Division, barely edging the New York Rangers for the final playoff berth. In fact, it was New Jersey's first-ever playoff appearance. The Devils upset the Patrick Division champion New York Islanders in the first round of the playoffs, then beat the Washington Capitals in a seven-game series.

I'll always remember Game 7 against New Jersey. Terry O'Reilly, my coach in Boston, grabbed Joyce and me before the game and said, "You never know—this could be your last chance ever to get to the finals."

Bobby and I were in the locker room, kind of laughing and joking a few hours before the game and saying we couldn't believe we were in this position. Four months earlier, we had been on our respective national teams, and all of a sudden, we were thrust into such an important game. When Terry grabbed us and said that to us, we both immediately realized how big it really was. It was enormous. To that point, through the whole playoffs, it had all been fun and games.

Bobby and I were very close. We had joined a team that had been going well without us, and we stepped in and took spots from other guys. We weren't exactly welcomed by veteran teammates, and I

didn't blame them. We were two kids off Olympic teams who had taken other guys' spots. We kind of formed a bond. We really wanted to contribute. For us to get to the finals was really hard to fathom.

I remember being able to help out the team, scoring a couple of goals. We ended up winning 6–2, but it had been a really tight game. We'd taken a 3–0 lead, but New Jersey had come back and cut it to 3–2.

I scored the first goal of the game, deflecting a slap shot by Ray Bourque on a power play midway through the first period. Moe Lemay scored three minutes after I did to make it 2–0. Then, off a face-off early in the second period, we got what proved to be the game-winning goal. Bourque came in off the point to take a face-off after the center got thrown out. Ray drew the puck back to Rick Middleton, who scored from there.

We weren't exactly welcomed by veteran teammates, and I didn't blame them.

John MacLean scored for the Devils late in the second period and New Jersey cut it to 3–2 when Kirk Muller scored early in the third. I was able to steal a clearing pass from Ken Daneyko and score against goaltender Sean Burke to restore our lead to two goals with just under eight minutes left. I think I caught Burke off guard—a quick turnover usually does that. He was out a little and I saw him shorten up on the stick. I thought he might poke at the puck, so I took a step in front, gave him a little deke, and put it by him.

I remember the pressure and the crowd, and all my friends were there. I scored a pretty big goal, looked through the glass, and a couple of my buddies from Boston College were right there. To see them and have them be a part of it with me was really a special moment. I was so caught up in the emotion, and wasn't until Cam Neely scored about a minute later that I relaxed a little. Ken Linseman added an empty-net goal in the final minute and we were in the finals. I couldn't believe it.

I couldn't believe, first of all, that I got a chance to contribute. Everything was so new. The crowd in Boston Garden was going cuckoo. I'll never forget the excitement of the crowd. I was just having fun and happy to be there. It was a more innocent time, the first time something like that had happened to me. I hadn't seen any of the negative parts of the game, guys being traded and things like that.

I remember after we won, we were carrying the conference championship trophy around, and afterward, when everyone was celebrating, Bobby and I went out by ourselves and were just hanging out. But mainly, I remember what led up to it: Terry pulling Bobby and I aside and saying it could be our only chance to get to the finals. It was a wild statement, but he was correct. I made it one other time, in 1990, but Bobby never did.

—As told to Don Wood

Craig Janney, a playmaking centerman, was traded by the Boston Bruins in February 1992. He scored 24 goals and a career-best 82 assists and 106 points the following season. Dealt to San Jose in March 1995, he later played for the Winnipeg Jets, who transferred to Phoenix. Janney spent his last NHL season, in 1998–99, with Tampa Bay and the New York Islanders.

I played on six Stanley Cup winners with the Montreal Canadiens and 15 years altogether in the National Hockey League.

FEBRUARY 23, 1972
OAKLAND-ALMEDA COUNTY COLISEUM, OAKLAND
BOSTON 8, CALIFORNIA 6

FIRST PERIOD
1. CA Redmond (Carleton, Marshall) 2:51.
2. CA Redmond (unassisted) 13:22.
3. BOS Stanfield (McKenzie) 17:37.
4. CA Croteau (Leach) 19:52.
No penalties.

SECOND PERIOD
5. CA Carleton (R. Smith) 3:58.
6. CA Croteau (J. Johnston, Shmyr) 7:34.
7. CA Patrick (M. Johnston, Jarrett) 8:53.
8. BOS Cashman (Orr, Walton) 14:36.
9. BOS Stanfield (Orr) 17:15.
Penalties: BOS Walton (fighting) 0:43; CA Shmyr (fighting) 0:43; CA Marshall (tripping, penalty shot awarded to Stanfield) 16:41.

THIRD PERIOD
10. BOS Orr (Westfall) 2:52.
11. BOS Stanfield (Orr, Awrey) 5:59.
12. BOS Esposito (Westfall, Smith) 14:31.
13. BOS Esposito (Cashman, Smith) 17:11.
14. BOS Sanderson (Westfall, Orr) 19:46 (EN).
Penalty: BOS Westfall (hooking) 8:17.

SHOTS ON GOAL:

BOS	10	12	15	**37**
CA	11	12	10	**33**

Goalies: BOS Johnston; CA Meloche
Referee: Lloyd Gilmour
Linesmen: John D'Amico, Pat Clarke

In all that time, I was in a lot of playoff games, and as everybody says there's something special about them. There's the extra tension because of what's at stake, there's the added incentive to win, and everyone is keyed up all the time.

You feel the same way, although I never showed it, I guess, when you're coaching a team in the playoffs, as I did the Boston Bruins in 1971 and '72. People always say I show no emotion on my face, although that's not quite true. I showed plenty when we won the Stanley Cup at Boston in 1972.

The game I'll never forget was one played that 1971–72 season, although not in the playoffs, which might surprise some people. I guess it'll surprise even more when you consider it was played against the California Seals, who didn't have much of a record.

At the time, Boston was really going strong. We lost just one game in December, one in January and one in February. But we did have some worries about Bobby Orr's knees. His left knee had been operated on twice by that time and at the start of a long road trip in February, he hurt it again.

By the time we got to Vancouver on our swing, he was limping a little and he admitted that his knee was locking on him. Then, during the Vancouver game that we won, he fell and hit the goalpost. That made the knee even worse.

Our next stop was at Oakland to play the Seals. That's the game that I always remember because I learned something about coaching that I'd never thought about.

Orr's knee was causing us a lot of concern. The way things were going, we didn't know if he'd be able to play the rest of the season or would be available for the playoffs. We felt we had to do something to make sure of our defense. We made a deal with the Seals before the game for defenseman Carol Vadnais. We also got another player, Don O'Donoghue, and gave them defenseman Rick Smith, who had played quite a bit for us, and forward Reg Leach and defenseman Bob Stewart, who hadn't.

Vadnais was an All-Star defenseman and played like that the rest of the season for us. He gave us insurance in case Orr's knee got worse but he was a standout player on his own. Not in that first game at Oakland, though. That's one of the reasons I remember that game.

The Seals started out as if they were going to rip us apart that night. Eddie Johnston was in goal for us, and he had a tough time of it, although you couldn't really blame him. Everybody—and I mean everybody—was playing so badly in front of him. He got no help.

At the end of the first period, we were down 3–1. Dick Redmond had scored a pair of goals for the Seals and Gary Croteau another. Fred Stanfield got our only goal.

I remember walking into the dressing room after that first period and noticing that all the guys were hanging their heads. I could see they were expecting a little heat, some rough words from me. I never was one to say much, but the way that had looked up on the ice had been incredible. And they knew it.

But I didn't give it to them. They'd looked so bad I couldn't think of anything to say. I just shrugged my shoulders and spread my hands, saying "What can you do?"

What I didn't know was that it would get worse. The first half of the second period was unbelievable. The Seals scored three more goals, going through our defense like it was paper. Our forwards weren't checking and Johnston couldn't stop anything. We were down 6–1.

I couldn't believe what I was seeing. And Vadnais? We'd just got him—this was his first game with us—and he was on the ice for five of California's six goals. Could we have made a mistake?

We got a couple of goals to end the second period and now we were behind 6–3, worse off than we'd been at the end of the first period. But we'd showed a little life.

I was still fuming when we went down to the dressing room. And the guys were still hanging their heads. But I resolved not to say a word. I could see that they were expecting a blast, but I wasn't going to give it to them.

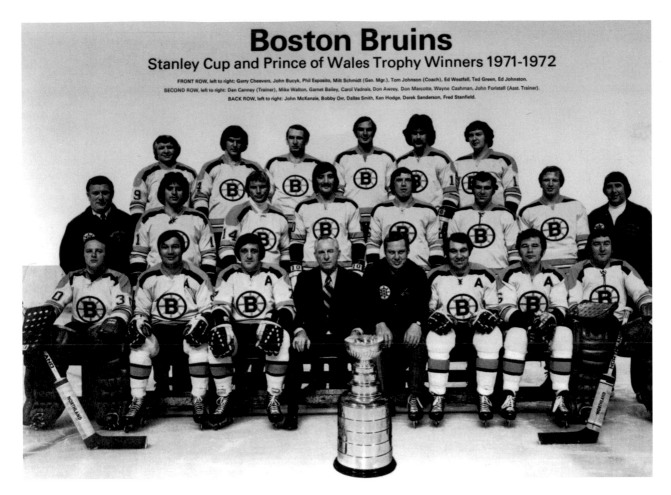

Boston Bruins
Stanley Cup and Prince of Wales Trophy Winners 1971-1972

FRONT ROW, left to right: Gerry Cheevers, John Bucyk, Phil Esposito, Milt Schmidt (Gen. Mgr.), Tom Johnson (Coach), Ed Westfall, Ted Green, Ed Johnston.
SECOND ROW, left to right: Dan Canney (Trainer), Mike Walton, Garnet Bailey, Carol Vadnais, Don Awrey, Don Marcotte, Wayne Cashman, John Forristall (Asst. Trainer).
BACK ROW, left to right: John McKenzie, Bobby Orr, Dallas Smith, Ken Hodge, Derek Sanderson, Fred Stanfield.

The Seals scored three more goals, going through our defense like it was paper. Our forwards weren't checking and Johnston couldn't stop anything.

A goal or two down and I might have spoken up. But 6–3!

Somehow, when they got back on the ice for the final period, they were all charged up. Gilles Meloche, who was in goal for California, soon found that out. First, Orr scored a goal on a shot from the point. That started it. Before it was all over, Phil Esposito had a pair of goals— I think one of them was his 54th of the season—and Stanfield got a hat trick.

We scored five goals that final period and won the game 8–6. We won a game we'd been losing 6–1. There were 14 goals in that game but not one of them was on a power play. Fact is, there were hardly any penalties. It was just one of those nights when everybody was skating up and down with nobody checking.

As I said, usually when I'm behind the bench coaching, I show no emotion, win or lose. If you took a photograph of me at the end of a game, there'd be no clue to what

had happened. This was different, though. This game showed me what we were capable of doing. We had a team with a lot of power. Esposito scored 66 goals that year. Orr, despite his bad knees, had a fine season. We had Johnny Bucyk, Wayne Cashman and a lot of other good players. We could score, you knew that. But winning that one showed me that we could pick ourselves up off the ice and come back, something that's tough to do, especially on the road, and almost incredible when you're down 6–1.

Vadnais got that bad game out of his system and was an All-Star for us the rest of the season and through the playoffs.

We went on to win the Stanley Cup and the final game will always be memorable for me. But the game I'll never forget is the one at Oakland.

—As told to George Vass

Tom Johnson, seated fifth from the left in the front row in the photo above, coached Boston to a 1972 Stanley Cup victory. Johnson began a decades-long association with the Bruins in the summer of 1963, after 14 seasons with Montreal. The 1959 Norris Trophy winner, Johnson helped Montreal win six Stanley Cups. A 1965 leg injury ended his playing career in Boston and he retired as team vice-president in 1999.

When you've played on eight Stanley Cup winners and been in the playoffs 19 of 20 years as an active player, there are bound

FEBRUARY 10, 1960
MAPLE LEAF GARDENS, TORONTO
MONTREAL 4, TORONTO 2

FIRST PERIOD
No scoring.
Penalties: TOR Ehman (holding) 5:45; MON Talbot (hooking) 11:15.

SECOND PERIOD
1. MON M. Richard (H. Richard) 2:32.
2. MON Backstrom (McDonald, Geoffrion) 4:15.
3. TOR Harris (Baun, Duff) 17:36.
4. MON M. Richard (H. Richard, Harvey) 19:59 (PP).
Penalties: MON Langlois (kneeing) 15:00; TOR Horton (tripping) 18:39.

THIRD PERIOD
5. TOR Harris (Wilson, Stanley) 14:28.
6. MON Provost (Marshall) 19:50 (EN).
Penalty: TOR Brewer (tripping) 12:07.

SHOTS ON GOAL:

MON	11	12	17	**40**
TOR	13	13	12	**38**

Goalies: MON Plante; TOR Bower
Referee: Vern Buffey
Linesmen: Bruce Simms, Loring Doolittle

to be a few highlights. It's hard to sort them out, but the first thing that comes to mind isn't a Stanley Cup game or one that was decisive in any way at the time. I don't even remember much about the game other than we lost it to the Montreal Canadiens. But I know for sure it's the game I'll never forget because of the things leading up to it and because it was the first one I ever played for the Toronto Maple Leafs.

It's all old stuff, of course, and I don't really like to talk about it too much, but it was a big story at the time so I guess there's no harm in going over it again. I came from Toronto and played my junior hockey at St. Michael's College. When I was ready to turn pro, the scouts took a good look at me. The Leafs didn't want me because their scout said I wasn't good enough to last 20 games in the National Hockey League. Detroit didn't see it that way, so the Red Wings signed me and I played 12½ years for them as a defenseman, starting in 1947 when I was 17 years of age.

We won eight league championships and four Stanley Cups in that time. We had some great teams. But in early 1960, the Wings weren't doing well. They'd finished last the previous season and now were fighting Toronto for second place behind Montreal. Jack Adams, who ran the Detroit club at the time, figured he had to make some changes. He and I had had a hard time agreeing on a contract before the 1959–60 season started and maybe that had something to do with Adams' decision to trade me a few months later.

Anyway, about February 1, 1960, Adams made a trade with the New York Rangers. The Red Wings sent Billy McNeill and me to the Rangers for Bill Gadsby and Eddie Shack. When I heard about the trade, it didn't take me long to make up my mind about what I was going to do. I decided to retire rather than go to New York. So did McNeill. So the deal was snagged. All kinds of pressure was brought on me to change my mind. But I wouldn't budge. So Adams had to call off the

deal. But he wouldn't take McNeill and me back. He suspended us both. The National Hockey League then stepped into the picture. President Clarence Campbell sent me a form advising me I had five days in which to report back to Detroit or go on the retirement list. If I went on the retirement list, I couldn't become active again if even one NHL club objected.

The whole thing had started on a Friday and on Sunday I was home wondering what was coming up next when I got a phone call from King Clancy, the Leafs' assistant coach, who was in Boston with the team. Clancy asked me what my plans were and I told him I was going to quit hockey and spend my time with the bowling alley and tobacco farm I owned. Clancy said, "Hey, don't do that. Punch wants you on his hockey club."

I was a little hesitant but Clancy kept talking, insisting that Punch Imlach, who coached the Leafs, was ready to make a deal for me with Detroit. I told him I'd think about it. He said to come to Toronto Tuesday and he and Punch and I could discuss it some more.

Tuesday, I packed up a small bag and flew to Toronto to meet Punch and Clancy at the airport. I only brought a small bag so it wouldn't look as if I'd made up my mind but I had it packed really tight with everything I needed to stay. We talked over my contract at dinner and I agreed to go with the Leafs. Imlach worked out a deal with the Wings, sending them a defenseman, Marc Reaume. There were a few other details to straighten out and even the NHL Board of Governors had to approve the transaction. I had to call up Adams in Detroit and tell him I was reporting back to the Wings so he could reinstate me and trade me to the Leafs.

The next night, Wednesday, February 10, 1960, I was to play my first game with the Leafs against the Canadiens in Toronto. At the team meeting that day, Tommy Naylor, the equipment man, gave me uniform No. 4. When I skated out on the ice that night before a full house at Maple Leaf Gardens, I felt like I was playing in my first NHL game all over again. I was finally where I'd always wanted to be. When the people stood up and clapped and cheered me I felt so tight I nearly burst. I'd never had anything happen like that before.

Before the game, Imlach told me he wanted me at center ice. I'd played defense for almost 13 seasons with Detroit but had seen a little service at left wing. Imlach wanted me up against Jean Beliveau, the great Canadiens center. I was up against Beliveau on the first face-off and I got the draw straight into the Canadiens' end. Jacques Plante was in goal for them and he came out to get the puck. I went right down

there like a shot and somehow got tangled up and went head over heels into the net.

I felt like a rookie that night and played center, left wing and defense. Imlach had me all over the ice. We lost that game 4–2, but it was the start of some great years in Toronto. We won four Stanley Cups in the seven and a half seasons I was there, so you can see why that game is so important to me; why it was such a big thing. There are other games I could recall, but that one I'll never forget.

—*As told to George Vass*

Red Kelly, shown in close against Montreal netminder Jacques Plante, above, concluded the second chapter of his remarkable playing career with the Toronto Maple Leafs. An eight-time All-Star Team defenseman with Detroit in the 1950s, Kelly helped the Wings to four Stanley Cup victories. Converted to a centerman in 1960 with the Leafs, Kelly won four more Cup rings with Toronto before beginning a successful coaching career in 1967–68.

DAVE KEON

**GAME 6, 1967
STANLEY CUP FINALS**

I was never good at talking about myself. I always figured that if you played the game, worked hard, did your job, that

**MAY 2, 1967
MAPLE LEAF GARDENS, TORONTO
TORONTO 3, MONTREAL 1**

FIRST PERIOD
No scoring.
Penalties: TOR Conacher (interference) 2:30; MON Backstrom (holding) 5:16; MON Beliveau (cross-checking) 10:21; TOR Conacher (interference) 13:25; MON Ferguson (elbowing) 18:50.

SECOND PERIOD
1. TOR Ellis (Kelly, Stanley) 6:25.
2. TOR Pappin (Stemkowski, Pulford) 19:24.
Penalties: MON Harper (holding) 3:05; TOR Stemkowski (cross-checking) 7:14; TOR Stanley (hooking) 13:23.

THIRD PERIOD
3. MON Duff (Harris) 5:28.
4. TOR Armstrong (Pulford, Kelly) 19:13 (EN).
Penalty: TOR Pappin (slashing) 11:46.

SHOTS ON GOAL:

TOR	11	16	9	**36**
MON	17	14	10	**41**

Goalies: TOR Sawchuk; MON Worsley
Referee: John Ashley
Linesmen: Matt Pavelich, B. Castleman

spoke for itself. Hockey is a team game. You have 18 guys and if they play together, you're going to have some success.

I was fortunate enough to be a player a long time, more than 20 seasons, the first 15 with the Toronto Maple Leafs, then seven more until I finished up with the Hartford Whalers. When you look back over a period of time like that, you almost wonder that you lasted that long. But I always thought that as long as you could help a team, you could play, and I guess other people thought so too.

Perhaps I never put as much emphasis on goal-scoring as some people did, though I scored close to 500. If you play the game the way you're supposed to—skate, check and do your job defensively—the opportunities will present themselves and the goals will come.

We had some goal scorers in the 1960s when we won four Stanley Cups at Toronto, but mostly we were a hard-working, checking team, with a lot of veteran players who knew how to play the game.

In my first eight or nine years in the NHL, I figured the only centers in the league were Norm Ullman, Alex Delvecchio, Stan Mikita, Jean Beliveau and Henri Richard. When they were on the ice, I was on the ice. It seemed to me they were the only guys I played against. When you're up against players of that caliber, you are out on the ice primarily to check. You feel you've done your job if you can keep them from scoring, not if you've scored yourself. All the same, in those years I'd get my share of goals, better than 20 a season. A lot of them came when somebody on the other team would make a mistake and you'd get an opportunity. A goal like that would be an accident, but then that's often the result of good forechecking.

It's difficult to remember all the high spots of a long career. That stands to reason when you've played on four teams that won the Stanley Cup. If I had to put my finger on a particular year it might be 1967 when we won the fourth Cup at Toronto. That might have

been the most gratifying, because not many people expected us to do it. The Chicago Blackhawks and Montreal Canadiens were the teams that looked to have the upper hand.

Chicago finished first in the league that year and some people thought it was their best team ever, with players like Mikita, Bobby Hull, Glenn Hall, Pierre Pilote, etc. The Canadiens, as usual, had a fine team, though I think we won as many games as they did, even if they finished second while we finished third. Not too many people gave us a chance against Chicago in the first round of the playoffs. They seemed to be at their peak and we had a mixture, but a lot of players who had been around a long time—Tim Horton, Red Kelly, George Armstrong, Allan Stanley and the two goalkeepers, Johnny Bower and Terry Sawchuk.

Well, we surprised them. I remember the fifth game in particular, the one that Bower started in goal. He looked shaky and early in the second period Imlach brought in Sawchuk. He hadn't been in the game more than a few

Imlach put the veterans on the ice....
Not a man under 30, and they did the job.

minutes when Hull let go with a slap shot that hit him in the shoulder, then glanced up and hit his mask. Sawchuk went down as if he had been knocked out.

Sawchuk just shook it off, got up and he must have made 40 saves the rest of the game as we beat Chicago, then won the sixth game to knock them out of the playoffs. That put us into the finals against Montreal, which had eliminated the New York Rangers.

I don't know if I can pick out any one game against Montreal as standing out above the others, but that was certainly as memorable a series of games as I ever played in. Well, let's say I could forget the first game. The Canadiens slaughtered us 6–2, and everybody started to write us off. But we came back in the second game to win 3–0, with Bower playing one of his best games in goal.

We won the third game, Montreal the fourth, and then we beat them in the fifth to take a 3–2 lead in the series. I got my

only goal of the finals in that game, but my job was mainly penalty killing and checking, stopping Beliveau and Henri Richard, and if I could do that, I'd done my job. That brought us to the sixth game, easily one of the most memorable games I played in, the one I'll never forget.

You couldn't ask for a better finish for the Stanley Cup. Gump Worsley started in goal for Montreal, Sawchuk for us. Nobody could get anything past them the first period. In the second period, we got a couple of goals—I think by Ron Ellis and Jim Pappin—and the Canadiens cut our lead to 2–1 in the third period. It stayed that way to the final minute of play, when the Canadiens pulled Worsley.

Imlach put the veterans on the ice: Horton, Stanley, Kelly, Armstrong and Bob Pulford in front of Sawchuk. Not a man under 30, and they did the job. On the face-off, Stanley shoved Beliveau off the puck, Kelly picked it up and passed to Armstrong, who put it into the empty net.

Dave Keon (14) breaks up the Montreal attack in front of his goaltender Terry Sawchuk. Keon, 1961 NHL rookie of the year, played a tenacious checking game yet won the Lady Byng Trophy twice. He captained the Toronto Maple Leafs from 1969 to 1975 before joining the WHA. Keon returned to the NHL for three seasons with the Hartford Whalers, retiring in 1982.

We won 3–1 and took the Cup. It was the fourth Stanley Cup winner I'd been on but in many ways it was the most satisfying, not because I'd scored so many goals [three in the playoffs] but because I'd done the job I had been asked to do. Afterward, I was given the Conn Smythe Trophy as the outstanding player in the playoffs. I thought there were other guys who might have won the Smythe instead of me; the big thing was winning the Stanley Cup and it took 18 players to do it.

—As told to George Vass

I played much of my career with the Montreal Canadiens, so when I say there are many good games to remember, you

know what I mean. Those were some good years for the Canadiens, in the 1960s and 1970s when I was with them, and there were many fine players and good teams.

What first comes to mind, when I think of one game that stands out for me personally, is the last game of the 1973 playoffs. We won the Stanley Cup in Chicago and I broke my leg near the end of the first period. That is a good reason to remember a game—you win the Cup and you break your leg at the same time!

My first full season with Montreal was 1964–65 and that was a big thrill for me, not only being with the Canadiens, but scoring 21 goals. At that time, 20 goals was a pretty good season.

I did pretty well the next two seasons, but in 1967–68 I got hurt. I didn't play regularly and did not play well. In those days, the Canadiens always had good kids coming up, so if you fell back they would trade you. So they sent me to the Minnesota North Stars in 1968, and I had two really good years there.

It was a good break for me to go to the North Stars. I got a lot more ice time than I would have with the Canadiens, and I had good linemates. I played with Danny Grant, who like me had come over from Montreal, and Danny O'Shea. We had one of the better lines in the league that year.

That first season with Minnesota [1968–69] was one of the best years I had in hockey—25 goals, I was voted to the West All-Star team—the All-Star Game was to be played in the Forum at Montreal—though I had been injured a few weeks before. I had pulled a groin muscle, missed 10 games, but was still among the top scorers in the West Division. It was a great feeling, to come back to the Forum as an All-Star the year after I'd been traded. That was the first year they had the All-Star Game between the East and West Divisions, and no one thought the West had much of a chance. But you have to remember the West had some great goalies—Glenn Hall, Jacques Plante and Bernie Parent.

Anyway, the game was tight all the way, though the East had the great scorers—Gordie Howe, Frank Mahovlich, Bobby Hull, Stan Mikita, Bobby Orr and a lot of others. Early in the third period, the East was ahead 3–2 and that held up until there were about five minutes to go. I was on the ice with my North Star linemates, Grant and O'Shea, when we got a bit of a break.

I headed for the net and O'Shea and Grant got the puck to me. I put a deflection past the goalie, Eddie Giacomin, and that tied the game 3–3. I can't remember many bigger thrills in hockey, especially because the crowd, maybe remembering I'd been a Canadien, and even though they were pulling for the East, cheered as loudly as if I'd been one of their players.

Montreal made a trade for me in the summer of 1970 and I spent the next four seasons in Montreal. We played the Chicago Blackhawks in the 1973 Stanley Cup finals and were greatly favored to defeat them for the Cup. My job in that series was to check the Hawks' left wing, Dennis Hull. At the time, he, Pit Martin and Jim Pappin were Chicago's top scoring line.

We had to go back to Chicago for the sixth game, the one that proved a turning point in my career. In the last minute or so of the first period, the score was 2–1 for us when there was a two-on-one break with Dennis Hull and Pit Martin. I was covering Dennis on the left side, and I came back. I saw Martin was going to pass to Dennis and Dennis had me beaten by a couple of strides, so I just dove to intercept the pass.

When I woke up, I heard I had gone right through the net. I had hit the back of my head on one of the metal bars and there was blood all over the place. They stitched me up, something like 20 or 22 stitches, between periods, and told me I was all right.

But when I tried to get up and put my foot on the floor, I couldn't walk. The doctor had me taken to the hospital where they put a cast on it. Lucky enough, they took me back to the Stadium before the end of the game, and I was able to go back with the team to Montreal and celebrate the winning of the Stanley Cup.

**MAY 10, 1973
CHICAGO STADIUM, CHICAGO
MONTREAL 6, CHICAGO 4**

FIRST PERIOD
1. CHI Martin (Mikita, Stapleton) 10:35.
2. CHI Martin (Pappin) 11:31 (PP).
3. MON Richard (F. Mahovlich) 19:48.
Penalties: MON Roberts (roughing) 3:40; CHI Korab (roughing) 3:40; CHI Martin (holding) 8:21; MON Roberts (hooking) 10:35; MON Wilson (elbowing) 12:29.

SECOND PERIOD
4. MON P. Mahovlich (Laperriere, Lefley) 5:05.
5. MON Houle (P. Mahovlich, Lefley) 6:37.
6. CHI Cryskow (Maki, Backstrom) 8:32.
7. MON F. Mahovlich (Lapointe, Cournoyer) 10:54 (PP).
8. CHI Martin (Hull) 17:05 (PP).
Penalties: CHI White (interference) 2:25; CHI Russell (holding) 10:20; CIII Korab (hooking) 12:26; MON Roberts (tripping) 16:58.

THIRD PERIOD
9. MON Cournoyer (Lemaire) 8:13.
10. MON Tardif (Cournoyer, Lemaire) 12:42 (PP).
Penalty: CHI Russell (hooking) 11:29.

SHOTS ON GOAL:

MON	7	15	11	**33**
CHI	9	14	4	**27**

Goalies: MON Dryden; CHI Esposito
Referee: Lloyd Gilmour
Linesmen: Matt Pavelich, John D'Amico

I had hit the back of my head on one of the metal bars and there was blood all over the place. They stitched me up, something like 20 or 22 stitches, between periods, and told me I was all right.

I had a hunch that would be the end of my career at Montreal. By the time I came back to play, it was late December and the season was pretty well shot for me. I expected it when the Canadiens traded me to St. Louis the next year. When you've broken your leg and you are around 31, they bring the kids in. That's what they always did in those days.

I had a lot more years of hockey left, mostly with the Blues, and they were good years. But I'll never forget that last game of the 1973 playoffs, and considering what happened, you can't blame me.

—*As told To George Vass*

Claude Larose was on three Stanley Cup winning teams in Montreal before the Habs traded him in the summer of 1968. After two strong seasons with the Minnesota North Stars, the Canadiens reacquired him in the summer of 1970. Larose won two more Cup rings in Montreal before being sold to St. Louis. Larose scored a career-best 29 goals in 1976–77 but retired a year later.

REGGIE LEACH

I remember when I first came into the league with Boston in 1971, I'd look up to some of the guys like Phil Esposito, Bobby

---

MAY 6, 1976
PHILADELPHIA SPECTRUM, PHILADELPHIA
PHILADELPHIA 6, BOSTON 3

FIRST PERIOD
1. PHI Leach (Barber) 5:45.
Penalties: BOS O'Reilly (tripping) 0:31; BOS Marcotte (hooking) 0:57; BOS Doak (roughing) 10:23; PHI Schultz (roughing) 10:23; PHI Dupont (cross-checking) 12:48.

SECOND PERIOD
2. BOS Sheppard (Smith, Bucyk) 0:59.
3. PHI Leach (Clarke, Barber) 2:02.
4. PHI Leach (Crisp, Kindrachuk) 8:51.
5. PHI Leach (Clarke) 17:09.
Penalties: BOS Savard (fighting) 5:42; PHI Bridgman (roughing, fighting) 5:42; PHI Clarke (hooking) 12:38.

THIRD PERIOD
6. BOS Marcotte (Hodge, Ratelle) 6:09.
7. PHI Leach (Clarke, Bladon) 8:07.
8. PHI Goodenough (Kindrachuk, Crisp) 17:13.
9. BOS Savard (Bucyk, Park) 17:57.
No penalties.

SHOTS ON GOAL:

PHI	7	9	5	**21**
BOS	7	9	12	**28**

Goalies: PHI Stephenson; BOS Gilbert
Referee: John McCauley
Linesmen: Matt Pavelich, Gerard Gauthier

Orr and Johnny Bucyk. They were great players and every day they went out and gave it their best. Now, after more than 10 years in the league, it's sort of gratifying to think I'm a little bit like those guys were then, that the younger guys on our club are looking up to me for an example. It puts a little pressure on you, but you don't mind that if you can help the club, if you feel the guys are looking to you for leadership. You're all working toward the same thing, the Stanley Cup, and it's up to those of us who have been in the finals, have won the Cup, to show the way. If we do that, the kids will follow along.

There's no doubt about what has been the biggest game of my career, the one that means the most. That came in 1975, the game that clinched the Cup for us at Philadelphia when we beat Buffalo. I was lucky. The first year I came to the Flyers we won the Cup. Some guys go through a whole career, play 15, 20 years, and never have that experience. I hope to have it again before my career ends.

The next year after we won—and that was the second Cup in a row for the guys who'd been at Philadelphia before me—I thought we'd do it again. We had a good chance, but Montreal outplayed us in the finals and it was disappointing. A lot of people mention those 1976 playoffs, in fact the whole season leading up to it, as being special in my career. And I guess it was from the standpoint of scoring goals. I did a lot of that in the season and the playoffs but it would have meant a lot more if we'd won the Cup too. It may sound strange, though, but I don't really look at the goals. I'm used to scoring them. I've been doing it all my life. What counts is what the goals accomplish, if they win something.

When I was a kid in Riverton, Manitoba, I had a shed where I lived. I'd make ice and shoot the puck maybe three, four hours a day. I made targets and some of the other kids and me would have shooting contests. I got so I could hit a certain spot almost every time. Within 15 to 20 feet of the net, you'd

have to say I'm deadly. I liked the game. I couldn't play it enough when I was 10 years old. I skated eight hours a day four winters. Even took figure skating for three years, mostly to get ice time on Wednesday and Saturday. There were a lot of days when I was at the rink after school they'd have to kick me out at midnight.

Our family was poor, with 12 children, and my dad died when I was 12 years old. I never even had my own skates until I was 15. My mom didn't have the money, what with work so scarce and 12 kids in the family. But I got by and I got good at the game. I was playing with the older kids when I was 12 and 13, but I never thought I'd be a pro until I got to Flin Flon as a junior and played with Bobby Clarke. He'd give the puck to me and I'd score. He made the big difference. He helped me build up my confidence.

It's worked like that for us with Philadelphia, once Bobby and I got together again. It figures that if you get the shots you have a better chance of getting the goals. With Clarkie, my job is pretty simple: just find a spot because I know Clarkie will get the puck to me. When you're scoring, it's like hitting a baseball. You get in a groove and you can't miss. When you're not hitting, it seems like everything you do is wrong. You go through stretches both ways.

I scored a lot of goals in the juniors, but with Boston I didn't play all that much. After the Bruins traded me to Oakland in February 1972, it was hard to get motivated. The owner, Charlie Finley, didn't care about the club, so the players didn't care. We were out of the playoffs by November. Then came the trade to Philadelphia on May 24, 1974. That turned things around for me, first being back with Clarkie, and then being with a club that cared, that was good, that could win and did.

As I said earlier, we won the Cup the first year I was with the Flyers, and you can't top the game that clinched it for being the most memorable. But the next season, the one in which I scored 61 goals and got a record 19 more in the playoffs, had its highlights too. Naturally, the most memorable game would have to be the playoff game in which I scored five goals against Boston. If you talk

I don't remember all
the details, except that
I took seven shots in the
game and five went in.
We won, 6–3, and were
in the finals.

about games you'll never forget, that's one. Never did I have anything to match that night. Everything I touched went in.

We were in the semifinals against Boston and after they won the first game, we won the next three. All we needed was one more win and we were in the finals. We had the home ice and the crowd in the Spectrum behind us and that always helps. I think it must have been about five minutes into the first period when I got the first goal, a backhander that got past goalie Gilles Gilbert's right pad. That pave us a 1–0 lead that stood up until Boston got a goal early in the second period.

I got the next three goals, all in the second period. I can't remember all the details, but I think Clarkie fed me on the first two. I think

on the first one Bobby was on the left boards and I was alone on the right side. I put it through Gilbert's pads. The third one was sort of weird. I was on the left side again and a Boston player was checking me to the outside. I just figured I'd throw a shot at the net and, as it happened, Gilbert went down and the puck hit the upper part of the net. Like I said, I don't remember all the details, except that I took seven shots in the game and five went in. We won, 6–3, and were in the finals.

Montreal was too much for us and they won the Cup but I got the Conn Smythe Trophy for being the outstanding player in the playoffs. It was an honor to receive it, but I would have preferred to win the Cup.

—*As told to George Vass*

Reggie Leach was drafted by the Boston Bruins with the third pick in the 1970 draft, but got little ice time on the talent-laden squad. Traded to California in February 1972, he didn't really blossom until joining Philadelphia in 1974–75. After notching 45 goals in his first season with the Flyers, "The Riverton Rifle" scored a league-leading 61 times in 1975–76. He played his final NHL season with Detroit in 1982–83.

GAME 1, 1968
STANLEY CUP FINALS

You have to be ready for anything every second that you are on the ice. Sounds simple enough, right? Sounds like

MAY 5, 1968
ST. LOUIS ARENA, ST. LOUIS
MONTREAL 3, ST. LOUIS 2 (OT)

FIRST PERIOD
1. STL Bob Plager (unassisted) 9:19.
2. MON Richard (Larose) 9:42.
Penalties: STL Picard (interference) 6:38; MON Vadnais (high-sticking) 12:07; STL Moore (high-sticking) 12:07; MON Provost (cross-checking) 14:03.

SECOND PERIOD
3. STL Moore (Bob Plager, Berenson) 8:16 (PP).
4. MON Cournoyer (Harris, Ferguson) 18:14.
Penalties: MON Harris (holding) 7:21; STL Moore (holding) 19:59.

THIRD PERIOD
No scoring.
Penalties: MON Ferguson (high-sticking) 2:23; STL Bob Plager (high-sticking) 2:23; STL Barday Plager (interference) 6:49.

FIRST OVERTIME PERIOD
5. MON Lemaire (unassisted) 1:41.
No penalties.

SHOTS ON GOAL:
MON	13	13	11	1	**38**
STL	6	18	11	1	**36**

Goalies: MON Worsley; STL Hall
Referee: Vern Buffey
Linesmen: Neil Armstrong, Pat Shelter

common sense. Sounds like the kind of advice a father might give his son before the boy's first game: "OK, Johnny, keep your head up at all times." But you would be surprised how many times a highly paid, highly skilled player in the world's top league won't be concentrating on the puck and ends up costing his team a game.

I had heard those words of wisdom so often growing up in Quebec—practicing in the driveway of my parent's house by shooting pucks at their garage door—that they seemed to echo in my head. I had a lot of learning to do during my rookie season with the Montreal Canadiens, but keeping focused at every minute of the game was one thing I had down pat. In fact, that little trait, that attention to detail, helped me help the Canadiens win the Stanley Cup that season.

The 1968 Stanley Cup finals were billed as a matchup between the Old Canadiens and the New Canadiens. The Old Canadiens—officially known as the St. Louis Blues—emerged from the Western Division. The Blues finished with a sub-.500 record in the regular season, but on the shoulders of one of the greatest goalies ever, Glenn Hall, the Blues battled their way into the finals.

The expansion Blues were a concoction of young, raw talent and stars who had passed their prime years. Many of those veterans had direct ties to the Canadiens. Dickie Moore had been a perennial All-Star with the Canadiens for 12 seasons, helping the Habs win five consecutive Stanley Cups in the 1950s. The Blues picked him up late in the year and gave him a chance. His teammate for many years was Doug Harvey, a do-everything defenseman who, at age 45, was still a valuable player. Red Berenson, a speedy center, never scored more than seven goals in the parts of five seasons he played in Montreal, but he found a home in St. Louis, scoring 24 goals that year. Similarly, Jim Roberts, a hard-charging winger who scored a total of 11 goals in four years with the

Canadiens, potted 14 goals in his first year in St. Louis. Noel Picard and Jean-Guy Talbot also had spent some time wearing the *bleu, blanc et rouge*. Even the Blues coach, Scotty Bowman, had coached me, Serge Savard and many other Canadiens youngsters in the minors before he took the job in St. Louis.

The real Canadiens were overwhelming favorites. We finished third in the league with 236 goals. Gump Worsley and Rogie Vachon shared the Vezina Trophy, allowing just 167 goals. Jean Beliveau was the runner-up for the Hart Trophy, J.C. Tremblay was the runner-up for the Norris Trophy and Claude Provost became the first recipient of the Masterton Trophy—awarded for dedication and perseverance. Henri Richard, Yvon Cournoyer and Jacques Laperriere also enjoyed great seasons.

I was the runner-up for the Calder Trophy that year. I finished with 22 goals and 20 assists that season, although I barely played before Christmas. Around that time, Richard went down with an injury and coach Toe Blake threw me into the line-up. Centering a line with Dick Duff on one wing and Bobby Rousseau on the other, I fulfilled a lifelong dream by becoming a part of the Canadiens.

After eliminating Bobby Orr and the Boston Bruins in four games and Bobby Hull and the Chicago Blackhawks in five games, we traveled to St. Louis for the first game of the finals—the game I'll never forget.

Anyone who thought this was going to be a breeze for us learned otherwise almost immediately. The Blues were a tenacious bunch, hunkering down in the corners, clearing the front of the net and tying up anybody wearing a Canadiens jersey. Finding scoring chances was like trying to find a French-language newspaper in Albuquerque.

The Blues turned that defense into offense, getting on the board 10 minutes into the game. Rugged defenseman Bob Plager's slapper had given the Blues a lift, bringing the crowd to its feet. When Henri Richard scored 23 seconds later to tie the game, many people figured the Habs were on their way—but those Blues came back again. This time, Moore scored in the ninth minute of the second period, bringing the fans back into the

The Blues were a tenacious bunch, hunkering down in the corners, clearing the front of the net and tying up anybody wearing a Canadiens jersey.

game. But late in the period, Cournoyer beat Hall to knot the score.

After a scoreless third period, both teams went back into the locker room knowing full well that the next goal would win the game and could set the tempo for the entire series. If the Blues scored, they had confidence, momentum and Game 2 at home. They had nothing to lose, no pressure, no expectations. They could be a dangerous team. If we won, we could start exerting our edge in talent, rob them of their spirit and make it a short, painless series.

When we returned to the ice to start the overtime period, coach Toe Blake tapped me on the shoulder to tell me I was on the ice next. The voice of every coach I've ever had must have been in the back of mind somewhere—"Be ready...pay attention"— because I was alert enough to follow the play from the bench and to jump right into the

flow the second my skates hit the ice.

In an instant, I was on the ice and was coming down on the Blues. I took a pass at their blue line, let the shot go, and all of a sudden the net behind Hall bulged. The red light went on and my teammates huddled all around me patting me on the head. The goal had stopped the clock 1:41 into overtime, sending the St. Louis faithful home, vowing the Blues would be back.

Although they didn't roll over and die, they didn't win another game. Blake retired after capturing his 13th Stanley Cup as a player or coach, enjoying one last championship parade. And I thought back to every coach who ever whispered the words "be ready." I say to them: "Thanks for the words of wisdom."

—*As told to Chuck O'Donnell*

Jacques Lemaire played his entire 12-season NHL career for the Montreal Canadiens. The winner of eight Stanley Cup rings, he had his best offensive season in 1972–73, when he scored 44 goals and 51 assists. Lemaire retired after the 1978–79 campaign to begin a successful coaching career. He returned to Montreal in 1983 to coach the team. He was behind New Jersey's bench for the Devils' 1995 Cup win. Lemaire was named the Minnesota Wild's first coach in June 200.

The first game that comes to mind is the one we played the night some crank threatened to shoot Gordie Howe and me.

MARCH 24, 1956
MAPLE LEAF GARDENS, TORONTO
DETROIT 5, TORONTO 4 (OT)

FIRST PERIOD
1. TOR Armstrong (Duff, Hurst) 0:29.
2. DET Kelly (Ullman) 12:27.
3. TOR Cullen (Reaume, Armstrong) 16:33 (PP).
Penalties: TOR James (tripping) 4:32; DET Pronovost (tripping) 5:40; DET Ferguson (tripping) 8:54; TOR Migay (tripping) 13:28; DET Lindsay (slashing) 15:08.

SECOND PERIOD
4. TOR James (unassisted) 13:20 (SH).
Penalties: DET Pavelich (high-sticking) 0:05; TOR Harris (tripping) 4:30; TOR Harris (tripping) 10:26; TOR Migay (hooking) 12:46; TOR Hennigan (holding) 18:59.

THIRD PERIOD
5. DET Prystai (unassisted) 2:46.
6. TOR Armstrong (Duff, Bolton) 7:40.
7. DET Howe (Kelly, Hillman) 9:11.
8. DET Lindsay (Reibel, Goldham) 14:25.
Penalty: DET Lindsay (high-sticking) 5:58.

FIRST OVERTIME PERIOD
9. DET Lindsay (Goldham, Howe) 4:22.
No penalties.

Goalies: DET Hall; TOR Lumley
Referee: Red Storey
Linesman: George Hayes, Sam Babcock

There were a lot of highlights in my career playing for the Detroit Red Wings in the 1950s, when we had the great team that finished first year after year and won the Stanley Cup four times.

One Cup game I remember in 1955, I was fortunate enough to score four goals against the Montreal Canadiens. Another game, the year before, I was lucky enough to score a goal in the second overtime to beat the Toronto Maple Leafs to win the first round of the playoffs. But it was that other game, the one in Toronto in 1956, that is the first one I think about whenever anyone asks me about high spots.

We opened the first round of the Stanley Cup series against the Leafs that year in Detroit. We won the first game and also beat the Leafs the second game, which got a little rough before it was over. First, Tod Sloan of the Leafs and I got into it, which wasn't unusual. Later in the game, Gordie and Sloan slid into the boards together. They had to carry Sloan off the ice. He had suffered a broken shoulder and the playoffs were over for him.

Naturally, the Leafs' fans were a little upset with the way things were going, their team losing the first two games to us in Detroit and Sloan hurt. After a day off, the series moved to Toronto for the third game in the Gardens. The day of the third game, a man who refused to give his name telephoned the Toronto newspapers. He threatened, "Don't worry about Howe and Lindsay tonight. I'm going to shoot them if they play in the game." He said it over and over again.

We didn't know anything about the threat at first. We were staying at a hotel in Hamilton and we weren't told about what the man had said until we arrived at the Gardens. Everybody else knew about it because it was big news. One Toronto newspaper had a headline: "Will Shoot Howe, Lindsay To Avenge Sloan, Is Threat."

In that day and age, assassins weren't as common as they seem to be today. Threats were uncommon and even when made were never carried out. It just didn't happen that way 20 years ago. Nevertheless, nobody wanted to take any chances, so extra police were sent out to patrol the Gardens. They made sure nobody was coming in with suspicious looking packages which might contain a rifle. Of course, we heard about the threats within minutes of arriving at the Gardens. We figured it was just a crank call and didn't take it seriously. We had to think about it, though. In fact, that's all we talked about while we suited up for the warm-ups. All the guys were sitting around and kidding Gordie and me.

"Don't skate close to me—the guy's liable to be a bad shot," one player said. Another player—I think it was Bob Goldham—suggested we use a rookie, Cummy Barton, as a decoy. He was just kidding, but his idea was that we have Gordie's No. 9 sewn on the back and my No. 7 sewn on the front of Barton's sweater. Barton was then supposed to skate up and down the ice to see what would happen. Everybody else was in favor of the idea except Barton, who wouldn't agree to it.

There was a lot of kidding around, but there was a serious side to the incident. Gordie was worried his mother, who was ailing, might hear about it back home in Saskatoon. He phoned and told her there was nothing to worry about. I guess I was more angry than worried. I thought it was the stupidest thing I'd ever heard of and wasn't worth making such a fuss about. But on reflection, considering what's happened in the world since, I guess you can't take things like that lightly even if the odds are that it was just a crank.

I have to admit, we might have been a little nervous during the warm-up and when the game first started. Later, Gordie said, "We were lucky nobody threw a firecracker or Ted and I would have dug a hole in the ice."

The game was a real battle, like all playoff games should be. Gordie showed the threat hadn't affected his play by scoring a goal early and we stayed with the Leafs through

He threatened, "Don't worry about Howe and Lindsay tonight. I'm going to shoot them if they play in the game."

Ted Lindsay, jumping up to screen the Montreal goalie, above, helped Detroit win four Stanley Cups. An almost perennial All-Star, Lindsay won the 1950 scoring title and finished runner-up to his linemate Gordie Howe three times. Lindsay's efforts to form a Players' Association earned him a ticket to Chicago in July 1957 and he quit after three seasons with the Hawks. "Terrible Ted" came out of retirement to rejoin the Wings for the 1964–65 campaign and later served the team as coach and general manager.

the first two periods. But they had a 4–3 lead early in the third period. I can't remember now how I scored the tying goal. All I know is I got it late in the third period off Harry Lumley, who was in goal for the Leafs and had played in earlier years with us at Detroit.

That goal sent the game into overtime and I got lucky again. I think at just about four minutes of overtime play I got the winning goal.

Going off the ice afterward—we all have a lot of ham in us—I decided to put my stick with the blade up under my arm as if to pretend it was a rifle. I skated around, pretending the hockey stick was a rifle, and kept chattering, "rat-ta-ta-tat."

That victory gave us three in a row in the series and we went on to win it four games of five. But then we lost in the finals to Montreal. Maybe there were other games that I could think of that meant more to me but that one, because of the death threat, is the one I can be sure I'll never forget.

—*As told to George Vass*

To be honest with you, I don't remember very much about the actual game. My memories of the Montreal Canadiens

MAY 24, 1986
CALGARY SADDLEDOME, CALGARY
MONTREAL 4, CALGARY 3

FIRST PERIOD
1. MON Gingras (Lemieux, Naslund) 6:53 (PP).
Penalties: CAL Fotiu (roughing) 2:45; CAL McDonald (hooking) 5:53; MON Skrudland (high-sticking, misconduct) 15:21; CAL Risebrough (misconduct) 15:21; CAL Fotiu (slashing) 18:26.

SECOND PERIOD
2. CAL Bozek (Hunter, Peplinski) 7:17.
3. MON Skrudland (McPhee, Lemieux) 10:49.
Penalties: MON Lalor (roughing) 1:28; MON Chelios (slashing) 3:26; CAL Fotiu (high-sticking) 14:40.

THIRD PERIOD
4. MON Green (Maley, Lalor) 10:11.
5. MON Smith (Naslund) 10:30.
6. CAL Bozek (Macoun) 16:46.
7. CAL Mullen (Quinn, MacInnis) 19:14.
Penalties: MON Ludwig (roughing) 6:31; CAL Fotiu (roughing) 6:31; MON Lemieux (interference) 13:01; CAL Hunter (high-sticking) 13:01.

SHOTS ON GOAL:

MON	12	10	11	**33**
CAL	7	12	14	**33**

Goalies: MON Roy; CAL Vernon
Referee: Don Koharski
Linesmen: Ron Finn, Ray Scapinello

defeating the Calgary Flames in the fifth game of the 1986 Finals to win the Stanley Cup are almost entirely of what happened before and after the game.

I was in my fourth season as an American in Montreal, this kid from Wisconsin loving every moment of life as a Canadien. My teammates were some of the best players and guys in the game: Rick Green, Ryan Walter, Larry Robinson, Guy Carbonneau, Chris Chelios and budding star Stephane Richer, to name a few. In those four short years, I grew a lot as a player in this fine organization. All I wanted at that point was a Stanley Cup.

One of the best things about being a Montreal Canadien is that, no matter how high or low the quality of your personnel may be, you always feel like you're a Cup contender. For the 1985–86 season, we knew we didn't have a line-up of superstars. But we had something better: A terrific chemistry of young talent and veterans who knew what it took to win.

When we defeated Ted Sator's Rangers in the conference finals in five games in May of '86, we knew this would be our chance. Our ability to win big games on the road helped us through the entire season and carried into the playoffs. When we took two in a row at the Montreal Forum to take a 3–1 lead over the Flames in the finals, we knew we had them just where we wanted them. But our captain, Bob Gainey, wanted to make sure we took advantage of the situation right away. After our practice the day before Game 5 we were all goofing around, trying to stay loose, soaking up the finals atmosphere. Then "Bo" spoke, and we all fell to a hush.

"OK guys, I want to say something," Gainey said. That's all we needed to hear, because Bo had so much respect in our dressing room. When he had something to say, we knew it was worthwhile. What followed was the greatest speech I ever have heard in my life. He spoke about how some players never get the opportunity to be in the position we were that day, and that we better

not wait until we returned to the Forum to try and bring the Cup back to Montreal.

It wasn't a condescending speech; it wasn't a phony one. As I'm sure Bo's trying to do now as coach of the Minnesota North Stars—the guy was born to lead—he explained everybody's role and told us to focus on the job at hand. After Bo spoke, I remember telling Chris Nilan, who was sitting next to me, "Geez, I wish Bo would have saved that for tomorrow. I'm dying to go out there and kick some tail right now." I still get chills thinking about what Bo said.

As I said, I don't remember too much about what occurred between 7:30 and 10:30 p.m. on May 24, 1986. As always, "Chelly" [Chelios] was my partner, and we logged at least 20 minutes of ice time. Our plan was to shut down Joey Mullen and Al MacInnis, especially on the power play where they had this deflection thing going.

We played Canadiens hockey, or what it was at the time. It meant playing as tight a defensive game as possible and capitalizing on offense when the opponent made mistakes. The Habs played it to perfection, and we took the game 4–3. Bobby Smith scored the winning goal with just under 10 minutes left in the third period. We had some tense moments in the last minute, when we had the one-goal lead and the Flames were really pressing, but Rick Green cleared the puck out of Patrick Roy's crease with five seconds left to end the game.

I was on the bench yelling on the outside, but my stomach was churning on the inside. In addition to what Bo said, I really wanted to win the Cup that night because it was the first birthday of my twin boys, Trevor and Taylor. I envisioned grabbing the Cup and going on television and saying "Happy birthday, guys," although, of course, they wouldn't understand a word I was saying. I felt it would be a cool thing to have on tape for the future.

Well, us winning and the kind folks at ESPN made it all possible. They put me in front of the camera and started asking me all these technical questions about the game. I answered as politely as possible, and then when I got the chance I yelled "Happy birthday" to my boys back in Eagle River,

Wisconsin. After my television stint, I grabbed a beer and sat in the trainer's room all by myself for a few minutes. I just wanted to take some time and reflect on how lucky I was. Not only was I playing for one of the greatest organizations in the history of sports, but now I would have my name engraved on the Stanley Cup as a member of that team. To think that I would be there with Bo, Larry Robinson, Mats Naslund and the rest of the guys was overwhelming.

When we arrived in Montreal the morning after the victory, there was this incredible burst of heat when we stepped off the plane that I'll never forget. We expected a crowd, but there were so many people there you could actually feel the warmth as you stepped off the plane. They say there are two million people in the city of Montreal, and 1.5 million were at our parade the next day.

Maybe the topper was that now I had a championship ring to give to my dad. This man taught me so much about all of the sports and put up with a lot of stuff, like driving me to practices and coaching my games. I felt the best way to say "Thank you" would be by giving him a symbol of having made it to the big time. My dad's never taken the ring off since I gave it to him. You have to see him. Back home, he's always cutting wood or chopping chickens, and he's still wearing It. I can only imagine what kind of shape it's in.

—*As told to Chris Botta*

After eight seasons in Montreal, the Canadiens traded **Craig Ludwig** to the New York Islanders. Ludwig, the quintessential big defensive defenseman, spent one season on Long Island before being dealt to Minnesota. The North Stars moved south in 1993 and it was as a Dallas Star that Ludwig picked up his second Stanley Cup ring. Shortly after his team won the 1999 Cup, Ludwig announced his retirement.

GRETZKY'S GOODBYE

The match itself paled in comparison to the postgame festivities. While Wayne Gretzky celebrated the notching of his final assist in his incomparable career, the retirement of "The Great One" made this a game to remember. Owner of 61 NHL records, including every scoring record of note, Gretzky's final helper brought his assist total to 1,963 and his overall points to 2,857. Pittsburgh's Jaromir Jagr scored in overtime, but all eyes immediately turned to Gretzky.

The standing ovation ebbed and flowed for almost 45 minutes of an emotional farewell. While his teammates followed at a respectful distance, Gretzky skated several laps of the rink, moving from laughter to tears and back several times. Among the numerous gifts Gretzky received came a pronouncement from NHL Commissioner Gary Bettman: Gretzky's No. 99 is henceforth officially retired from league play.

—*Chris McDonell*

APRIL 18, 1999
MADISON SQUARE GARDEN, NEW YORK
PITTSBURGH 2, NEW YORK RANGERS 1 (OT)

FRANK MAHOVLICH

MARCH 21, 1973

When you've been on six Stanley Cup winning teams, four at Toronto and two at Montreal, the big games, those that are

MARCH 21, 1973
MONTREAL FORUM, MONTREAL
MONTREAL 3, VANCOUVER 2

FIRST PERIOD
1. VAN Boudrias (Lemieux, Lalonde) 1:07 (PP).
2. MON Tardif (Lafleur) 3:51.
Penalties: MON Robinson (hooking) 0:48; VAN O'Flaherty (hooking) 11:44; MON Tardif (hooking) 17:55.

SECOND PERIOD
3. MON M. Wilson (Richard, Roberts) 3:07.
4. VAN Wright (Kurtenbach) 5:42.
Penalty: VAN Guevremont (tripping) 9:47.

THIRD PERIOD
5. MON F. Mahovlich (Richard, Lapointe) 1:27.
Penalty: VAN Tallon (cross-checking) 8:57.

SHOTS ON GOAL:

MON	12	8	5	**25**
VAN	15	12	14	**41**

Goalies: MON Dryden; VAN D. Wilson
Referee: Bob Myers
Linesmen: Gerard Gauthier, J. Christison

memorable, pile up on you. It's pretty hard to rate one above the other, though there can be no doubt that nothing quite matches a final game, the one in which you win the Stanley Cup.

Sometimes a game stands out in your memory not so much because it was great but because it was out of the ordinary. There was a game like that in the Stanley Cup finals in 1973 when I was with the Canadiens, playing the Chicago Blackhawks. Ken Dryden was in goal for Montreal and Tony Esposito for Chicago, two of the best ever. Each team had good defensemen and forwards who played both ways. Yet, the final score was 8–7, Chicago winning. How do you explain so much scoring, the most ever in a playoff game, with the defensive ability that was on the ice? I guess once a game starts out wide open it is difficult to change it. And in playoff hockey, when you're down by one goal, you can't play for a tie as you do in the regular season. You have to press and gamble. When you're down by two, there's even less reason to be cautious. Thus, a crazy score is more logical in playoff hockey than during the season when a tie game can earn you a point.

So that's one game to remember, one out of many in 17 years in the National Hockey League. Another, of course, was the game in which I scored the 500th goal of my career. It was an individual achievement, of course, not providing quite the feeling you get with a team accomplishment. Still, it is in some ways the game I'll never forget. At the time, only four players had scored 500 career goals in the NHL. To be ranked with them was quite an honor, when you realize they were Gordie Howe, Bobby Hull, Rocket Richard and Jean Beliveau.

I'd scored my 499th goal four days earlier, and I don't know that there was any real pressure on me in the game against Vancouver at the Montreal Forum. Sure, you like to get a milestone goal like that before your own fans, but you know that it's

something that will come sooner or later. Play your regular game and the goals will come for you. But sometimes they do come in unusual ways, when you least expect them. And at times when you think you're going to get a goal for sure, you miss and there's no real explanation. That night, both things happened to me, which is another reason to think about that game.

I think I got three shots on goal in the first period against Vancouver, though I don't remember the first two as being exceptional chances. It is the third one that stands out because it proves you can never count on a goal until the puck is in the net. I don't recall exactly how the play developed, but I got a clean breakaway from our own blue line. There wasn't anyone between the Vancouver goaltender, Dunc Wilson, and me. Often, when you've got a situation like that, the goaltender will come out, then back up as you move in. It's a question of who's going to commit himself first.

Wilson decided to stay in the crease. I must have been about 15 feet out when I deked to the right and at the same time took a shot to the left side of the net. Wilson stayed low, moved a little with my deke, but got back quickly to deflect the shot with his arm. He'd played it perfectly and I really couldn't fault myself for the play, though I hadn't got my 500th goal.

I think I got a couple of more shots in the second period, not real good chances, but whenever you shoot you've got to hope it will go in. After two periods, it looked that this might not be the night. Still, when you play hockey a long time, you tend to realize nothing is predictable about it; it's that kind of game. We went into the final period tied 2–2.

I got a shot early in the third period, but didn't get much wood on it. I can't recall getting frustrated at that point, but maybe that was the case. I'd had all those shots with nothing to show for it, and besides, the game was tied. More than anything else, we wanted to win the game.

The opportunity came less than two minutes into the third period. I was moving down left wing when Henri Richard got the puck over to me. I don't remember how long

> **I swung so hard that I went off balance. I even went down on one knee. As so often happens when you swing that hard, you don't get really good wood on the puck.**

a shot it was, but I do recall that the moment the puck got to me from Richard I just took a whack at it. I swung so hard that I went off balance. I even went down on one knee. As so often happens when you swing that hard, you don't get really good wood on the puck. I must have just ticked it. If it were golf, you'd call it a shanked shot. Being over-anxious, I slapped while off balance and the heel of my stick barely nicked the upper edge of the puck on the upswing. I was down on one knee, sliding toward a corner as I watched the puck sliding slowly. I wasn't sure it would make it, but eventually it slipped into the empty right side of the net. What had happened was that the blade of my stick was aimed toward the left side and Wilson had fallen that way, leaving an

opening for the puck on the right side. It shows you the nature of the game. He'd made a great save on my breakaway, but on this slow shot he had been helpless. Another thing: I was even thinking about giving the puck another nudge—that's how slow it was going—when a Vancouver defenseman took me out of the play. We both watched the puck sliding over the goal line.

So that was number 500. Not only that, but it won the game, 3–2, and the win clinched the East Division title for the Canadiens to make it even more memorable for me. Of course, there were many other big games in my career, but you'd have to agree that one is bound to stick out. It was certainly one of the ones I'll never forget.

—*As told to George Vass*

Toronto rookie **Frank Mahovlich** won the 1957–58 Calder Trophy. An almost perennial All-Star, he helped the club win four Stanley Cups before being dealt to Detroit in March 1968. Mahovlich joined the Canadiens in January 1971. He won two more Cup rings as a Hab (No. 27, above) before jumping to the WHA. Mahovlich entered the Hall of Fame in 1981 and became a member of the Canadian Senate in 1998.

SEPTEMBER 4, 1972

I had eight and a half wonderful years in Montreal, playing for the Canadiens, and I left with no hard feelings when I was

SEPTEMBER 4, 1972
MAPLE LEAF GARDENS, TORONTO
CANADA 4, SOVIET UNION 1

FIRST PERIOD
No scoring.
Penalties: CAN Park (cross-checking) 10:08; CAN Henderson (tripping) 15:19.

SECOND PERIOD
1. CAN P. Esposito (Park, Cashman) 7:14.
Penalties: SOV Gusev (tripping) 2:07; SOV (bench, delay of game, served by Zimin) 4:13; CAN Bergman (tripping) 15:16; SOV Tsigankov (slashing) 19:54; SOV Kharlamov (misconduct) 19:54.

THIRD PERIOD
2. CAN Cournoyer (Park) 1:19 (PP).
3. SOV Yakushev (Zimin, Liapkin) 5:53 (PP).
4. CAN P. Mahovlich (P. Esposito) 6:47 (SH).
5. CAN F. Mahovlich (Mikita, Cournoyer) 8:59.
Penalties: CAN Clarke (slashing) 5:13; CAN Stapleton (hooking) 6:14.

SHOTS ON GOAL:
CAN	10	16	10	**36**
SOV	7	5	9	**21**

Goalies: CAN T. Esposito; SOV Tretiak
Referees: Steve Dowling, Frank Larsen

traded during the 1977–78 season to the Pittsburgh Penguins. It goes almost without saying that there were many memorable moments with the Canadiens, particularly because we won the Stanley Cup four times during the years I played at Montreal. There is no describing the feeling of pride, of achievement, that goes with being on a Stanley Cup championship team.

Undoubtedly, the most memorable Stanley Cup game I ever played in was the seventh game of the 1971 finals, in which we were down, 2–0, to the Blackhawks in Chicago, but rallied to win 3–2. Those come-from-behind victories are always the sweetest. But there are other games that stand out just as vividly, especially two or three in international play against the Russians.

Hockey is our national game. This makes the 1972 Canada–Soviet Union series particularly memorable for me, as it does for almost every player who participated in it.

How could you ever forget the eighth game in Moscow, when we were down, 5–3, and came back to win, 6–5, on three goals in the final period, the last by Paul Henderson with just 34 seconds left to play? Yet, most memorable for me is the second game of the series, in which I scored a goal that helped us beat the Russians.

Today, we respect the Russians. We know that they are good hockey players, that they can play the game well, and that we have to be at our best to beat them. It's a totally different climate than it was in 1972 before that first great series against them opened.

The public and the media were convinced we'd beat the Russians eight straight games, that Team Canada would breeze through. We had pretty much the same feeling. We were confident that there was no way the Russians could beat a team of the finest NHL professionals. In short, we were prepared to walk over them.

Well, you know what happened in the first game in Montreal. The way it started

out, as we jumped to a 2–0 lead, made us even more confident, if that was possible. But before the game was over, we found out different. The Russians quickly tied us, then beat us, 7–3, to shock everybody in the world, except maybe themselves.

Naturally, we were a little better prepared for the second game, one of the most memorable games I've ever played in. We knew we'd have to play a controlled game, a team game and tighten the defense in our own end. The Russians had controlled the puck much of the first game and we had lost our heads. We had to break up their quick, crisp passing game, control the puck more.

We played much better right from the start in the second game. Chicago's Tony Esposito was in goal and he came up with some big saves, but he got a lot of help. Unlike the first game, our defensemen stayed up and kept the Russians from buzzing the net. Boston's Wayne Cashman and Minnesota's J.P. Parise played a particularly strong forechecking game, mucking with the Russians in the corners all night.

Cashman's persistence in the corners finally paid off in a goal early in the second period. Cashman got a pass out to Phil Esposito, his Boston teammate, who was moving for the net. Esposito fired from his favorite spot, about 20 feet out in the slot, and put one past the Soviet goalie Vladislav Tretiak to give us a 1–0 lead.

We knew enough now about the Russians not to change our game just because we were up by a goal. We continued to play them tight and carried the 1–0 lead into the third period. We got a power-play advantage right at the start of the final period and made good use of it. Montreal's Yvan Cournoyer broke down right wing, took a perfect pass from New York's Brad Park, and walked in on Tretiak, scoring the goal that made it 2–0.

A two-goal lead made us breathe a little easier, but not much. It was just as well because around the five-minute mark, the Russians got a power-play going after Bobby Clarke of Philadelphia was called for slashing. Our defensemen got caught and Aleksandr Yakushev got a breakaway to score the power-play goal for the Russians that cut our lead to 2–1.

I was able to shake the defensemen and went in alone on Tretiak. I gave him two or three head fakes, hoping he'd commit himself, and he finally did.

The crowd got pretty quiet at that point, no doubt thinking about the first game. It got even quieter about a minute later when Chicago's Whitey Stapleton drew a hooking penalty. Phil Esposito and I were sent out as the penalty killers. In that kind of situation, you really concentrate. You can't afford to make a mistake. Luckily, the Russians made one.

Somehow, Phil got the puck and slid it up to me at center ice. I had a couple of Russian defensemen with me but I had a little room and I went for the net.

I was able to shake the defensemen and went in alone on Tretiak. I gave him two or three head fakes, hoping he'd commit himself, and he finally did. I was able to slide a backhander in behind him into the open net for a shorthanded goal.

That gave us a 3–1 lead with about 13 minutes to play. I haven't scored many goals that have given me more satisfaction. But what made the night even more complete was that my brother Frank, then also with Montreal, scored the fourth goal for us a few minutes later. We went on to beat the Russians 4–1, to even up the series at a game apiece. It was the start of turning things around after that disaster in the first game.

There were a lot of other high points in that series, in which we won four of the eight games and tied another to edge the Russians. But there haven't been too many thrills in hockey for me to match that second-game goal.

—*As told to George Vass*

Peter Mahovlich played for Detroit in 1965–66 but it wasn't until after his 1969 trade to Montreal that he earned a full-time NHL job. Mahovlich, younger brother of Frank, played a big part in the Canadiens' 1971 Stanley Cup victory, contributing 10 goals and six assists in the playoffs. Three more Cup wins followed before Montreal traded him to Pittsburgh in November 1977. Mahovlich concluded his NHL career in 1980–81 after two seasons with Detroit.

I guess two games stand out for any player—his first in the NHL and, if he is lucky enough to be in one, an All-Star

FEBRUARY 14, 1979
MADISON SQUARE GARDEN, NEW YORK
NEW YORK RANGERS 5, BOSTON 1

FIRST PERIOD
1. NYR Don Maloney (Esposito, Farrish) 5:14.
2. NYR Esposito (Don Maloney, Murdoch) 6:00.
3. NYR Nilsson (Marois, Hickey) 7:39 (PP).
Penalties: BOS Park (holding) 0:24; BOS Jonathan (hooking) 6:33; NYR Fotiu (interference) 9:15; NYR Marois (roughing) 13:24; BOS Secord (roughing) 13:24; BOS Doak (charging) 13:56; NYR Plante (high-sticking) 17:12; BOS Schmautz (boarding) 18:15.

SECOND PERIOD
4. NYR Vadnais (Hedberg, Greschner) 8:14 (PP).
Penalties: NYR Talafous (tripping) 4:01; BOS Milbury (interference) 7:49; BOS Wensink (high-sticking, delay of game) 9:34; NYR Fotiu (high-sticking, delay of game) 9:34; NYR Farrish (interference) 12:19; BOS Milbury (unsportsmanlike conduct, misconduct, game misconduct) 15:21.

THIRD PERIOD
5. NYR Hickey (Nilsson, Hedberg) 8:50.
6. BOS O'Reilly (McNab) 14:59.
Penalties: NYR Esposito (holding) 5:26; BOS McNab (holding) 15:11.

SHOTS ON GOAL:

NYR	15	10	7	**32**
BOS	8	0	14	**22**

Goalies: NYR Davidson; BOS Gilbert
Referee: Bob Myers

Game. It's that way for me, but I've also got another special memory from when we beat the Islanders in the 1979 playoffs. My most vivid memory was coming up on February 14, 1979—Valentine's Day—from New Haven. The week before, we'd had a little break in the schedule because of the Challenge Cup between the NHL and the Soviet Union. We played an exhibition with the Rangers and I played my worst game of the year—of my life. I couldn't stand up or do anything right. There had been talk I'd be called up soon. I broke my thumb at the start of the year, and that pushed me back a couple of months. I knew if I was called up, it would be a short stay if I played like that. When the call came for me to go to New York, I brought a carryover bag. You could see I didn't expect a lot.

I had dinner with Don Murdoch, who was living with my brother Dave. He said, "Do what brought you here. If you are a scorer, then score. If you are a checker, then check." My forte was going into the corners, getting the puck and getting it out in front of the net. I never thought twice about giving it up.

I was kind of content in New Haven. It was the first winning team I had been on in so long, and I was scoring pretty well. But I was pleasantly surprised when I was called up. I also was scared to death. Dave picked me up and drove me to the game, and I remember all this traffic. I was thinking how we'd be late to the Garden for my first game in the NHL. And Dave is not a patient driver by any means. He was making me more nervous.

In the locker room, I felt out of place. There was Espo [Phil Esposito], Walter Tkaczuk, Steve Vickers, the Swedes Anders Hedberg and Ulf Nilsson. I watched them for years. I was thinking, "What am I doing here?"

It was the hardest warm-up I've ever taken. I was skating like crazy—my nerves were so jumpy. My parents had come down from Canada on top of it all. We were playing Boston, and I was put on the ice for the fourth shift of the game. I went out with Espo and Murdoch. Espo was not having a successful season, and Murder [Murdoch] was just back from his suspension [40 games for violating the league's drug policy].

The puck went into the corner, and I got it after bumping the defenseman off it. I swung around the net, and there was nobody to pass to. I took a shot at [Boston goalie] Gilles Gilbert. The puck came back out and I put the rebound between his pads.

I'll never forget that. I jumped about 10 feet off the ground. What a feeling to score on your first shift, your second shot in the NHL! In those days, the team came off the bench to celebrate a goal. The players all rushed off the bench and were patting me on the back. And the fans were going crazy. They all hated Boston, "the Big, Bad Bruins." It was amazing.

On the next shift, I got an assist on Espo's goal, and he told me not to get spoiled. In the second period, we held the Bruins without a shot on goal. It was the first game I ever played in where a team got no shots on goal. We won 5–1, and there was a party for the wives and families. It was all so new, and I enjoyed it the most of all the games I'd played until then. The bright lights, being on Broadway, it was all the right setting.

I had a feeling after that start that I'd be staying. Then Espo was praising the way he would get the puck from me, that he loved having a winger who went into the corners and got him the puck. That was my strength. It's lucky I didn't believe how great I was from the way Espo talked about me.

The next night at Buffalo, I got an assist. Espo was happy and scoring again. It was the right place at the right time. What really helped was having Dave there. He'd been around the block for four years. He was a barometer for things, someone to bounce things off of.

By the time we got into the playoffs, nobody expected much. The Islanders were the best team in the league and beat us the last game to finish first. But the city got so involved in the series. It was the semifinals, mostly on the back pages of the newspapers but sometimes on the front, and on TV. It was not just hockey anymore; it made the

> I jumped about 10 feet off the ground. What a feeling to score on your first shift, your second shot in the NHL!

city come alive. For once, New York was crazy for hockey.

There was not a lot for us to be confident about, I guess. But when you looked at the way J.D. [goalie John Davidson] was playing, you knew we had a chance in any game. We also had a lot of guys with strong character. Carol Vadnais, Espo—they knew what it took to win. We had a good combination of youth and experience. But I don't know if we ever realized we could beat the Islanders.

We won the first game, then we lost the second in overtime, both at the Coliseum. So we knew we could play with them. That was a pretty strong showing. We also won the third game but lost the fourth in overtime when Bob Nystrom scored a weird goal. But we went out to the Coliseum and beat them again.

Maybe I was too young and didn't know any better. There was no reason in my mind to think we wouldn't beat them. The last game was 2–1, tight and exciting, the way Stanley Cup games should be. The Garden was in absolute bedlam, as loud as it could get after our victory.

There were hundreds, maybe thousands, milling around outside after the game. The police had to put down barriers because the people were leaning on the glass at the restaurant outside the Garden, trying to get a glimpse of the players. I'll never forget the fans.

—*As told to Barry Wilner*

Don Maloney played with his brother Dave for the New York Rangers from 1979 until Dave was traded in December 1984. Don, who hit his career high with 29 goals and 40 assists in 1982–83, stayed with the Rangers until December 1988. After half a season with Hartford, he signed a free agent contract with the New York Islanders. He retired two seasons later to move into management.

JACK MCCARTAN

MARCH 6, 1960

It goes almost without saying that nothing can match the satisfaction of having been a member of the U.S. team that won the

MARCH 6, 1960
MADISON SQUARE GARDEN, NEW YORK
NEW YORK RANGERS 3, DETROIT 1

FIRST PERIOD
1. NYR Brian Cullen (Bathgate, Hebenton) 18:29.
Penalties: DET Ullman (hooking) 11:47; NYR Prentice (slashing) 11:47.

SECOND PERIOD
2. DET Delvecchio (Oliver, Howe) 16:18.
3. NYR Hebenton (Prentice, Brian Cullen) 11:30.
Penalties: DET Aldcorn (hooking) 17:07; NYR Fontinato (holding) 18:36.

THIRD PERIOD
4. NYR Prentice (Brian Cullen) 11:30.
Penalties: NYR Brian Cullen (holding) 3:44; NYR Spencer (hooking) 6:38; NYR Spencer (cross-checking) 15:47.

Goalies: NYR McCartan; DET Sawchuk
Referee: Frank Udvari
Linesmen: R. Williams, A. Reichert

Olympic gold medal in 1960 at Squaw Valley. Not too many people gave us a chance. Most people figured that either the Canadians or the Russians, who were the defending champions, would win it. At that time, the Russians had been coming along fast on the world hockey scene and their national program was improving quickly. The Canadians, as always, had a strong team,

Our winning the gold medal in 1960 was something like the situation in 1980 when the U.S. team surprised everyone by winning it again. It was just as much of a surprise in 1960, though maybe it didn't quite get the attention it got 20 years later.

Being the goaltender on that 1960 team, I have good reason to remember the games. They were all memorable in their way, especially the ones in which we beat Canada and then the Soviet Union. The one in which we beat the Russians, 3–2, was probably the key game, though in order to win the gold we had to beat Czechoslovakia in the final game, which we did, 9–4.

An added benefit of winning the gold medal was that it probably helped make possible my continuing to play hockey as a professional. I loved hockey—I'd played it almost all my life—and I thought it would be a great way to make a living. The Olympic Games helped make that possible.

Right after the Games, Muzz Patrick, who then was general manager of the New York Rangers, signed me to a contract. I was still in the U.S. Army at the time, but I got a 30-day leave to go to New York and join the Rangers. The attention I got in my first workout with the Rangers was overwhelming. The press was all over me. Most of them were straightforward, but there were some who criticized the Rangers for signing me, saying it was all a publicity stunt to boost attendance for a game or two, and that I didn't have enough experience to stick in the National Hockey League.

I knew when the Rangers signed me that they intended to give me a start in goal, so it was no surprise that three days after I arrived in New York I was told I'd be in the nets. That first NHL game was certainly one I'll never forget. Here I was, a kid from St. Paul, Minnesota, in Madison Square Garden, playing for the Rangers, getting a chance to show what I could do.

We were playing the Detroit Red Wings that night and I was going to take shots from some great players: Gordie Howe, Norm Ullman and Alex Delvecchio. The moment I skated out on the ice, I knew the fans were behind me, that they were pulling for me. They raised the roof. I tried to hide my nervousness, but it wasn't easy. I felt a couple of beads of sweat trickle down my jersey. My mouth felt parched and my tongue was thick, hut I kept talking to myself. I kept repeating, "Take it easy kid. Try to look like you belong here."

I knew that stopping the first shot by the Red Wings was critical. When a goalie makes a good save on a tough shot early, that bolsters his confidence. If he makes a mistake, he's really in trouble. It can set off a chain of worrying, overreaction, anxiety. The man I was most aware of was Howe. I had my eye on him even before the game started. Detroit had a lot of great scorers, but Howe was especially dangerous. As much as I could, I kept my eye on him. I figured he'd be in on me first.

I don't remember if he got the first shot on me, but I know he got the first good one. He gave me my first real test in the NHL. The way the play developed, Howe stole the puck from one of our players and only one man, defenseman Bill Gadsby, was between him and the goal. Somehow, with his great strength, Howe bulled his way past Gadsby and skated in on me.

I hugged the near post and he faked a shot at the far corner, but he held the puck and tried to pull me out of the net so he could put it in behind me. But I was ready for him, and when he took a wrist shot low, I dove at the puck and got my body in front of it for my first big save.

That save was a shot in the arm for me. I played a pretty good game the rest of the way

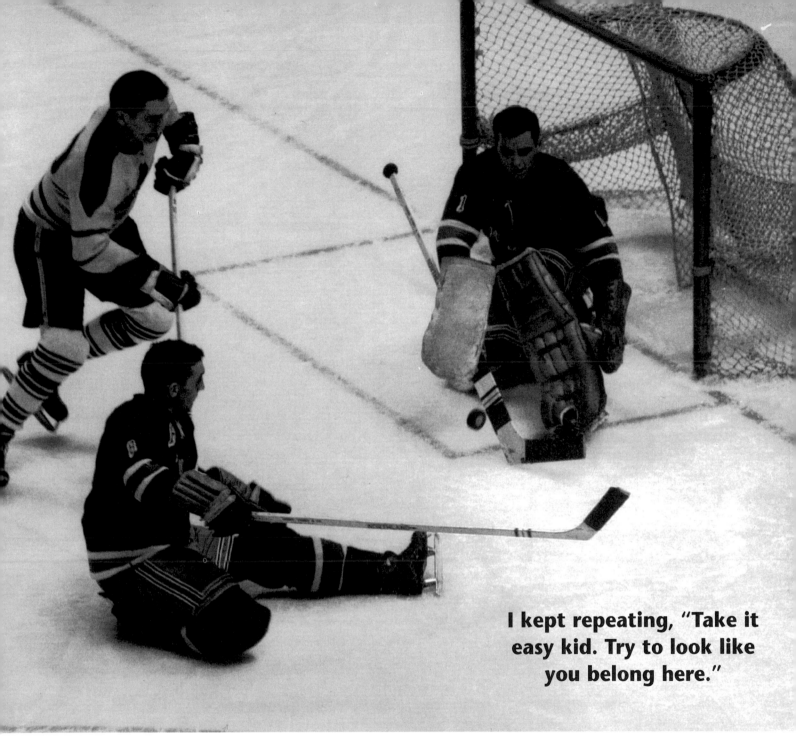

I kept repeating, "Take it easy kid. Try to look like you belong here."

and we won 3–1. I think I had 33 saves, so it wasn't as if I hadn't been tested in my first NHL game. I looked on that game as one of my biggest tests in hockey. Before I went in, I felt that I might be out of my league and that maybe the Red Wings would bomb me right back to St. Paul in one game. When I came through that game, I felt I was going to be all right.

I played three more games with the Rangers before my Army leave was up and we lost only one of them. The next year, I played eight more games with the Rangers and didn't do as well. I spent most of the season in the minors, but it was the start of a 13-year career as a professional hockey player.

I played in a lot of places—near the end with the Minnesota Fighting Saints of the World Hockey Association in my home town of St. Paul. I loved hockey and it was a great way to earn a living. I never minded the traveling, though it was a special thrill to wind up playing in Minnesota.

Nothing can top winning the Olympic gold medal, but that first game in the NHL, that game against Detroit in the old Madison Square Garden, ranks high among the thrills of my career. It's certainly a game I'll never forget.

—*As told to George Vass*

Jack McCartan played a huge role in the United States gold medal victory at the 1960 Winter Olympic Games. The New York Rangers quickly signed him to a five-game tryout. McCartan fared well initially in the NHL but his average ballooned in 1960–61. He bounced around the minor leagues for years and concluded his professional career with the WHA's Minnesota Fighting Saints in 1974–75.

STAN MIKITA

This is my 14th season with the Chicago Blackhawks and you can bet there have been a lot of big moments in that time.

MARCH 26, 1961
CHICAGO STADIUM, CHICAGO
CHICAGO 2, MONTREAL 1 (3OT)

FIRST PERIOD
No scoring.
Penalties: MON Langlois (high-sticking) 1:26; CHI Balfour (charging) 6:44; MON Richard (roughing) 7:18; CHI Fleming (roughing) 7:18; CHI Hay (high-sticking) 11:04; MON Gendron (high-sticking) 11:04; CHI St. Laurent (high-sticking) 18:00; MON Backstrom (high-sticking) 18:00.

SECOND PERIOD
1. CHI Balfour (Hay, Hull) 18:33.
Penalties: CHI Balfour (holding) 7:47; CHI St. Laurent (tripping) 8:12; MON Johnson (hooking) 12:59; CHI Murphy (roughing) 14:07; MON Provost (roughing) 14:07.

THIRD PERIOD
2. MON Richard (Goyette), 19:24.
Penalties: CHI Mikita (fighting, misconduct) 13:09; MON Hicke (fighting, spearing, misconduct) 13:09; CHI Hay (tripping) 18:40.

FIRST OVERTIME PERIOD
No scoring.
No penalties.

SECOND OVERTIME PERIOD
No scoring.
Penalties: MON Talbot (tripping) 4:20; CHI St. Laurent (tripping) 10:21; MON Langlois (hooking) 14:18.

THIRD OVERTIME PERIOD
3. CHI Balfour (Pilote, Mikita) 12:12 (PP).
Penalties: CHI Murphy (tripping) 0:08; MON Moore (tripping) 11:44.

SHOTS ON GOAL:

CHI	7	6	7	8	13	4	**45**
MON	13	4	13	8	10	6	**54**

Goalies: CHI Hall; MON Plante
Referee: D. McArthur
Linesmen: George Hayes, Ron Wicks.

One of the most memorable days I recall is the day in 1967 we clinched the Prince of Wales Trophy for the first time in the history of the team. We really went crazy over that one in the locker room, and though we've finished first four times since, there was never a party like that.

It had taken 40 years to set it up. I've seen films of the celebration in the dressing room and it was a wilder scene than I even remember. The champagne bubbling down throats, over shirts and hair and squirting in all directions. It's hard to imagine a bunch of grown men acting like kids, but we couldn't have been happier.

Usually, a division title isn't as big a cause for celebration as, say, winning the Stanley Cup. But that time in 1967, it was because all our efforts had been aimed at finishing first, maybe partly to wipe out the memory of the years in which we had just missed making it. No Hawk team ever had done it before, from the time the club started in 1926. Unfortunately, we didn't go on to win the Stanley Cup that year. We got knocked out of contention in the first round by Toronto, which went on to win the Cup in 1967.

We've won the Cup only once since I've been with the Hawks, in 1961, which brings me to the game I'll never forget. That was the third game of the first round against the Montreal Canadiens, on March 26, 1961, in Chicago Stadium. The Canadiens won the first game 6–5 and we came back in the second game to win 4–3, with Eddie Litzenberger getting the deciding goal. That gave us a split of the first two games, both at Montreal, and our chances looked pretty good going into the third one, at Chicago.

It was a close-checking game, although there were enough chances on both sides to score in the first two periods. We had a 1–0 lead going into the last minute of play but you knew that anything could happen with Montreal having the big bombers like Boom Boom Geoffrion, Dickie Moore, Jean

Beliveau and others.

I don't remember what started it now, but with about a minute or so to go in the game, I got into a fight with Bill Hicke. Both of us went to the penalty box, each getting two minutes for roughing. We hadn't even sat down when Hicke said something uncomplimentary to me and I answered him back. We started swinging and it took a couple of minutes before the linesmen could separate us. And this was in the penalty box! Referee Dalt McArthur gave us each five minutes more plus 10-minute misconducts.

That was a total of 17 minutes in penalties with only a minute to go in the game, so McArthur said, "You guys might as well go down to the dressing room. You won't be playing any more tonight."

All right. I figured we had the game down. I went downstairs to the dressing room, then started taking off my uniform. Suddenly there was this tremendous shout, although I didn't know what it was about until my teammates came into the room a couple of minutes later. With half a minute left, Henri Richard had scored the tying goal for the Canadiens and we were going into a 20-minute "sudden death" overtime.

"Kid, you'd better get dressed," Rudy Pilous, our coach, told me. "We might need you." I put on a clean uniform and took a seat in the penalty box when the overtime period started. I didn't think I'd play, since I still had almost 16 minutes in penalties left. I figured a goal would come before that. But when my penalty time elapsed we were still tied 1–1, although Donnie Marshall hit our goal post with a shot and we hit their post twice.

In the second overtime, Dickie Moore twice hit the post with shots. Finally, in the third overtime we got a break, McArthur calling a penalty on Montreal. Now we could finish it! I was playing right point on the power play but somehow I ended up on the left side when the puck came out to me. I wound up for the slap shot but half fanned on it in my eagerness. I got just enough of the puck to get it past the first Canadien who was charging into me, and it reached Murray Balfour, who was standing in front of the net. He just wheeled around with a back-

Sporting the No. 21 that Chicago retired after back surgery ended his playing career in 1979, **Stan Mikita** slips the puck past Toronto goalie Johnny Bower. A constant innovator, Mikita invented the curved stick and an improved helmet that many players began wearing. Over 22 seasons for the Blackhawks, Mikita won a Stanley Cup ring, eight All-Star berths, four Art Ross Trophies, two Lady Byng Trophies and the Hart Trophy twice.

hand shot and put the puck through the goalie's legs, and we had won the game 2–1.

Canadiens coach Toe Blake was so infuriated by McArthur's penalty call that had set up our power play goal that he took a swing at the referee after the game. That cost him a $2,000 fine.

There were three games left in the series but that was the "big one." The three over-times really sapped the Canadiens. They won the next game to tie the series 2–2, but it didn't really matter. We knew we could beat them and we did, Glenn Hall shutting them out twice. We beat Detroit in six games in the final to take the Stanley Cup.

—*As told to George Vass*

Some people have said that this was one of the greatest games of all time, and who am I to argue? What I can say for certain is

**APRIL 10, 1984
NASSAU COUNTY COLISEUM,
UNIONDALE NY
NY ISLANDERS 3, NY RANGERS 2 (OT)**

FIRST PERIOD
1. NYR Greschner (unassisted) 12:06.
2. NYI Bossy (unassisted) 19:49.
Penalties: NYI Nystrom (roughing) 7:24; NYR Dave Maloney (tripping) 15:34.

SECOND PERIOD
No scoring.
Penalties: NYI Bourne (high-sticking) 1:18; NYR Hanlon (high-sticking, served by Laidlaw) 1:18; NYI Jonsson (hooking) 16:42; NYR Hanlon (slashing, served by Erixon) 18:39.

THIRD PERIOD
3. NYI Jonsson (D. Sutter, Gillies) 7:56.
4. NYR Maloney (Pavelich, Patrick) 19:21.
Penalty: NYI Bossy (elbowing) 8:35.

FIRST OVERTIME PERIOD
5. NYI Morrow (B. Sutter) 8:58.
No penalties.

SHOTS ON GOAL:

NYI	5	6	8	7	**25**
NYR	10	13	13	8	**44**

Goalies: NYR Vanbiesbrouck, Hanlon; NYI Smith
Referee: Dave Newell
Linesmen: Ron Finn, Ray Scapinello

that it ranks at the top of my list, even though I had previously played on four straight Stanley Cup championship teams with the New York Islanders, from 1980 through 1983. This was the spring of 1984, and we had embarked on what the front office had dubbed "The Drive for Five." Our goal was to equal the Montreal Canadiens' run of five straight Stanley Cups during the 1950s when the NHL still was a six-team league.

The Islanders of 1984 remained a very confident club, and why not? We had Billy Smith, one of the best money goaltenders of all time, Denis Potvin, a future Hall of Famer on defense, and such outstanding scorers as Mike Bossy, Bryan Trottier and Clark Gillies up front. But no matter how confident we were, the Islanders always had an extra bit of respect when it came to our cross-county rivals, the New York Rangers.

The Rangers had upset the Isles a year before I got to the team [1979] in a classic playoff, and anytime the teams met there was always that emotional factor that could lift the underdog to greater heights. What made the series even more meaningful to me was my 1980 [gold medal-winning] Olympic coach, Herb Brooks, was now behind the Rangers bench.

We took the Rangers in the first game 4–1, but the score wasn't all that indicative of the play. We found that out pretty quickly in Game 2 when Glen Hanlon, playing the goal of his life, shut us out 3–0. That sent us to Madison Square Garden for the next two games in what was a best-of-five series.

We got clobbered 7–2 in Game 3, and just about everybody in New York City had counted us out, especially since the next game was at the Garden. Call it what you will—Islanders spirit or whatever—but we shrugged off the home-ice disadvantage and got right back in the series with a 4–1 victory. That sent us back to Nassau for the deciding game.

Up to this point, the Rangers had been outplaying us, even though we were tied at

two games apiece. As it happened, they continued to outplay us in Game 5, but somehow we managed to move ahead of them 2–1 in the third period as the clock wound down to the finish. Our plan was to play strict defensive hockey and kill the clock. Certainly, we had the players to do it, and Smitty once again was playing well for us in goal. Then it happened.

With little time left in the third period, I was on the ice when the Rangers went on the attack. Their young rushing defenseman, James Patrick, was coming toward me across our blue line. I made a mad rush to stop Patrick but only got a piece of him—not quite enough. Patrick moved the puck across to Mark Pavelich, who had been my 1980 Olympic teammate and was now one of the best Ranger forwards. By this time I was out of the play and in the unfortunate position of watching its culmination.

I held my breath as Pavelich took the shot. Smitty made the save, but as he went to his knees to make the block, Don Maloney cruised in for a rebound. The puck ricocheted up over Smitty and was over Maloney's shoulders as Don made his move. As the puck started descending, Maloney swung his stick and connected. The puck went right into the net!

Maloney's goal was a terrific deflation for Islanders fans, but surprisingly it had little effect on our club. We went into the dressing room with an amazing amount of confidence. Some other teams might have dwelled on the Rangers' comeback, but we didn't do that. Our morale was positive going into the overtime, although I certainly didn't even think I'd figure in the scoring.

Once the overtime began, it had overtones of the regulation three periods. There was incredible action at both ends, but once again the Rangers had an edge in play. Lucky for us, Smitty was at the very top of his game. The play that led to my most memorable moment occurred in our end. Bob Brooke, who had been one of the Rangers' better forwards, got the puck just off the right face-off circle. His shot was labeled to the lower far right corner, and I know a lot of the spectators thought that would be the

> **Once I fired the puck and it went into traffic, I lost sight of it. I didn't know the puck had gone in until I heard it clang off the bottom of the back of the net.**

end of the series—and our reign. But somehow Smitty got a piece of the puck, and it rebounded back to us.

I had been on the bench at the time of the play, but when we counter-attacked, coach Al Arbour sent me out as part of a line change. Brent Sutter, who was just a kid then, took a bad-angle shot, and the puck rebounded. The Rangers tried to clear it along their right boards, but John Tonelli kept it in. Then, Reijo Ruotsalainen, the Rangers' Finnish defenseman, tried to clear the puck again along the boards. That was the fatal mistake.

The puck bounced off the boards on my right side. I saw an opening and didn't hesitate; I just put the shot right on goal. Fortunately, Patrick Flatley, our young right wing, had camped right in front of Glen Hanlon, so the goalie was perfectly screened on the play. Once I fired the puck and it went into traffic, I lost sight of it, but I was told that it went right between Hanlon's legs. If Flatley hadn't screened him, I'm sure Hanlon would have made the save. I didn't know the puck had gone in until I heard it clang off the bottom of the back of the net.

Why was it so memorable? It was one of the best games I ever played in, and, as I mentioned, the opposition was terrific. That triumph gave us our 17th straight playoff series victory, and we went on to win an unreal 19 in a row until Edmonton beat us in the finals. It was a great run, but even if we didn't complete our "Drive for Five" I'll never forget my goal, which kept us alive.

—*As told to Stan Fischler*

Ken Morrow was part of the USA's "Miracle on Ice" at the 1980 Winter Olympics, winning a gold medal. He then joined the New York Islanders and won a Stanley Cup ring that spring, the first of four consecutive championship seasons. A hard-hitting but clean defensive defenseman, Morrow retired from the Islanders in 1989 after a couple of injury-plagued seasons.

BILL MOSIENKO

I've told the story a thousand times, maybe ten thousand times, so there's no danger I'll ever forget that game, not that I'd ever

MARCH 23, 1952
MADISON SQUARE GARDEN, NEW YORK
CHICAGO 7, NEW YORK RANGERS 6

FIRST PERIOD
1. CHI Bodnar (Gadsby, Mosienko) 0:44.
2. NYR Eddolls (unassisted) 4:50.
3. NYR Raleigh (Stewart, Stanley) 17:12.
4. NYR Slowinski (Raleigh, Stewart) 18:35.
5. CHI Horeck (Finney, Hucul) 18:47.
No penalties.

SECOND PERIOD
6. NYR Stewart (Slowinski) 13:19.
7. NYR Dickenson (Ronty, Hergesheimer) 15:55.
No penalties.

THIRD PERIOD
8. NYR Slowinski (Raleigh) 3:37.
9. CHI Mosienko (Bodnar) 6:09.
10. CHI Mosienko (Bodnar) 6:20.
11. CHI Mosienko (Bodnar, Gee) 6:30.
12. CHI Finney (Hucul, Fogolin) 13:50.
13. CHI Finney (Gadsby) 19:22.
No penalties.

Goalies: CHI Lumley; NYR Anderson
Referee: George Gravel
Linesmen: D. Bialto, Doug Davies

want to. It's a wonderful thing that so many people remember it and want to hear about it again.

Those three goals in 21 seconds on March 21, 1952, in Madison Square Garden are the most vivid memory of my hockey career. I still get a great feeling thinking about them and recalling just how it happened. It's just a coincidence, of course, but three days before the game I was visiting a friend in Toronto. We were going through the record book and I remarked how nice it would be to have my name in there with some of the hockey greats. Isn't it remarkable that just a few days later I'd earn the right to be listed in that book?

When we went to New York for that game, it didn't mean a thing as far as the league standings were concerned. It was the final game of the season and my Blackhawks were buried deep in last place. The Rangers were way ahead of us but they were locked in fifth.

There weren't too many people there in old Madison Square Garden, maybe somewhat over 1,000 and they were pretty happy with the way the game went the first two periods. The Rangers were leading 6–2 early in the third period, Ed Slowinski getting a hat trick for them by that time, which most people forgot about later.

I was on a line with Gus Bodnar, the centerman, and George Gee, the left winger. Bodnar had scored the first goal of the game at just 44 seconds of the first period but after that Lorne Anderson, a rookie who was in the nets for the Rangers, had settled down pretty well, allowing just one more goal while his team got six. He stopped me a few times. So it looked like we were headed for a beating to round out the season when things started to happen for me. I sort of caught lightning in a beer bottle, like they say.

I remember what happened just like it was last night. Bodnar won a face-off and he got me the puck in center ice. I took off and went in around Hy Buller, the Ranger defenseman, on top of the goalkeeper, Anderson. I got off a low wrist shot along the ice, and it went in on the right side.

That was my 29th goal of the season, which was quite a few in those days, so I reached into the net for the puck as a souvenir. I skated back to the bench and handed the puck to our coach, Ebbie Goodfellow. That goal was at 6:09 of the third period and, of course, we faced off right away at center ice.

Right off the face-off, Bodnar got the puck and put it on my stick when I hit the blue line. I was really going and, just like the first time I went around Buller, again moved in on Anderson pretty quickly. I had him all to myself and I figured since I'd been able to beat him on the right side, his glove hand, I'd try it again. Just like the first time, I slid the puck along the ice. I don't think Anderson was ready for the quick shot and it got by him for my second goal, at 6:20, just 11 seconds after I'd scored the first one.

Anderson was naturally unhappy about what had happened and I'll never forget the look he gave me as I reached into the net for the puck. That was my 30th goal and I skated back to the bench and added the puck to the one I'd given Goodfellow before. Naturally, I was thinking about the hat trick, not that I was prepared for what actually happened. After all, there was more than 13 minutes left in the game. But the Rangers were still leading by two goals, 6–4, and figured to tighten up their defense. Even if the game didn't mean a thing, still it would be nice to end the season by winning.

Bodnar won the draw again, though. He got it back to our left wing, Gee. When Georgie got control of the puck, he began moving toward the blue line. I was skating with him and as he reached the line I made my move. He saw me cutting over the line and laid a perfect pass on my stick. Buller was waiting for me, but like the first two times, I cut around him and went in on Anderson. He'd been burned twice on the right side and this time he moved to his right, figuring I'd try it again.

I knew what he was thinking so I decided to change my strategy. So instead of shooting the puck along the ice to the right side, I

I'd scored three goals in 21 seconds for a new record but I was so dazed I hardly realized what had happened.

pulled him out of the net to the left, then put one over him high into the top right hand corner. That was the third goal, at 6:30, just 21 seconds after the first and 10 seconds after the second. I'd scored three goals in 21 seconds for a new record but I was so dazed I hardly realized what had happened.

I started to skate back to center ice for another face-off when Jimmy Peters grabbed me, yelling, "Hey, you'd better grab that puck, too. I think you've got a record." I went for the net to get the puck and Anderson was really hot. You can imagine what he said to me.

Funny thing is that 45 seconds later, I could have had a fourth goal. I was in alone again, I faked Anderson out of position and had an open net to hit, but I missed the far post by a matter of inches. When I went back to the bench after missing that one, Goodfellow yelled at me. "Hey, what's the matter, Mosie? Are you slowing down?" Isn't that something?

Oh, yes. We won 7–6.

—*As told to George Vass*

Bill Mosienko, still remembered most for his 21-second hat trick record, was a two-time NHL Second All-Star Team member. He hit a career high in the 50-game 1943–44 campaign, with 32 goals and 38 assists. Mosienko won the Lady Byng Trophy the following season after scoring 28 goals and 26 assists without picking up a single penalty.

The game I remember most was the game that won us the Stanley Cup in 1989. Everything pretty well went our way

**MAY 25, 1989
MONTREAL FORUM, MONTREAL
CALGARY 4, MONTREAL 2**

FIRST PERIOD
1. CAL Patterson (Murzyn, MacInnis) 18:51.
Penalties: CAL Mullen (hooking) 0:54; MON Chelios (elbowing), 5:09; MON Naslund (interference) 8:20; CAL M. Hunter (roughing) 9:53; MON Skrudland (roughing) 9:53; CAL Murzyn (tripping) 10:26; CAL Roberts (roughing) 18:30; CAL Ramage (roughing) 18:30; MON Corson (roughing) 18:30; MON Smith (roughing) 18:30.

SECOND PERIOD
2. MON Lemieux (Skrudland, Chelios) 1:23.
3. CAL McDonald (Nieuwendyk, Loob) 4:24.
Penalties: CAL M. Hunter (roughing) 4:53; CAL M. Hunter (roughing) 4:53; MON Walter (roughing) 4:53; CAL Vernon (roughing, served by Roberts) 6:37; MON Corson (roughing) 6:37; MON Ludwig (slashing) 11:08; CAL Nattress (hooking) 16:36.

THIRD PERIOD
4. CAL Gilmour (Otto, MacInnis) 11:02 (PP).
5. MON Green (McPhee, Lemieux) 11:53.
6. CAL Gilmour (Mullen, Macoun) 18:57.
Penalties: CAL M. Hunter (holding) 2:17; MON Skrudland (roughing) 2:17; MON Courtnall (boarding) 10:46; CAL MacInnis (roughing) 18:34; MON Lemieux (roughing, misconduct) 18:34.

SHOTS ON GOAL:

CAL	4	8	7	**19**
MON	9	7	6	**22**

Goalies: CAL Vernon; MON Roy
Referee: Denis Morel
Linesmen: Ron Finn, Swede Knox

through the whole playoffs. We snuck through in the first round—Vancouver probably outplayed us—but we stuck it out and went on to win it all. Game 6 of the finals in Montreal was definitely a dream come true and the highlight of my career.

We had taken the first game of the finals in Calgary, and we had them on the ropes going into the second game, but they came back and won that one. Going into Montreal for the third game, we had them down, and I had a shot at an open net to ice the game. But I wound up missing the net, and then they came down and tied the game up and won in double overtime. That was tough.

In the fourth game, again I had a shot at an open net to ice the game and I missed it again, although we held on for the win. The fifth game we pretty much dominated, taking an early lead on Joel Otto's goal. That set up Game 6.

Everyone talked about the mystique of Montreal never losing a Cup game in their building, and it gave us something to think about. In a way, it helped us, because we were pretty determined. We were ready to go in and play our best game. The waiting was hard, though. You're so psyched up for the game, it's tough to do anything. It's tough to sleep or even to do your routine. You're just really nervous, and you wish the game would start right away. But we relaxed as soon as the puck dropped and the game got under way. We felt great right from the opening face-off, and we played really well.

I was playing on a line with Dougie Gilmour and Colin Patterson, and Colin got the first goal. We dumped the puck in, and Chris Chelios knocked it down. It came right to Colin, right over the blue line, and he took a wrist shot and scored. Colin was the checker on the line, did most of the defensive work on our line, and he played tremendously throughout the series. He struggled to score goals, and that was probably the biggest goal of Colin's career. To

see him get it was a big lift for the rest of us, knowing that he's not the goal-scoring type but does some other jobs better than some of the other guys. It was great for him to help out in the offensive capacity.

Playing us was kind of tough, because at times our line was hot and at times Joe Nieuwendyk's line was very hot. It was tough for the Montreal checking line, and I ended up playing mostly against Ryan Walter.

Montreal tied the game early in the second period, but then Lanny McDonald got the lead right back. He hadn't dressed in the previous couple of games, and Terry Crisp elected to sit out Jim Peplinski and Tim Hunter and play Jiri Hrdina and Lanny. It was funny because we were talking with Lanny before the game and Lanny told us that he had scored his first goal ever in the Montreal Forum. He said, "Maybe I'll get my last one here."

The Flames broke out three-on-two, with Nieuwendyk, Hakan Loob and Lanny. Lanny came a little bit late on the right side. Loob came up the middle, with Nieuwendyk on the left. Loob gave it to Nieuwendyk, and he threw it all the way over to Lanny. Lanny just put it top shelf. It was quite a goal. He had told us the story, and then all of a sudden he went out and got the goal. The guys who heard the story that day remembered it and were happy for him. It probably meant just as much to all of us as it did to him. He had been such a great player through his career— it was nice that Lanny got the big goal. It would have been sad for him to retire after not having played at all. I think the coaches had that in their minds—that Lanny had had a great career and he deserved to play in the final game.

Dougie got two goals that game. His first one came on the power play in the third period. We knew we had a good offensive team, and the power play was working for us. That really helped, because in the past when we went into the playoffs, our power play kind of got lost on us. It was really a tremendous help and probably carried us through most of the games. The Canadiens made it 3–2 right after that, but we were sticking to our basic game plan. We knew it

Everyone talked about the mystique of
Montreal never losing a Cup game in
their building, and it gave us something
to think about. In a way, it helped us.

was going to be a battle, and we tried not to take penalties. But we tried to hit them and get them off their game. Sticking to the game plan was the main thing we did right. Not giving them the power play was our biggest advantage. In the past, we were known to take retaliatory penalties, but we kept our cool and didn't take those stupid penalties. You can get into situations where there's pushing and shoving, taking bad penalties, but we didn't do that throughout the series.

I'll never forget seeing Dougie score the open-net goal at the end. I had an assist on that. After the game, it was very, very crowded in our locker room. It is very small, and there were people wall to wall, with everybody trying to go crazy. It was such a relief, a load off everybody's mind, to know that we were the team they said we could be. We were not still trying to find out if we could be that good.

—As told to Bob Grove

He recorded two 40-goal seasons as a member of the St. Louis Blues but **Joe Mullen** was traded to Calgary in February 1986. He helped the Flames win the 1989 Stanley Cup and won a second Cup ring in 1992 as a member of the Pittsburgh Penguins. Mullen became the first American-born player to score 500 NHL goals, on March 14, 1997. He entered the Hall of Fame in 2000.

I was your typical 19-year-old, zit-faced, peach-fuzzed kid who had just put in a four-goal night. Sitting on the bench as the

OCTOBER 12, 1976
MET SPORTS CENTER, BLOOMINGTON
NEW YORK RANGERS 10, MINNESOTA 4

FIRST PERIOD
1. NYR Hickey (Vadnais, Hodge) 1:12.
2. MIN Hogaboam (Sharpley, Jensen) 1:37.
3. NYR Hodge (Greschner, Farrish) 5:15.
4. NYR Polis (McEwen, Tkaczuk) 6:02.
5. MIN Eriksson (Barrett, Jensen) 12:14.
6. NYR Hodge (Hickey, Esposito) 13:10.
Penalties: NYR Polis (hooking) 1:44; MIN O'Brien (hooking) 6:39; MIN Nanne (high-sticking) 7:52; MIN Young (hooking) 14:26; MIN Younghans (interference) 18:25; NYR Gilbert (roughing) 18:25; MIN O'Brien (fighting, game misconduct) 18:25; NYR Dillon (fighting, game misconduct, gross misconduct) 18:25.

SECOND PERIOD
7. NYR Murdoch (Newman, Stemkowski) 8:23.
8. MIN Sharpley (Jensen, Hogaboam) 9:46.
9. MIN Young (Jarry, Talafous) 11:31 (PP).
10. NYR Murdoch (Tkaczuk, Polis) 12:31.
11. NYR Murdoch (Vadnais, Hodge) 19:50 (PP).
Penalties: NYR Hickey (tripping) 10:06; MIN Young (hooking) 18:06; NYR Gilbert (cross-checking, roughing) 18:53; MIN Younghans (roughing) 18:53.

THIRD PERIOD
12. NYR Gilbert (Stemkowski, Newman) 11:28.
13. NYR Murdoch (Tkaczuk, Polis) 17:32.
14. NYR Murdoch (unassisted) 19:55.
Penalties: NYR Farrish (tripping) 6:51; NYR Vadnais (boarding) 14:48.

SHOTS ON GOAL:

NYR	23	14	12	**49**
MIN	13	10	6	**29**

Goalies: NYR Gratton; MIN Smith
Referee: Alf LeJeune
Linesmen: Ryan Bozak, Gordon Broseker

final seconds were ticking away in our win over the Minnesota North Stars, I was trying not to break out into a big smile as I relived each goal in my mind. It was the fourth game of the 1976–77 season—and only the fourth game of my NHL career.

I didn't score in the first period, but things began to heat up for me and my Rangers teammates in the second period. My first goal came on a rebound, with assists from Dan Newman and Pete Stemkowski. That gave us a 5–2 lead.

The lead wasn't safe; the North Stars had come to play. Minnesota wasn't known as a physical, tough team, but they had stirred it up a little in the first period when Tim Younghans tangled with one of our best players, Rod Gilbert, and Dennis O'Brien put a licking on another one of our young guns, Wayne Dillon. After my goal, Glen Sharpley and Tim Young each beat our goaltender, Gilles Gratton, to cut the lead to 5–4. But then the puck continued to follow me around no matter where I went on the Met Center ice.

One such time, I found myself breaking past North Stars defenseman Fred Barrett. From about 25 feet out, I let go a shot that beat goalie Gary Smith. Then, with just 10 seconds remaining in the period, the puck found me again. This time, we were on the power play.

As I look back at the players on the ice when I scored that third goal, I can really see that this was a team in transition. The Emile Francis era produced several great moments for the Rangers, but John Ferguson had taken over as general manager in 1976. As any G.M. and coach would, Fergie was looking at the players he had inherited and was trying to mold the team as he saw fit.

One thing Fergie had going for him was that he inherited an organization stocked with good, young talent. I was only 19. And Ron Greschner—what a defenseman—was manning one of the points as we lined up for the face-off. He was only in his third year. Soon, Mike McEwen, Greg Polis, Don

Maloney, Dave Farrish, Nick Fotiu, Pat Hickey, Ron Duguay, Lucien DeBlois and Ed Johnstone, to name a few, would be coming up through the system and joining us in the Rangers line-up.

Also on the ice at the time were Phil Esposito and Ken Hodge. Espo and defenseman Carol Vadnais were still trying to fit in after coming to the Rangers the year before in the trade that sent Brad Park and Jean Ratelle to the Boston Bruins. In order to make Espo feel a little more at home, the Rangers had brought in Hodge, Espo's former linemate in Boston.

The fifth guy joining me, Gresch, Espo, and Hodge on the ice was Gilbert. He was a holdover from the Rangers' glory years in the early 1970s under Francis' leadership. Gilbert, Steve Vickers, Walt Tkaczuk and Pete Stemkowski had been stalwarts with the Rangers for years and knew how to handle the ups and downs of playing in New York. They brought a sense of leadership to the locker room.

So here we all were, a motley crew of players at different points in their careers, ready for the drop of the puck. Espo, one of the greatest face-off men I have ever seen, won the puck and sent it back to me. I just slapped it past Smith to make it 7–4 at the end of the second period.

If there had been any doubt about the outcome of the game, Gilbert put an end to it with a goal early in the third period. However, the puck wouldn't leave me alone. I scored my fourth goal of the night with less than three minutes left in the game. I couldn't believe this was happening to me. I was off to a great start that season. I scored in my first shift and now I had seven goals in my first four NHL games. I would have never dreamed of such a beginning.

I was beaming on the inside with happiness, on the verge of giddiness, as the clock ran down. There was a face-off in the Minnesota end, and Espo came over to our bench. I was just sitting there in my own little world when he began to talk to the coach.

"Fergie, put the kid in," said Espo. "Let him score another one."

Fergie looked at me, shrugged his shoulders, and said, "Get out there, kid." I

Finally, after a few seconds that seemed like hours, Espo won it over to me. I cocked my stick back and let fly with everything I had.

jumped out onto the ice like a kid in a candy store and glided down to the Minnesota end of the ice. That's where Espo pulled me aside.

"Listen, kid," said Espo, "Stay here. Don't move from here. If I win the draw, you'll get it. If I lose the draw, don't move. I'll get it to you." I just looked at him and nodded. When a guy who scored as many goals as Espo talks, you don't question what he's saying.

I went over and stood in the exact spot where Espo told me to, my stick ready, my heart pounding, and history just a swipe away. Espo never loses face-offs, but it looked for a second as if he wasn't going to win this time. But Espo's instruction was echoing in my mind: "Don't move kid...Don't move kid."

I kept my skates planted in the ice as Espo fought for the puck. Finally, after a few seconds that seemed like hours, Espo won it over to me. I cocked my stick back and let fly with everything I had. Smith didn't have a chance. The back of the net rippled, the red light came on and, with 10 seconds remaining in the game, I had my fifth goal of the night.

I had never scored that many goals in one game in my life. When I got back to the locker room, reporters were crowding around me and my teammates were patting me on the back. People were telling me only one other rookie had ever scored five goals in a game in the NHL.

That's the kind of night you never forget.

—*As told to Chuck O'Donnell*

Don Murdoch (No. 14, above) scored 32 goals and 24 assists as a rookie in 1976–77. He notched 55 points the following season but, found to have used cocaine, was suspended for the entire 1978–79 campaign. The suspension was lifted after 40 games but Murdoch's NHL career never got back on track. Traded to Edmonton in 1980 and to Detroit in 1981, he retired in 1986 after spending more than four seasons in the minor leagues.

VACLAV NEDOMANSKY

JANUARY 2, 1978

When you have played hockey for 20 years, like I have, it is difficult to choose one game, one goal, over all the others, to

say that it is the one you will never forget. But maybe I can do it. I'll tell you why. It is because one goal I scored made me feel so good, because it showed some old friends, men I had played with or against years before, that even when I was 35 years of age I could still play the game well, that I was not, as they say, "washed up."

Hockey is a popular sport in Czechoslovakia and it was so when I was a small boy growing up. I remember when I got older, when I started to play and began to do well, Stan Mikita, who played so long for the Chicago Blackhawks, was a hero to so many players in Czechoslovakia, the country he had left as a small boy to go to Canada. Like so many other youngsters in Czechoslovakia who played hockey, I dreamed of playing in Canada some day, of even playing in the National Hockey League. It was a dream that sometimes seemed nothing more than that, but in my case it came true.

I played many years in Czechoslovakia and there were many good moments to remember. We have good players there, I can tell you, and our national team was sometimes as good as any in the world. We won some big championships in Europe and we did pretty well when we played in Canada. Even in my early days, in the late 1960s, I began to think seriously about playing for a Canadian team, in the NHL. I knew that some of the teams wanted me, but Czechoslovakia would never let me go.

There was one time, in 1967 I think it was, that I almost got my wish. Our team from Czechoslovakia was on a tour of Canada and we were playing in Kitchener [Ontario]. Emile Francis, who then was general manager of the New York Rangers, and I had talked earlier. He had arranged to drive me away after the game. But the people who were in charge of our team must have suspected something. They did not play me in that game. They kept close watch on me, so the chance never came, not until many years later.

In 1974, some people from the Atlanta Flames and Toronto in the World Hockey Association talked to me again. Some arrangements were made and I felt sure that if I left Czechoslovakia, I would be able to play hockey in Canada, which always had been my dream. I arranged that summer for a vacation in Switzerland with my wife Victoria, who had been born in Toronto, and my son Vasik. We drove through Austria to Switzerland. From there, I let the people in Canada know that I wanted to play for them. After some bargaining, I got a very good contract for the time, more than I could ever have dreamed of in my home country, from Mr. John Bassett, who owned the Toronto Toros of the WHA. I was 30 years old then, and it had taken a long time to get my wish, but finally it had come true. I could not have been happier.

The Toros played two more seasons in Toronto and I did pretty well, then we moved to Birmingham [Alabama] and they renamed the team the Bulls. We had some good players, such as Frank Mahovlich and Mark Napier, but the team did not attract many fans. It was strange to play hockey there. Still, I never regretted leaving Czechoslovakia, even though I still had not completely achieved what I had dreamed of, playing in the NHL.

That finally came in 1978 when Birmingham traded me to the Detroit Red Wings. Most of the four seasons I played with the Red Wings, I enjoyed very much. We did not have much success, but I think I proved I belonged in the NHL. My only regret was that I couldn't have proved it when I was younger. And I did get to play in the Stanley Cup playoffs one year, my first [1977–78], and scored three goals, so that was something to remember. But even more pleasing was something that happened just a few weeks after I joined Detroit, early in 1978.

The Czechoslovak team Pardubice was touring the U.S. and Canada and we played a game against them at the Olympia in Detroit. More than anything, I wanted to play in this game against some of the players I had played with and against all those years. There were some of them on the Pardubice team. But for a time it did not look as if I would get the opportunity.

I dreamed of playing in Canada some day, of even playing in the National Hockey League.

The Pardubice officials did not want me to play. They even asked the NHL to make sure that I did not. What I will never forget is that the guys on the Red Wings backed me up, they helped me. They had a meeting and told the Detroit officials that if I was not allowed to play they would not play either. I think that made it clear to Pardubice that either they agreed to let me play or there would be no game. They finally gave in.

There were not many people in the Olympia for the game but I cannot remember one that I was more excited to play in or wanted to do better in. Luckily, I was able to do well.

I was very early in the game when I went on the ice. I got the puck and went around a Pardubice defenseman and passed to Dennis Hull. He scored a goal on a shot that went just under the crossbar past the Pardubice goalie, Jiri Crha, to make it 1–0. A few minutes later we had a power play. I was near the net when Dan Maloney passed to me and I scored a goal.

We won the game 5–4, and I don't know that I was ever more excited. I really wanted to win that one, and the guys helped me. I had wanted to show that I was as good as ever, that I was playing even better than when I had left Czechoslovakia. What's more, we didn't have any players from a national team on the Red Wings. We were just a regular team.

So that's the game I'll never forget. And why not? It meant a lot to me. I felt fantastic after I scored that goal.

—As told to George Vass

Vaclav Nedomansky starred for Czechoslovakia on the world stage and helped his homeland win the 1972 World Championships. He defected in 1974 and scored an average of more than 44 goals over three seasons in the WHA. Traded to Detroit in November 1977, Nedomansky had NHL seasons of 38 and 35 goals at 35 years of age. He retired after playing for both the New York Rangers and St. Louis in 1982–83.

BERNIE NICHOLLS

GAME 7, 1994
EASTERN CONFERENCE FINALS

People don't realize that winning championships means everything to athletes. The summer workouts, the

MAY 27, 1994
MADISON SQUARE GARDEN, NEW YORK
NEW YORK RANGERS 2, NEW JERSEY 1
(2OT)

FIRST PERIOD
No scoring.
No penalties.

SECOND PERIOD
1. NYR Leetch (Graves, Messier) 9:31.
Penalty: NJ Lemieux (interference) 12:13.

THIRD PERIOD
2. NJ Zelepukin (Lemieux, Richer) 19:52.
Penalty: NYR Kovalev (elbowing) 6:32.

FIRST OVERTIME PERIOD
No scoring.
No penalties.

SECOND OVERTIME PERIOD
3. NYR Matteau (Tikkanen) 4:24.
No penalties.

SHOTS ON GOAL:

NYR	11	11	6	15	5	**48**
NJ	10	5	9	7	1	**32**

Goalies: NYR Richter; NJ Brodeur
Referee: Bill McCreary
Linesmen: Kevin Collins, Ray Scapinello

practices, the 82-game regular season—you can't imagine all the hard work that we go through just to be the team that wins the Stanley Cup.

That's why getting so close with the New Jersey Devils in 1994 and not winning was a difficult pill to swallow. We ultimately lost to the New York Rangers in double overtime of Game 7 of the Eastern Conference finals. That was the game I'll never forget.

The series matched up pretty equally. They had an outstanding defenseman in Brian Leetch and we had one in Scott Stevens. They had a great coach in Mike Keenan, and we had a great coach—although he had a different style—in Jacques Lemaire. They had a hot goalie in Mike Richter, and we had a hot goalie of our own in Martin Brodeur. They had guys who rose to the occasion in the playoffs like Mark Messier, and we had a few playoff heroes in Stephane Richer and Claude Lemieux. I think the Rangers had the better individuals if you looked up and down the roster, but we played better as a team.

We took a 3–2 lead in the series. I had been suspended in Game 4 for cross-checking Alexei Kovalev. I was pretty disappointed about being suspended because it was more of a push. It looked bad, but it wasn't like I broke my stick or hit him hard. Kovalev even admitted I didn't hit him hard. It was frustrating to be suspended because when you get to the point in the season, you want to play every minute of every game.

When I got back into the lineup in Game 5 at Madison Square Garden, I scored two goals. Both came off two-on-one opportunities. On one, John MacLean fed me for a one-timer. On the other one, I scored the rebound of Lemieux's shot.

That victory gave us a lot of momentum going into Game 6 at home. We had a 2–0 lead in the second period, and I think if we had got to the locker room 2–0, we would have won. But they scored late, and Messier had a hat trick in the third period to send the series to a Game 7.

Heading back to the Garden, the momentum had shifted in their favor, but I think we were confident we could still win. We had won twice at the Garden earlier in the series.

I can't imagine anything will ever be able to top Game 7. Before the game, I had butterflies. If a guy tells you he doesn't have butterflies before an emotional game like that, he's fooling you. Even Messier, who had won five Cups to that point, got butterflies. If you don't, you shouldn't be playing. Game 7, Madison Square Garden, the two best teams so evenly matched—I was just excited to be there.

In games of that magnitude, it's very easy to get too excited before the game. As an older player, I had learned to control my emotions. When I was younger, I tended to let my emotions get the best of me. When I was playing for the Los Angles Kings with Wayne Gretzky, we ended up playing the Edmonton Oilers in the playoffs. I was so nervous before the first game that my body felt like I had played a game before the contest even began.

Game 7 against the Rangers was played pretty much the same as the rest of the series. In the first 59 minutes, Leetch's goal in the second period was the only goal of the game. We came close a few times but could not get the equalizer.

Finally, it came down to the last minute. There was a face-off in the Rangers zone to Richter's right. Coach Lemaire chose me to take the face-off. I had to go against Messier. He's my pick as the best face-off guy in the league. But I was having a good night on draws against him, and I won it.

Our defenseman, Bruce Driver, made a nice play pinching in down the left wing. Eventually we got the puck in front, and we all went to the net to jam away. Valeri Zelepukin found the puck and put it in with eight seconds remaining.

Going into overtime tied 1–1, I thought we had regained the edge. When you're on the road, all you want is the score to be close late in the game. This was a perfect situation. The game went into double overtime. Even though both teams had everything riding on the next goal, neither team was holding back.

> It was like a funeral in the dressing room after the game. A lot of grown men cried. I really felt low that night. It was the worst feeling I know.

Both teams had a lot of chances as the game wore on, even though fatigue was starting to take a toll. This was the third overtime game of the series. Unfortunately, our fatigue took the biggest toll. Late in that second overtime, Stephane Matteau scored for the Rangers. He wrapped the puck around the net, and it went off either Slava Fetisov or Brodeur—I'm not sure—and went in. It wasn't a pretty goal, but most double-overtime goals aren't.

It was a heartbreaker. I thought that the winner of that series would be the best team in hockey. Sure enough, the Rangers went on to win the Stanley Cup. I think we would have beaten the Vancouver Canucks in the finals, too.

Losing that series just ripped my heart out. I started skating when I was three, played hockey for almost my whole life and worked out every day all for the chance to win the Stanley Cup. To come so close and not get there, it just rips your heart out. It was like a funeral in the dressing room after the game. A lot of grown men cried. I really felt low that night. It was the worst feeling I know. Those kind of chances don't come around very often. I think that was mine. Will I come close again? I don't know. Maybe that was my year to win.

—*As told to Chuck O'Donnell*

Bernie Nicholls had his most prodigious scoring seasons with the Los Angeles Kings, where he played from 1981–82 until January 1990. His career-best campaign came in 1988–89, when he tallied 70 goals and 80 assists. Traded to the New York Rangers, Nicholls also played for Edmonton, New Jersey, Chicago and San Jose before ending his career in 1999 with 475 goals and 734 assists.

I would have to say my most memorable game was my first NHL game in Toronto, as a rookie with the Detroit Red Wings.

MARCH 1, 1986
MAPLE LEAF GARDENS, TORONTO
DETROIT 6, TORONTO 4

FIRST PERIOD
1. DET Young (Oates, Barrett) 4:16.
2. DET Larson (Kisio, Loiselle) 7:37 (PP).
3. DET Oates (Gallant, Snepsts) 13:57.
Penalties: DET Larson (holding) 0:56; TOR Clark (boarding) 6:54; DET Leavins (holding) 7:52; DET Kisio (hooking) 11:09; TOR Courtnall (slashing) 15:16.

SECOND PERIOD
4. TOR Clark (Nylund) 0:53.
5. DET Klima (Foster, Loiselle) 7:17.
6. DET Duguay (Ogrodnick, Kisio) 10:20.
7. TOR Vaive (Thomas) 12:32.
8. DET Oates (unassisted) 19:01.
Penalties: DET Snepsts (fighting) 3:03; TOR Clark (fighting) 3:03; DET Gallant (fighting) 4:05; TOR McGill (fighting) 4:05; DET Barrett (holding) 13:04; TOR Kotsopoulos (high-sticking) 15:33; DET Leavins (roughing) 20:00; TOR Courtnall (double minor roughing) 20:00.

THIRD PERIOD
9. TOR Vaive (Maxwell, Thomas) 11:55 (PP).
10. TOR Terrion (unassisted) 18:14 (SH).
Penalties: DET Ogrodnick (holding) 1:30; TOR Nylund (roughing) 4:30; DET Kisio (holding) 6:24; TOR Kotsopoulos (high-sticking) 8:41; DET Ladouceur (roughing) 11:08; TOR McGill (major slashing) 14:37; DET Larson (hooking) 15:01; DET Oates (high-sticking) 19:10.

SHOTS ON GOAL:

DET	17	12	10	**39**
TOR	11	16	5	**32**

Goalies: DET Stephan; TOR Edwards, Wregget
Referee: Dave Newell
Linesmen: John D'Amico, Ron Finn

I got three points, we won the game 6–4 and I was named the first star of the game. I was really pumped up to play at Maple Leaf Gardens, and I had a lot of people at the game to watch me. To play where you grew up, and to play great with your mom and dad and your friends there, that was really something.

Every time I play at the Gardens, I think it's hard. First of all, the rink is small, it has no corners, and there isn't much room to work. And I'm really nervous every time I go in there, because I'm playing in front of all the guys I grew up with. When you're a Toronto boy, everybody you played with knows when you're playing. As a kid, I was at the Gardens all the time. When I played in Tier II Juniors, my team was like a Leafs farm team, but about five levels down. We wore the Leafs crest on our sweaters and everything. And I used to go to the [major junior] Marlies games at the Gardens all the time.

I can't really say I was mad that the Maple Leafs didn't draft me. It's really tough to say that, now that I've made it in the NHL. I mean, you're one of thousands of kids playing in the Toronto area. How can you say they should single out a kid playing Tier II hockey—as a 20-year-old? I was lucky I met a scout from RPI [Rensselaer Polytechnic Institute], and he gave me a scholarship and a chance to keep playing in college. That was toward the end of my season of Tier II. I don't know what I would have done without that opportunity.

My first time in Toronto with the Red Wings came early in my rookie year, and they made me sit out. Like a lot of guys who were from Toronto, I had about 20 people at the game. I skated in the warm-ups, and then they told me I wasn't playing. That really hurt. They knew I was from Toronto, and they wanted to make me think a little bit. I had played about 15 games before we went up to Toronto, and then I didn't play. I guess it was a little psychology. Coaches do that sort of thing all the time.

I was really, really struggling. I came to the team after we won the national championship at RPI, and I signed as a free agent. It was a tough adjustment, and I guess there was a little pressure on me to perform. With the way I play, I'm the kind of player who has to have a lot of ice time. A lot of guys are that way. Not even Wayne Gretzky could do anything getting one or two shifts a game. That's the way it was for me at the beginning of the year—I wasn't playing a lot. You second-guess yourself, and it gets worse. It was a real adjustment getting ready to play every night after playing 30 games a year in college.

The Red Wings weren't as bad as we looked [17–57–6, with two coaches fired]. But we got off to a bad start, and it just snowballed. We did have a lot of quality players on the team, but it seemed like the first couple of months we couldn't win a game. It was total hell; the whole year was hell.

I went down to the minors to Adirondack for a couple of months and played for Bill Dineen. He was really good for me. I got my confidence back, and by the time I came back up, it was a no-lose situation for the team. Brad Park, who had taken over for Harry Neale as the coach, was really good to me.

The best thing was that first game I got to play in Toronto. During the anthem, I couldn't help but stand there on the bench and look around the Gardens. I was playing on a line with Warren Young and Joey Kocur. Warren is a really nice guy who had signed as free agent too, and he had helped me a lot. And he's another guy from Toronto.

I got an assist on my first shift, and it was on kind of a fluke goal. I had a little give-and-go play with Warren; I passed him the puck, and he whiffed on it a little bit. It rolled through about 15,000 legs and went in. It was lucky, but, hey, we'll take it. Don Edwards was playing goal for the Leafs. I didn't go out of my mind or anything on the ice, but inside, it felt really good. Things were alright after that; it gets all those butterflies out. It's like getting your first hit in the big leagues—it gets you going. It's like getting out of a slump.

I scored a goal on my next shift, and then I scored a goal in the second period on a slap shot, which isn't me at all. A slap shot? Have

> **I had a little give-and-go play with Warren; I passed him the puck, and he whiffed on it a little bit. It rolled through about 15,000 legs and went in.**

I scored 20 slap shot goals in my NHL career? Come on, not even close. That's what kind of game that was.

After I came up and played with the Red Wings to finish up the season, I went back down to Adirondack and we won the Calder Cup. Did the way I played at the end make that a good year? No, I'd have to say it was an awful year. All in all, I'd have to say the year was a wash.

—As told to Jeff Gordon

Adam Oates played his first four NHL seasons with Detroit. His 1989 trade to St. Louis matched him with Brett Hull, an ideal linemate and Oates made the 1991 Second All-Star Team. Traded to Boston in February 1992, Oates hit career highs with 45 goals and 97 helpers in 1992–93. The consummate playmaker, Oates continued to tally high assist totals after his trade to Washington in March 1997. He joined Philadelphia at the March 2002 trade deadline.

ED OLCZYK

I had played in only two games during the last four-and-a-half months of the 1993–94 season. We went through the first two

MAY 25, 1994
MEADOWLANDS ARENA, EAST RUTHERFORD
NEW YORK RANGERS 4, NEW JERSEY 2

FIRST PERIOD
1. NJ Niedermayer (unassisted) 8:03.
2. NJ Lemieux (Niedermayer, Nicholls) 17:32.
Penalties: NYR Larmer (roughing) 9:15; NJ Holik (hooking) 15:12; NJ Driver (high-sticking) 19:07.

SECOND PERIOD
3. NYR Kovalev (Messier) 18:19.
Penalties: NJ Nicholls (unsportsmanlike conduct) 14:07; NYR Messier (unsportsmanlike conduct) 14:07; NYR Tikkanen (tripping) 18:51.

THIRD PERIOD
4. NYR Messier (Kovalev, Leetch) 2:48.
5. NYR Messier (Kovalev, Leetch) 12:12.
6. NYR Messier (unassisted) 18:15 (SH, EN).
Penalties: NJ Niedermayer (roughing) 11:32; NYR Tikkanen (roughing) 11:32; NYR Anderson (slashing) 17:11; NJ Stevens (misconduct) 19:40; NJ Nicholls (high-sticking, roughing, misconduct) 19:40; NYR Anderson (unsportsmanlike conduct, misconduct) 19:40; NYR Gilbert (slashing) 19:43; NJ Daneyko (slashing) 19:43.

SHOTS ON GOAL:

NYR	9	13	14	**36**
NJ	13	13	4	**30**

Goalies: NYR Richter; NJ Brodeur
Referee: Kerry Fraser
Linesmen: Gerard Gauthier, Pat Dapuzzo

rounds of the playoffs and I didn't get into one game.

I was resigned to my role on the team. Coach Mike Keenan wanted me to be a leader off the ice. I was there to keep the players loose and be supportive. Going into Game 6 of the Eastern Conference semifinals against the New Jersey Devils, Brian Noonan had a shoulder injury. I thought there was a chance I would get to play, but I had been let down so many times before I didn't want to get my hopes up.

Before the morning skate, I was sitting there taping my stick and Mike [Keenan] came up to me. He asked me, "What's your best year? What's the most goals you've scored in one season?"

I looked at him to make sure he was serious. So he asked me again. I thought it was a little weird, because that's something he could have just looked up. I told him I scored 42 goals one year and scored over 30 four other years.

He said, "Oh yeah? We need you to play tonight."

I was really pumped. After hardly playing for so long and then to dress in such a critical game—that was the game I'll never forget.

The Devils were leading the series three games to two. By then, there were so many subplots to the series: the suspensions to Jeff Beukeboom and Bernie Nicholls; Mike benching Brian Leetch and Mark Messier in Game 5; the long drought between Stanley Cups in New York; and the Devils defense, which made life hell for us. Then, before Game 6, Mark made the prediction that we were going to win. It was quiet, almost dead silence in the locker room. Finally, Kevin Lowe spoke. I remember him saying, in his smirky voice, "Well Mess, I guess we gotta win this one." That really broke the ice and settled everyone down a little.

I wasn't nervous going into the game, just more intense. I had never been on a team that won anything. When I played in Chicago, we made it to the semifinals one year, but we didn't have the horses.

I wanted to help the team by going out, scoring two or three goals, and really make Mike look like a genius for putting me in there. I wanted to be Kirk Gibson, coming off the bench to hit a homer or Bobby Baun scoring an overtime goal. I wanted to come out and be aggressive, but I didn't want to do anything too risky, either. I went out and gave Bruce Driver an elbow in the chops and he retaliated by bringing his stick down on my head, drawing a penalty.

I ended up playing 12½ minutes that game. I think it was Don Koharski who refereed the game, and I remember him yelling at me to get out of the crease on the power play. I remember vividly getting whacked a couple of times by their goalie, Martin Brodeur.

I wish I could say I had a goal or an assist or something, but I didn't. In fact, through almost two periods, we could not sustain any

I thought there was a chance I would get to play, but I had been let down so many times before I didn't want to get my hopes up.

pressure. They were carrying the play and winning face-offs and getting to loose pucks. We were trying hard to do things, but our chances were not materializing. But our goalie, Mike Richter, made some nice saves to keep the game close.

We were trailing 2–0 when Alexei Kovalev scored for us in the final few minutes of the second period to cut the deficit to one. The tide started to turn from that point. Of course, Mess scored three in the third period to lead us to a 4–1 win. After he scored for the third time, he came over to the bench. Just to be a part of that will be something I'll never forget.

He knew what he was talking about when he predicted we would win. He was trying to reassure us that we could do it, and rise to the occasion. Just when you thought he was as big as he could get, he put on a performance like Babe Ruth or Joe Namath or Muhammad Ali.

We won the series two nights later when Stephane Matteau scored in double overtime. At one point, he went down to get his skate repaired during the game. He saw me and, in broken English, he said, "Go ahead, give me some luck. Give me some luck." So I kissed his stick. Later, he scored. I guess it was meant to be.

I've had some other memorable games during my career. Playing for the Toronto Maple Leafs in the 1989 playoffs, I had five points in Game 5 of a series against Detroit. I scored the overtime goal to complete the hat trick. Also, although I didn't assist on either, Gary Leeman's 50th goal in 1988 against Toronto was exciting, as was Keith Tkachuk's against Los Angeles last year. It's satisfying when people you like reach milestones like that.

—As told to Chuck O'Donnell

Ed Olczyk, above, crowds New Jersey goalie Martin Brodeur during his 1993–95 stint with the New York Rangers. Olczyk won a Stanley Cup ring in 1994. The Blackhawks drafted Chicago native Olczyk third overall in 1984 and he scored 20 goals and 30 assists as a rookie. Dealt to Toronto in September 1987, he also played for Winnipeg (twice, interrupted with his term with the Rangers), Los Angeles and Pittsburgh before concluding his career with the Blackhawks in 2000.

> **A lot of people ask me what my most memorable game was, and most of them think I will say it was my first game. Well,**

JANUARY 1, 1961
BOSTON GARDEN, BOSTON
BOSTON 3, MONTREAL 2

FIRST PERIOD
1. MON Hicke (Richard) 12:35 (PP).
2. BOS Bucyk (Horvath, Boivin) 15:04 (PP).
Penalties: MON Gendron (slashing) 1:03; BOS Bartlett (high-sticking) 1:03; BOS Bartlett (cross-checking, spearing, fighting) 5:25; MON Hickey (spearing, fighting) 5:25; MON Langlois (hooking) 7:30; MON Gendron (slashing) 14:00; BOS Flaman (high-sticking, roughing) 15:21; MON Talbot (roughing) 15:21.

SECOND PERIOD
3. BOS Boivin (unassisted) 7:18.
Penalties: MON Gautier (cross-checking) 2:27; MON Backstrom (roughing, misconduct) 5:47; BOS Mohns (roughing) 5:47; BOS Flaman (hooking) 8:06; MON Beliveau (holding) 8:37; BOS Erickson (holding) 10:00; MON Moore (tripping) 10:48; MON Beliveau (slashing) 15:24.

THIRD PERIOD
4. BOS O'Ree (Boivin) 10:07.
5. MON Richard (Geoffrion) 13:06.
Penalties: MON Gendron (hooking) 1:42; MON Talbot (roughing) 6:24; BOS Burns (roughing) 6:24; MON Beliveau (roughing) 9:18; BOS Bartlett (roughing, misconduct) 9:18; MON Backstrom (fighting, cross-checking) 11:30; BOS Mohns (fighting) 11:30; MON Beliveau (roughing) 11:30; BOS Armstrong (roughing) 11:30.

Goalies: BOS Gamble; MON Hodge
Referee: Dalton MacArthur
Linesmen: Neil Armstrong, George Hayes

that first game when I broke the NHL's color barrier with the Boston Bruins was very memorable and very special to me. It always will be. But, I think scoring my first goal was the biggest thrill for me.

Let's first go back to my first game. I broke the color barrier on January 18, 1958, in Montreal. If it happened today, there would be a media circus, with TV reporters and newspaper writers and everyone swirling around. And I think since then, there has been a lot written about my first game. It's gotten got a lot of publicity and a lot of people come up to me and want to know what it was like to be the first black player in the NHL. They'll ask me what happened in that first game.

But actually, there was no big deal made about it at the time, if you can believe that. Just a week earlier, I was just Willie O'Ree, playing for the Quebec Aces against the Montreal Royals in the Quebec Professional League. When I stepped on the ice at the Forum, everyone said, "Oh, there's that black hockey player, Willie O'Ree. He's with the Bruins. He must have been called up." So no one up there thought much of it. More was made of the fact that we had beaten the mighty Canadiens, which was a feat in itself.

We were very fortunate to beat the Canadiens 3–0 that night. I played on a line with Don McKenney and Jerry Toppazzinni. After the game, both teams got on the train after the game and went to Boston for a rematch. The Canadiens beat us 5–3 in the next game.

Montreal was a great team. I had just missed playing with Jean Beliveau in the minors by a few years, so it was great to play against him in the big leagues.

One thing I'll never forget about my first game was how supportive my Bruins teammates were and how they welcomed me to the team. Johnny Bucyk, Doug Mohns, Charlie Burns and Leo Labine—they all said to me, "No matter what, we're behind you

100 per cent, so don't worry about a thing. Just go out and play."

But I only played two games when I was up with Boston that time and I didn't get to score a goal before I was sent back down. I ended up playing in the minors for another two-and-a-half seasons before I got called up again.

That period of watching and waiting seemed to gon on forever. I wanted to get back into the NHL so badly. I tried to play well and hustle and keep myself in good shape in the minors. I never gave up hope that I was going to get the call back. I had broken the color barrier — which was great — but I didn't just want to be a footnote. I wanted to be a regular, everyday NHL player.

Then, all of a sudden, out of the blue, it came. The Bruins brought me up and I got to stick around for a while this time. I ended up staying for more than half the season. It was great to play so much. I loved playing in Boston. A lot of people give it a bad rap, but I really enjoyed playing there. I'd take the train into the Garden. The whole time I played there, I never heard one racist remark.

Those weren't the best of times for the Bruins on the ice. Bobby Orr and the "Big Bad Bruins" were still in the future, and the Milt Schmidt and the Kraut Line era was in the past. We just didn't have a lot of good players. But I'll say one thing: We always played hard. That's all you can really ask of a player.

So I finally scored my first goal on January 1, 1961. We were playing the Canadiens. In the third period, I was playing left wing. I took a pass from one of our defensemen, Leo Boivin. He hit me in stride as I was going down the left wing. Luckily, I was always blessed with good speed, so I just accelerated. Then I cut in, went around a defenseman, made a shift, put on a few moves and broke in around the other defenseman. Suddenly, I found myself one-on-one with the goalie.

The Canadiens' goalie that night was Charlie Hodge, who was filling in for the legendary Jacques Plante, who was hurt that night. So here I was, going to the net. Hodge did what any goalie would do. He came out a little, then started moving back in.

I had broken the color barrier which was great—but I didn't just want to be a footnote. I wanted to be a regular, everyday NHL player.

As I was going in on goal, everything started moving in slow motion. I began to think about some advice Bronco Horvath had given me. In 1959–60, Bronco tied Bobby Hull for the league lead in goals, so he knew a thing or two about scoring. He once said to me, "Willie, if you ever get in on Hodge, shoot low. He's weak on the low shots. Don't put the puck up where you can handle it. Shoot low. Don't forget it."

As I was going in on the net, the only thing that kept going through my mind was, "Shoot low. Shoot low." I had my head up. I made a couple of fakes, and I shot the puck right along the ice. It was a lucky shot because I could have easily missed the net, but it hit just inside the left post and went in. That gave us a 3–1 lead.

I went into the net, grabbed the puck and gave it to coach Milt Schmidt to hold. The fans gave me a standing ovation that lasted for more than two minutes. It was tremendous.

Six or seven minutes later, the "Pocket Rocket," Henri Richard, scored for Montreal. That made it 3–2. But we managed to hang on. That goal turned out to be not only my first goal, but the game-winning goal, too.

That goal helped me feel like an established player, like I belonged up there in the big leagues with the big boys. I still have that puck from my first goal in my home. I'll never forget that goal. Or that game.

— *As told to Chuck O'Donnell*

Willie O'Ree was the first black NHL hockey player. Although he had a 23-year professional hockey career, his games in the NHL were few. O'Ree joined the Boston Bruins for two games in 1958 and played 43 games for the Bruins in 1960–61. He retired from active play in 1979 and was named Director of Youth Development for the NHL and USA Hockey Diversity Task Force in 1998. O'Ree continues to meet and motivate young people in inner cities.

I had a long way to go to prove myself when I first came up to the NHL. I was far from the most polished player around and

MAY 10, 1979
MONTREAL FORUM, MONTREAL
MONTREAL 5, BOSTON 4 (OT)

FIRST PERIOD
1. BOS Middleton (Redmond, Cashman) 10:09 (PP).
2. MON Lemaire (Savard, Lapointe) 14:19 (PP).
Penalties: BOS Miller (high-sticking) 1:16; MON Tremblay (roughing) 1:16; MON Lambert (holding) 4:57; MON Chartraw (high-sticking) 9:47; BOS Miller (hooking) 12:55; BOS Marcotte (holding) 16:56.

SECOND PERIOD
3. BOS Cashman (Middleton, Ratelle) 0:27.
4. BOS Cashman (Ratelle, Middleton) 16:12.
Penalties: BOS Ratelle (hooking) 9:20; BOS Marcotte (slashing) 9:55; MON Lapointe (holding) 9:55; MON Shutt (cross-checking) 10:48.

THIRD PERIOD
5. MON Napier (Lafleur, Tremblay) 6:10.
6. MON Lapointe (Lafleur, Gainey) 8:16 (PP).
7. BOS Middleton (Ratelle, Sims) 16:01.
8. MON Lafleur (Lemaire) 18:46 (PP).
Penalties: BOS Redmond (hooking) 7:11; BOS (too many men, served by McNab) 17:26.

FIRST OVERTIME PERIOD
9. MON Lambert (Tremblay, Houle) 9:33.
No penalties.

SHOTS ON GOAL:
MON	15	12	17	8	52
BOS	10	10	7	3	30

Goalies: MON Dryden; BOS Gilbert
Referee: Bob Myers
Linesmen: John D'Amico, Ron Finn

I had to work hard to improve my skating and balance. I was forced to be a physical player in order to make up for my shortcomings. I wasn't stylish or graceful as a skater and to stop the guys who were, I had to make the most of what I could do. But I think that through hard work and with experience I've improved a great deal and proved I belong. I'm still not a great skater and my style of play may not be as graceful as that of some players, but I get the job done.

In my years at Boston, I've been very fortunate to have coaches who appreciated what I was trying to do and stuck with me. I've also been fortunate enough to play on some outstanding teams, including the one that won the Stanley Cup in 1972.

Playing on that '72 championship team, naturally, has been one of the highlights of my career. It's what every hockey player strives for and I was lucky to be on a Stanley Cup team so early in my career. Some players never experience the feeling that comes with winning the Cup. In the years since 1972, we've had some good teams at Boston, and I don't think any was better than the 1978–79 team.

We were a hard-working club with a lot of balance. Don Cherry did an excellent job of coaching to get the most out of the talent we had. He had us working—some writers called us the "Lunch Pail Brigade," meaning we were a team of good, hard-working, honest hockey players.

Going into Stanley Cup play in the spring of 1979, we honestly felt we had a good shot at it. Being the champions, the Montreal Canadiens naturally were favored. They'd won it three years in a row and had great players. The New York Islanders also had an outstanding team, with players such as Denis Potvin, Bryan Trottier, Mike Bossy and Glenn Resch, among others, having had a great season. And the New York Rangers had been coming on. But we felt that the Cup was really between the Canadiens and us. We'd had good luck playing them during the

regular season and we saw no reason that would change in the playoffs.

We won our quarterfinal series four straight over the Pittsburgh Penguins and then went up against Montreal in the semifinals. The way we looked at it, if we beat Montreal, we'd have a tremendous chance at the Cup. We thought we could handle either the Islanders or the Rangers in the finals.

The semifinal series opened at Montreal and the Canadiens won the first two games. I'm not going to say anything about the officiating, but it's amazing how seldom the Canadiens get a cheap penalty called on them in the Forum. Their power-play goals killed us. But we came back, winning the next two games at Boston, the second one in sudden-death overtime on a goal by Jean Ratelle, who had a hat trick.

Montreal won the next game on their ice, and then we tied the series again, at three wins apiece, by beating them in Boston Garden. I think Stan Jonathan had a hat trick for us in that game. So it came down to the seventh game of the semifinals, the game I'll never forget.

I had the feeling that if we could win this one we'd go on to win the Cup in the finals. You'd have to say the odds were against us in one way. We hadn't won a game at the Forum in three years. I think we'd lost 14 straight games to the Canadiens on their ice. But a thing like that had to come to an end and there couldn't be a better time.

I don't think we've ever been more steamed up for a game than we were for that one. We knew what we were up against in the Forum, but we also remembered the first two games, each of which we could have won, if we hadn't made a few mistakes.

We got the first goal in the seventh game. It came in the middle of the first period, and though the Canadiens tied it quickly, we came out of the period tied 1–1 feeling pretty good about our chances. The second period was all ours. We scored a couple of goals, both by Wayne Cashman, to take a 3–1 lead. We didn't get many shots, but we made the most of our opportunities. The Canadiens, at the same time, were getting a lot of chances, but Gilles Gilbert was playing outstandingly for us in goal.

All we had to do was hang on for less than four minutes and we'd beat the Canadiens. They were pressing, but if we played it smart we'd come out all right and then go on to the finals.

We couldn't hang on to that two-goal lead in the third period, Montreal tying the game early. But with less than four minutes left, Rick Middleton put a shot past Ken Dryden, the Canadien goalie, and we had a 4–3 lead. All we had to do was hang on for less than four minutes and we'd beat the Canadiens. They were pressing, but if we played it smart we'd come out all right and then go on to the finals.

Somehow, though, whenever you've got the Canadiens in trouble, they seem to get out of it. There were only a couple of minutes left when we got a stupid penalty for too many men on the ice. As usual, the Canadiens made the most of it. Guy Lafleur scored a power-play goal with just over a minute to go to tie the game 4–4 and it went into sudden-death overtime.

We should have won in the overtime. We had plenty of chances to score, though the Canadiens had theirs, too. I remember hitting a goalpost with one shot, but most of all I remember a shot that should have won the game for us. There was a scramble in front of the Montreal net and Dryden left one post open. I got the puck and took the shot, but it went wide of the net. If I'd been more accurate, the game would have been over and we'd have gone to the finals. But I shot wide, and after about nine minutes of overtime Yvon Lambert scored the goal that won it for the Canadiens.

That's the game I'll never forget. If we'd beaten the Canadiens we would have met the Rangers for the Stanley Cup and I think we'd have beaten them. So, actually, the Stanley Cup was on the line there.

—As told to George Vass

In 1971–72, **Terry O'Reilly** scored in the only game he played for the Boston Bruins. He hit personal bests with 29 goals and 61 assists in 1977–78. Yet it was O'Reilly's tough and physical approach to the game, rather than his scoring ability, that made him a fan favorite. He retired in 1985 after 891 games with 204 goals, 402 assists and 2,095 penalty minutes. Team captain for his last two seasons, O'Reilly later coached the team.

BOBBY ORR

I can still remember the first National Hockey League game I played like it was yesterday. That's one game I'll never forget.

MAY 10, 1970
BOSTON GARDEN, BOSTON
BOSTON 4, ST. LOUIS 3 (OT)

FIRST PERIOD
1. BOS R. Smith (Sanderson) 5:28.
2. STL Berenson (Bob Plager, Ecclestone) 19:17.
Penalties: BOS Sanderson (butt-ending) 0:40; STL Fortin (holding) 4:41; STL Picard (roughing) 4:41; STL Ecclestone (roughing) 4:41; BOS Orr (roughing) 4:41; BOS McKenzie (roughing) 4:41; BOS McKenzie (slashing) 7:13; STL Picard (interference) 8:07; BOS Stanfield (high-sticking) 12:58; BOS Awrey (charging) 16:04; STL Boudrias (roughing) 18:36; BOS Stanfield (roughing) 18:36.

SECOND PERIOD
3. STL Sabourin (St. Marseille) 3:22.
4. BOS Esposito (Hodge) 14:22.
Penalties: BOS Sanderson (elbowing) 4:21; STL Berenson (hooking) 6:32; BOS McKenzie (slashing) 11:55; BOS D. Smith (interference) 18:52.

THIRD PERIOD
5. STL Keenan (Goyette, Roberts) 0:19 (PP).
6. BOS Bucyk (McKenzie, R. Smith) 13:28.
Penalties: STL Fortin (holding) 6:15; BOS Esposito (roughing) 6:15; STL Bob Plager (tripping) 8:25.

FIRST OVERTIME PERIOD
7. BOS Orr (Sanderson) 0:40.
No penalties.

SHOTS ON GOAL:
BOS	10	8	13	1	**32**
STL	14	7	10	0	**31**

Goalies: BOS Cheevers; STL Hall
Referee: Bruce Hood
Linesmen: Matt Pavelich, Ron Ego

The other one was the game in which we won the Stanley Cup for Boston in 1970. Those are the two games out of many hundreds that have meant the most to me.

I suppose every player remembers his first NHL game, how nervous he was, and a lot of the things that happened. As for the Stanley Cup winner, I wish every player could have that experience because there's nothing like it. There's no thrill to match that.

Everybody knows how much was made of it when I first reported to the Boston Bruins in 1966. I was only 18 and a lot was expected of me. I know I was nervous before the first game, but once I got on the ice it started to wear off. We played the Detroit Red Wings in Boston Garden [Oct. 19, 1966] and, of course, I was awed, especially by Gordie Howe. I guess you could say he introduced me to the National Hockey League. I took the puck around behind the net and when I made the turn I passed off. Instead of keeping my head up, I was admiring my pretty pass when Gordie hit me. He gave me a good jolt. I don't remember if he said anything, but he got the message across.

I picked up my first point in that game. The funny thing about it was that afterwards everybody said I'd made a beautiful pass when actually I fanned on a shot and the puck went over to Johnny McKenzie, who scored a goal. It was my first assist.

That's the first game I'll never forget. The other one was the last game of the Stanley Cup finals in 1970. The 1969–70 season was the beginning of our best years in Boston. We finished second during the regular season behind Chicago in our division, but we won a lot of games [40–17–9] and gained the confidence we needed to win the Stanley Cup.

As it turned out, the first playoff series was the toughest. We got a battle from the New York Rangers, but we took the series in six games, winning the final one in Madison Square Garden. We expected just as tough a second round from the Chicago Blackhawks.

They had Bobby Hull, Stan Mikita and one of the best goaltenders in hockey in Tony Esposito. But Ed Westfall did an incredible job of shadowing Hull in that series. I don't think Bobby got off six shots in the first three games. We got a tremendous effort out of everyone on our team and we swept the Blackhawks to go into the finals.

The St. Louis Blues were our opponents and we were heavily favored to win the series. We didn't have any doubt that we could beat them, but you can never be sure of anything in hockey. There was always the chance of an upset and you can't afford to take anyone lightly. Fortunately, we were all keyed up. We wanted that Cup in the worst way, both for ourselves and for our fans. The Bruins hadn't won the Cup since 1941, long before I was born, and the fans had supported them loyally through some hard years. They deserved a winner. I know they were always good to me.

Most of all, we wanted to win the Cup on our own ice. I'm glad it worked out that way, that our fans got to see us win at home. The Blues gave us a battle in the first three games, largely because of the way old Glenn Hall played goal for them. He was outstanding, but in each of the first three games, we wore him down. We had the shooters: Phil Esposito, Johnny Bucyk, Ken Hodge, Derek Sanderson, John McKenzie and the rest.

We went into the fourth game [Sunday afternoon, May 10, 1970] with a chance to win the Cup in front of our own fans, but the Blues refused to buckle easily. They gave us a fight. They might lose, but they were determined to make us earn our victory.

Rick Smith scored the first goal for us, on a shot from the point, early in the first period. That set our fans off to roaring, but the Blues, checking us tightly, didn't buckle. Late in the period, Red Berenson scored a goal to tie the game 1–1.

Early in the second period, the Blues took a 2–1 lead. I think Gary Sabourin scored a goal for them. We kept putting on the pressure, but Hall was having a good day, and it wasn't until most of the period was gone that Phil Esposito scored to tie it, 2–2.

You've got to give St. Louis credit. They could have died right there but they didn't.

I got off a shot just as a defenseman tripped me up with his stick. I was flying through the air—I thought I was going to leave the rink— when the puck hit behind Hall in the cage.

They got a goal from a young kid, Larry Keenan, in the first minute of that third period to take a 3–2 lead. It was beginning to look like this wasn't going to be our day.

We went 12 minutes without being able to tie the game. Then, with seven minutes left in the game, Bucyk got a pass along the boards from McKenzie and fired a shot that got past Hall to tie the game 3–3. That fired us up, but we couldn't get the game-winner. The clock ran out to send the game into overtime.

When the overtime period started, Sanderson won a face-off and got the puck back to me on our blue line. I gave the puck back to him as he took off along the boards, and headed for the net myself. It was a give-and-go, and I flew into the Blues' zone, cut around a defender and took the return pass from Sanderson. I got off a shot just as a defenseman tripped me up with his stick. I was

flying through the air—I thought I was going to leave the rink when the puck hit behind Hall in the cage. We'd won the Stanley Cup.

I don't remember having many happier moments than the one when I saw Bucyk skate around the Garden holding the Stanley Cup high so all the fans could see it. Then the parade, the fans, the excitement, the sheer joy of winning the greatest prize in hockey. It wasn't me who scored the winning goal. It was the whole team. The credit belongs to all the guys I play with, unbelievable guys.

We won the Stanley Cup again two years later, and that was great. But the first one, that was the one that gave me the greatest thrill. That and my first game in the National Hockey League.

—As told to George Vass

Bobby Orr rewrote the book on playing defense in the NHL. Winner of the 1967 Calder Trophy, Orr won eight consecutive Norris Trophies and First All-Star Team nominations. He also won two scoring titles, in 1970 and 1975, and earned the Conn Smythe Trophy both times when the Bruins won the Stanley Cup in 1970 and 1972. He left Boston for Chicago as a free agent in June 1976 but knee injuries soon ended his career. Despite taking off the entire 1977–78 season, Orr retired after only six games the following season.

JOEL OTTO

APRIL 15, 1989

Some guys can remember the smallest details of the games they played years ago. I have trouble remembering things from a

game I played last week. So the fact that I remember anything about the overtime goal I scored in the first round of the 1989 playoffs demonstrates that it was quite a game. It was the seventh game of the series, and it lifted us, the Calgary Flames, past the Vancouver Canucks. It was a game even I could never forget.

We'd had a great regular season that year. We finished with a league-high 117 points and outscored our opponents by more than a hundred goals overall. Our team was deep. Our first line was Doug Gilmour, Joe Mullen and Colin Patterson. Doug was just coming into his own at that point, and Mullen would finish with more than 100 points. Our second line was Joe Nieuwendyk, Hakan Loob and Gary Roberts. Nieuwendyk scored more than 50 goals that season. In fact, we were so talented that Theo Fleury was on the fourth line, if you can imagine that.

I centered the third line. Jim "Pepper" Peplinski and I played with Mark Hunter for a while, until he got hurt. We also had Lanny McDonald, Brian MacLellan, Jiri Hrdina and Tim Hunter playing with us at different times during the season. On defense, we had guys like Al MacInnis, Gary Suter, Brad McCrimmon, Jamie Macoun and Rob Ramage. And, of course, Mike Vernon was our goalie.

Since we had so many great scorers, we left the job of putting the puck in the net up to them. Pepper and I considered ourselves the checkers. We contributed our fair share of goals, but our primary job was to go out and bang and get the puck into the corners. Since we'd had such a great regular season and had so much depth at every position, we were big-time favorites to beat Vancouver in the Smythe Division semifinals.

It didn't go quite as easily as we had hoped. The Canucks didn't have much to lose, and they played like it. They were loose—they played without the fear of losing a lot of teams have—and they battled us

tooth and nail. They won one of the first two games in our building: in overtime. We managed to come back and take the lead in the series, but they won Game 6 to set up a seventh and deciding game in our building.

Going into the game, the pressure was just enormous. We had been such big favorites going into the series. I remember being nervous. You might be surprised that NHL players get nervous, but even Wayne Gretzky would have been nervous if he were in our situation. Of course, I don't remember many of the details of the game. The biggest thing was Vernon—he made at least four or five incredible saves. Without Vernon, we would have been toast. He made a glove save on Greg Adams. He made a toe save on Petri Skriko. He stopped Stan Smyl on a breakaway. At one point, I was sitting on the end of the bench with our backup goalie, Rick Wamsley. We just looked at each other after one of the saves, rolled our eyes, and said, "Oh, my god."

When I spun around, the puck hit off my skate and went past Vancouver goalie Kirk McLean. I turned around and went nuts.

I can't even tell you who scored late in the game, but the goal tied the game at 3–3 and sent it into overtime. Going into overtime, the pressure got even worse. I remember sitting there saying to myself, "Oh, goodness—I can't imagine losing." Luckily, it didn't happen.

On one shift in the first overtime, we came down the ice into their zone. Loob was on the wing with Peplinski and I on that particular shift. Pepper went wide with the puck, so I went to the net like players are taught since they're little kids. The Canucks had had so many chances that we just wanted to get the puck to the net at that point, not make the pretty play.

I was trying to get position in the slot. Doug Lidster was cross-checking me in the back. The only reason I know that is because I have a picture of it. Pepper had centered the puck into the slot. I was so busy trying to elude the defense that I didn't even see it coming. When I spun around, the puck hit off my skate and went past Vancouver goalie Kirk McLean.

I turned around and went nuts. I don't know if the Canucks were protesting—I was too busy celebrating. It was an innocent play and the referee and linesmen knew it. I wish I could tell my grandchildren it was a beautiful goal, but it wasn't. It wasn't a pretty goal at all. What I can tell them is that it won the game and the series for us.

I was more relieved than excited at that point. The goal set us in the right direction. We had dodged a big bullet, and we never looked back after that. We went through the next three rounds and eventually won the Stanley Cup. Gilmour scored an empty-netter in the last game of the finals against the Montreal Canadiens. It was a great feeling to know that we had come so close to losing, but that we were still going to win.

—As told to Chuck O'Donnell

Joel Otto, shown squeezing Montreal's Bobby Smith out of the play, above, made his NHL debut with the Calgary Flames in 1984–85. At six-feet, four-inches and 220 pounds, his physical presence contributed to the Flames' 1989 Stanley Cup victory. Philadelphia signed Otto as a free agent in September 1995. He took one last trip to the Cup finals with the Flyers in 1997 and retired after the 1997–98 season.

CZECH MATE

Vezina- and Hart Trophy-winner Dominik Hasek elevated his stellar game to an even higher level at the 1998 Olympic Games. While teams from Canada and the USA included NHL players exclusively, almost half the team from the Czech Republic had never played in North America. With a defensive team system, however, and backstopped by "The Dominator," the Czechs grew stronger and stronger as the tournament progressed.

Due to Hasek's heroics, the Czechs defeated the USA (4–1) before meeting Canada in the semifinals. Hasek, with a one-goal lead, completely repelled the Canadian attack until the last minute of the third period. Team Canada's Trevor Linden finally got a puck by him, but Hasek was invincible against five Canadians in a tie-breaking shootout. The Czechs met Russia in the gold medal game. This time, Hasek (shown stopping "The Russian Rocket" Pavel Bure) was truly flawless, posting a shutout for a remarkable victory. A national hero, Hasek was celebrated by hundreds of thousands in Prague's central square before he returned to the NHL.

—*Chris McDonell*

FEBRUARY 22, 1998
NAGANO, JAPAN
CZECH REPUBLIC 1, RUSSIA 0

The first time is the best, and if there's a moment among the many high spots I've had as a goalie that I rate above the others,

MAY 19, 1974
PHILADELPHIA SPECTRUM, PHILADELPHIA
PHILADELPHIA 1, BOSTON 0

FIRST PERIOD
1. PHI MacLeish (Dupont) 14:48.
Penalties: PHI Dupont (interference) 0:32; PHI Clement (roughing) 10:18; PHI Cowick (elbowing) 10:18; BOS Forbes (roughing) 10:18; BOS O'Reilly (hooking) 13:58; PHI Clarke (roughing) 14:22; BOS Orr (roughing) 14:22.

SECOND PERIOD
No scoring.
Penalties: PHI Dupont (tripping) 0:40; BOS Hodge (hooking) 1:15; BOS Sims (cross-checking) 5:44; PHI Joe Watson (holding) 9:22; PHI Joe Watson (tripping) 15:02; BOS Vadnais (tripping) 17:46.

THIRD PERIOD
No scoring.
Penalties: BOS O'Reilly (hooking) 8:12; PHI Schultz (holding) 11:15; BOS Bucyk (tripping) 14:54; BOS Orr (holding) 17:38.

SHOTS ON GOAL:

PHI	8	14	4	**26**
BOS	16	9	5	**30**

Goalies: PHI Parent; BOS Gilbert
Referee: Art Skov
Linesmen: Neil Armstrong, C. Bechard

it is the game that won the Stanley Cup for the Philadelphia Flyers in 1974.

Whenever I think of that game, I think of what went on before because a year earlier I had been playing in the World Hockey Association. The Flyers traded me to the Toronto Maple Leafs in the middle of the 1970–71 season. I really hated to leave because I'd grown to love Philadelphia. Besides, my wife Carol is from Cherry Hill, New Jersey, and all her family and friends lived in or around Philadelphia.

Then, in the summer of 1972 came the WHA with all the promise of big money. When you're a professional athlete, you have to listen. You've got a family to think about.

Right from the start, things went wrong with the Philadelphia Blazers, the WHA team. I broke a bone in my right foot almost at the beginning, and that was just the start of a confusing year. The team played at the most before 3,000 or 4,000 people. There were broken promises about money, and finally I decided I'd like to get back to the Flyers if I could, though my NHL contract belonged to Toronto.

In the summer of 1973, the Flyers made a deal with the Leafs to get me back. That made for one of the happiest days of my life. It also paved the way for Philadelphia's first Stanley Cup, and the game I'll never forget.

Not that the final game of the 1974 playoffs was the best game I ever played. That's hard to choose. I remember another playoff game in '68 against St. Louis that I consider to have been my sharpest. I made 63 saves that night, so I kept busy. If I remember right, we were trailing 1–0 in that game in the St. Louis Arena with just 15 seconds left in regulation when Andy Lacroix scored a goal for us to tie it.

The game went into the middle of the second overtime when Don Blackburn finally scored the winning goal for us. I was so worn out that I couldn't even hold a cup of water steady when the game was over.

The strange thing about it was that game, which tied the series 3–3, should have given us a shot in the arm, especially since we won it on St. Louis ice. Instead, we went home for the seventh game and were knocked out of the playoffs before our own crowd in Philadelphia. All the same, I can't ever remember playing a better game than that one. Those 63 shots! But it was the finish of the 1974 season, our first Stanley Cup, that was the most satisfying for me, as it probably was for all the Flyers.

We got off to a rocky start, but we soon put everything together in the early stages of the season and by Christmas of '73 we were really believing in ourselves. A big win near the end of the regular season, one that probably contributed to our winning the Cup later, was beating the Boston Bruins. Not only did the game clinch our division championship, but it was our first victory since '67 over the Bruins, who had either beaten or tied Philadelphia in 27 games.

We won the first round of the playoffs over Atlanta in four games, but had a rougher time against New York in the second round. We finally won it in seven games in our building, though it was only by a goal, 4–3.

Now we were up against Boston in the finals. They were tough then, with Bobby Orr, Phil Esposito and a gang of other good players riding high. They'd won the Cup before, so it figured to be an uphill battle for us. In fact, nobody really thought we'd beat Boston. Most of the press picked the Bruins to win the Cup in five games. And they had the home ice advantage on us, the series opening with the first two games in Boston Garden.

What's more, they had rested a week after beating Chicago in six games, while we had to open the series on Tuesday after the seventh game against New York on Sunday. But we surprised them. We had a 3~2 edge in games coming home to the Spectrum for No. 6 and a good chance to win the Stanley Cup before our own fans, who had supported us so tremendously all season. Naturally, we had Kate Smith singing "God Bless America," because this was the game, of all games, that we most needed and wanted.

We knew what we had to do, and most of all it was to stop Orr, to wear him out any

> **We knew what we had to do, and most of all it was to stop Orr, to wear him out any way we could.... Orr was the heart of the Boston team.**

way we could, to give him a shot after he gave up the puck, to slow down his skating. Orr was the heart of the Boston team, the man who controlled play every minute he was on the ice, and it seemed like he was on it 40 minutes of the 60.

We got the only goal of the game in the first period. Rick MacLeish scored it, deflecting a power-play shot from the point by Moose Dupont. Gilles Gilbert, the Boston goalie, never had a chance to stop it. That one goal wasn't much to work with, but our defense gave me great protection, and we outskated Boston most of the night. The Bruins' best scoring chance came with about three minutes left. Kenny Hodge fired a slap shot at me from 30 feet and I was fortunate enough to get my stick on the puck and deflect it.

Our big break came with just over two minutes left. Orr was caught holding Bobby Clarke and when he went off the ice we felt the Cup was in our grasp. All we had to do was hang on, protect that 1–0 lead, and the champagne would be flowing.

I'll never forget the explosion of sound in the Spectrum when time ran out, and the swarm of fans who poured onto the ice. It was so jammed that Clarke and I, who were to carry the Cup around the ice, had to give up. But the Cup was ours. We'd won it, and we won it again the next year. But the first time, that's something special; and that's a game I'll never forget.

—*As told to George Vass*

Bernie Parent, who played part of two seasons with the Boston Bruins, joined the Philadelphia Flyers for the franchise's inaugural season in 1967–68. Traded to Toronto in 1971, he sharpened his game under the tutelage of his goaltending partner Jacques Plante. After spending 1972–73 in the WHA, Parent returned to the Flyers and promptly won two Vezina Trophies, two Conn Smythe Trophies and two Stanley Cup rings. He retired in 1979 after sustaining a major eye injury.

BARCLAY PLAGER

GAME 7, 1968
STANLEY CUP SEMIFINALS

There's no game that sticks out more clearly for me than the seventh game of the Stanley Cup semifinals in 1968, a game

MAY 3, 1968
ST. LOUIS ARENA, ST. LOUIS
ST. LOUIS 2, MINNESOTA 1 (2OT)

FIRST PERIOD
No scoring.
Penalties: MIN J.P. Parise (high-sticking) 5:43; STL Picard (holding) 5:43; STL Bob Plager (high-sticking) 5:43; MIN Woytowich (holding) 10:27.

SECOND PERIOD
No scoring.
Penalties: MIN Balon (high-sticking) 8:41; STL Sabourin (hooking) 18:30.

THIRD PERIOD
1. MIN McKechnie (McCord) 16:49.
2. STL Moore (Keenan, Barclay Plager) 17:20.
No penalties.

FIRST OVERTIME PERIOD
No scoring.
No penalties.

SECOND OVERTIME PERIOD
3. STL Schock (Melnyk, McCreary) 2:50.
No penalties.

SHOTS ON GOAL:

STL	5	6	12	10	5	**38**
MIN	10	9	11	14	1	**45**

Goalies: STL Hall; MIN Maniago
Referee: Art Skov
Linesmen: Neil Armstrong, Pat Shetler

against the Minnesota North Stars that put us into the finals against the Montreal Canadiens. It wasn't just the game itself that was memorable for me, but all that led up to it that year, the first season of expansion in which the National Hockey League had gone from six teams to 12. It was sort of a turning point in hockey as well as in my career.

Like a lot of other young players at that time, I spent years in the minors waiting for a chance to get into the NHL. With six teams, there weren't as many opportunities then as there are now. I started the 1967–68 season playing for Buffalo, which at the time was in the American Hockey League. I had hopes that the New York Rangers, who owned my contract, might call me up soon. It didn't quite happen that way, but it worked out well in any case.

In November, I was traded along with Red Berenson to the St. Louis Blues by the Rangers for Ron Stewart and Ron Attwell. I was really glad. For one thing, my brother Bobby already was with the Blues, and so was Jimmy Roberts, with whom I'd played in junior and minor professional. Noel Picard, too, was a good friend on the Blues. I'd played for coach Scotty Bowman six years previous to that.

When I got there in November, the Blues were struggling. But in mid-season, there were a lot of changes and they began to bring in some veteran players with great records: Dickie Moore, Jean-Guy Talbot, Al Arbour and some others. Some of these players had been with the Montreal Canadiens and they knew how to win. They set the tone for our team and we began to pick up.

Philadelphia finished first in the West that year, Los Angeles second, the Blues third and Minnesota fourth. That put us up against Philadelphia in the first round, and nobody gave us much of a chance. We beat them only one game during the regular season and we played them 10 times. You could say then

that winning the quarterfinal series against the Flyers was a surprise. And we could have won it in six games. We were leading, 1–0, in the sixth game on our own ice with 20 seconds to go. Philadelphia pulled its goalie and scored the tying goal, then went on to win in overtime.

The series went back to Philadelphia for a seventh game, in a rink in which we hadn't won all year. This time we won. We were ahead, 2–1, in the final seconds when the Flyers again pulled their goalie. Berenson won a face-off in the Flyer zone and put the puck into an open net to make sure.

That win put us into the semifinals against Minnesota, which won two of the first three games, then was leading 3–0 in the fourth game midway through the third period. Somehow, we came back. Roberts scored the tying goal for us with 11 seconds left after we pulled our goalie, Glenn Hall. In overtime, Gary Sabourin scored the winning goal for us and we were even with the North Stars at two wins apiece, rather than being down 3–1 as it looked like we were going to be.

It came down to a seventh game, the one I'll never forget, in St. Louis. It had been a tough, bruising series, but we felt pretty good about the situation. We'd had some exceptional play from our veterans, who had a lot of playoff experience. Doug Harvey joined us midway in the playoffs from Kansas City, where he had been coaching and playing. He was 43, but he could still play. Just watching him was a hockey education. He set the tone.

During the season, the crowds hadn't been too big in our rink. But as the playoffs progressed, they began to build up. For that seventh game against Minnesota, they had the biggest crowd ever to see a hockey game in St. Louis up to that time. They were singing and cheering and it made chills run up and down my spine.

It couldn't have been a tighter game. Both teams played like they knew they were one step away from getting into the finals against the Canadiens. You wait for the other team to make the mistake. Nobody made one, not until there was less than four minutes to go in regulation time. Then it was me who made it.

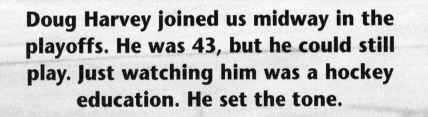

Doug Harvey joined us midway in the playoffs. He was 43, but he could still play. Just watching him was a hockey education. He set the tone.

The score was 0–0 when Walt McKechnie of Minnesota flipped the puck to one of his players just as I was charging into the man. I happened to get my stick on the puck and, bang, I put it in our own net to make it 1–0 for Minnesota. I could have killed myself. I was wishing the ice would melt and swallow me. It looked like I had put us out of the playoffs.

Luckily, 30 seconds later, Dickie Moore scored the tying goal for us and the game went into overtime. I was still kicking myself, thinking we could have won it 1–0 except for my mistake. At a time like that, to put in a goal for the other team! I had to think about that all of the first overtime, and into the second before Ronnie Schock scored

the winning goal for us to beat Minnesota, 2–1, and put us into the finals.

Realistically, I suppose, we knew we didn't have much of a chance against the Canadiens in the finals, but we did give them a battle. They beat us in four games, but one of the games went into overtime and in each one the margin was only one goal. What's more, our goalie, Glenn Hall, won the Conn Smythe Trophy for being the most valuable player in the playoffs. He was outstanding. Still, what I remember most about the playoffs that first year in the NHL is the goal I put in for the other team. I'm just glad we won the game I'll never forget.

—*As told to George Vass*

Assisting his goaltender Ernie Wakely, defenseman **Barclay Plager**, above left, stretches to help foil New York Ranger Brad Park. Plager played his entire NHL career for the St. Louis Blues, between 1967–68 and 1976–77. His brothers Bob and Bill both played with him for several years with the Blues. Team captain for almost six seasons, Plager saw his No. 8 retired in 1982. He was diagnosed with cancer while serving the team as an assistant coach and died in 1988.

JACQUES PLANTE

Never have I been so nervous as I was the night of March 20, 1960, in the old Madison Square Garden in New York. No,

it was not a Stanley Cup game. It was the last game of the regular season.

We Montreal Canadiens had already clinched first place, so the game didn't mean anything to us or to the New York Rangers. What made me nervous was that I was going after my fifth Vezina Trophy in a row in this last game. Nobody had ever done that before. Bill Durnan of Montreal had won four in a row in the 1940s and everybody thought that would stand forever as a record. Toe Blake, our coach, kept telling us before the game, "Jacques says Durnan won it four times and he's got a chance to make it five. If he does, I don't think anybody is ever going to match it or beat it."

Blake turned to me and said, "I hope you can break the record. Durnan was a big friend of mine but I've got to say that winning the Vezina in our day and age is much tougher than it was in his time because of the slap shot and the longer schedule. The season was 50 games long when Durnan played and with 70 like we have now there is more pressure. The slap shot was just starting when Durnan played. What you're doing is much tougher."

Blake told me all these things before this game in which I was going for my fifth Vezina. I kept thinking about Glenn Hall, who was playing for Chicago that year. We were tied for least goals going into the last game and Glenn was playing at Boston that same night. I knew that Glenn never allowed more than two goals in a game in Boston and that I always had trouble in New York.

All the time I was playing, I was waiting for the results from Boston. I played pretty well the first period, though, although the Rangers scored on me. Andy Bathgate put in a backhander from a short distance and I don't think I could blame myself on that one. That made it 1–0 in New York's favor after one period. When we went down for the intermission, we got the score from Boston. It was 1–1 there, which meant Glenn

and I were still tied for the Vezina.

I got through the second period all right and it was still 1–0. But we hadn't heard yet from Boston. I was trying not to let the pressure get to me but I could feel it building up. It was as if I could not move.

Just after the third period opened, Maurice Richard put in a goal for us and that made it 1–1. It was fine that we could tie the game. You always want to win, but it was the goals against us, not the goals for us, that were important that night. A few minutes later Brian Cullen of the Rangers got in on me and snapped a wrist shot. I reached out for it with my glove but missed it and it went in. That made it 2–1. I could not believe I had not stopped the shot. I could feel the Vezina chances disappearing.

There was a little more than seven minutes left in the game when Bathgate took a slap shot just 15 feet away. I had a clear view of the shot and it was on the glove side. I raised my glove but the puck went just over it into the left corner. I was too tense and I couldn't move. I know that normally I could have picked up two of the shots that went for goals with my bare hand, but that day I just froze on the shots. This was a game that I felt as much pressure as I could stand.

As soon as the third New York goal went in, I said to myself, "Well, there goes the Vezina. There's no way that Glenn can have more than two goals scored against him in Boston." I was just thinking this when there was a stoppage of play and one of my teammates came to me from the bench. "Hey, Boston and Chicago are tied 4–4," he said.

I could not believe it. That meant I was ahead of Hall by one goal. Bobby Hull of the Blackhawks and Bronco Horvath of Boston were fighting for the scoring championship that year. Chicago went all out offensively to give Bobby the chance to win the championship so they left Glenn un-protected. I did not know this until later, but I got through the rest of the game in New York without being scored on again. Our game ended 3–1 and the Boston-Chicago game ended 5–5. I won the Vezina by two goals over Glenn. Hull won the scoring title over Horvath.

MARCH 20, 1960
MADISON SQUARE GARDEN, NEW YORK
NEW YORK RANGERS 3, MONTREAL 1

FIRST PERIOD
1. NYR Bathgate (Prentice, Hebenton) 17:25.
Penalty: NYR Fontinato (charging) 13:42.

SECOND PERIOD
No scoring.
Penalties: MON Turner (tripping) 2:58; MON Pronovost (hooking) 8:43; MON Hicke (high-sticking) 17:22; NYR Fontinato (high-sticking) 17:22.

THIRD PERIOD
2. MON M. Richard (H. Richard, Moore) 1:17.
3. NYR Cullen (Bathgate) 5:00.
4. NYR Bathgate (Prentice, Cullen) 12:44.
Penalties: MON Talbot (slashing) 13:18; NYR Fontinato (misconduct) 13:18.

Goalies: NYR Rollins; MON Plante
Referee: Vern Buffey
Linesmen: Bill Morrison, George Hayes

> **I know that normally I could have picked up two of the shots that went for goals with my bare hand, but that day I just froze on the shots.**

The $1,000 that I got for the Vezina was not important. Just the honor, that you've won something, meant so much to me. When I was a youngster all I wanted to do was play one game for the big team, Montreal. I never thought of contending for the trophy and here I had won my fifth Vezina in a row, a record.

Even now, I think about the second one I won, in 1957, because of what was written in the papers. Going into the second last game of the season, I was two goals behind Glenn Hall, Detroit's goaltender at the time. He won 5–3 for Detroit at Toronto while I passed him by shutting out Chicago 3–0 in Montreal. The next night, after I had won the Vezina, I read in the papers, "Jacques Plante won his second Vezina, but there is no way he can come close to Durnan's record of four in a row. He has asthma, isn't strong enough and won't play in the league long enough to come close to Durnan's mark." I look back and laugh. I am still here, playing, 15 years later.

—*As told to George Vass*

Jacques Plante won his first of six Stanley Cup rings with the Canadiens as a 1952–53 rookie. He played barefaced until finally negotiating the right to don a mask in 1959. Plante also won six Vezina Trophies and the 1962 Hart Trophy with Montreal but was traded to New York in June 1963. He retired in 1965 but returned in 1968–69 to star for St. Louis, when he shared the Vezina Trophy with Glenn Hall. Plante made 1971's Second All-Star Team as a Maple Leaf and concluded his NHL career with Boston in 1973.

Anyone who has played in the NHL as long as I did is going to have a trunk full of memories and certainly more than one

MARCH 22, 1979
MONTREAL FORUM, MONTREAL
NEW YORK ISLANDERS 5, MONTREAL 3

FIRST PERIOD
1. NYI Bossy (Persson, Tonelli) 1:40.
2. MON Lemaire (Lapointe, Napier) 11:27 (PP).
3. NYI Price (Trottier) 12:33.
4. NYI Henning (Harris, Potvin) 17:42.
Penalties: MON Langway 2:12; NYI Gillies 2:33; NYI Persson 9:34.

SECOND PERIOD
5. MON Tremblay (Gainey, Jarvis) 3:38.
6. MON Lemaire (Engblom) 8:12.
7. NYI Potvin (Gillies, Kaszycki) 10:09.
No penalties.

THIRD PERIOD
8. NYI Bourne (unassisted) 17:33.
No penalties.

SHOTS ON GOAL:

NYI	7	9	14	**30**
MON	8	15	10	**33**

Goalies: NYI Resch; MON Dryden

game that stands out as special. It's no secret that every one of us who has taken up professional hockey as a vocation has one primary goal in mind, and that is to win the Stanley Cup. Naturally, the game in which my team, the New York Islanders, won its first championship in 1980 remains indelible in my mind, from Bobby Nystrom's winning goal in overtime to Bill Smith's huge saves in the third period after Philadelphia stormed back to tie the score.

As wonderful as those games were, the most memorable game for me took place a year before we actually won our first Stanley Cup. It happened at the Forum in Montreal; that, for me, has always been the cathedral of hockey. The special aura of a Montreal Canadiens home game can never be duplicated anywhere else, because the Forum is the oldest NHL arena and because the Habs have such a rich tradition of winning Stanley Cups.

Perhaps because I'm a French Canadian from Hull, Quebec, the Forum and the Canadiens meant even more to me than other players who were not as steeped in the Montreal lore. Whatever the case, I had not been very successful whenever the Islanders played there, and this was a source of annoyance to me. It didn't help that the Habs had beaten us in the 1976 and 1977 playoffs. But our club had been getting progressively better by the year.

We had made the playoffs for the first time in 1975 and repeated in 1976, 1977 and 1978. Starting in 1976, the Canadiens were playing fantastic hockey and—with guys like Ken Dryden, Guy Lafleur and Bob Gainey—had won the Cup four straight seasons. But by 1978, we had become a formidable team. Even though Toronto beat us in a seven-game playoff, there was no question that we would be heard from for some time. We had players like Mike Bossy, Bryan Trottier, Clark Gillies, Morrow and Nystrom, as well as Al Arbour behind the bench.

But I have to add that this and the other accomplishments that followed might never have happened had I not come through an earlier episode that could have torpedoed my career before it had ever started.

This was in my rookie year with the Islanders, 1972–73. I was general manager Bill Torrey's first draft pick, and I came to the club with a fair amount of fanfare, so it was no secret that the spotlight was on me. Everything had gone along pretty well until a Sunday morning in December following a home game against the Blackhawks. I knew we had a game at the Spectrum in Philadelphia the following night, and I was aware that our team bus was to leave from the Coliseum at 10 a.m. for the ride to Philly. Unfortunately, my alarm didn't go off—or if it did, I didn't hear it—and the first sound I heard was at 9:50 as the telephone nearly rang off the hook. I finally picked it up and heard Nystrom's voice at the other end, "Denis, where the heck are you?"

He told me that Arbour was pacing the aisle of the bus and was going to give the signal to the driver pretty soon. "Tell him I'll be outta here in a minute," I shouted, and hung up. I threw on my clothes, jumped in my car—it was snowing and the highway was wet—and sped to the Coliseum. My luck, there was a red light at the last crossing, and that hurt. When I finally got to the parking lot, the radio blared, "WINS news time, 10:06." But the bus was gone.

I dashed down to the dressing room but no one was there, so I returned to the parking lot and tried to get hold of myself. It was snowing hard. I debated whether I should drive to Philly but decided against it. We were in a fuel crisis, gas was impossible to obtain, and my tank already was close to empty—just enough to get me home.

I got back to my apartment, took off my wet clothes, and tried to figure out what to do next. If I had been thinking clearly I might have tried to get to Manhattan and grab the train to Philly, but my head was too clouded at the time, so I sat in my living room and waited.

It wasn't until six o'clock that the phone rang. It was my brother Jean, at the time an Islanders defenseman, and he was calling from the Spectrum. Arbour was right there,

The first sound I heard was at 9:50 as the telephone nearly rang off the hook. I finally picked it up and heard Bobby Nystrom's voice at the other end, "Denis, where the heck are you?"

and I explained the story. "Okay," said Al, "just stay there and don't move out of your house tonight. Be at practice at 10:00 tomorrow."

The Islanders lost 4–0 at Philadelphia that night, and soon after the reporters were calling me. The next day's headlines really hurt: "Potvin, Game Were Lost" and "A Sad Story By AWOL Potvin."

By Monday morning, I was the most humiliated athlete in the world. I showed up in the dressing room, and eventually Arbour walked in and strolled past me without even a hello. A few minutes later, the trainer told me to get on the ice, and eventually Al put me through a grueling series of stops and starts. Soon the players arrived, and then Bill Torrey told me he'd have to fine me and that

I'd have to apologize to my teammates.

So, 48 hours after the incident, I told my pals that I had goofed, I was sorry and that it would never happen again. Our captain, Eddie Westfall smiled and said, "Next time Baby Bear won't hibernate in his house." The guys laughed, and from then on everything was okay.

At that point in time, the incident could have had a detrimental effect on my career. I was only 18, and conceivably I could have been ruined by the episode. In retrospect, I still get upset. After all, they could have waited a few more minutes. But, as the old saying goes—all's well that ends well.

—As told to Stan Fischler

Denis Potvin played his entire 15-season Hall of Fame career with the New York Islanders. The first pick in the 1973 amateur draft, he didn't disappoint and won the 1974 Calder Trophy. A premier playmaker with a hard shot, and a devastating body checker, Potvin won the Norris Trophy three times. He captained the Islanders to four consecutive Stanley Cup victories in the early 1980s and entered the Hall of Fame in 1990.

It is very difficult to choose one game out of so many when you have played 18 seasons in the National Hockey League and

MAY 3, 1979
BOSTON GARDEN, BOSTON
BOSTON 4, MONTREAL 3 (OT)

FIRST PERIOD
1. BOS Ratelle (O'Reilly) 15:15.
2. MON Mondou (Lapointe) 18:59 (PP).
Penalties: MON Robinson (high-sticking) 5:59;
BOS Milbury (high-sticking) 5:59; BOS O'Reilly
(roughing) 18:13.

SECOND PERIOD
3. MON Lafleur (Engblom) 7:58.
4. BOS Ratelle (Schmautz, Marcotte) 13:21.
Penalty: MON Jarvis (interference) 4:52.

THIRD PERIOD
5. BOS McNab (O'Reilly) 16:18.
6. MON Lapointe (Napier, Gainey) 17:54.
No penalties.

FIRST OVERTIME PERIOD
7. BOS Ratelle (Middleton, Smith) 3:46.
No penalties.

SHOTS ON GOAL:

BOS	8	6	15	3	**32**
MON	13	6	5	0	**24**

Goalies: BOS Gilbert; MON Dryden
Referee: Wally Harris
Linesmen: Claude Bechard, Jim Christison

to say that game is the most memorable. It is something I have to think about.

In the 13 years that I played for the New York Rangers, there certainly were many games that were outstanding for the team and myself. In the early years the team did not do so well, but, in the early 1970s, we had an outstanding team. I was particularly fortunate to play on a line with Rod Gilbert and Vic Hadfield. They made the game particularly enjoyable for me because we fit together so well.

I recall being greatly encouraged in 1967 when I scored three goals for the first time. That hat trick came not long after I had undergone spinal fusion surgery. Back problems had kept me from playing much of the previous season. After the operation, I naturally wondered if I would be able to play without pain and well again.

My doubts were eased early in 1967–68. I believe I got three goals in a span of less than five minutes against the Toronto Maple Leafs, which helped to restore my confidence. And so much of goal-scoring and playing hockey in general depends on confidence. That hat trick somehow made up for all the time I lost with my bad back. I would say it was to me what a Pulitzer Prize is to a reporter.

I had many enjoyable seasons at New York. My only regret was that we could not win the Stanley Cup, especially when we came so close when we lost to Boston in the finals in 1972. I would have been happy to continue with the Rangers and finish my career with them, if it had not been for the trade to Boston early in the 1975–76 season.

At the time, the trade was a terrible shock for me. I did not really want to leave New York. It was something to think about at the age of 35. And it was the first time I had been traded. Trades are part of a professional athlete's life, but the transition requires some adjustment. It took me some time to make a decision, to talk matters over with my wife Nancy and my lawyer, before agreeing to stay with the Bruins.

As it happened, one of the earliest games I played for Boston was against the Rangers in Madison Square Garden [November 26, 1975]. It was a strange feeling to be in another uniform, playing against the team for which you had been playing for so long, in the rink that you considered home. I believe I scored a goal and got an assist as the Bruins beat the Rangers. If I remember correctly, it was a game that also was memorable in another way, being the last game Bobby Orr played for Boston.

It took me a while to get over the worry, the uncertainty, after the trade to Boston. The biggest help was that I became convinced that I was wanted and needed by the Bruins. As it turned out, that trade was the biggest break of my career. If I had stayed in New York, I wouldn't be playing hockey. I would have retired long ago. Becoming a Bruin gave me a new lease on hockey life.

The style of play of the Bruins under, first, coach Don Cherry and Fred Creighton kept hockey enjoyable for me. Enjoyment of what you're doing is important. I enjoy playing hockey very much but the pleasure is relative to the caliber of the team. The Bruins have been a good team in the years I've been with them, making it easier for me to play as well as I like to. If you are on a team that's not doing well, the pressure is so much greater that it takes the fun out of playing. And as you get older, there has to be fun in hockey.

I have been fortunate, and since I have been with Boston, there have been many great games. As I said, it is extremely difficult to choose one of them above the rest. One that was most certainly outstanding from a personal point of view is the fourth game of the 1979 Stanley Cup semifinals against the Montreal Canadiens.

I really thought, as did all our other players, that we had a good chance to win the Stanley Cup that year. We had a good season and we were playing well going into the playoffs. We figured that the semifinal series would go seven games and that we would win. It was disappointing but not a surprise to us that we lost the first two games at Montreal. We knew we could come back at Boston in the next two games, and we did. We won the third game,

A hat trick is especially a thrill in Stanley Cup play, and even more so when the third goal wins the game in overtime.

2–1, and then evened the series in the fourth game, the one that was memorable to me.

I was fortunate enough to score the first goal, then another in the second period. That one tied the game, 2–2. We took a 3–2 lead late in the third period on a goal by Peter McNab, but you know how Montreal is. Just a minute later, Guy Lapointe scored a goal for them to send the game into overtime, tied 3–3. After almost four minutes of overtime, we took advantage of a two-on-one opportunity. I was moving into the slot when Rick Middleton gave me a pass right on my stick. I was in close and got the shot off so quickly that goaltender Ken Dryden had very little chance of stopping it.

That goal won the game, 4–3, to even the series at two games apiece. A hat trick is especially a thrill in Stanley Cup play, and even more so when the third goal wins the game in overtime. That was certainly a highlight of my career. It would have been even more satisfying if we could have gone on to defeat the Canadiens in the semifinals. We came very close to doing it, having them down several times. But they came back to win the seventh game and go on to win the Stanley Cup by beating New York in the finals.

There are many other games, of course, that are memorable. But most of all, I've always enjoyed hockey and still feel good about playing the game. As long as I feel that way and I can help the team, I hope to continue playing.

—As told to George Vass

Jean Ratelle played his first NHL games for the New York Rangers in 1960–61 but spent some time in the minors until the 1965–66 campaign. His apprenticeship served, Ratelle had matured into one of the NHL's most gentlemanly but effective scorers and playmakers. He hit personal bests with 46 goals and 63 assists in 1971–72, when he won the Lester Pearson Award. Traded to Boston in November 1975, he continued to produce until 1981, when he retired with 491 career goals. Ratelle entered the Hall of Fame in 1985.

I'll tell you, I have memories of many games, those I've played in and those I've coached, and it's a difficult job to choose

MAY 8, 1973
MONTREAL FORUM, MONTREAL
CHICAGO 8, MONTREAL 7

FIRST PERIOD
1. MON F. Mahovlich (unassisted) 2:47.
2. CHI Hull (Jarrett, Russell) 9:34.
3. CHI Mikita (Stapleton) 11:24.
4. MON P. Mahovlich
(F. Mahovlich, Robinson) 14:52 (PP).
Penalties: CHI J.P. Bordeleau (tripping) 12:52; CHI Pappin (misconduct) 15:17.

SECOND PERIOD
5. MON Larose (unassisted) 0:37.
6. CHI Kryskow (Backstrom, Maki) 3:10.
7. MON Larose (Wilson) 4:23.
8. CHI Mikita (Stapleton, Marks) 6:21.
9. MON Cournoyer (Lemaire, Lapointe) 7:09.
10. CHI Pappin (unassisted) 11:24.
11. CHI Frig (Mikita) 16:21 (PP).
12. CHI Pappin (Mikita, Hull) 19:03.
Penalty: MON Bouchard (interference) 15:14.

THIRD PERIOD
13. MON Savard (Wilson, Larose) 1:15.
14. CHI Angotti (White) 4:06.
15. MON Richard (F. Mahovlich) 11:43.
No penalties.

SHOTS ON GOAL:

CHI	11	11	7	**29**
MON	6	17	8	**31**

Goalies: CHI Esposito; MON Dryden
Referee: Bruce Hood
Linesmen: Neil Armstrong, Claude Bechard

one as standing above the others. During my playing days with Montreal, one game I'll never forget is the one in the 1953 Stanley Cup playoffs in which the Rocket [Maurice Richard] got the winning goal against Jimmy Henry of Boston with blood streaming down his eyes. That was one of the greatest individual efforts I ever saw.

I won't forget the seventh game of the finals in 1971. I was coaching the Blackhawks against Montreal and we led them 2–0 in our building when Jacques Lemaire scored from 70 feet and gave them life. They beat us 3–2 for the Cup.

There is one game that stands out, though, and that was against the Canadiens in the finals again two years later. Maybe it was not an artistic game, but it was amazing. I never thought I'd see a game like that.

We went into Montreal down 3–1 in the finals. They'd beaten us 4–0 in Chicago Sunday and couldn't have played better. Most of the people in the Montreal Forum Tuesday night came figuring this would be the last game, that the Canadiens would wrap up another Stanley Cup.

It figured to be a tight game. The two best goaltenders in hockey, Tony Esposito for us and Ken Dryden for Montreal, were playing. Both teams had good defensive records. And when you think about it, both goaltenders played well at times. They each made good saves, particularly in the first period. But things just built up.

When you go into a game like that, with so much depending on it, you're looking for the first goal. Most of the time, the team that gets the first goal wins. This time Montreal got the first goal. We made a mistake in our end. Later, defenseman Pat Stapleton admitted the puck had bounced over his stick. Whatever happened, Frank Mahovlich got to it and scored the first goal to put the Canadiens ahead, 1–0.

That "1" looks very big in the Forum against Montreal in the seventh game of the

finals. But we got a little lucky. Anyway, Dennis Hull let one fly from 50 feet out and Dryden got a shoulder on it. But not enough. The puck deflected off his shoulder into the net and it was 1–1.

Before the first period ended, Pete Mahovlich scored another goal for the Canadiens and we tied it up. Stan Mikita scored the goal to tie it 2–2, but it didn't come easily. Before he scored, Dryden made a couple of tremendous saves and Lou Angotti hit the post.

I was pretty pleased between periods. We were still in the game, we weren't disgracing ourselves. With a break or two, we could win. It figured to be tight, but I wasn't prepared for what happened in the second period.

It was a period of Stanley Cup hockey you couldn't believe. It was 20 minutes of wide open play, skating from one end to the other and it produced eight goals. I couldn't tell you now how they were scored or who scored them, except that Jim Pappin scored twice for us and Claude Larose twice for Montreal.

No, I'll take that back. I do remember that Yvan Cournoyer scored the fifth goal of that period to put Montreal ahead 5–4. I think it was his 14th goal of the playoffs, a record. Then we got three straight goals and I do remember Pappin's, the one that tied it 5–5. He had spent 10 minutes in the penalty box for bumping referee Bruce Hood and maybe the rest had done him good. Whatever the reason, he tore down the ice, faked out defenseman Serge Savard, who fell down with another Montreal defenseman tripping over him, and put a backhander past Dryden.

We got two more goals before the buzzer sounded and were leading 7–5 after two periods. Eight goals had been scored in the period, five for us, three for the Canadiens. It was probably the wildest period of playoff hockey ever. When you're a coach and see something like that, all you can do is hold your breath and hope the score comes out in your favor. It's not the kind of hockey you're looking for, but if it gives you the edge, you take it.

I'll tell you, that two-goal edge didn't look like much going into the last period. It didn't hold up long, either. With less than two

It was over, but I couldn't believe it. Still can't. How can you explain an 8–7 game—15 goals in a playoff game—with the two greatest goalies in hockey facing each other?

minutes gone, Montreal scored on a long screen shot by Savard and we were ahead just 7–6.

You're always concerned by a quick goal like that. It can pick a team up, give it momentum, and no team more than Montreal in the Forum, especially in a game that means the Stanley Cup. But we held them. All that season, our club had proved it could come back in key games and it still had something left. About three minutes after Savard's goal, Angotti scored for us on a shot that went between Dryden's legs, to make it 8–6.

There were still 15 minutes left in the game, so that seemed like next to no lead at all, especially the way things were going that night. And when Henri Richard scored for them to make it 8–7, well, I just held my breath.

It was still 8–7, though, with just a second or two left in the game. But the final face-off, with Montreal having pulled Dryden for an extra forward, was in our end. Luckily, Backstrom won the draw and sent the puck into the Canadiens zone to kill the clock.

It was over, but I couldn't believe it. Still can't. How can you explain an 8–7 game—15 goals in a playoff game—with the two greatest goalies in hockey facing each other? We lost the next game in Chicago and Montreal won the Stanley Cup, but that 8–7 game is the one that stands out for me. I never expected to see anything like it and I doubt if I ever will again.

—*As told to George Vass*

Billy Reay earned NHL respect as both a player and a coach. He played four games for Detroit before joining the Montreal Canadiens in 1945–46, when he won his first of two Stanley Cup rings. Reay became a playing coach in the Western Hockey League in 1953 and was back in the NHL behind the Toronto bench for two seasons in the late 1950s. He coached the Chicago Blackhawks from 1963–64 until 1976–77.

MARK RECCHI

**GAME 6, 1991
STANLEY CUP FINALS**

It's funny that a blowout game is the one I'll never forget, but it was the most exciting moment of my career. We were in

**MAY 25, 1991
MET SPORTS CENTER, BLOOMINGTON MN
PITTSBURGH 8, MINNESOTA 0**

FIRST PERIOD
1. PIT Samuelsson (Taglianetti, Trottier) 2:00 (PP).
2. PIT Lemieux (Murphy) 12:19 (SH).
3. PIT Mullen (Stevens, Taglianetti) 13:14 (PP).
Penalties: MIN Broten (interference) 0:09; MIN Johnson (high-sticking) 6:20; PIT Stevens (holding) 10:25; PIT Roberts (roughing) 10:59; MIN Modano (interference) 11:17; PIT Roberts (interference) 13:58; PIT Taglianetti (tripping) 17:35.

SECOND PERIOD
4. PIT Errey (Jagr, Lemieux) 13:15.
5. PIT Francis (Mullen) 14:28.
6. PIT Mullen (Stevens, Samuelsson) 18:44.
Penalties: PIT Samuelsson (roughing) 8:03; PIT Recchi (roughing) 8:03; MIN Tinordi (double minor roughing, served by Modano) 8:03; MIN Churla (roughing) 8:03; MIN McRae (misconduct) 8:03; MIN Gagner (roughing) 15:18.

THIRD PERIOD
7. PIT Paek (Lemieux) 1:19.
8. PIT Murphy (Lemieux) 13:45 (PP).
Penalties: MIN McRae (slashing) 12:27; PIT Stevens (slashing) 13:03; MIN Gavin (slashing),13:03.

SHOTS ON GOAL:

PIT	11	9	8	**28**
MIN	16	7	16	**39**

Goalies: PIT Barrasso; MIN Casey, Hayward
Referee: Don Koharski
Linesmen: Gord Broseker, Kevin Collins

Minnesota for the 1991 Stanley Cup finals. It was Game 6, we were leading the North Stars 3–2 and we knew we would have had to go home for Game 7 if we lost. So we wanted to end it there.

We got off to a really great start in the game. We scored three quick goals, and then we knew the Stanley Cup was going to be ours. We won easily, 8–0, and we couldn't wait for the game to get over. We wanted to get on with it and party. Personally, it wasn't my greatest game as far as goals and assists go, but really it was because winning the Stanley Cup is something you dream about for a long time. I had hurt my neck in the third period, so I was sitting there watching the clock, waiting. I was the countdown guy, and it was a long 10 minutes, I'll tell you that. I'd yell out very minute that came off the clock. We just couldn't wait for it to get over.

It was a lot of fun. The playoffs had been a war for two months, but when it was over we came out champions. It was such a great feeling to hold the Cup over your head out on the ice. That's why I want another chance. It's like a blur, it goes by so quickly. You're so excited and time races past. I want another chance to win it. I might be getting greedy because some guys don't get a chance to win it at all, but I'd like that chance again.

It was an outstanding feeling, but we were tired too. Everyone was worn out, but we still found the energy after it was all over. The pictures of me from those two months of the playoffs look like I was beaten up. I guess I was, too.

Having Bob Johnson as our coach was special. He never stopped coaching until the very last moment. We were up 7–0 or 8–0, and he was still back behind the bench coaching. I finally turned to him and said: "Bob, forget it. We did it." I don't think he could believe it. Winning the Cup was something he had dreamed of, and it was an outstanding feeling to see how excited he was because he had worked all his life for

this. It was a good memory of him, because he was so happy. Unfortunately, things happened to Bob later with cancer, but he finally got what he really wanted.

We finished 41–33–6 and beat the Rangers out for first place in the Patrick Division that year. We had a good team, but the playoffs are different. After we beat New Jersey in the first round, we really believed we could win it. We felt Jersey was going to be our toughest battle. Once we got by them, we felt we were ready to roll on. It was a matter of getting things in order. We just got better every round. And so did Mario Lemieux. Mario got better every series. Once he got a sniff of what was to come, he just took over.

In the first two series, he was there and

played well. He had been hurt in the first series against Jersey, but in the second series he really started to play well. Against Boston and Minnesota, he was the best. He showed he was the best player in the world. He just dominated like no one else. It was scary.

That was a special team, though. It was a lot like it is here in Philadelphia. We're getting that chemistry here. We're a lot younger than we were in Pittsburgh, but we have the same types of people, and I look for the same types of things here.

Chemistry is a very important part of the game—it can win a series for you. If you have a close bunch of guys, you can do a lot of things. After we won, we had a great time. Finally all the pressure was off. We celebrated

with the Cup, and it found its way into the swimming pool. It was great just being around the guys after the playoffs. It had been such a long haul that you could see the relief on everyone's face. Everyone started to get a little color back in their faces after two months. We were pale from being so drained.

We got our rings at the beginning of the next season, and that really brought it back again. I really want another crack at winning the Cup again.

—*As told to Phil Coffey*

Mark Recchi, above, hoists the Stanley Cup after Pittsburgh's 1991 Stanley Cup victory. The Penguins traded Recchi to Philadelphia in February 1992. He hit personal bests with the Flyers in 1992–93, tallying 53 goals and 70 assists. Traded to Montreal in February 1995, Recchi was returned to the Flyers late in the 1998–99 campaign. He led the league with 63 assists the next season, finishing third overall in scoring with 91 points.

CHICO RESCH

Whenever you think of the great games you've played in, 95 per cent of the time they're games that your team happened to

APRIL 26, 1975
CIVIC ARENA, PITTSBURGH
NEW YORK ISLANDERS 1, PITTSBURGH 0

FIRST PERIOD
No scoring.
Penalties: NYI Gillies (major) 2:44; PIT Paradise (major) 2:44; PIT Burrows 3:48; NYI Lewis 6:06; NYI Westfall 7:27; PIT Owchar 11:17; NYI Lewis (major) 17:25; PIT Kelly (major) 17:25; NYI St. Laurent 18:07; PIT Campbell 18:07; NYI Hart 20:00; PIT MacDonald 20:00.

SECOND PERIOD
No scoring.
Penalties: PIT Pronovost 1:11; NYI J. Potvin 3:11; PIT Arnason 15:35.

THIRD PERIOD
1. NYI Westfall (Marshall) 14:42.
Penalty: NYI Howatt 5:48.

SHOTS ON GOAL:

NYI	5	6	6	**17**
PIT	14	11	5	**30**

Goalies: NYI Resch; PIT Inness
Referee: Wally Harris
Linesmen: Neil Armstrong, Ray Scapinello

win. We've won a few with the New York Islanders in recent years but there's no doubt in my mind which was the most memorable game for me. The game that I'm thinking of is the seventh game of the Stanley Cup quarterfinals in 1975 against the Pittsburgh Penguins. It was the series in which we came from behind after losing the first three games to win the next four, something that hadn't been done in Stanley Cup play in more than 30 years.

I was a rookie, so that was an especially big game and series for me, but it was even bigger for the Islanders as an entire team. We were a relatively new team and lightly regarded, even though we'd beaten the Rangers in the best-of-three preliminary round. The victory over Pittsburgh, especially because of the way it came about, gave us a lot of confidence, it gave us a lot of credibility and it gave us a lot of following. By the latter I mean that we became a "Cinderella team" for the rest of the playoffs and the following season.

So I think the seventh game was the game that did the most for everybody concerned with the Islanders. It was the turning point for the franchise. That was the first year we made the playoffs and by showing not only that we could come back from being three games down, but by finishing it off by winning four straight, we came that extra step.

Billy Smith played goal for us at the start of the Pittsburgh series and he deserved to play. But we lost the first three games and our coach, Al Arbour, decided to make a change, not because Smitty wasn't playing well but maybe because he figured it might help pull our guys together in front of a rookie goalie. I don't suppose anyone thought we could win the series, being down three games to none. People had us pretty much written off, for which you could hardly blame them. But I remember Al saying, "You know, guys, there's a way to look at it that might help. If you look at it from the standpoint that you have to win the next four games in a row it seems insurmountable, but if

you think of it one period at a time, it doesn't seem that impossible."

He said this just before the first period of the fourth game and as it happened we won that one, 3–1. I was in goal and I think Pittsburgh got something like 35 shots against me but things went my way. The next game was at Pittsburgh and we won that one, too. Then we won one at home to even the series at 3–3. The games were close and I remember there was a feeling—you could just feel the guys surging. We took the approach Arbour suggested and it seemed to have an effect. Even after we won the first two, I felt really confident. It was just one of those times I felt that we were going all the way.

The seventh game was in Pittsburgh, which meant the advantage was with them. But we were so confident now that we didn't think that made much difference. The guys were playing the kind of game in front of me that a goalie needs. Pittsburgh was getting shots, but they weren't getting too many rebounds. I don't think I've ever seen our guys forecheck better than they did in that series, and the defensemen, too, were outstanding, especially Bert Marshall and Denis Potvin, who both had a great series.

Pittsburgh came right at us from the start of the seventh game and I remember a couple of things vividly from the first period. Syl Apps came down right in the slot, got off a good shot, and the puck hit me right in the mask. The puck rebounded off into the corner, then skidded to the point outside the blue line. Another Pittsburgh player picked it up and hit Jean Pronovost, their top scorer at the time, with a pass.

Pronovost came down right wing and let go with a blast that hit me in the face again, just like Apps had done. If it hadn't been for the mask, I don't know what would have happened on either shot. But I made both saves with my mask and in each case I was sort of going down, so I'm sure both shots would have been goals if they hadn't hit me. I remember thinking, "Boy, do I have it going tonight."

I really did have it going for me, and luck always helps when you're in goal because Pittsburgh had its chances but couldn't

Pronovost came down right wing and let go with a blast that hit me in the face again, just like Apps had done.

score. I know they threw 30 shots at me and I remember one in particular besides the two that hit me in the mask in the first period.

It was still 0–0 past the midway point of the third period when Pierre Larouche got a breakaway. He was coming in and he slowed down to try to get me to commit myself first when Denis Potvin caught up with him. While Denis slowed him down, I came out and got a stick on the puck and Larouche never got off a shot.

A minute later, with less than six minutes left in the third period, we got the breakthrough goal. Pittsburgh had the puck in its own zone but lost control. Somehow, Bert Marshall got the puck and fed it to Eddie Westfall. Eddie put a 20-foot backhander past Gary Inness, who'd been playing well in goal

for Pittsburgh. That's all we needed because we won the game, 1–0.

I don't have to tell you how excited we all were at the finish. I remember kissing the goalposts. Later we were told that it had been the first time since 1942 that a team had lost the first three games of a Stanley Cup series then won the next four.

Like I said, it was a step forward, a big one, in the building of the Islanders. Our confidence showed in the next round of those playoffs, against Philadelphia. We took them to seven games, though we lost. We became a "Cinderella team," and that's why I'll never forget that seventh game against Pittsburgh in 1975.

—*As told to George Vass*

Glenn "Chico" Resch earned his nickname for his resemblance to *Chico and the Man* TV comic Freddie Prinze. For more than seven seasons, Resch shared goaltending duties with the up-and-coming New York Islanders with Billy Smith. After winning the 1980 Stanley Cup, the Islanders decided to go with Smith in the playoffs and dealt Resch to Colorado. Traded to New Jersey in June 1982, Resch concluded his NHL career with Philadelphia in 1986–87.

MAURICE RICHARD

GAME 2, 1944
STANLEY CUP PLAYOFFS

Hockey isn't much different than when I was playing. The rules haven't changed and the stars of today would have been

MARCH 23, 1944
MONTREAL FORUM, MONTREAL
MONTREAL 5, TORONTO 1

FIRST PERIOD
No scoring.
Penalty: MON Lamoureaux 6:43.

SECOND PERIOD
1. MON Richard (Blake, McMahon) 1:48.
2. MON Richard (Blake, Lach) 2:05.
3. TOR R. Hamilton (Carr, Morris) 8:50 (PP).
4. MON Richard (Lach, Blake) 16:46.
Penalties: MON Richard 8:34; TOR Webster 12:20; MON Richard 12:20; TOR Morris 19:24.

THIRD PERIOD
5. MON Richard (Blake, Lach) 1:00 (PP).
6. MON Richard (Blake, Lach) 8:54.
Penalty: MON Heffernan 14:57.

SHOTS ON GOAL:

MON	5	20	17	**42**
TOR	3	11	6	**20**

Goalies: MON Durnan; TOR Bibeault
Referee: Bill Chadwick
Linesmen: Bert Hedges, Stan McCabe

stars when I was on the ice. The game may be a little faster now and there are a lot more goals scored, although there aren't as many nice plays as there used to be. But I suppose I would have scored more goals if I were playing now. After all, they were only 50 games then and they've got 78 today.

There are a lot of games I can look back on to be proud of. In some, I set records. Others were Stanley Cup winning games. I never have been too much concerned with records, but there is one that I take special pride in. That's the record of scoring six goals in overtime play in Stanley Cup games. That alone gave me six games to choose from as the one that I'll never forget and there are a lot of others over the years, like the one in which I scored my 50th goal in 1945. Yet there's a game from my early years that people have often asked me about. And I know I won't forget that one.

It was in 1944 [March 23], the second game of the opening round of the Stanley Cup playoffs between the Montreal Canadiens and Toronto Maple Leafs. The Leafs won the first game 3–1 and this game was in the Montreal Forum, When the season started coach Dick Irvin put me on a line with Elmer Lach at center and Toe Blake at left wing. We worked well together and pretty soon people were calling us the "Punch Line."

I scored 32 goals playing with Lach and Blake that season and when the playoffs opened the Leafs put Bob Davidson, a big, good-checking forward on me. He must have done a good job because I didn't score in the first game. In the second game, Davidson was all over me again and I don't even remember getting off any shots in the first period. We didn't score and neither did Toronto so we went into the second period with a 0–0 tie.

But soon after the second period started, I got my chance. I think it was defenseman Mike McMahon who passed the puck to Lach to start the play going. Lach gave it to me and I went in on the Leaf goalie Paul Bibeault, I gave him a deke, then the shot. It went in at 1:48 of the second period.

Less than 20 seconds later, I scored my second goal. It was a nice line play this time, Blake and Lach setting me up for the shot. So we were ahead 2–0, which meant Toronto had to open up a little. That's always good because it gives you a chance to take advantage of such a situation. But it worked for them this time. Reg Hamilton scored for them about halfway through the period and our lead was now just 2–1.

We kept working. Davidson was still checking me and I wasn't getting any chances. I think my goals had been my only chances in the first 30 minutes or so of the game. I'd been in the penalty box twice, too. But near the end of the second period, Blake and Lach set me up again. It has been so long ago, I forget exactly how I scored, but I put the shot past Bibeault to get the hat trick. All three goals in one period!

We had a 3–1 lead but in hockey you never know. It may not be enough. If never hurts to get one or two more if you still play your game defensively. As long as you don't let up on defense and wait for your chances, you play the game right.

When we came back on the ice for the third period, we were ready to go. We did not want to lose this one at home. It would be hard to come back after losing the first two games of a series. The third period started and the Forum crowd was really alive, cheering us. It gave us a lift. It always did. It was a minute, maybe—not much more— when Blake and Lach again set me up in the Toronto zone. I put a wrist shot past Bibeault for my fourth goal of the game.

Something like halfway in the third period I scored another goal, my fifth. The funny thing is that I don't think I had more than six or seven shots on goal all game and each goal was scored in a different way. A couple of nights later, when we beat the Leafs 11–0, I scored only two goals. But this night I got all five. And we beat Toronto 5–1.

When they picked the three top stars of the game after the final buzzer, like they always do in Montreal, they picked Richard

When they picked the three top stars of the game after the final buzzer, like they always do in Montreal, they picked Richard as Star No. 1, Star No. 2 and Star No. 3.

as Star No. 1, Star No. 2 and Star No. 3. Later, I learned that the five goals were a Stanley Cup game record [which still stands]. Getting them against the Leafs was something extra. They were always a close-checking club. Davidson was always out there shadowing me. Sometimes he stayed so close that I'd get angry. Maybe that night I took it out on him and the puck.

There are a lot of other games that I could talk about. We won a lot of them at Montreal in those days—and still do. But that five-goal game in 1944, only my second season in the league, was something special.

—As told to George Vass

Maurice "Rocket" Richard's passion and scoring feats made him the biggest star to have ever played for the most decorated team in NHL history. He joined the Montreal Canadiens in 1942–43, then won his first of eight Stanley Cup rings the following season. Richard tallied 50 goals in 50 games in 1944–45, although he never won a scoring title. He did lead the league in goal-scoring five times and his name now graces the NHL's award for the achievement.

JEREMY ROENICK

GAME 3, 1992
CAMPBELL CONFERENCE FINALS

No question, the biggest game of my career so far took place in the Campbell Conference finals between my club, the

MAY 20, 1992
NORTHLANDS COLISEUM, EDMONTON
CHICAGO 4, EDMONTON 3 (OT)

FIRST PERIOD
1. EDM Nicholls (Murphy, Richardson) 2:08.
2. EDM MacTavish (Lamb, Buchberger) 13:00.
Penalties: CHI Graham (unsportsmanlike conduct) 7:17;
EDM Mellanby, (unsportsmanlike conduct) 7:17; CHI
Matteau (holding) 7:17; CHI Hudson (elbowing) 10:14;
EDM Glynn (interference) 13:32; CHI Lemieux (high-
sticking, game misconduct) 16:07.

SECOND PERIOD
3. CHI Noonan (Roenick, R. Brown) 6:36 (PP).
4. CHI R. Brown (Goulet, Noonan) 13:31 (PP).
5. CHI Chelios (unassisted) 18:49.
Penalties: EDM Maciver (holding) 5:26; EDM Richardson
(cross-checking) 6:55; CHI Hudson (slashing) 11:04; EDM
Lowe (slashing) 11:04; EDM Tikkanen (tripping) 12:04.

THIRD PERIOD
6. EDM Glynn (unassisted) 7:13.
Penalties: CHI Larmer (roughing) 3:31; EDM Lowe
(roughing) 3:31; CHI Hudson (high-sticking) 3:40; CHI K.
Brown (high-sticking) 7:24; EDM Damphousse (roughing)
7:24; CHI Goulet (roughing) 18:58; EDM MacTavish
(roughing) 18:58.

FIRST OVERTIME PERIOD
7. CHI Roenick (Chelios, Goulet) 2:45.
Penalties: None.

SHOTS ON GOAL:
CHI	6	10	8	5	**29**
EDM	13	4	7	0	**24**

Goalies: CHI Belfour; EDM Ranford
Referee: Bill McCreary
Linesmen: Gord Broseker, Kevin Collins

Chicago Blackhawks, and the Edmonton Oilers. Until that time, the game that had meant the most to me, purely at a level of personal achievement, took place in my rookie year. That was the playoff game against St. Louis in which all my teeth got knocked out. I wound up with 14 stitches and scored the winning goal—and that closed out the Blues.

Beating Edmonton was something else because you have to take into consideration the team we were playing. The Oilers had won the Stanley Cup five times going into the 1992 playoffs and still had some classy players with them: Kevin Lowe, Esa Tikkanen, Craig MacTavish and Bill Ranford. They had beaten us in six games in the 1990 playoffs—and that still hurt.

Things were different this time, though. Our club had already knocked off St. Louis in the opening round and then handled Detroit. By the time we got to my special game, we had won nine playoff games in a row. The club had as much confidence as a team can have. Our feeling was, "Let's just go do it!"

We certainly did it in the first two home games of the Edmonton series. In the opener at Chicago Stadium, we beat them 8–2, and in the second game we came out on top 4–2. None of us figured the Oilers were dead, though, especially with the series shifting to Edmonton.

Perhaps the most remarkable aspect of my memorable game against Edmonton was the lousy start I had. I began having a very tough time, not getting many chances. Steve Larmer and Michel Goulet were working their butts off, and even though the line got a couple of chances, we were not threatening. I give Edmonton full credit. Oilers coach Ted Green had Esa Tikkanen shadowing me, and he just about had a blanket over me. You could tell how Edmonton was outplaying us by the score. After one period, they were up 2–0 on goals by Bernie Nicholls and Craig MacTavish.

Even down by two, we weren't worried. There was no reason to let down with 40

minutes left. A team effort could reverse the flow. We already had positive signs. In the first period, we killed three Edmonton penalties totaling nearly eight minutes, including most of a five-minute major to Jocelyn Lemieux for high-sticking David Maley.

Our comeback began in the second period. First, Brian Noonan beat Ranford at 6:36, and I got an assist on that one during a power play. I had drifted in and got past their defenseman, Craig Muni. I took a low-angled shot and Brian jammed in the rebound. We tied it 2–2 at 13:31 on a goal by Robbie Brown and then took a 3–2 lead with 1:11 left in the second. That goal shocked Edmonton a bit because Ranford had been almost invincible. We had outshot them 10–4 and stopped Edmonton's two power plays.

Any thoughts we had of cruising to the win were dashed by Brian Glynn, who scored at 7:13 of the third. The score remained tied through the third period, setting up sudden-death overtime.

Not that I was worried. Before the game, I had one of those premonitions that athletes get every once in a while. We were sitting in the dressing room earlier when a thought came to me and I could see the whole game before me, including the end. I turned to our captain, Dirk Graham, and said, "This game is going to end with a pass out from the side and then I'm gonna put it in! I'm gonna one-time it."

What shocked the hell out of me was the fact that I hadn't been doing a thing in the minutes before the climax. In overtime, I was out with "Larms" and Michel, and we were in the Edmonton zone. Michel had the puck near the blue line. I was near the net looking for an opening. Michel just threw the puck on the net. Chris Chelios dropped down, and I did a swing from the corner to the slot.

When I saw Chelly move in, I knew I had one Oiler behind me. I yelled to him—I had just skated over the red dot on the left side. Chelly got the puck and fired across the slot. I just wanted to deflect it to the net. I got a good piece of it, directing the puck past Ranford off the far post, then the crossbar, and down the far corner.

I never actually saw the puck enter the net, but I did hear the "cling" as it bounced off the crossbar. When Larms' arm went up, I knew it was in and the game was over.

The hockey media like to ask, "What does it feel like when something like that happens?" First, there's the feeling of sheer ecstasy knowing the puck went in. Second, there's a feeling of relief, knowing that the game is finally over and we won.

Perhaps the best part comes about two seconds after the goal is official. I enjoy the feeling of the guys coming over and jumping all over me and, of course, the postgame festivities in the dressing room.

I imagine my parents liked what Oilers coach Ted Green said and what I read in the papers the next day: "A great kid made a great play, and that was the game for the Hawks." My feeling of euphoria lasted all night, right back to the hotel room where my roommate, Brent Sutter, shared the joy with me. The next morning, I was at breakfast reading the headlines: "Roenick, Hawks Dump Oilers in OT." It was so enjoyable, I didn't even mind the snow outside—even in May.

I don't know what would have happened had Edmonton taken the game in overtime. Who knows? They might have come back and tied the series. But I do know that my goal gave us a three-games-to-nothing lead, and we wrapped up the series in four straight with a 5–1 win at Northlands.

—As told to Stan Fischler

Shown, above, muscling Mark Messier for position, **Jeremy Roenick** has brought an aggressive approach to his game since his 1988–89 rookie season with Chicago. He had back-to-back 50-goal seasons with the Blackhawks in the early 1990s. Traded to Phoenix in August 1996, "J.R." spent five seasons with the Coyotes before signing as a highly sought after free agent with Philadelphia in 2001.

TEAMMATES FOREVER

The Detroit Red Wings ended a 42-year drought when they won the 1997 Stanley Cup. Although Detroit goaltender Mike Vernon earned the Conn Smythe Trophy as most valuable player, many votes went to hard-hitting Wings defenseman Vladimir Konstantinov. A stalwart on Russia's famed Central Red Army team until he joined Detroit for the 1991–92 season, Konstantinov had earned the nickname "Vlad the Impaler" for his decimating open-ice body checks and "take no prisoners" approach to defense.

Unfortunately, while returning with several teammates via limousine from a victory celebration, Konstantinov suffered massive brain trauma in a July 13, 1997, car accident. Months of rebalitation brought only the most rudimentary improvement in memory, speech and mobility. When Detroit successfully defended their title in 1998, their fallen comrade was not forgotten. Captain Steve Yzerman handed the Stanley Cup to an elated Konstantinov, who was wheeled to center ice (shown left) to join the celebration. His injuries have proved career-ending, yet the Wings continue to keep Konstantinov's dressing room stall open for his return.

—Chris McDonell

JUNE 16, 1998
MCI CENTER, LANDOVER MD
DETROIT 4, WASHINGTON 1

It's difficult to single out a moment in a hockey career that goes back 40 years and includes many highlights. We had some

MARCH 18, 1952
BOSTON GARDEN, BOSTON
BOSTON 4, CHICAGO 0

FIRST PERIOD
1. BOS Kryzanowski (Chevrefils, Schmidt) 17:14 (PP).
Penalties: CHI Peters (tripping) 9:08; CHI McFadden (hooking) 16:53.

SECOND PERIOD
2. BOS Schmidt (Dumart, Bauer) 12:58.
Penalty: BOS Kyle (hooking) 9:23.

THIRD PERIOD
3. BOS Bauer (Schmidt, Chevrefils) 6:40.
4. BOS Chevrefils (Schmidt, Kryzanowski) 13:41.
No penalties.

Goalies: BOS Henry; CHI Lumley
Referee: George Gravel
Linesmen: Sam Babcock, Bill Morrison

good teams at Boston when I was a player in the late 1930s and '40s. And it was a great satisfaction to me as a general manager when the Boston Bruins won the Stanley Cup in 1970, for the first time since 1941.

We went through some lean times in between those Cup years. That made it all the more gratifying when, with players like Bobby Orr and Phil Esposito, we were able to build up our team to the point where we became consistent winners. You never forget your days as a player, though, and I have some great memories of the early years of my career. Still, one of the greatest moments came near the end of my playing days.

The story of how Woody Dumart, Bobby Bauer and I got together to become known as "The Kraut Line" often has been told. We first played together 40 years ago for a team at Kitchener, about 70 miles west of Toronto. Woody was the left wing, Bobby the right wing and I played center at Kitchener. Later, we moved up as a line to Providence, the Bruins' farm club. Albert Leduc, the Providence coach, tagged us the "Sauerkraut Line," which was changed to the "Kraut Line" when we began playing together at Boston in 1937–38.

We finished first at Boston four years straight and won two Stanley Cups. Then came World War II and we enlisted. We didn't return to Boston until it was over.

That last game before we left for the Royal Canadian Air Force was something to remember. We beat the Montreal Canadiens 8–1. Our line got eight scoring points, and when the game was over the players from both teams picked us up and carried us off the ice while the organist played "Auld Lang Syne."

It wasn't quite the same when we came back three years later. We weren't as successful as a team and after a couple of seasons Bobby retired as a player. We missed him. He was our team, my right arm. Those were the beginning of some lean years at Boston, though we usually made the playoffs. We never finished first or won the

Cup and the attendance dropped, maybe because television was coming in.

But there was one great night that surely was one of the high spots of my career. That was the night in 1952 when they honored us. They called it Schmidt-Dumart Night and what really made it outstanding was that after four years of retirement, Bobby came back to play with us. The Bruins signed him to a one-game contract just for that night. It was great to see him in uniform again.

It was an important game for us, even though it was near the end of the regular season. We were still in contention for a playoff spot, just a step ahead of the New York Rangers. We were playing the Chicago Blackhawks that night, but they were out of the playoffs.

One other thing: I had 199 career goals going into that game.

The pregame ceremonies naturally were very emotional. Woody and I got a lot of gifts and Bobby wasn't overlooked either. The place was almost packed, with a crowd of more than 12,000, which was quite a change from the small turnouts we'd had lately.

Woody, Bobby and I were reunited as a line for that game and it was a great feeling to be back together again. You could see that Bobby, not having played in four years, was struggling a little, but I knew he'd give it his best. We needed that game. As I said, we were struggling with New York for fourth place, which meant a playoff spot those days in the six-team league. If we won that night and New York lost, we'd clinch it.

Chicago had Harry Lumley in the net and he was a good goaltender. We got our first goal off him, though, in the first period. Ed Kryzanowski was switching off with Bobby on our line at right wing and he put one in to give us a 1–0 lead.

Fortunately, we were able to protect that lead until we got our second goal midway in the second. That was the one that made the evening for me, because it was just like the old days. Bobby gave a pass to Woody at center ice and he skated in on Lumley.

Woody got off a good shot, plenty of wood on it, but Lumley got in front of it somehow. The puck rebounded off his body

Our line got eight scoring points, and when the game was over the players from both teams picked us up and carried us off the ice while the organist played "Auld Lang Syne."

and came back to me. With Lumley down, I fired the puck into the net over his sprawling body. Bobby retrieved the puck and gave it to me as a souvenir.

That was the 200th goal of my career but the real thrill came when the announcement was made: "Boston goal by Schmidt, assists from Dumart and Bauer!" It was a thrill to hear that again.

Later, in the third period, I slipped a pass to Bobby. He was clear on the right wing and

he deked out Lumley and slipped a goal into the net. The crowd roared just as loudly as it did on my goal.

We won the game 4–0, and clinched the playoff spot. Bobby retired after the game, but that's one I know I'll never forget.

—*As told to George Vass*

Milt Schmidt was a dominant NHL centerman for six seasons, helping Boston to two Stanley Cup victories and winning the 1940 scoring crown, before he interrupted his career to enter the Canadian military in 1942. Returning to the Bruins more than three years later, Schmidt continued to lead his team. He won the 1951 Hart Trophy, retiring in 1955 to coach the team. He later served the team as general manager, his position when Boston won the Cup in 1970.

The Cold War was running hot in 1976. The socialist Soviet Union and the capitalist Western world continued to

JANUARY 11, 1976
PHILADELPHIA SPECTRUM, PHILADELPHIA
PHILADELPHIA 4, CENTRAL RED ARMY 1

FIRST PERIOD
1. PHI Leach (Barber) 11:38 (PP).
2. PHI MacLeish (Lonsberry) 16:37.
Penalties: CRA Alexandrov (elbowing) 2:24; CRA Glazov (tripping); PHI Dornhoefer (interference) 3:34; PHI Dupont (hooking) 7:00; PHI Van Impe (hooking) 9:10; CRA (bench, delay of game) 11:21; PHI Dornhoefer (boarding) 17:56.

SECOND PERIOD
3. PHI Joe Watson (Saleski, Kindrachuk) 2:44 (SH).
4. CRA Kulyergin (Popov) 10:48.
Penalties: PHI Dupont (hooking) 1:08; PHI Van Impe (high-sticking) 11:31; CRA Alexandrov (roughing, misconduct) 17:08; PHI Leach (roughing) 17:08.

THIRD PERIOD
5. PHI Goodenough (Clarke, Dornhoefer) 4:01 (PP).
Penalty: CRA Volchenkov (hooking) 3:14.

SHOTS ON GOAL:

PHI	17	14	18	**49**
CRA	2	8	3	**13**

Goalies: PHI Stephenson; CRA Tretiak
Referee: Lloyd Gilmour

produce weapons of mass destruction in a race for global superiority. Somehow, the Philadelphia Flyers were dragged into this international theater, called upon to defend the honor of hockey in the free world.

The visiting Central Red Army, the perennial champions of the Soviet Union, was going through NHL cities like a hot sickle through butter. The Soviets drubbed the New York Rangers, 7–3. A few nights later, they tied the Montreal Canadiens, 3–3. In Boston, they shredded the Bruins, 5–2.

In the first meaningful hockey meeting between East and West since the 1972 Summit Series, the Soviets were embarrassing the NHL's best. Establishing a puppet government behind the Iron Curtain was one thing, but come over here and skate circles around us—this was serious. So serious that all of the hockey world was watching the night of January 11 when the Red Army entered the Spectrum for its fourth and final "exhibition" game—the game I'll never forget.

Our playing styles were as different as East and West. The Soviets were incredibly gifted skaters and passers, but didn't do much body checking, didn't do much dump and chase, and weren't especially great in the corners. They hardly ever displayed emotion on the ice and only shot the puck when they had a good, clear chance. They were robotic, yet highly efficient.

Their best forward was winger Valeri Kharlamov, a smooth skater with a wicked shot. Kharlamov was very familiar with the Broad Street Bullies style of hockey. Our captain, Bobby Clarke, put Kharlamov out of the Summit Series, breaking the Soviet star's ankle with a vicious slash. Clarke was just playing Flyers hockey. Whether we were fighting or just throwing our weight around along the boards, we thrived on intimidation. Just ask the rest of the league; it stood by and watched us win the previous two Stanley Cups.

The question remained: How were we going to match up against the Soviets? I remember Kelly saying to me before the game, "Dave, you can't skate with them; you can't stickhandle like them; you're not allowed to fight. What are you going to do?"

Coach Fred Shero knew what to do: He devised one of his famous systems. He wasn't going to send us chasing the Soviets around the ice; he wanted us to lay back in the neutral zone and dare the Soviets to try to skate through us. When they came forward, he wanted us to greet them with ill will. And when one of the officials came into the locker room before the game to tell us that Lloyd Gilmour was refereeing that night and wanted us to play our game, I knew this was going to be fun.

Sparked by the tremendous buildup to the game, the pressure from the league to win and Kate Smith's rousing rendition of "God Bless America," we came out of the gate flying. We threw a few jarring hits and the Spectrum crowd was whipped into a frenzy. Then came the big moment: Defenseman Ed Van Impe, who had just finished serving a penalty for tripping, rushed across the ice and lodged either his forearm or elbow into Kharlamov's face. The Soviet star went down on his knees, holding his face in his hands.

The Central Red Army coach, Konstantin Loktev, was irate. He waved for the officials to come over. Then he delayed putting his next line on the ice. After a few seconds, Gilmour had enough. He skated toward the Soviet bench holding up two fingers, one for each penalty minute the Soviets were being assessed for delay of game. When Loktev realized what was happening, he ordered his players into the locker room.

I just shrugged. This was par for the course for the Flyers. We had been hauled into courts, brought before the commissioner, and had stormed into enemy stands after rowdy fans. What's a little international incident compared to our years of hell-raising?

We just skated around and peppered Stephenson with a few practice shots while everything unfolded in the bowels of the Spectrum. Legend has it that the Soviets were refusing to return and were going to pack up

When one of the officials came into the locker room before the game to tell us that Lloyd Gilmour was refereeing that night and wanted us to play our game, I knew this was going to be fun.

and return home until someone pointed out that they wouldn't get paid for the game unless they came back out and played. Chagrined, the Soviets re-emerged after 17 minutes. We got the distinct feeling that this team was scared of us, scared of what we could do to them.

Play resumed with us on the power play, and just 17 seconds after the Soviets returned to the ice, Leach tipped a pass from Barber past Tretiak to give us a 1–0 lead. Feeling the momentum, MacLeish made it 2–0 late in the period, getting a nice pick from Dornhoefer and beating Tretiak with a wrist shot.

The second period was more of the same: a couple of big checks, our Berlin Wall defense in the neutral zone and another goal. This time Watson took a pass from

Saleski and backhanded in a shorthanded goal. By now, the outcome was decided—we had three goals and the Soviets didn't even have three shots.

The Soviets finally got on the board when Viktor Kutyergin's slap shot eluded Stephenson, but they were never able to mount a serious rally. Larry Goodenough added a third-period goal, and when the final buzzer went off, we had won 4–1. We became the toast of the hockey world. Those same people who had reviled us now revered us for beating the Soviets and stemming the surging Red Tide...on the ice.

—*As told to Chuck O'Donnell*

The most notorious of Philadelphia's Broad Street Bullies, **Dave "The Hammer" Schultz** led the league in penalties four times. His 472 penalty minutes in 1974–75 remains an NHL record and his fighting ability and intimidating presence contributed to two Stanley Cup wins for the Flyers. Dealt to Los Angeles in September 1976, Schultz was traded to Pittsburgh just over a year later. He concluded his NHL career with Buffalo in 1979–80.

My first couple of years with the Montreal Canadiens were among the most frustrating of my life. I spent most of my

APRIL 23, 1977
MONTREAL FORUM, MONTREAL
MONTREAL 4, NEW YORK ISLANDERS 3

FIRST PERIOD
1. NYI Harris (Trottier, Gillies) 8:39 (PP).
2. MON Mahovlich (Houle, Wilson) 12:14.
3. NYI Harris (Lewis, Trottier) 12:56.
Penalties: NYI Hart (holding) 3:31; MON Lemaire (hooking) 7:25.

SECOND PERIOD
4. NYI Harris (Gillies, Hart) 0:49.
5. MON Wilson (Savard) 9:40.
Penalties: NYI Marshall (interference) 12:15; NYI Smith (slashing) 12:48; MON Robinson (interference) 12:48.

THIRD PERIOD
6. MON Lafleur (Lapointe, Lemaire) 2:25.
7. MON Shutt (Lemaire) 4:07.
No penalties.

SHOTS ON GOAL:
MON   15   9   14   **38**
NYI   8   6   5   **19**

Goalies: MON Dryden; NYI Smith
Referee: Brian Lewis
Linesmen: Matt Pavelich, Willard Norris

time not even suited up or, when I was, sitting on the bench.

I had a pretty good opinion of myself when I first joined the Canadiens in 1972. I had scored 70 goals in my last year as a junior and 63 the year before. I was a big star with the Toronto Marlboros. The way I looked at it, there was no reason I couldn't step into the NHL and do the same thing—score a lot of goals right from the start. It took me a while, but I learned different.

When I first got to the Canadiens' camp and counted the left wings—Frank Mahovlich, Murray Wilson, Marc Tardif and Chuck Lefley—I began to have my first doubts about where I was supposed to fit in. These were all solid players and here I was, a kid fresh from the juniors, hoping to break in. It took a lot longer than I expected. Maybe I was a little too cocky as a kid. That sort of drained out of me as I spent more games the first two years watching from the press box than I did playing. We won the Stanley Cup my first year but I wasn't even dressed for the final game. I didn't feel I had contributed anything.

Later on, I realized I didn't know a lot of little things it took to play in the NHL, especially about the defensive side of the game. It was something I hadn't taken enough time to learn as a junior, something that could only come from making adjustments, from the experience of playing in the NHL.

It took me two years to learn how to play the game the way the Canadiens wanted me to. I played in spots, scored eight goals the first year, 15 the next. I got to wondering whether I could even play the game, whether I could skate hard enough, learn all the little things it took to be able to play regularly in the NHL. The frustration was tremendous. I suppose that now I would agree that the Canadiens were right in taking their time breaking me into the lineup, but I sure didn't think so at the time.

It may have been hard to take, but I had to bide my time and wait for my chance. My fourth year [1975–76], was when things really began to fall into place. The odd thing about it was that things began to pick up just when they looked at their worst. We weren't going too well in the early season and coach Scotty Bowman threatened to bench me. Then he changed his mind, put me on a line with Pete Mahovlich and Yvan Cournoyer and we got hot right away. I think we scored something like 19 goals in the next eight games and I got eight of those.

From then on, things went really well. That was my first really big scoring season—45 goals—and we went on to win the Stanley Cup, the first of the four we were to win in a row. The goals began to come regularly and I built up my confidence, which is the key to success in everything. When you haven't got it, you're in trouble.

But I was on track now, and more or less to stay. Not all my goals were pretty. Some people called me a garbage collector, as if scoring goals the way I did it was easy. Well, maybe I'm not individually a good player, but I always worked hard, and I was always there for the rebound, the chance. I made a point of being in the right place at the right time. And I was fortunate in having the right linemates.

For the 1976–77 season, when I scored 60 goals, I played mostly with Pete Mahovlich and Guy Lafleur. We fit together well. I can't stickhandle through a team like Pete Mahovlich or skate circles around everybody like Lafleur. With those two out there, a lot of people didn't even notice me. But that was all the better. I was always there for the rebound or the loose puck, I had the anticipation. Some people can score goals, and some can't. I could always do it and it isn't as easy as it looks. When a Lafleur comes down the right side, you've got to figure where the rebound is coming out and you've got to be there. That takes a knack and I've been fortunate enough to have it.

As I said, 1976–77 was the year I came into my own and it was a great year for the Canadiens. We lost only eight games all season and went into the playoffs with a head of steam. I remember one of the playoff games in particular. Though I scored in several, the most memorable game for me came in the

> **Not all my goals were pretty. Some people called me a garbage collector, as if scoring goals the way I did it was easy.**

semifinals against the New York Islanders.

The Islanders were beginning to come on that year. It took us six games to beat them. The first game is the one that stood out for me. The Islanders came out strong and took a 3–1 lead, something you don't see a club do too often in the Montreal Forum. The odd thing about it was Billy Harris, who had been a good friend of mine as a junior, scored all the goals for the Islanders. We were still trailing 3–1, early in the second period, and the Islanders were hot. They'd won six straight in the playoffs, taking two from Chicago in the opening round, then four straight from Buffalo. So far, everything had been falling into place for them.

All of a sudden, we started to turn the game around. First, Murray Wilson tipped in a shot from the point by Serge Savard to make it 3–2, still early in the second period. Then, just a couple of minutes into the third period, Lafleur tied the game at 3–3.

It must have been a couple of minutes later that I got what was to be the winning goal. Jacques Lemaire set me up and I beat Islander goalie Billy Smith on a wrist shot. We held on to win the game, 4–3.

There have been a lot of other games memorable in their own way, especially those that clinched the Stanley Cup. But that's one of them, one of the best, because it was one of the first in which I really felt I had contributed.

—*As told to George Vass*

Steve Shutt won five Stanley Cup rings with the Montreal Canadiens in the 1970s. His league-leading 60 goals in 1976–77 broke Bobby Hull's record for a left-winger. Shutt's 45 assists were also a personal best, lifting him into third place overall in league scoring. He made 1977's First All-Star Team and the Second Team in 1978 and 1980. Traded to Los Angeles in November 1984, Shutt retired at season's end. He entered the Hall of Fame in 1993.

GAME 3, 1982
SMYTHE DIVISION SEMIFINALS

The fans, except for the diehard ones, were getting up and leaving. The ones that stayed began to boo. The Edmonton Oilers

APRIL 10, 1982
GREAT WESTERN FORUM, INGLEWOOD CA
LOS ANGELES 6, EDMONTON 5 (OT)

FIRST PERIOD
1. EDM Messier (Anderson) 10:39.
2. EDM Gretzky (unassisted) 19:23 (SH).
Penalties: LA Bozek, 0:08; EDM Anderson 0:08; LA Korab 4:37; EDM Gretzky 7:34; LA Taylor 8:25; EDM Messier 13:15; LA Simmer 15:37; EDM Hunter 18:46; LA Nicholls 18:50; EDM Unger 18:50.

SECOND PERIOD
3. EDM Fogolin (Gretzky, Lowe) 0:43 (SH).
4. EDM Siltanen (Gretzky) 5:15.
5. EDM Gretzky (Anderson, Gregg) 14:02 (PP).
Penalties: LA Hardy 1:15; LA Lewis 2:52; EDM Messier 2:52; LA L. Murphy 4:16; LA Wells 4:16; EDM Unger 4:16; EDM Hunter 4:16; EDM Coffey 6:39; LA Hopkins 10:01; EDM Lumley 10:01; LA Taylor (double minor) 11:10; EDM Hunter (minor, misconduct) 11:10; LA Smith 13:03; EDM Huddy 13:03; EDM Unger 14:51; EDM Fogolin 15:51; EDM Roulston 16:07.

THIRD PERIOD
6. LA Wells (Dionne, L. Murphy) 2:46.
7. LA Smith (Hardy, Korab) 5:58 (PP).
8. LA Simmer (Hopkins) 14:38.
9. LA Hardy (Bozek, L. Murphy) 15:59.
10. LA Bozek (Hardy, Dionne) 19:55 (PP).
Penalties: LA Smith 1:03; EDM Lumley (minor, major) 2:23; LA Nicholls (major) 2:23; LA Simmer (misconduct) 2:23; EDM Gregg (misconduct) 2:23; EDM Hughes 5:51; EDM Callighen 6:33; EDM Lumley (major) 10:04; LA Bonar (major) 10:04; LA Lewis (misconduct) 10:04; EDM Kurri (misconduct) 10:04; EDM Siltanen (misconduct) 10:04; LA Evans (misconduct) 10:04; EDM Huddy (misconduct) 10:04; LA Korab (misconduct) 10:04; LA M. Murphy (misconduct, game misconduct) 10:04; LA Nicholls (double minor, misconduct) 10:13; EDM Unger (major, misconduct) 15:00; LA Lewis (minor, misconduct) 15:00.

FIRST OVERTIME PERIOD
11. LA Evans (Smith) 2:55.
No penalties.

SHOTS ON GOAL:

LA	14	17	18	3	**52**
EDM	13	12	10	1	**36**

Goalies: LA Lessard; EDM Fuhr
Referee: Ronald Fournier
Linesmen: Gord Broseker, Gerard Gauthier

began to laugh at us. Even our owner got up and left. Game 3 of the 1982 Smythe Division semifinals against the Oilers was turning into an embarrassment for everyone associated with the Los Angeles Kings organization. After two periods, we were trailing 5–0.

From the outset, most people didn't think this was going to be a close series. The Oilers had amassed 48 more points than us in the regular season, and we had the worst record [24–41–15] of any of the 16 playoff teams that season. We were living down to everyone's expectations after the teams split the first two and fell behind in Game 3. Early on it was all Wayne Gretzky. And Mark Messier. And Paul Coffey, Jari Kurri, Glenn Anderson, Kevin Lowe and Grant Fuhr. These guys are going to form their own wing in the Hall of Fame some day, and against us, it seemed as though they were playing about as good as they could. This team had blazing speed throughout the line-up and they were using it to beat us to loose pucks and create scoring chances.

Not only was losing the game a foregone conclusion, but we were going to be in a deep hole in this best-of-five series. Crawling out from under a 2–1 deficit is about as difficult as body checking a zamboni.

With the Oilers enjoying their lead a little too much, we started chipping away in the third period. The first goal should have been a sign to us that something strange was going to happen. It was defenseman Jay Wells who got us on the board. Don't get me wrong—Jay was a big, strong, solid defense-man who would eventually find his scoring touch in the NHL, but considering he had one goal in 60 regular season games that year, he wasn't the guy you would expect to ignite a rally. But after rookie center Doug Smith added a second goal, we felt a groundswell of momentum.

Then it was my turn. I tucked in a loose puck to cut the Oilers' lead to 5–3. It wasn't a pretty thing. All I did was jam a loose puck

in, but it was about time our line had started pulling its weight.

People had come to expect big things from the "Triple Crown Line." With me at left wing, Marcel Dionne at center, and Dave Taylor on the right wing, we became the first line to boast three 100-point scorers during the 1980–81 season. Over the next few seasons, we enjoyed a lot of success.

I give the bulk of the credit for the line's success to Dionne. He was just an amazingly gifted player who really put everything into motion. He wasn't big, but when the team needed a goal, he always seemed to be there, either setting up Dave or me, or scoring it himself.

Speaking of scoring; it wasn't as if the Oilers had let down as we began to crawl back. They were still getting great chances in the third period. Since we needed goals, we had pushed up and had slightly forsaken the defense. This gave the Oilers some odd-man breaks, but when they came down the ice, they were being rebuffed by goalie Mario Lessard.

Even when they beat Mario, we apparently had luck on our side. If I remember correctly, they hit a few posts or a post and a crossbar in the third period. If they had scored a goal during final period, it would have really deflated us. Instead, we kept coming on strong, trimming the deficit to 5–4 when Mark Hardy, one of the best—and most underrated all-around defensemen in the league at that time—scored with about four minutes remaining in the game.

Even though the Forum was half-empty, it was the loudest I ever heard it in the eight seasons I played there. The fans couldn't believe that this team that looked dead in the second period was suddenly back in this game. They were loving it.

So we had momentum, a hot goalie, luck and the support of a roaring crowd. The only thing we needed was the fifth goal to tie the game. But as we pressed on, it seemed as though we were destined to fall that much short. But destiny had other ideas. It smiled on a rookie named Steve Bozek. Bozek, a 22-year-old center from a place called Kelowna, British Columbia, put in a rebound with just five seconds remaining.

> **We had momentum, a hot goalie, luck and the support of a roaring crowd. The only thing we needed was the fifth goal to tie the game.**

We had come all the way back from a five-goal deficit. I can remember sitting in the locker room between regulation and the first overtime. I couldn't wait to get back on the ice. I think the whole team just wanted to keep riding the momentum and finish what we had started. And thanks to a 5-foot, 8-inch, winger who had two goals in 14 regular season games that year, the game will always be remembered as "The Miracle on Manchester".

At 2:35 of overtime, Daryl Evans controlled a face-off win by Smith and slapped the puck goalward. Little did he know his shot was going to cap one of the greatest rallies in playoff history. In a flash, the crowd was roaring, the players were jumping off the bench and mobbing Evans and the Oilers

were hanging their heads in disbelief. Evans had become the third rookie to score for us that night.

You would think that the momentum would have carried over into Game 4 and we would have been able to wash the Oilers off our hands, but they rebounded to tie the series and send it back to Edmonton for Game 5. If we had lost the fifth and final game, the huge comeback in Game 3 would have been a bittersweet memory. But we won, and that third period rally will always be the sweetest memory of the game I'll never forget.

—*As told to Chuck O'Donnell*

Charlie Simmer went from journeyman to superstar in 1979 when he joined center Marcel Dionne and right-winger Dave Taylor on what became known as the "Triple Crown Line." Simmer led the league with 56 goals in 1979–80, making the First All-Star Team that season and the next, when he tallied an identical 56 goals. Traded to Boston in October 1984, he concluded his NHL career with the Pittsburgh Penguins in 1987–88.

CRAIG SIMPSON

**GAME 5, 1990
STANLEY CUP FINALS**

I think one of the most exciting games I've ever played wasn't necessarily my best game. It was Game 5 of the 1990 Stanley

---

**MAY 24, 1990
BOSTON GARDEN, BOSTON
EDMONTON 4, BOSTON 1**

FIRST PERIOD
No scoring.
Penalties: BOS Bourque (cross-checking) 2:56; EDM Tikkanen (holding) 4:32; BOS Galley (holding) 4:45.

SECOND PERIOD
1. EDM Anderson (unassisted) 1:17.
2. EDM Simpson (Anderson) 9:31.
No penalties.

THIRD PERIOD
3. EDM Smith (Messier, Simpson) 6:09.
4. EDM Murphy (Lamb, Gelinas) 14:53.
5. BOS Byers (Sweeney, Bourque) 16:30.
Penalties: EDM Huddy (hooking) 7:04; BOS Bourque (holding) 11:46.

SHOTS ON GOAL:

EDM	10	5	7	**22**
BOS	10	10	10	**30**

Goalies: EDM Ranford; BOS Moog
Referee: Andy Van Hellemond
Linesmen: Ray Scapinello, Swede Knox

Cup playoffs against the Boston Bruins. I had success in the game, but more than anything, we were on a roll as a whole team. We were playing in synch, with such unity, that we just kept getting better with every game. I don't think I've ever been as excited to play hockey as I was at that particular point in time.

The Bruins were on their last breath with us leading three games to one. They'd brought their level up probably to the best it had been in the series. I remember thinking in the first period that this is the most exciting hockey I'd ever been involved in. It was a thrill to be part of it. I was so focused and playing so well at that particular time. We had a Halloween party a few years ago and somebody put a tape of that game on. Being early in the regular season, our level of play was nowhere near what it was in that playoff game. Everybody was in shock at how quick we were skating and how we were jumping.

Early in the second period, Glenn Anderson took the puck out of our end, beat one guy at our blue line, split two defensemen and beat [Boston goalie] Andy Moog. That was a real key turning point in the game, when we felt we were going to win the Stanley Cup. In the middle of the period, Andy [Anderson] and I had a two-on-one. He took the defenseman wide and did a spin-around, behind-the-back pass right to me for a breakaway. I got cross-checked into the net after scoring, but that ended up being the Stanley Cup–winning goal.

In terms of goals for me, it was just a fantastic play by Glenn and, of course, it's one I'll always remember. In terms of importance, you'll always have your name listed as scoring a Stanley Cup–winning goal.

As the game progressed, we kept grinding away and Billy Ranford was unbelievable in net. But I remember it as a bittersweet thing. I was so excited because it was my second Stanley Cup, but, in a lot of ways, I was kind of depressed it had to end. There had never been another time in hockey when I'd felt so

into it. To reach the finals and win is an incredible feeling. But at the same time, I wanted those games to go on because of the great experience of playing at that level. That's what teamwork is all about.

We were fortunate we had a bunch of guys who cared about each other. Everybody wanted to do better to help the team. As our confidence grew, everybody got that feeling and it was so uplifting. It's like having an extra guy on the ice.

One of the key experiences came in the first period. The Bruins came out strong and played their best hockey of the series. Our feeling when we went back into the dressing room after the first period was, "Hey, we've raised our game above that." We felt that was their best shot. They gave their all. The Bruins showed so much character. It was an unbelievable effort. But we raised our game

---

> **He took the defenseman wide and did a spin-around, behind-the-back pass right to me for a breakaway. I got cross-checked into the net after scoring, but that ended up being the Stanley Cup–winning goal.**

above that or at least to their level. I think the guys were all feeling, "We've got them now."

The first game of the series set the tone when we went three overtime periods. There were times in that game when we lined up for a face-off and thought, "This game is never gonna end." They had great chances and so did we. They had great goaltending and we had great goaltending. It really typified the entire series. But in Game 5, you could really feel our team coming closer together by the minute. Everybody's play picked up quite a bit over the course of the game.

I think that team marked the end of the Oilers dynasty. There were probably better Oilers teams on the other four Edmonton Stanley Cup teams and certainly there was more talent in other years. But this was a different type of team. We always needed a total team effort. We were without Wayne Gretzky; it was Mark Messier's team. We had four lines that were really solid. Everybody could say "Hey, I contributed for us to win."

In the last minute of play, we were winning 4–1 and hugging each other. The commitment we made to each other is what sticks out in my mind the most when I think back to that moment. That's a special moment in sports, when you realize you may never have it again, and if it does happen again, it probably won't be with the same group of guys who you just battled with to victory.

—As told to Phil Coffey

A quarter of the way through his third NHL season, Pittsburgh traded **Craig Simpson** to Edmonton in a multi-player deal that sent Paul Coffey to the Penguins. Simpson erupted with 43 goals (giving him 56 for the season) in 59 games for the Oilers, helping them win the 1988 Stanley Cup. Traded to Buffalo in September 1993, he suffered a back injury three months later. Simpson scored 247 goals in 634 NHL games but his back problems forced him into retirement in 1994–95.

HARRY SINDEN

DECEMBER 21, 1968

The most memorable game for me was the eighth game of the Canada-Russia series in 1972, no doubt about it. No other game,

not even the game in which we won the Stanley Cup at Boston in 1970, could equal that one for what it meant to me as coach of Team Canada, for the players, for Canada as a nation. The emotion, the elation, the pride that went into it can't be topped. And I suppose everyone who participated in that game would choose it as the one they'll never forget. Nobody possibly could have played in a hockey game that had more meaning.

Yet there's another game I remember, one that nobody won, that nobody scored in, yet might have been the greatest I ever saw. I don't think I ever was involved in a better game though no goals were scored. It's memorable to me because of the tremendous skating, the great shooting, the unbelievable goaltending and the way the fans at the Montreal Forum reacted. Would you believe it, nobody scored a goal but no fan could have gone home unhappy? But that's the kind of game it was.

I was coaching the Bruins in 1968 when we went into Montreal to play the Canadiens. We were an up and coming team then, with good young players like Phil Esposito, Bobby Orr, Derek Sanderson, Don Marcotte and veterans like John Bucyk, Johnny McKenzie and Ted Green. The Canadiens—well, they were the Canadiens—with Jean Beliveau, Henri Richard, Ralph Backstrom, Terry Harper, Ted Harris and the usual depth. A great team.

They had a rookie in goal that night, Tony Esposito. We had Gerry Cheevers. But all the talk, the stories in the newspapers, were about Phil Esposito against brother Tony. Phil already had a reputation as a scorer but Tony was a kid trying to win a job. We'd played Montreal a few weeks before and Tony was in goal for that game, too. Phil scored the only goals for us, but Tony handled himself well and the game was a 2–2 tie.

As a coach, you know that there's no brotherly love on the ice. Once that puck is

dropped, it's team against team and no one is related to the guys in the other uniform. That's the way it was that night. We got a great scoring chance right at the start. Phil had Tony dead-to-rights from the slot but that glove shot up and Tony picked the puck out of the air.

Up and down, that's the way it went all night. Beliveau must have had three or four good scoring chances in the first period, but Cheevers wasn't letting anything get by. I know Phil had at least five good opportunities to beat Tony at close range. But he might as well have been shooting at a wall in front of the net. Nothing was going to go in.

The crowd was wild, much louder than usual in the Forum. It was nonstop hockey and up and down the ice. I don't think I ever saw two teams go more all-out for 60 minutes. But Cheevers and Esposito were out

---

DECEMBER 21, 1968
MONTREAL FORUM, MONTREAL
BOSTON 0, MONTREAL 0

FIRST PERIOD
No scoring.
Penalties: MON Backstrom (hooking) 7:15; BOS Webster (boarding) 7:30; MON Beliveau (holding) 8:21; BOS McKenzie (charging) 14:00; MON Richard (elbowing) 19:14; BOS Cashman (slashing) 19:48.

SECOND PERIOD
No scoring.
Penalties: MON Savard (cross-checking) 7:43; MON Harris (slashing) 9:42; BOS Sanderson (spearing) 10:34; BOS Awrey (interference) 13:16; BOS Sather (high-sticking) 13:57; MON Duff (high-sticking) 13:57.

THIRD PERIOD
No scoring.
Penalties: BOS Orr (high-sticking) 3:09; MON Harris (high-sticking) 3:09; BOS McKenzie (fighting) 8:50; MON Richard (fighting) 8:50; MON Savard (interference) 9:57; BOS Hodge (hooking) 11:43.

SHOTS ON GOAL:

BOS	14	8	19	**41**
MON	10	13	11	**34**

Goalies: BOS Cheevers; MON T. Esposito
Referee: Bill Friday
Linesmen: Brent Casselman, Matt Pavelich

All the talk, the stories in the newspapers, were about Phil Esposito against brother Tony. Phil already had a reputation as a scorer but Tony was a kid trying to win a job.

of this world! When it was over, Esposito had stopped 41 shots and Cheevers about the same number. I never saw better goaltending on each side.

Somebody told me later that Danny Gallivan, the Montreal broadcaster, called it "the best all-around contest played at the Forum in 10 years." That was a pretty strong statement, considering the kind of team the Canadiens had from 1958 to 1968, and the Stanley Cups they'd won. But I'd agree with it. In fact, I haven't seen a better game yet.

Sure, it was 0–0. But unlike most 0–0 ties, which are close-checking, cautious games, there were about 40 shots on goal by each team. I'll never forget the crowd reaction, the excitement, the applause as long as I live. It was probably the best game from the standpoint of exciting and skilful play, for goaltending, for the fans to see, that hockey's ever had. It easily could have been 10–9 the

way both teams played. But it was 0–0 and, strange as it may sound, that's the game I'll never forget because it was the best one I've ever seen.

That eighth game of the Russian series in Moscow has a special place in my heart. It was a fantastic game and we won it 6–5 to take the series 4–3–1. I'll always remember Paul Henderson's goal in the last 34 seconds to win it for us. I'll always remember the bedlam in that Moscow Arena when the referee called a misconduct on J.P. Parise that nearly set off a riot and delayed the game 10 minutes. There's nothing I'll forget about that game, how Henderson slid the puck under Vladislav Tretiak to break the tie and how we celebrated afterward.

But that 0–0 game, believe it or not, that's the greatest game I ever saw.

—As told to George Vass

Harry Sinden captained the Whitby Dunlops, representing Canada, to the 1958 World Championship gold medal and won silver at the 1960 Olympics. He is shown, above, being hoisted by the Boston Bruins after he coached them to the 1970 Stanley Cup. Sinden retired but returned to hockey to coach Team Canada in 1972 before returning to Boston to become general manager. He held the position for 29 seasons and remains club president.

FEBRUARY 7, 1976

One game provided me with the greatest thrill of my life. In another I broke a record. I can't really choose between them

FEBRUARY 7, 1976
MAPLE LEAF GARDENS, TORONTO
TORONTO 11, BOSTON 4

FIRST PERIOD
1. TOR McDonald (Sittler) 6:19.
2. TOR Turnbull (Sittler, Thompson) 7:01.
3. BOS Ratelle (Schmautz) 16:54.
Penalties: BOS Sims (high-sticking, fighting) 13:00; TOR Boutette (roughing, fighting) 13:00.

SECOND PERIOD
4. TOR Sittler (Salming, McDonald) 2:56.
5. TOR Salming (Sittler) 3:33 (PP).
6. BOS Schmautz (Bucyk, Ratelle) 5:19.
7. TOR Sittler (unassisted) 8:12.
8. TOR Sittler (Valiquette, Ferguson) 10:27 (PP).
9. BOS Bucyk (Ratelle, Schmautz) 11:06.
10. TOR Ferguson (Hammarstrom, Garland) 11:40.
11. TOR Salming (McDonald, Sittler) 13:57.
12. BOS Ratelle (Schmautz, Bucyk) 14:35.
Penalties: BOS Park (boarding) 3:29; BOS Sheppard (slashing) 8:45; TOR Ferguson (interference) 16:27; BOS Forbes (interference) 19:44.

THIRD PERIOD
13. TOR Sittler (Salming, Thompson) 0:44 (PP).
14. TOR Sittler (Thompson) 9:27.
15. TOR Sittler (McDonald) 16:35.
Penalties: TOR Salming (tripping) 3:46; BOS Edestrand (holding) 9:50.

SHOTS ON GOAL:

TOR	9	21	10	**40**
BOS	11	9	12	**32**

Goalies: TOR Thomas; BOS Reece
Referee: John McCauley
Linesmen: Ray Scapinello, W. Norris

because they are both games I'll never forget.

I don't know whether I played any better the night I broke the scoring record with 10 points than I did some other nights. It was just one of those things that happen. Almost every time I touched the puck it resulted in a goal, scored either by me or by one of my teammates. I've played hockey almost all my life and it's still a mystery to me how unpredictable a game it is.

We played the Boston Bruins at Toronto midway through the 1975–76 season and they came in to Maple Leaf Gardens with a hot hand. They'd won seven games in a row, while we were having our troubles. We'd won just one of our last seven. Gerry Cheevers had just come back to the Bruins from the WHA but he wasn't ready to play yet. Boston started young Dave Reece, a rookie, in goal.

The first period was pretty much the usual tight-checking game. I was on a line with Errol Thompson and Lanny McDonald, as I had been most of the season. In the first period, I got an assist on a goal by Lanny and another one by Ian Turnbull, a defenseman. We skated off the ice at the first intermission with a 2–1 lead. I had two points. Now I can't tell you in detail what happened after that, how I scored each goal or assist. Things happened so fast that it all sort of flows together in my mind. It was unbelievable. Unreal!

All I know is that every time I got my stick on the puck it headed straight for the net. Other nights you may handle the puck even more, get some good shots, and nothing happens. Then, on a night like this, the red light's going on every minute. I scored three goals and added two more assists in the second period. The assists were on goals by Borje Salming, and I scored the last two goals close together. So after two periods I had seven points—three goals, four assists—and we were leading Boston 8–4.

I really wasn't thinking about records at the time, though I knew I had the seven points, with a period left to play. I was just glad we were ahead. I suppose if I'd thought about it I would have figured things couldn't go on like this. I'd already had my share. Like I said, though, there's no explanation for what happens in hockey. That third period was incredible for me, though I remember only the last goal exactly. I scored my fourth goal of the game early. At the halfway point, I scored another, on a pass from Thompson. I'll never forget how the crowd responded when the public address announcer said I'd broken the record of eight points in a game. They gave me a standing ovation. It sent chills down my spine. Nine points.

The 10th, my sixth goal, is the one I remember clearly. I had nine points already and I went behind the net with the puck. I was looking for someone out front, and I saw one of our players. I passed it out to him. The puck hit Boston defenseman Brad Park in the leg and bounced off, through Reece's legs into the net for my sixth goal, and my 10th point. The noise was incredible, the fans yelling their heads off, my teammates mobbing me, pounding me. I set a record with the 10 points, and even if someone breaks it someday, I'll never forget that night.

Even so, I don't think it topped the other game I'll never forget, the one in which we won the Canada Cup against Czechoslovakia [September 15, 1976] at Montreal. There's something special about playing for your country in an international series like that. You have tremendous pride, an intense desire to do your best for the greatest country in the world. I'm proud of being a Canadian and always will be. We had a great team in that series, probably the best team ever assembled. Players like Bobby Orr, Bobby Hull, Rick Martin, Rogie Vachon…you name the best players and most of them were on that team.

The Czechs were good, too. They were the world champions, and they had to beat an outstanding Russian team to be that, so you couldn't take anything away from them. It was a round robin series and the final game between the Czechs and us was for the championship. They'd beaten us 1–0 in the preliminary round but we came back to beat them 6–0 in the opener of the best-of-three

The noise was incredible, the fans yelling their heads off, my teammates mobbing me, pounding me.

championship round. They had tremendous goalkeeping in both Jiri Holecek and Vladimir Dzurilla. Dzurilla shut us out in the preliminary round game.

Holecek started for them in the game the Czechs had to win to stay alive, and we had Vachon. But we got two quick goals on Holecek and Dzurilla replaced him. The Czechs came back and I remember we were losing 4–3 with just a couple of minutes left when Bill Barber scored for us to send the game into overtime, tied 4–4.

Both goalies did a tremendous job in overtime. I remember Vachon making an incredible stab of a shot by Vladimir Martinec to save the game. We went on like that for more than 11 minutes of overtime before we got the break we needed. Marcel Dionne hit

me with a pass and I broke into the Czech zone. Someone had told me that when you got a breakaway, Dzurilla would come rushing out. The thing to do was give him a move, then go to the side. I did it, and I had an open net to shoot at. I was lucky enough to score the winning goal for the Canada Cup.

We exchanged sweaters with Czech players and stood on each other's blue line. When they carried the Canadian flag around the stadium and played the national anthem, I felt a surge of pride that's indescribable. That was one of the most memorable and touching moments of my career.

——*As told to George Vass*

Darryl Sittler joined the Maple Leafs in 1970–71 and by 1975–76 had earned the captaincy. He hit personal highs with 45 goals and 72 assists in 1977–78, making the Second All-Star Team. Despite turmoil with Toronto owner Harold Ballard and coach/ manager Punch Imlach, Sittler notched consecutive 40-goal seasons before being traded to Philadelphia in January 1982, Sittler concluded his NHL career in 1984–85 with Buffalo. He currently works with the Leafs in community relations.

Having played with four Stanley Cup championship teams with the Edmonton Oilers, I've had plenty of memorable

**MAY 31, 1987
NORTHLANDS COLISEUM, EDMONTON
EDMONTON 3, PHILADELPHIA 1**

FIRST PERIOD
1. PHI Craven (Eklund, Crossman) 1:41 (PP).
2. EDM Messier (Nilsson, Anderson) 7:45.
Penalties: EDM Messier (cross-checking) 0:34; EDM Coffey (holding) 1:13; PHI Poulin (hooking) 4:22.

SECOND PERIOD
3. EDM Kurri (Gretzky) 14:59.
Penalties: PHI Sinisalo (hooking) 3:39; PHI Marsh (holding) 12:15; PHI Mellanby (roughing) 15:27; EDM Smith (roughing) 15:21; EDM Messier (charging) 16:02.

THIRD PERIOD
4. EDM Anderson (Huddy) 17:36.
Penalties: PHI Tocchet (roughing) 4:31; PHI Hextall (roughing) 4:31; EDM McSorley (roughing) 4:31; EDM MacTavish (roughing) 4:31; PHI Crossman (holding) 14:16; EDM Tikkanen (roughing) 14:16.

SHOTS ON GOAL:

PHI	12	6	2	**20**
EDM	18	13	12	**43**

Goalies: PHI Hextall; EDM Fuhr
Referee: Andy Van Hellemond
Linesmen: John D'Amico, Ron Finn

games during my career. But if I had to pick the one game that sticks out in my mind the most, it would have to be Game 7 of the 1987 Stanley Cup finals against Philadelphia.

As a kid, you dream about winning the Stanley Cup. For me, that was the first time my dream came true. We had taken a 3–1 lead in the series, but the Flyers came right back and won the next two games to tie things up at 3–3. Philadelphia had the momentum going into the final game but we were playing on our home ice at the Northlands Coliseum. There was no doubt in our minds that we were going to win the game.

We all knew what we had to do. But before the game the normal leaders we had on our team—Mark Messier, Wayne Gretzky and Kevin Lowe—all had some famous words of inspiration that got all of us pumped up and ready to go. We got off to a slow start, though, and took a couple of penalties very early in the game. Philadelphia ended up scoring before the game was two minutes old. But we got that goal back when Messier scored for us later on in the first.

In the second period, I clearly remember Jari Kurri scoring what proved to be the game-winning goal. I wasn't in on the goal but I was standing pretty close to Jari when he scored. Gretzky was behind the net and passed the puck out to Jari, who was in the slot. Jari went for the far side and beat the Flyers goalie, Ron Hextall, on his glove side.

We knew it was too early to start celebrating just yet. But then, late in the third period, we started to feel a little bit more comfortable when Glenn Anderson put us ahead 3–1. He scored on an unbelievable end-to-end rush, turning a defenseman inside out and then beating Hextall.

It was such a great relief for our whole team when Glenn scored that third goal. It was at that point we realized, if we could just bear down for the last few minutes, the Stanley Cup would be ours.

Throughout the game, one of the most difficult things to control was the mental battle with yourself. It's hard not to think about what sort of festivities you're going to have after the game if you win. It was tough trying to get a hold of yourself and stay focused on winning the game first.

Another reason why I remember this game is because I played a couple of shifts at left wing. I was a defenseman throughout my career, but they put me out on the wing for the power play. Glen Sather was our coach at the time. I didn't bother asking him why he was putting me out there. But I at least knew to stand in front of the Philadelphia net and not move. As it turned out, I didn't get any good scoring chances. Since it was Game 7 of the Stanley Cup finals, it was weird to play a position I never had played before. During my six years in Edmonton, it was the only game I played up on the wing on the power play.

During the last 20 seconds of the game, we had control of the puck and knew for sure we were going to win. The guys on the bench all started celebrating. Our trainer started to collect our gloves and helmets so we wouldn't throw them into the stands. The wildest thing about it all was that as exciting as that moment of winning the Stanley Cup was, there was also a feeling of a letdown. We had worked so hard all season towards this goal and after this game it would all be over.

Parading around the rink with the Stanley Cup was just an incredible feeling, though. After Wayne Gretzky accepted the Cup, he turned around and handed it to me first. I looked up to the stands and found my parents while I was holding the Cup. Then I let out this big yell. It felt so great.

Afterwards, I had all my family in the dressing room. We all went out together later and ended up celebrating all night.

I have all my Stanley Cup playoff games on tape. They're all worth remembering. I don't have time to take them out and watch them now, but some time down the road, I'll show them to the kids.

—As told to Sam Laskaris

I looked up to the stands and found my parents while I was holding the Cup. Then I let out this big yell. It felt so great.

Steve Smith, a classic defensive defenseman, won three Stanley Cup rings with the Edmonton Oilers. Traded to Chicago in October 1991, he played six seasons for the Blackhawks before retiring to become Calgary's assistant coach in 1997–98. Smith returned to action with the Flames the following season. Named team captain for 1999–2000, he missed most of the campaign with a bruised spinal cord. The potentially paralyzing injury flared again the following season and Smith retired for good in December 2000.

When it happened, I didn't realize what was going on. Sure, I knew I was cut, I was aware of the blood running down my

MAY 6, 1971
CHICAGO STADIUM, CHICAGO
CHICAGO 5, MONTREAL 3

FIRST PERIOD
1. CHI B. Hull (Maki, Angotti) 4:39 (PP).
2. MON Lemaire (Tremblay) 9:06 (PP).
3. MON P. Mahovlich (Tremblay, Laperriere) 17:58.
Penalties: MON Beliveau (holding) 4:18; CHI Maloney (holding) 7:20; MON Ferguson (high-sticking) 19:28; CHI Mikita (high-sticking) 19:28.

SECOND PERIOD
4. CHI Maki (Angotti, B. Hull) 11:58.
5. CHI Pappin (O'Shea, Foley) 13:50.
Penalties: CHI Magnuson (cross-checking) 2:09; MON Houle (elbowing) 16:39; CHI Martin (elbowing) 16:39.

THIRD PERIOD
6. CHI Angotti (unassisted) 7:27.
7. MON F. Mahovlich (unassisted) 8:56.
8. CHI Angotti (unassisted) 16:47.
Penalties: MON Harper (high-sticking) 11:11; CHI Mikita (elbowing) 11:11.

SHOTS ON GOAL:

CHI	11	12	12	**35**
MON	10	11	6	**27**

Goalies: CHI Esposito; MON Dryden
Referee: Art Skov
Linesmen: Matt Pavelich, John D'Amico

throat, but I didn't feel a thing. It was as if someone had taken a razor and slashed my face. The strange thing was that there was no pain. Absolutely none. It never hurt.

It happened in the 1970–71 Stanley Cup finals in which we played the Montreal Canadiens and had them down two goals in the seventh game but still lost. We started the series in Chicago Stadium. We won the first game and went into the second feeling pretty good, though we knew we had to take it too. You can't go into Montreal with a 1–1 start in a playoff series and expect to come out alive. You've got to win your home games.

I can't tell you how that second game went, other than it was a Thursday night and we won it. All I can remember is what happened to me.

I'd had a tough time getting started that season because I'd injured my left knee the previous February. I tried to deflect a puck with my hand, sliding along my knees in front of our net, and slid into the post. I knew I was hurt bad. I can remember the net bouncing up and down after the collision and thought I'd broken my leg.

What happened was that the ligaments in my knee were torn. It took a long time to get over that, maybe until mid-season of 1970–71. Luckily, I was playing with Bill White as my defensive partner and maybe he carried me a little bit. But the previous summer had been a rough one. I had to wear a cast for six weeks and I was on crutches until August 1, when I finally got permission to skate. My injury seemed so severe and took so much longer than usual to come around than I thought it would that I began to have doubts.

Once I got back to playing, I would have been in serious trouble if it hadn't been for White. He carried me on his back for a while. But I got going and we had a good season, finished first in our division, won the first two rounds in the playoffs and were up against Montreal in the finals.

As I said, all I remember about the scoring in the second game is that we won it, although I wasn't around for the finish. It happened in the second period. The Canadiens, as always, were buzzing around in our end. I went down to my knees in front of our net when Rejean Houle came in and spun around on his skates. Houle was off balance and one of his skates caught me across the face when he fell.

It went clear through my lip, cut clear through the right cheek. The cut was clean, from my lip almost to my eye. It was as if a razor had slashed through everything. Yet I didn't feel hurt. There was no pain. I could feel the blood gushing but I didn't realize at first what had happened, the extent of the injury.

I skated over to the bench for help and our trainer, Skip Thayer, didn't waste any time. He took me down to the dressing room and saw this was no ordinary stitching job. He put in a call for a plastic surgeon, Dr. Randell McNally.

Notice the doctor's name, Rand McNally, which was fitting, because my face looked like a road map for a few days. The stitching took two hours at the hospital. The only thing that hurt about it at all was the shot of painkiller every 20 minutes. Isn't that something?

The doctor told me he wasn't so worried about the cut near the lip opening again. He was concerned about the upper part, where he had to repair some muscles. After the stitching, I drove back to the Stadium, took a shower and drove my family home.

The next morning, I was back at the Stadium for the practice and somebody asked me if I wanted a mask. I didn't want to put one on. I had to wear one a couple of years before when I got a stick across the face and it bothered me. The only thing I worried about was getting tired.

Maybe I should have worn a mask. I didn't look very pretty. A grayish-blue scar ran all the way up the right side of my face, with 52 stitches on the outside and at least that many more on the inside of my mouth. Everybody was asking if I was going to play in the next game, Sunday at Montreal. Heck, I never thought about not playing. There was

The cut was clean, from my lip almost to my eye. It was as if a razor had slashed through everything.

really nothing to worry about. If it opened up, the doctor could stitch it again.

I was in there taking my regular turns in the Sunday game. We didn't do well, lost to the Canadiens, but we didn't disgrace ourselves. Everybody made a big deal out of my playing with that cut, but it didn't bother me a bit. I was tired after the game, but I'm always that way, especially after killing a lot of penalties. And there were a lot of those, especially the three-against-five that take more out of you. Coach Billy Reay asked me to let him know if I got weak or tired. But I didn't feel unusually so during the game at any time.

It was a tough series, especially tough to lose, coming so close to a Stanley Cup. I've never been on a team that came that close. We led in the seventh game by two goals but the Canadiens came back and won it and the series. I won't forget that seventh game either, but the one I'll remember most is the second, the one in which that skate cut through my face from lip to eye. That's something you'll always carry with you, although I guess I don't look so bad after all these years.

—As told to George Vass

Pat Stapleton, shown moving the puck away from teammate Tony Esposito's goal, first broke into the NHL with the Boston Bruins in 1961–62. He returned to the minors the following season but made the made the NHL's Second All-Star Team for the first of three times when he joined Chicago in 1965–66. Strong defensively and an excellent passer, Stapleton jumped to the WHA in 1973. He retired after the 1977–78 season.

I have had many, many memorable games during my career, but if I have to select just one it would be a contest during the

**MAY 2, 1985
MONTREAL FORUM, MONTREAL
QUEBEC 3, MONTREAL 2 (OT)**

FIRST PERIOD
1. QUE Bell (Kumpel, Ashton) 3:27.
Penalties: MON Robinson (roughing) 1:25; QUE Paiement (interference) 10:23; MON Flockhart (slashing) 19:15.

SECOND PERIOD
2. QUE Sauve (Maxwell, Bell) 1:24.
3. MON Mondou (Naslund, Robinson) 9:23.
4. MON Naslund (Robinson, Kurvers) 17:14.
Penalties: MON Nilan (roughing, misconduct) 3:54; QUE Sauve (holding) 17:31.

THIRD PERIOD
No scoring.
Penalties: QUE Maxwell (slashing) 2:50; MON Naslund (slashing) 2:50; MON Tremblay (high-sticking) 17:11; MON Chelios (slashing) 17:53; QUE Goulet (slashing) 17:53.

FIRST OVERTIME PERIOD
5. QUE P. Stastny (Price) 2:22.
Penalties: None.

SHOTS ON GOAL:

QUE	8	6	8	3	**25**
MON	4	12	8	2	**26**

Goalies: QUE Gosselin; MON Penney
Referee: Kerry Fraser
Linesmen: John D'Amico, Ron Finn

1985 playoffs when I was with the Quebec Nordiques. What made that game, and that series, special was that we were playing the Montreal Canadiens, and the rivalry between the two teams and the two cities was just incredible.

The series was tied 3–3 going into the seventh game of the Adams Division finals at the Montreal Forum. The Nordiques had finished second in the division that season [41–30–9] and the Canadiens first [41–27–12], so we were only a few points behind them. We beat Buffalo in the first round, 3–2 in a best-of-five series, and then played Montreal.

We had played the Canadiens twice before in the playoffs. We beat them in 1982 in the first round but lost in the second round in 1984. But this was the most dramatic. It also was a hard, physical series. They had played Boston in the first round, so both teams were tired. Injuries also took a toll on the players. Quebec's Dale Hunter played despite a hand injury, and a back problem kept Michel Goulet's status in question. For the Canadiens, defensemen Rick Green and Chris Chelios were playing with injuries: Green with a shoulder problem and Chelios with a twisted knee.

There wasn't much offense in the first period, but we took an early lead when Bruce Bell scored on Steve Penney right after Montreal killed off a penalty. Jean Francois Sauve scored our second goal in the second period. He took a long shot, from perhaps 50 feet out, and the puck got between Penney's pads and went into the net.

We had a scary moment after that. Our goalie, Mario Gosselin, was hit in the throat by a Mario Tremblay shot, and we thought he might not be able to continue. Gosselin stayed in the game after taking a few moments to catch his breath, but Montreal pressed the attack and tied the score. I believe Pierre Mondou and Mats Naslund scored for the Canadiens, so the game was tied after two periods.

No one scored in the third period, so we all knew the next goal would be the game winner. We had a face-off in the Montreal zone early in the overtime, and I was fortunate enough to beat Guy Carbonneau, a strong defensive player. The puck went back to one of our defensemen, Pat Price, and I went to the net.

Penney stopped Price's shot. I got to the rebound, but Penney stopped that one too. The puck came free again, though, and I got the puck past him this time for the victory. It was a great moment and a great feeling—truly euphoric.

It was the first time the Nordiques had beaten the Canadiens in the playoffs, and to do it in overtime in the last game was just incredible. We were all so happy we had won, but we were exhausted too. The series had been played at such a high level that it was draining.

What I remember maybe even more than the game itself was the reaction of the Nordiques fans. Our departure from Montreal had been delayed for a couple of hours after the game, but when we got to Quebec City there were still several thousand fans jamming the airport to welcome us home. The scene was just incredible with all the people celebrating. When we finally got outside the airport, the roads were a mess with cars double-, triple- and even quadruple-parked all over. The series had been as much a victory for the fans as it had been for the players.

—As told to Phil Coffey

Peter Stastny, shown breaking away from Pittsburgh's Mario Lemieux, defected from Czechoslovakia in 1980. He and his brother Anton signed with the Quebec Nordiques; older brother Marian joined them a year later. Peter won the 1981 Calder Trophy and hit personal bests with 93 assists and 139 points the following season. Traded to New Jersey in August 1990, he carried the flag for Slovakia at the 1994 Olympics before signing with St. Louis. Stastny retired in 1994–95 and entered the Hall of Fame in 1998.

It was the first time the Nordiques had beaten the Canadiens in the playoffs, and to do it in overtime in the last game was just incredible.

PETE STEMKOWSKI

GAME 6, 1971
STANLEY CUP SEMIFINALS

I never wanted to be anything but a hockey player and when you look at it that way, you'd have to say I had a pretty

APRIL 29, 1971
MADISON SQUARE GARDEN, NEW YORK
NEW YORK RANGERS 3, CHICAGO 2 (3OT)

FIRST PERIOD
1. CHI D. Hull (Mikita, Koroll) 10:19.
Penalties: CHI White (interference) 4:46; CHI O'Shea (holding) 7:02.

SECOND PERIOD
2. CHI Maki (Martin, B. Hull) 1:54.
3. NYR Gilbert (Hadfield, Park) 7:07.
Penalties: CHI Pappin (hooking) 10:13; NYR Park (holding) 10:43.

THIRD PERIOD
4. NYR Ratelle (Hadfield, Gilbert) 4:21.
Penalties: CHI Magnuson (holding) 9:04; NYR Rolfe (hooking) 10:48.

FIRST OVERTIME PERIOD
No scoring.
No penalties.

SECOND OVERTIME PERIOD
No scoring.
Penalties: NYR Horton (tripping) 9:28; CHI Stapleton (tripping) 19:25.

THIRD OVERTIME PERIOD
5. NYR Stemkowski (Irvine, Horton) 1:29.
No penalties.

SHOTS ON GOAL:

NYR	10	14	8	8	7	1	**48**
CHI	6	3	7	3	7	0	**26**

Goalies: NYR Giacomin; CHI Esposito
Referee: Bruce Hood
Linesmen: C. Bechard, John D'Amico

satisfying career. I played 15 years in the NHL and had some good seasons and even got to be on a Stanley Cup winner.

At the time I got started, the NHL teams signed you at an early age. I was the "property" of the Toronto Maple Leafs by the time I was 16.

In 1963, when I turned 20, the Leafs sent me to Rochester, but it wasn't until the next season that I really got started as a pro. Late in the 1964–65 season, I was called up to Toronto and played about half the schedule, mostly in spot situations.

I must have been in awe of Punch Imlach, who was the coach and general manager of the Leafs at that time. I was very young and he was a tough, very strict man, like a sergeant in the army. Hockey was a serious business with him, and I guess I was a fun-loving guy. But I was very happy to be with Toronto, because as a youngster I'd always dreamed of playing for the Canadiens or Maple Leafs, like every kid in Canada did.

The Leafs had a good team then, with a lot of older players. If you were a rookie, the older players didn't pay much attention to you until you'd proved yourself. I was shy and it took me a while to feel at home with the older players. After a while, though, I began feeling as if I fit in, and Imlach gave me more and more playing time.

I began to get my share of goals, though that wasn't what I was chiefly on the ice for, and started to feel at home in the NHL. Not that Imlach ever let you feel as if you had it made. He was always on the guys to work harder. I never thought I'd play for any other club than the Leafs. It just never entered my mind. Later, I was to learn how easy it is to be traded, and I played for Detroit, New York and Los Angeles before my career ended. But those early years with the Leafs gave me one of the greatest thrills of my career and the opportunity to play in one of the two games that are the most memorable.

Of course, you can't top winning the Stanley Cup, which we did with the Leafs in 1967. That's the top goal of every hockey player, and I was lucky to experience it at least once. We went against Chicago in the first round of the playoffs and most everybody figured they'd walk over us. They might have, too, if it hadn't been for Terry Sawchuk's play in goal for us. He turned the series around in the fifth game in Chicago. The Hawks looked like they were going to tear us apart, and Johnny Bower, who started in goal for us, looked shaky. But Sawchuk came in [after the first period] and he played one of the greatest games in goal I've ever seen.

He held Chicago, which was just bombarding him, and we were able to come back. I scored the tie-breaking goal to give us a 3–2 lead, and we hung on, then won the sixth game to go into the finals against the Canadiens. That game will always stick out in my mind.

Just as against Chicago, nobody gave us a chance to beat the Canadiens, especially after they crushed us in the first game. But we came right back and beat them in six games. Winning the Cup—there's nothing like it. That's what you play for. Maybe you don't appreciate it as much at the time, but it stands out more and more as your career goes along, especially if you never have the experience again. And especially if you come close and don't quite make it, as happened a couple of times later on when I was with the Rangers.

In 1968 Imlach traded me in a deal that also sent Frank Mahovlich and Garry Unger to Detroit. It was a shock, but I enjoyed my couple of years in Detroit.

Then, in 1971, I was traded to the Rangers. I was to stay there seven years. And I played the most memorable game of my career with New York, the game I'll never forget.

It was the sixth game of the semifinal playoff series in 1971 in Madison Square Garden. It was one of the best-played series I was ever in. Three of the seven games went into overtime and, though we lost the series, we had nothing to be ashamed of. We gave Chicago a battle.

We needed that sixth game to stay alive in the playoffs. Eddie Giacomin was in goal for us and Tony Esposito for the Blackhawks.

By late in the second overtime period, both teams were so fatigued they needed oxygen between shifts and at the intermission. It looked as if the game would go on forever.

Chicago took a 2–0 lead early, but we fought back. Rod Gilbert got a goal for us late in the second period and a goal by Jean Ratelle early in the third period tied the game, 2–2. Meanwhile, Giacomin shut the door on the Blackhawks. We went into overtime after he made a particularly outstanding save on Dennis Hull, who had a breakaway with about a minute to go in regulation time.

Both clubs had some good chances to score in the first overtime and in the second. I remember, in particular, that late in the second period a shot by Stan Mikita hit Eddie in the mask, knocked him over, but he came right back. Another time, Giacomin was out of the net to make a save and Bill White and Mikita both missed the open net with rebound shots.

By late in the second overtime period, both teams were so fatigued they needed oxygen between shifts and at the intermission. It looked as if the game would go on forever when we opened the third period of overtime. It was near midnight in New York. It looked like we were in for more of the same, when we got a break. I think it was Ted Irvine who got the puck to me, and I let go a quick shot. It got past Esposito at 1:29 of the third overtime. I've never scored a goal that felt better. As tired as we were, we went crazy. We'd won, 3–2.

We played more than 100 minutes of hockey in that game, the longest game in Ranger history, and I scored the winning goal. That's got to be the game I'll never forget.

—*As told to George Vass*

Pete Stemkowski, seen above (21) asserting his position against the Atlanta Flames, won a Stanley Cup ring as a member of the Toronto Maple Leafs in 1967. Traded to Detroit in March 1968, he joined the Rangers in October 1970. "Stemmer" had his most productive season in 1973–74, when he scored 25 goals and 45 assists. He played his final NHL season in Los Angeles after signing as a free agent with the Kings in August 1977.

It has been more than 40 years now so if I don't recall all the details it wouldn't be surprising, but I remember enough of

APRIL 3, 1933
MAPLE LEAF GARDENS, TORONTO
TORONTO 1, BOSTON 0 (6OT)

FIRST PERIOD
No scoring.
Penalties: TOR Clancy; BOS Shore.

SECOND PERIOD
No scoring.
Penalties: BOS Chapman; BOS Shore.

THIRD PERIOD
No scoring.
Penalties: BOS Lamb; TOR Doraty; BOS Clapper; TOR Thoms; TOR Cotton; TOR Day.

FIRST OVERTIME PERIOD
No scoring.
Penalties: TOR Levinsky; TOR Levinsky (holding); TOR Sands.

SECOND OVERTIME PERIOD
No scoring.
Penalties: BOS Barry; BOS Shore; BOS Shore.

THIRD OVERTIME PERIOD
No scoring.
Penalties: BOS Stewart; TOR Conacher.

FOURTH OVERTIME PERIOD
No scoring.
Penalties: BOS Smith; TOR Clancy.

FIFTH OVERTIME PERIOD
No scoring.
No penalties.

SIXTH OVERTIME PERIOD
1. TOR Doraty (Blair) 4:46.
No penalties.

SHOTS ON GOAL:

TOR	12	20	11	8	19	12	15	14	3	**114**
BOS	9	5	15	8	12	12	16	13	3	**93**

Goalies: TOR Chabot; BOS Thompson
Referees: Odie Cleghorn, Eusebe Daigneault

them. That was a game that sort of stands out no matter whether you're on the winning or losing side.

Hockey was a little different in the 1930s when it came to stickhandling, shooting or skating, but it was the same in one respect—the idea was to put the puck in the net, or keep it out if you were the goaltender as I was.

My rookie year—that's something to remember, too. That was 1929 and we won the Stanley Cup for Boston against the Rangers in New York. That last game at New York in which we won 2–1—well. that's almost up there with my most memorable game. When your team finishes first in the league and goes on to win the Stanley Cup in your rookie season, that's quite a thrill.

But the game that was the highlight of my career was the one in 1933, I still think of it as the finest game I ever played on an individual basis, even though we lost. We had some players that year at Boston, I'll tell you. Eddie Shore, Dit Clapper, Red Beattie, Nels Stewart—those are just some of them. We went into the first round of the Stanley Cup playoffs [best of five] against Toronto and they were a strong club too. Lorne Chabot was their goalie and they had King Clancy, Joe Primeau and a raft of other good players.

What a series that was! Three of the first four games went into overtime. We'd each won a pair going into the fifth game and we had no idea what was ahead of us.

The fifth game, that's the one, the most memorable game of my career. It was at Toronto and everything depended on it. The winner would go to the finals.

Hockey was just as big in those days in Toronto as it is today. The place was packed. Something over 14,500, and with everything on the line, even the crowd felt the tension. They came early but they didn't have any idea how late they'd stay.

Everybody was a little careful, naturally, with so much riding on the game. But Toronto seemed to get more chances to score

during regulation time than we did. They tell me I stopped 111 shots that night. I can't tell you. I was too tired to count, because after a while it seemed the game would never end.

We almost won it in regulation time, in the third period. Alex Smith broke through and flipped one past Chabot, but he was ruled offside. Well, we argued loud and long but it didn't get us anywhere.

Now, 60 minutes of playoff hockey is a long, hard grind, but that was just a start. And the ice—that was incredibly bad. In those days, they didn't flood the ice between periods as they do now. It got sloppier and sloppier as the game went on.

And it did go on. Nobody even got close to scoring until the fourth overtime period. That's when Clancy rifled one past me. But I'd heard the whistle and just let it go. It was no goal, of course, because an official had blown the whistle.

At the end of the fourth overtime, Frank Calder, who was president of the National Hockey League, suggested a coin flip to decide the winner. Well, the crowd didn't like the idea and neither did the players, as tired as we were after 140 minutes of hockey. We all wanted to play until somebody won legitimately, even if it took all night. And it nearly did.

The fifth overtime was like a slow motion film. The ice was mush, and everybody was so exhausted they were skating around listlessly. Every once in a while somebody would get a second wind and there would be a rush on goal, but neither Chabot or myself let anything get past.

The fans seemed just as tired. But every once in a while, they'd get stirred up and cheer a little, and it would speed up the action briefly. But then the game would die down again.

It was after 1:30 in the morning when the sixth overtime period started. We were four minutes into it when the winning play began. Andy Blair was playing for Toronto, chiefly to shadow Eddie Shore, who was a great scoring threat despite being a defenseman. Blair was right on top of Shore all night and finally he got a break.

Shore tried to break away from Blair with

With everything on the line, even the crowd felt the tension. They came early but they didn't have any idea how late they'd stay.

the puck. He batted the puck ahead of him, meaning to go around Blair and pick it up. Instead, he put the puck right on Blair's stick. Blair saw his chance and made the most of it. He crossed the blue line into our zone, with Shore right on him. As Shore swung around to check him, Blair passed to Ken Doraty, who was heading for our net.

Doraty picked up the pass in full stride and snapped the puck past me to win the game for Toronto. The goal came at 4:46 of the sixth overtime—the longest game ever played at that time, and there has been only one longer since.

They tell me that the crowd gave me a standing ovation, even though we lost. I didn't hear a thing. I was just too tired. I don't think anyone cared at that point. But that's my most memorable game. I stopped 111 shots and played more than eight periods in goal.

—*As told to George Vass*

Cecil "Tiny" Thompson had a spectacular NHL rookie year in 1928–29. He posted 12 shutouts and had a 1.15 goals-against average during the 44-game regular season, then helped the Boston Bruins win the Stanley Cup by allowing only three goals in five playoff games. Thompson collected four Vezina Trophies before being sold to Detroit in November 1938. He retired after the 1939–40 season to become a minor league coach.

The game I'll never forget came during a year in which everyone, including me, did not expect our team to do much of

MAY 21, 1991
MET SPORTS CENTER, BLOOMINGTON MN
PITTSBURGH 5, MINNESOTA 3

FIRST PERIOD
1. PIT Stevens (unassisted) 0:58.
2. PIT Francis (Stevens, Mullen) 2:36.
3. PIT Lemieux (Recchi, Murphy) 2:58.
4. MIN Gagner (Bellows, Dahlen) 18:22.
Penalties: PIT Samuelsson (charging) 7:27; PIT Stanton (high-sticking) 7:44; MIN Propp (high-sticking) 7:44; MIN Johnson (holding) 14:45; PIT Samuelsson (holding) 18:38.

SECOND PERIOD
5. PIT Trottier (Errey, Jagr) 9:55.
6. MIN Propp (Gagner) 13:10 (PP).
7. MIN Modano (Propp, Gagner) 18:25 (PP).
Penalties: MIN Modano (slashing) 4:28; PIT Murphy (roughing) 11:22; MIN McRae (double minor roughing, served by Modano) 11:22; PIT Stevens (holding) 11:49; PIT Lemieux (roughing, served by Loney) 12:34; PIT Lemieux (roughing) 13:10; MIN Bellows (roughing) 14:34; PIT Murphy (roughing) 16:59; PIT Errey (high-sticking) 18:06; MIN Gagner (roughing) 18:50.

THIRD PERIOD
8. PIT Bourque (Mullen, Lemieux) 19:43 (EN).
Penalties: PIT Loney (high-sticking, served by Coffey, game misconduct) 13:03; MIN Casey (interference, served by Propp) 16:52.

SHOTS ON GOAL:

PIT	13	5	6	**24**
MIN	14	17	7	**38**

Goalies: PIT Barrasso; MIN Casey
Referee: Andy Van Hellemond
Linesmen: Gord Broseker, Kevin Collins

anything. In the first half of the 1990–91 season, we were awful. The Minnesota North Stars management had decided to go with a young team. That meant a lot of developing players, such as me, were getting a lot of ice time, and it showed. Up until the All-Star Game, our team didn't play anywhere near our potential.

Fortunately, we caught fire in the second half of the season, posting one of the best records in the NHL during that time. Even with that surge, however, we barely managed to squeak into the playoffs. We were the fourth and final team in the Norris Division to qualify for postseason play.

No one thought we would really do anything in the playoffs, especially since were going up against the Chicago Blackhawks in the first round. They led the league in points with 106. We managed to win the first game, and that gave us a big lift going into the rest of the series. Because of all the penalties Chicago took and the pure strength of our power play, we were able to overcome the Blackhawks' physical game. We gave up only two goals over the last three contests and won the series in six games.

Our momentum started to build, even though we really didn't know what we were doing. Being such a young team, I don't think it struck us that we were actually playing for the Stanley Cup. We were playing the underdog role the whole way, and I think we liked being in that position. It was just so much fun to play that we never felt the pressure.

Our team was between the ages of 20 and 23, with a few exceptions. It was the right time for all of us. It was definitely the right time for my defensive partner, Shawn Chambers, and me. Our ice time was adding up, and we had a lot of chances to play in key situations.

In the next series, we faced the St. Louis Blues. They were second in the league during the regular season with 105 points, but with hard work and determination we were able

to beat them in six games. If those two upsets weren't amazing enough, we then had to go against the defending Stanley Cup champion Edmonton Oilers. That hard-fought battle also lasted six games and ended with our team coming out as the victors.

Dethroning the defending champions put us on such a roll, and it kept going and going. Before we knew it, we found ourselves in the Stanley Cup finals against the Pittsburgh Penguins. This was a team with a lot of scoring power. Besides Mario Lemieux, they had guys like Larry Murphy, Joe Mullen, Paul Coffey, Mark Recchi and Kevin Stevens, who were all outstanding offensive players. In the net, they had a great goaltender in Tom Barrasso. In addition, Pittsburgh had made a late-season trade to acquire Ron Francis and Ulf Samuelsson, which rounded out an already talented team.

But we weren't intimidated and went into the series prepared. Our game plan was good, and we thought we would be able to win if we could stick to it. The Penguins had a lot of offense, but we never felt that they had too much for us. We won the first game of the series in Pittsburgh. They came back to win the second game, but we returned home to win Game 3 and took a 2–1 advantage. That set up a crucial Game 4, which turned out to be the game I'll never forget.

That contest was critical because we were in a good position to take total control of the series. A win would give us a 3–1 edge, which would be awfully hard for even the Penguins to overcome. The game was played in Minnesota. We really had the crowd behind us. I remember everything about Game 4 very well. What I remember most about that contest is that we played really good hockey. The entire game was played in their end, but we just couldn't score. We weren't able to finish our chances.

The one play I remember best was when Neal Broten and I had a two-on-one in the second period. It was a great scoring opportunity, but we couldn't convert. We played the whole third period just looking for one goal to tie the game, but it never happened. Barrasso came up big for Pittsburgh. It was just one of those things.

> Dethroning the defending champions put us on such a roll, and it kept going and going. Before we knew it, we found ourselves in the Stanley Cup finals.

I figured that was our best chance to win. That was our Stanley Cup. That game cost us the championship. We lost the game, which evened the series at 2–2. We went to Pittsburgh, where we still couldn't secure a victory. In what would be the final contest, Game 6, we came back to Minnesota, where we again really had the hometown crowd going. But as a team, we didn't have anything left. The feeling of confidence was gone, and we got destroyed that night.

After the game, I remember sitting in the locker room. I recall thinking to myself that we did everything we could. I felt pretty happy with the way we played. I can't say mistakes cost us against Pittsburgh or that we weren't ready to play them; we simply ran out of gas.

As for other big highlights of my career, playing in my first NHL game is a great memory. As a member of the New York Rangers in 1987, we had traveled to Edmonton to take on the Oilers. I'm from nearby Red Deer, Alberta, so it was a pretty amazing feeling to be able to play there in front of my parents and friends.

—*As told to Chuck O'Donnell*

Mark Tinordi, shown above left manhandling Pittsburgh's Mario Lemieux, played his rookie season for the New York Rangers before he was dealt to Minnesota in October 1988. Tinordi, a big and rugged defenseman, moved with the North Stars to Dallas for the 1993–94 season. Traded to Washington in January 1995, he spent five seasons with the Capitals. Atlanta claimed Tinordi in the 1999 expansion draft but he suffered a major knee injury before playing a single game for the Thrashers.

Maybe it was because we never won the Stanley Cup during my years as a player with the New York Rangers. A Cup winner

APRIL 11, 1970
MADISON SQUARE GARDEN, NEW YORK
NEW YORK RANGERS 4, BOSTON 3

FIRST PERIOD
1. BOS Speer (Esposito) 9:31.
2. NYR Ratelle (Kurtenbach, Gilbert) 13:07.
3. NYR Tkaczuk (Neilson) 14:24 (PP).
Penalties: BOS Sanderson (double major, misconduct, game misconduct) 1:31; NYR Balon (double major, misconduct, game misconduct) 1:31; BOS Marcotte (major) 1:31; BOS D. Smith (major) 1:31; NYR Brown (major) 1:31; NYR Tkaczuk (major) 1:31; BOS McKenzie 2:37; NYR Irvine 2:37; BOS McKenzie 4:36; NYR Kurtenbach 7:20; NYR Egers (major) 10:12; BOS Doak (major) 10:12; BOS Cashman (major, misconduct) 13:33; NYR Kurtenbach (major, misconduct) 13:33; NYR Park 16:51.

SECOND PERIOD
4. NYR Gilbert (Ratelle, Park) 13:48 (PP).
Penalties: NYR Awrey 0:23; NYR Horton 3:40; BOS Marcotte 6:56; BOS McKenzie 13:10; NYR Luce 14:48.

THIRD PERIOD
5. NYR Irvine (Tkaczuk, Fairbairn) 2:43.
6. BOS Orr (Bucyk, Stanfield) 5:59 (PP).
7. BOS Stanfield (D. Smith, McKenzie) 12:07.
Penalties: NYR Luce 4:44; BOS Cashman (minor, major, misconduct) 8:29; NYR Fairbairn (major) 8:29; NYR Kurtenbach 8:43; BOS Lorentz 9:02; BOS McKenzie 14:25; NYR Irvine 14:25.

SHOTS ON GOAL:

NYR	19	10	14	**43**
BOS	12	7	10	**29**

Goalies: NYR Giacomin; BOS Cheevers
Referee: John Ashley
Linesmen: John D'Amico, Pat Shetler

would have been something to remember. But whatever the reason, there is no one game that truly sticks out, not for its overall importance. All the same, there are some instances from games over the years, some things I liked and some things that I didn't that I'll never forget. One thing here, one thing there, things you always remember.

One of the most memorable was against the Boston Bruins in the first round of the playoffs in 1970, when they had a strong team and we had a strong team. But when we went into Boston to open the series, the Bruins won the first two games, and they beat us pretty soundly.

The third game was in New York and it was about a minute into the game when there was a face-off to our goalie Eddie Giacomin's left. Boston had a line out there of Derek Sanderson, Ed Westfall and Don Marcotte and I was out there with Bill Fairbairn and Dave Balon for the face-off. Just as referee John Ashley was about to drop the puck, Giacomin skated out from the net to Sanderson and said something to him. Nobody knew what he said, just Eddie and Derek. Giacomin skated back to his net just as if nothing happened, only you could see Derek Sanderson's hair starting to stand up. You could see he was all excited about something, but we didn't know what it was.

The puck was dropped with Sanderson facing off with me, and the puck went into the left corner. It had been a physical series anyway, so when Sanderson went into the corner I was chasing him. I hit him from behind and one of our other players, Arnie Brown, hit him from the front. We smashed him into the boards, then he collided with Balon. The gloves went flying, and Balon and Sanderson were at it and everybody was crowding in along the boards, gloves dropping. Sanderson was just wild, throwing punches at everybody in reach. The Madison Square Garden crowd went crazy, and debris was flying all over the ice. By the time the

officials restored order, 15 minutes had passed and everybody on the ice at the time got a penalty, including Sanderson, who was ejected from the game.

At the end of the period, on the way to the locker room, I asked Eddie, "What the hell did you say to that son of a gun? Whatever you said, you could see his hair was standing up and there was something bothering him."

Eddie said, "I told him that right after the face-off you're going to get killed. Keep your head up or we're going to get you."

That's what stirred up Sanderson. And it almost happened. And nobody knew it except him and Giacomin. We got into a big brawl because of something Eddie said. There was something like 38 penalties and 174 penalty minutes in that game. We won it 4–3, and I got one of the goals. But the brawl and the penalties and the way Giacomin set them off is what made the game so memorable. Sanderson made a lot of publicity out of the situation. He said Giacomin had said the Rangers had put a price on his head. He even got on the Johnny Carson show because of that incident.

It didn't really turn the series around, though we won the next game too, in New York. But when we went back to Boston, the Bruins won the fifth game, then won the series in the sixth game in New York. They went on to win the Cup that year, but that incident in the third game still sticks out for me.

Another instance always comes to mind when I think of my career as a player, something that was very disappointing to me. In fact, it might have been the biggest disappointment of my career. It came the last time we went to the Stanley Cup finals [1979] and we were playing Montreal.

Though Montreal had won the Cup the three previous years, we had a pretty good chance to beat them. We beat Los Angeles, Chicago and the Islanders in the first three rounds and we had a good head of steam going into the finals. Then we won the opening game in Montreal 4–1, and you don't do that often in the Forum. So things looked pretty good for our chances of winning the Cup. And we got a 2–0 lead on

Sanderson was just wild, throwing punches at everybody in reach. The Madison Square Garden crowd went crazy, and debris was flying all over the ice.

them in the second game. But things turned around; they scored the next six goals to win that game. They won the next three games to keep the Stanley Cup.

That was a disappointment in itself, but what I found out during the course of the summer made it all the more disappointing. I found out that some of the players on our team were out to the early hours every night after each game of the finals. Finding out that they had been so selfish toward the other players on the team, that they couldn't pass

up their pleasures even though the Stanley Cup was at stake, was one of the biggest disappointments of my career in hockey.

There are probably a lot more memories like those two. When you play hockey a dozen years and more they pile up. Like I said, some instances you recall are ones you like, others are ones you'd just as soon not have happened. But they are all ones you never forget.

—*As told to George Vass*

Walt Tkaczuk established himself as an NHL regular in 1968–69, his first of 13 seasons with the New York Rangers. One of the strongest centers in the league, he was often assigned a checking role against the opposition's top line. Tkaczuk had his best offensive season in 1969–70, when he scored 27 goals and 50 assists. He shared the Rangers' captaincy in 1980–81, shortly before he retired.

When I think about the most memorable game of my career, it definitely would be the final game of last year's Canada Cup,

when Team Canada beat the Soviets.

SEPTEMBER 15, 1987
COPPS COLISEUM, HAMILTON
CANADA 6, SOVIET UNION 5

FIRST PERIOD
1. SOV Makarov (Krutov) 0:26.
2. SOV Gusarov (unassisted) 7:04.
3. SOV Fetisov (Makarov) 8:00.
4. CAN Tocchet (Goulet, Murphy) 9:50 (PP).
5. CAN Propp (Tocchet, Sutter) 15:23.
6. SOV Khomutov (unassisted) 19:32.
Penalties: SOV Bykov (interference) 4:59; SOV Kravchuk (cross-checking) 9:10; CAN Sutter (holding) 10:16; SOV Makarov (high-sticking) 17:11.

SECOND PERIOD
7. CAN Murphy (Gretzky, M. Lemieux) 9:20 (PP).
8. CAN Sutter (Hawerchuk, Crossman) 11:06.
9. CAN Hawerchuk (Murphy, Propp) 15:32.
Penalties: SOV Bykov (tripping) 8:24; CAN M. Lemieux (slashing) 11:34; SOV Larionov (interference) 12:37; CAN Bourque (high-sticking) 16:05; CAN Bourque (hooking) 18:51.

THIRD PERIOD
10. SOV Semak (Lomakin) 12:21.
11. CAN M. Lemieux (Gretzky) 18:34.
No penalties.

SHOTS ON GOAL:

CAN	19	12	15	**46**
SOV	9	8	6	**23**

Goalies: CAN Fuhr; SOV Mylnikov
Referee: Don Koharski
Linesmen: John D'Amico, Micheal Golinovski

The first time somebody asked me about being picked for the team, I said I was surprised but not shocked. I was asked to the first camp, when they took 36 guys. When it came down to the actual training camp, they called five players in every day and let them go. Finally, coach Mike Keenan told me to be there at a certain time, and that meant I made it. I felt I had a secure job with the Flyers, but I really didn't know what would happen with the Canada Cup team.

During the actual tournament, I got hurt against the Soviets. I went to hit a guy, missed him and twisted my left knee. I strained some ligaments and was really disappointed. I said, "Here is my chance to represent my country in this type of tournament, and I might never have another chance." But I decided I was still part of the team and could be a cheerleader to the guys.

On the night of the first game of the finals, I felt a little better and told Mike I could play the game. He said OK because I knew best how I felt. We lost 6–5 in overtime to the Soviets, and my knee ballooned up after the game. When we went to Hamilton for the second game, I couldn't skate on it, and I had to sit out. Of course, I knew I might not get in again because if we lost, it would be over.

That could have been the most exciting game I have ever seen, as we beat the Soviets 6–5 in double overtime. It was unbelievable to watch. I was far more nervous than when I play. My stomach was in knots, and I had no way to release the tension.

After we won, we had the next day off and all I could think was, "I don't know about the knee." I said to myself, "I can play the final game; I've got the chance to do it and I will." So when the other guys went out after the game, I went to my room to be ready.

Mike called me in the morning, and they flew me to Philadelphia to see the Flyers' doctor. The doctor told me that if I didn't play, he wouldn't blame me, but I couldn't do any more damage to my knee, and he wouldn't stop me from playing. That was all I needed to hear.

When I got back to Hamilton, I told Mike I wanted to play. He said, "We'll see." The next day, game day, my uniform was hanging up in the dressing room and I got ready to play.

I expected it to be a pretty tense time, but the other guys on the team really relaxed me. I saw Ray Bourque and Wayne Gretzky and Paul Coffey talking and joking, and the music on the jukebox was on. Maybe they were nervous but they were acting ready and relaxed, not sweating at all.

I felt a twinge in my knee before the game in warm-ups, so I took it easy and didn't put pressure on it. I glided through warm-ups. Then I went to my dressing stall and never said a word. I wanted to be on the ice, but I didn't want to embarrass myself or make a key mistake. When we got onto the ice, I felt the responsibility of playing for my country and for the 22 million people in Canada and the people in the United States against the Soviets. That was on my mind.

I also thought about the things the Soviets can do. They are the best-trained team in the world. I would suggest to anyone playing them never to watch them practice; you'll think you can't beat them. They've also found that some of the North American hockey skills fit them. They have players who grind and hit, which they never had before. I appreciate that—there are always jobs for these types of players.

In the first period, the Soviets jumped out to a 3–0 lead, but there wasn't much panic on the bench. One of my most nervous moments was when Keenan put me on the power play instead of Gretzky or Mario Lemieux. I was thinking, "Why am I on?"

Somehow, the puck just came to me in the slot and I scored. The whole team got a lift from it. I think that was exactly what Mike had in mind. It was a gamble that paid off.

I hadn't played that much but after I scored I began playing more on a line with Brent Sutter and Brian Propp. We were just banging them, and then I got the puck to Brent and he sent it off Brian's skate into the net to make it 3–2.

The Soviets scored to make it 4–2 after the first period. But we all felt confident in the locker room. All through the tournament, we had come back for victories.

We were all over them in the second period, outhitting and outskating them, and we outscored them 3–0. It was our best period of the tournament. Grant Fuhr was playing great, and Dale Hawerchuk and Brent Sutter were just unbelievable. The fans were on their feet throughout the period, and they were generating great electricity throughout the building. It was the fastest paced game I've ever been through.

The Soviets tied the score with about eight minutes left. I didn't even remember I had a knee problem, there was so much adrenaline flowing.

We were taking the play to them, and we all knew somebody would score. But it happened so quickly. The Soviet defenseman pinched in and got caught for a three-on-one break. The whole play lasted maybe two seconds. Hawerchuk, Gretzky and Lemieux were on the fly. What were the odds of the puck going in? Pretty good. A frenzy of celebration broke out when Mario scored.

I can't say enough about the whole experience. The NHL is a business. The Canada Cup is played for the love of one's country. I don't think a team that good will ever be assembled again. Maybe a team will have Gretzky and Lemieux, but will they be on top of their games the way they were? We might never see it again.

—As told to Barry Wilner

Approaching 1,000 career points and 3,000 penalty minutes, **Rick Tocchet** has been one of the NHL's strongest power forwards since entering the NHL with Philadelphia in 1984–85. Traded to Pittsburgh in February 1992, he won a Stanley Cup ring with the Pens that spring. He had his best offensive season in 1992–93, notching 48 goals and 61 assists. Tocchet later spent seasons with Los Angeles, Boston, Washington and Phoenix before returning to Philadelphia in March 2000.

I've been fortunate to play with an outstanding team that has won four Stanley Cups in a row, so there are any

JANUARY 6, 1981
NASSAU COLISEUM, UNIONDALE NY
NEW YORK ISLANDERS 6, TORONTO 3

FIRST PERIOD
1. NYI Tonelli (Bossy, Trottier) 10:06.
2. NYI Trottier (D. Potvin, Bossy) 15:48 (PP).
Penalties: TOR Farrish (interference) 4:29; TOR Hotham (kneeing); NYI Howatt (holding) 18:10.

SECOND PERIOD
3. NYI Tonelli (Langevin, Bossy) 1:43.
4. TOR Vaive (Sittler, Hotham) 19:59.
Penalties: NYI Gillies (holding) 8:19; TOR Paiement (fighting) 14:29; NYI Lorimer (fighting) 14:29.

THIRD PERIOD
5. NYI Tonelli (Bossy, Persson) 1:53.
6. TOR Ellis (Farrish, Boschman) 9:56.
7. TOR Vaive (Farrish, Hickey) 16:06.
8. NYI Tonelli (Trottier, Bossy) 17:02.
9. NYI Tonelli (Bossy) 19:18 (EN).
Penalties: TOR Melrose (fighting, slashing) 5:31; NYI Howatt (fighting, slashing) 5:31; TOR Anderson (tripping) 7:34; TOR Boschman (high-sticking) 10:42; NYI Lorimer (interference) 10:42.

SHOTS ON GOAL:

NYI	17	9	10	**36**
TOR	7	12	12	**31**

Goalies: NYI Resch; TOR Crha
Referee: Bruce Hood
Linesmen: Gord Broseker, Wayne Bonney

number of games that would stick out in my mind as being memorable. You get a lot of those with the New York Islanders, and I hope there are a lot more to come.

Every game that wins a Stanley Cup is a new thrill, but I guess the first one is extra special because it's something you've never experienced. This is what you're working for, playing for your entire hockey career, and now it's come true. A lot of guys who play many years never get the chance to have that feeling. You're lucky if you do, especially when it happens early in your career, as it did for me in 1980.

We won the Cup the first time in my second year with the Islanders, when I was only 23. And there's no way I'll ever forget the final game against Montreal, because I was lucky enough to get the puck to Bob Nystrom for the goal that won the Cup in overtime. That rates up there with my top thrills in hockey, getting an assist on the Cup-winning goal.

I was fortunate in many ways when I got into hockey, always being associated with winning teams. Before the Islanders, I was with the Houston Aeros of the old World Hockey Association, and that was a tremendous experience for me. Here I was, 18 years old, and my first linemates at Houston were Gordie Howe and Mark Howe. I don't care who you are, you've got to be in awe of Gordie Howe.

I'll never forget that first training camp with the Aeros and the impression that Howe made on me. Here he was, 47 or 48 years old, and he was skating by everybody. He was unbelievable. I'll admit I was nervous and had to struggle to keep up with Howe. Gordie would go by me and wink and say, "Hurry up, kid." It was unbelievable. What a player he was. And this was after he'd played almost 30 years. He was the greatest athlete I ever saw. What's more, I can't think of a player who was more helpful to a young kid than Gordie. He was always willing to talk

hockey, to give you a tip. And just watching him play hockey was an education.

Like I've said, I was lucky to be on good teams and follow some good examples in improving my play. That makes a lot of difference. When you're with a team like the Islanders, you put team play first, not individual achievements. You work on contributing to a winning season; that's where you get the greatest satisfaction. Once in a while, though, a game comes along that you may remember mostly because of some individual achievement. And I guess the game that I remember most from those, one of the games I'll never forget, is the one in which I scored five goals.

In my first few years I wasn't known exactly as a goal scorer, though I got my share, about 20 a season. But until that big night, I never had a hat trick, though I think I'd scored two goals in a game a couple of times. We were playing Toronto on our ice and we'd had a little shakeup in our forward lines. That game, I'd been put on left wing with Bryan Trottier [center] and Mike Bossy [right wing]. There's an oddity in itself. On a line like that, which guys would you think might have a five-goal game?

But that was one of those games in which the puck seemed to follow me around. No matter where I was on the ice, the puck came on my stick. Of course, it helps when you're playing with great players like Bossy and Trottier. Still, there has to be some luck involved.

Jiri Crha was in goal for the Maple Leafs, and it wasn't his night, not that any of the goals were easy, other than the last one. I don't remember each goal in detail, but I do remember I scored in the first period. I think that gave me 14 goals for the season, as many as I'd scored the entire season before.

I got two more in the second period. The funny thing, I remember, is that after I'd got two goals, while we were on the bench, Bossy whispered, "We'll get you three." I just laughed. I'd never had a hat trick either in the NHL or the WHA. That third goal, when it came, was about all I could expect. It was a great feeling.

But in the third period, the Leafs came back and cut our lead to 4–3. We didn't want

> **I can't think of a player who was more helpful to a young kid than Gordie Howe. He was always willing to talk hockey, to give you a tip.**

to let the game get away and we soon got an opportunity. Trottier hit me with a pass as I moved into the slot. Crha came out, backed up and had the net pretty well covered, so I tried to jam the puck inside the left post. But to show you what kind of night it was, the puck went through Crha's legs. We had a 5–3 lead and I had my fourth goal.

I can't say I ever dreamed of a fifth one. I mean, not many guys have ever scored five goals. When you think of the great players that have scored that many, well, it takes you back. But I got it.

With about a minute and a half to go, the Leafs pulled Crha and we won a face-off in our end. I was at mid-ice when Bossy snapped a pass to me. The net was empty and all I had to do was keep the puck on my stick, skate and put it in the net. When it went in and that red light went on, it was a tremendous feeling. I almost hit the roof I was so elated.

That was really something special, getting five goals in a game, and it's something you never forget. It may not rank up there with the games in which we won the Stanley Cup, but in a different way, it's a great memory.

—*As told to George Vass*

A tenacious and inspirational player, **John Tonelli** spent three seasons in the WHA before joining the New York Islanders in 1978–79. He helped the Islanders win four Stanley Cups in the early 1980s, won the 1984 Canada Cup MVP Award, then scored a career-high 42 goals and 100 points for the Isles in 1984–85. Dealt to Calgary in March 1986, Tonelli later played for Los Angeles, Chicago and Quebec before retiring after the 1991–92 season.

There's no way I can forget it, because I've got a silver tea service from Leafs management to remind me of the night I

FEBRUARY 2, 1977
MAPLE LEAF GARDENS, TORONTO
TORONTO 9, DETROIT 1

FIRST PERIOD
No scoring.
Penalties: TOR Weir (interference) 3:46; DET Cameron (tripping) 6:06; DET Hextall (hooking) 11:30; DET Wilson (slashing) 19:42.

SECOND PERIOD
1. TOR Turnbull (McDonald, Salming) 1:55.
2. TOR Boutette (Weir) 2:35.
3. TOR Ashby (Thompson) 4:12.
4. TOR Williams (Alexander, Glennie) 8:15.
5. TOR Turnbull (unassisted) 10:26.
Penalties: DET Bergeron (slashing) 8:43; TOR Walker (double minor, roughing) 8:43; TOR Ashby (roughing) 8:43; DET Lapointe (slashing) 8:43; DET Hamel (holding) 9:28; TOR Ashby (slashing) 17:32.

THIRD PERIOD
6. TOR Turnbull (unassisted) 4:58.
7. TOR McDonald (Ashby, Alexander) 6:13.
8. DET Grant (Hextall, Harper) 16:18.
9. TOR Turnbull (Weir, Salming) 17:10.
10. TOR Turnbull (Salming, Valiquette) 18:30.
Penalties: TOR Turnbull (tripping) 2:32; TOR Walker (high-sticking) 8:14; DET Joly (high-sticking) 13:27; TOR Garland (high-sticking) 13:27; DET Bergeron (hooking) 19:06.

SHOTS ON GOAL:

TOR	8	0	14	**32**
DET	9	12	10	**31**

Goalies: TOR Thomas; DET Giacomin, Rutherford
Referee: John McCauley
Linesmen: Gord Broseker, John D'Amico

scored five goals against Detroit. Seriously, while I appreciate the significance people attach to hockey records, I can't say that scoring five goals in a game has changed me. I don't see how it could. Hockey players are portrayed to be living in a dream world, but it's simply not true. Most of them view themselves as just earning a living like most people, though I suppose they have more fun than many people do in other professions.

I can truthfully say the glitter and glamor of being a hockey player simply doesn't affect me because I never believed in it in the first place. Personally, I don't think hockey players should be idolized the way we are. Sure, hockey is in the public eye, I can see that. But it's really just a job.

I've never been one for seeking much attention. It's not something I enjoy. I don't even like to see my name in print, though I'm sure I would like it if it was in connection with the Leafs winning a Stanley Cup. But that's yet to come, and I hope it's not too far in the future.

Until that time, I'm sure that the outstanding game of my career will remain the one against Detroit in Maple Leaf Gardens in which I broke the record for goals scored by a defenseman. The record of four had stood many years, so the press really played up my achievement.

I can't say that any of the five goals was particularly significant because we beat Detroit 9–1 that night. In fact, if I remember right, that month we were scoring goals in clusters against everyone. The trouble is, we were giving up almost as many. I guess I sort of typified the Leafs that season. Offense always came naturally to me. I had to think more about defense. I know the coaches are usually after me to stay back a little more and I think I've been doing that year by year. But I have to make mental notes not to go up too much, because my natural style is to get the puck and go. I might be getting a little smarter now about chancing a risky play. I'm

becoming a little more defensive.

That night, there was no reason to complain about our defense, since we gave up only one goal. In fact, it looked at the beginning like it was going to be a tight-checking game all the way. Neither team scored in the first period. I know I didn't have a shot on net. In fact, at the end of the game I'd had only five shots—but all had gone in.

I remember talking to Darryl Sittler after the game. He sat it out because of a rib injury, but he said it reminded him of the big night he'd had against Boston the year before when he'd scored six goals and four assists. He said, "There's no explanation why you suddenly have a game like that. It happens when it happens." That's the way I looked at it, too.

I can't describe each goal in detail. They just kept going in on Eddie Giacomin, who was the Detroit goalie that night. The first one came early in the second period, after which we got three more goals. My second goal closed out a five-goal second period.

One of my two goals in the second period—I don't remember which one—was just lucky. I took a shot and it deflected off a Detroit defenseman's skates into the net. After getting two goals with a period left to play, it's only natural to think of a hat trick, even if you're a defenseman, and I'm sure it crossed my mind. It didn't take me long to get it, the third goal coming early in the third period.

We were ahead 6–0 at that point, so I guess Detroit opened up, which must have increased our opportunities to score. I got my fourth goal, then my fifth, the only one I really remember in any detail. That fifth goal, the one that broke the record, was one I didn't even take a shot on. Stan Weir let one go and it hit me as I was skating in front of the net. It bounced off me past Giacomin. Again, there was nothing he could do about it. He never had a chance.

It was just one of those nights when everything goes in. It was like a good day at the race track. I wish that the track had been going that afternoon. I probably would have cleaned up. I know I didn't do anything

> **The glitter and glamor of being a hockey player simply doesn't affect me because I never believed in it in the first place. Personally, I don't think hockey players should be idolized the way we are.**

differently than I had been doing. We stuck to the style of play we'd been using, which probably increased my scoring opportunities. It called for our wingers to pick up their wingers at their blue line rather than going deep to forecheck. That meant our wingers were more checkers than puck-carriers, so it meant our defensemen had to be more mobile and got more of a chance to carry the puck. But there's no explaining for why you have a game like that. It just happens, and it happened to me that night, like it had happened to Sittler the year before.

It got a lot of attention, that's for sure. And I understand it even if I'm not seeking it. I'm not in hockey for publicity. I don't care if I'm ever remembered as a hockey player. I don't care if the fans remember me or what I accomplished. But I suppose they'll remember this game. I will.

—*As told to George Vass*

Smooth-skating defenseman **Ian Turnbull** joined the Toronto Maple Leafs in 1973–74. He missed most of his sophomore season due to injury, but scored 20 goals and 36 assists in 1975–76 before setting career highs with 22 goals and 57 helpers in 1976–77. The Leafs traded Turnbull to Los Angeles in November 1981 but he finished out the season in the minors. He played his final six NHL games for Pittsburgh in 1982–83.

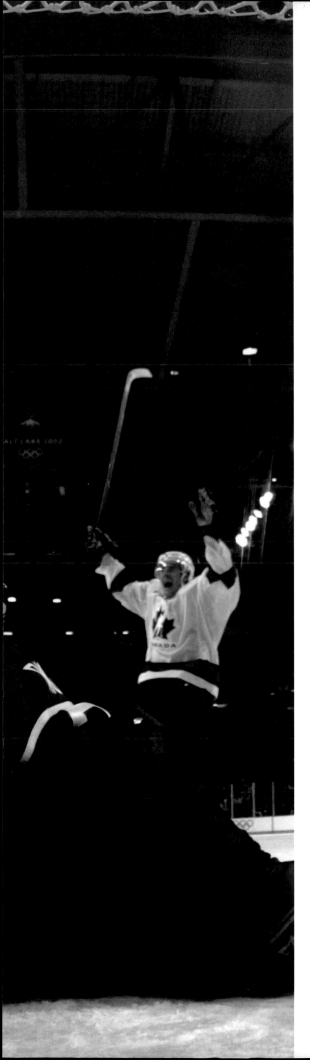

CANADIAN GOLD

The Canadian women's hockey team defeated the Americans for the women's gold medal (below), setting up Canada's dream scenario. The men's team did not disappoint. Jarome Iginla, far left, celebrates his second goal and the game-winner as splayed USA netminder Mike Richter and defenseman Gary Suter (20) realize the puck is in. Iginla, who also added an assist, sparked the Canadians to a hard-fought 5–2 victory. As Team Canada celebrated on the ice, fans across Canada were already pouring into the streets in jubilation.

—*Chris McDonell*

FEBRUARY 24, 2002
E-CENTER, SALT LAKE CITY
CANADA 5, USA 2

There's been nothing like it in my career, not when I was with Montreal, not during my seasons with the Los Angeles Kings.

SEPTEMBER 15, 1976
MONTREAL FORUM, MONTREAL
CANADA 5, CZECHOSLOVAKIA 4 (OT)

FIRST PERIOD
1. CAN Perreault (Lafleur, Potvin) 1:25.
2. CAN Esposito (Potvin) 3:09.
Penalties: CZS Cernik (interference) 0:25; CAN Leach (high-sticking) 0:25; CZS B. Stastny (interference) 3:40; CAN Potvin (elbowing) 9:38; CAN Gainey (hooking) 16:15.

SECOND PERIOD
3. CZS Novy (Martinec, Machac) 9:44.
Penalties: CZS Pouzar (tripping) 5:49; CAN Barber (hoarding) 8:07; CZS B. Stastny (holding) 10:38; CZS Augusta (hooking) 15:39.

THIRD PERIOD
4. CZS Pouzar (M. Stastny, Chalups) 2:14.
5. CAN Clarke (Hull, Perreault) 7:48.
6. CZS Augusta (Machac, Martinec) 15:01.
7. CZS M. Stastny (Holik, Bubla) 16:00.
8. CAN Barber (Leach, Clarke) 17:48.
Penalties: CZS Pospisil (elbowing) 6:10; CAN Potvin (elbowing) 14:22.

FIRST OVERTIME PERIOD
9. CAN Sittler (Dionne, McDonald) 11:33.
Penalty: CZS (bench, intentionally knocking net off mooring) 8:30.

SHOTS ON GOAL:

CAN	9	11	14	5	**39**
CZS	8	6	7	4	**25**

Goalies: CAN Vachon; CZS Holecek, Dzurilla.

Not all the shutouts, not all the Stanley Cup games, can match the final game when Team Canada beat the Czechs in the Canada Cup competition in 1976.

I played goal in every one of the seven games of that series. I am still surprised about that, pleased about that. I feel for the other guys who worked so hard and didn't get to play but I was the hot goalie and I guess the coaches wanted to stick with me. I'm glad they did.

I was never so excited in my life. I usually don't get too excited. Goaltending is a job, like any other job. Maybe not like any other job, but you've got to look at it that way. If you give up a goal, a good goal, you still eat well, sleep well. If you give up a bad goal, well, you still must live, sleep and eat. You do the best you can. If you let it upset you, it's foolish.

This Canada Cup series in the fall of 1976 was just like the Stanley Cup finals, the same excitement, the publicity, the full arenas, the noise, the hard play. It didn't make me nervous. I don't get that way too much. But it made me sharp, enthusiastic, inspired, determined to do my best.

It was thrilling just to be on the ice with the great players on my team—the best team ever—with players like Bobby Orr, Bobby Hull, Guy Lafleur, Phil Esposito, Rick Martin and all the others. I don't think there was ever a team so good.

This was not like the first big series in 1972 when Canada was overconfident. This time, we knew the Russians were good, the Czechs were good. We knew it would not be easy. The Czechs that year already had won the World Cup. They play up and down hockey, much like the NHL style, and pass and skate very well. Unlike the Russians, they don't drop back into their own zone and pass the puck around trying to get the checkers to make a mistake. They work the puck up the ice right away, going for the net.

There were six nations in the round robin competition, and we finished atop the standings, winning four of the five games

before the playoffs. The Czechs finished second; winning three, losing one, with a tie. The only game we lost was to the Czechs, who beat us 1–0, in what was one of the best games ever played. The Czech goalie, Vladimir Dzurilla, had one of those nights you dream of. He could do nothing wrong. I had a good night, too, but late in the third period Milan Novy, one of the best forwards I've ever seen, beat me with a shot on the stick side, a good shot.

I had a shutout, too, in the first five games, over Sweden. It was not easy. I had to stop 28 shots, and the Swedes are great skaters and shooters. We beat them 4–0. But the playoffs were the most important. They would decide who was the best, Team Canada or the Czechs. They'd shown us in the 1–0 game what we could expect of them. They had good goaltending, good defensive play and forwards who could make the most of the opportunities.

It was best-of-three series and the first game was in Toronto. I don't know whether Dzurilla had a bad night, or our team was exceptionally fired up, but we scored four goals in the first period and went on to win easily, 6–0. It was my second shutout of the series, but it is easier for a goalie with a big lead. He can play more relaxed; more of the pressure is on the shooters.

That brings us to the most memorable game of my career, the one at Montreal. I'd given up only six goals in the first six games so I knew I was hot, and I was playing with confidence. I think more people watched that game on TV than ever saw another hockey game. The excitement was tremendous. I could feel it, I was inspired, even before I took the ice in the Forum before that roaring crowd.

The Czechs started Jiri Holecek in goal. He was supposed to be their best, even better than Dzurilla. We expected a tight game, good checking, waiting for the breaks. Instead, nine goals were scored. In fact, three more than that, all by Canada, but they were disallowed.

We got the first two goals, right at the start of the game, by Gil Perreault and Phil Esposito, with less than four minutes gone. The Czech coaches must have figured Holecek was shaky, or that a change might lift the team, because

Vladimir Martinec put a shot on me from close range and I was lucky to get my glove up and catch it. It was instinct, nothing more.

they put Dzurilla in there right away. I don't remember all the goals. All I remember is that the Czechs showed tremendous courage, because they fought right back. They kept working and they cut our lead to 2–1 going into the third period.

I can't recall a more exciting period than that third one. The Czechs made the most of their chances and they scored three goals. All of a sudden, we found ourselves trailing 4–3, with less than three minutes to play.

We were just as determined as they were. We went up and down the ice with them and with just 2:12 left, Bill Barber scored the tying goal. All the same, the Czechs came close to winning it in regulation time. Novy got a breakaway right after Barber's tying goal when he beat our defenseman, Guy Lapointe. But Guy made a great recovery and slowed down Novy so I could hook the puck off his stick.

The overtime was electric. I had to make my best save of the game right at the beginning to keep us alive. Vladimir Martinec put a shot on me from close range and I was lucky to get my glove up and catch it. It was instinct, nothing more. Either I caught it, or the game was over.

The overtime was in its 12th minute when we got a break. Darryl Sittler got a breakaway. He'd noticed that Dzurilla rushed out to meet a player on a break. Sittler gave him a move and went around him. He beat Dzurilla with a wrist shot from the left side and it was all over, 5–4.

We felt like the world champions, and we were. We'd beaten the Czechs, who had played great hockey. I can't think of a bigger thrill. That was the most memorable game of my life. Nothing like it!

—*As told to George Vass*

Rogie Vachon won three Stanley Cup rings with the Montreal Canadiens, but rookie Ken Dryden usurped his position. Vachon was dealt to Los Angeles in November 1971, where he played for seven seasons. Vachon made the Second All-Star Team in 1975 and 1977 and signed with Detroit as a free agent in August 1978. Traded to Boston in the summer of 1980, he concluded his playing career after two seasons with the Bruins. He returned to Los Angeles where he has served as coach, general manager and president.

Every guy on the Toronto Maple Leafs in the early 1950s was good friends with Bill Barilko. He was an easygoing guy—the

APRIL 21, 1951
MAPLE LEAF GARDENS, TORONTO
TORONTO 3, MONTREAL 2 (OT)

FIRST PERIOD
No scoring.
Penalties: MON Dawes (slashing) 0:27; TOR Barilko (charging) 16:04.

SECOND PERIOD
1. MON Richard (MacPherson) 8:56.
2. TOR Sloan (Kennedy) 12:00.
No penalties.

THIRD PERIOD
3. MON Meger (Harvey) 4:47.
4. TOR Sloan (Bentley, Smith) 19:28.
Penalties: TOR Barilko (roughing) 10:36; MON Johnson (roughing) 10:36; MON Reay (misconduct) 10:36.

FIRST OVERTIME PERIOD
5. TOR Barilko (Meeker, Watson) 2:53.
No penalties.

Goalies: TOR Rollins; MON McNeil
Referee: Bill Chadwick
Linesmen: Sam Babcock, Bill Morrison

kind of guy who would light up the room when he walked in. Barilko had a big, broad smile and a shiny head of blond hair. He was a real team guy. He kept everyone's spirits up in the dressing room.

Barilko was a pretty raw talent when he came up with the Leafs. He was a real diamond in the rough, but his game got a lot of polishing from coaches Hap Day and Joe Primeau. They brought Barilko along and made him one of the best defensemen at the time. He was quite a hitter; after all you have to be a good hitter to get the nickname "Bashin' Bill."

Since he was so well liked and such a good player, it made it even more of a tragedy when he was suddenly killed in the summer of 1951. Four months after scoring the deciding goal in the Stanley Cup Finals against the Montreal Canadiens, Barilko was flying with a friend in a single-engine plane back to Timmins, Ontario, after a fishing trip. The plane vanished. At first, there were hopes that they would be found alive, but as time went on, you just knew they wouldn't. Eleven years later, they found the wreckage.

I was a pallbearer at Bill's funeral. On that sad day, my mind drifted back to the overtime goal Barilko scored to clinch the 1951 Stanley Cup, in the game I'll never forget.

The Canadiens were our biggest rivals back then. We hated them, especially Maurice "Rocket" Richard. He was a great skater, and once you caught him, you couldn't knock him down. For some reason; I always had good luck checking Richard. Don't ask me why, but I did. When I was with the Detroit Red Wings [before I was traded to Toronto], coach Jack Adams once said to me, "I wish we played the Canadiens every night," because he liked the way I played Richard.

There were other teams we wouldn't get as up for, like the Chicago Blackhawks and the Boston Bruins. But Richard's Canadiens—we were always ready for them.

I always thought that checking was my specialty as a player, although back in those days, you were expected to also play defense and score. I didn't really have a strategy against Richard. He was tough to check. He would circle all the time, just trying to get some daylight. Then, all of a sudden, he would dart in toward the net like an arrow. And he had a great shot. He would hardly ever miss the net. Richard had a great backhander, too.

We had a strong team. In goal we had the tandem of Turk Broda and Al Rollins. On defense, we featured Barilko, Jim Thomson, Bill Juzda, Fernie Flaman and Gus Mortson. Up front, we had a lot of firepower in Tod Sloan, Sid Smith, Teeder Kennedy, Max Bentley and Fleming Mackell. Back then, I mostly played with Howie Meeker and Cal Gardner.

Everyone knew the series was going to be close, but I don't think anyone had any idea it was going to be as tight as it really was. We won the opener at home in overtime, on a goal by Smith. A few nights later, Montreal evened up the series when Richard scored in overtime.

The series then switched to Montreal, where Game 3 went into overtime—again. This time, Teeder got the game-winning goal. Game 4 went into overtime, and I managed to score the goal to win it.

The Canadiens took an early 2–1 lead in Game 5 and sat on it for most of the third period. In desperation, we pulled our goalie, Rollins, for an extra attacker in the final minute. Off a face-off in the Canadiens' zone, the puck came back to the point. There was a sea of bodies in front of the net, but Sloan found the puck and put it past Gerry McNeil. We were headed for another overtime.

We got an early jump in the overtime and worked the puck into their zone. I hit Meeker with a pass and he took a shot that hit the outside of the net and then settled behind the goal. Meeker went behind the net with Tom Johnson, battling for the puck. Meeker won the battle and threw it in front, hoping someone would be there. I took a crack at the puck, but I missed it. That's when Barilko spotted his chance.

Barilko was supposed to stay off the blue line. But he saw the puck coming out, so he just roared in and sent it toward the goal.

Bill Barilko scores the overtime goal against Montreal, above, to win the 1951 Stanley Cup for Toronto. **Harry Watson**, in the inset photo, laughs as Barilko is carried off the ice by his jubilant teammates. Watson broke into the NHL with the Brooklyn Americans in 1941–42. He helped Detroit win the Cup the following season. Traded to Toronto in September 1946, Watson won four more Cup rings in five seasons. Sold to Chicago in 1954, he concluded his NHL career with the Blackhawks in 1956–57.

The Leafs were always a defensive team back in those days. Barilko was supposed to stay on the blue line. But he saw the puck coming out, so he just roared in and sent it toward the goal.

There have been a lot of great overtime goals in the history of the NHL, but to me, Barilko's was one of the best—a perfect ending to a tremendous series. It's just a shame that it was also the end of a great man's career too.

—As told to Chuck O'Donnell

Defeating the Soviet Union in the 1972 Summit Series made every player on Team Canada an instant national hero. It may be

SEPTEMBER 28, 1972
MOSCOW
CANADA 6, SOVIET UNION 5

FIRST PERIOD
1. SOV Yakushev (Maltsev, Liapkin) 3:34.
2. CAN P. Esposito (Park) 6:45.
3. SOV Lutchenko (Kharlamov) 13:10.
4. CAN Park (Ratelle, Hull) 16:59.
Penalties: CAN White (holding) 2:25; CAN P. Mahovlich (holding) 3:01; SOV Petrov (hooking) 3:44; CAN Parise (interference, misconduct, game misconduct) 4:10; SOV Tsigankov (interference) 6:28; CAN Ellis (interference) 9:27; SOV Petrov (interference) 9:46; CAN Cournoyer (interference) 12:51.

SECOND PERIOD
5. SOV Shadrin (unassisted) 0:21.
6. CAN White (Gilbert, Ratelle) 10:32.
7. SOV Yakushev (Shadrin) 11:34.
8. SOV Vasiliev (unassisted) 16:44.
Penalties: CAN Stapleton (cross-checking) 14:58; SOV Kuzkin (elbowing) 18:06.

THIRD PERIOD
9. CAN P. Esposito (P. Mahovlich) 2:27.
10. CAN Cournoyer (P. Esposito, Park) 12:56.
11. CAN Henderson (P. Esposito) 19:26.
Penalties: CAN Gilbert (fighting) 3:41; SOV Mishakov (fighting) 3:41; SOV Vasiliev (tripping) 4:27; SOV Petrov (elbowing) 15:24; CAN Hull (high-sticking) 15:24.

SHOTS ON GOAL:

CAN	14	8	14	**36**
SOV	12	10	5	**27**

Goalies: CAN Dryden; SOV Tretiak.
Referees: Josef Kompalla, Bata.

the biggest moment in Canadian hockey history. The Canadian people threw parades to welcome us back. Before I knew it, our faces were on postage stamps and coins, if you could believe that. Even today, not a week goes by where someone doesn't come up to me at the supermarket or bank or wherever and ask me about the Series. But if we lost, I would be telling you this story from under a rock somewhere in the wilderness of northern Ontario.

As the minutes ticked away in Game 8, it looked as if we were going to lose. The Soviets had a 5–3 lead as we filed back into the dressing room after the second period of the eighth and final game of the series. Outside, people in the streets of Moscow had begun to celebrate. Even if we had come back to tie the game—and that seemed nothing short of a miracle at that point—the Soviets would have won the series. Without an overtime period, the series would have ended 3–3–2, and the Soviets would have won by virtue of scoring the most goals in the series.

What we needed was a win. It may surprise you to hear this, but in that locker room that night there were no long faces. There were fire-and-brimstone speeches. There was only focus. There was just a job that had to be done. We knew what I think all professional athletes know: If you panic, you'll get off your game.

I still remember finding out that I had been picked. It was a great honor because they had so many players to choose from. I reported to camp in Toronto in August with the other 34 guys and began an intense training program. My defensive partner on the Chicago Blackhawks, Pat Stapleton, and I didn't dress for the first game of the series, a loss in Montreal.

Coach Harry Sinden put Stapleton and me in the line-up for Game 2, a win in Toronto. Pat and I stayed together through a tie in Game 3 and a loss in Game 4, in which the Vancouver crowd gave us a cold send-off for the next four games in Russia.

Before we resumed the series, we played some exhibition games in Sweden against its national team. It had been weird since training camp to look around the room at the guys you had played against for years and then, suddenly, you were all on the same team. It was a big adjustment. The Soviets, on the other hand, had played together for years.

Even when we lost Game 5, I could see the team coming together. Game 6 was a big win for us. Ken Dryden played terrific in net. So did Tony Esposito in Game 7, which we also won. Suddenly, there was hope we could win the series after all.

That hope began to dissipate late in the second period in Game 8—the game I'll never forget. It began as a seesaw battle: They scored, we scored, they scored, we scored, they scored, we scored. My second-period goal at about the halfway point of the game made it 3–3. We were on the power play when the Rangers' Rod Gilbert was just cradling the puck by the boards. He was being patient and the Soviets wouldn't move out of position to go after him. So he stayed there a little longer. I think he got them a little spellbound because I began to sneak unnoticed in the back door. Finally, with every Soviet defender on the ice mesmerized by Gilbert's stickwork, he slipped the pass to me and I shot it past their goalie, Vladislav Tretiak.

A minute later, however, the Soviets regained the lead. And five minutes later, they had a two-goal lead and a firm stranglehold on the series. We went back to the dressing room in a hole, but we weren't about to quit.

Phil Esposito got us back to within a goal. Then Cournoyer found a loose puck in front of the net and somehow stuffed it past a pile of bodies in the goalmouth. In fact, the red light didn't go on and NHLPA president Alan Eagleson got tangled up with some Soviet guards trying to make his way to the scorekeeper's area. When peace was restored, there were about seven minutes left.

We still needed one more goal. We knew a tie wouldn't help us. With less than a minute to go, one of the Soviet defensemen made a play he'll probably remember for the rest of his life. He tried to make a pass up to a

Outside, people in the streets of Moscow had begun to celebrate. Even if we had come back to tie the game—and that seemed nothing short of a miracle at that point—the Soviets would have won the series.

winger on the right side. Espo—he was so clutch for us that whole series—intercepted it and threw it on Tretiak in desperation. Tretiak stopped it, but left a rebound.

Paul Henderson happened to be there. He had moved in on a forecheck behind the net, and had started back up the ice when Espo stole the puck. Henderson slammed on the brakes and found a rebound sitting there. He took one shot, but Tretiak made a save. He took another and scored.

It was a moment to celebrate, but just for a moment. There was still 34 seconds to play. Stapleton and I talked briefly about how explosive these guys were and how we couldn't fool around in those final 34 seconds.

When the puck was dropped, you could tell they pretty much had it. We had taken a lot of wind out of their sails. About the most tense moment came when I had the puck just inside my blue line and just wanted to bump it out. The puck started to go down the ice and it looked like it would be icing. That would have led to a face-off in our zone, which could have led to a problem. One of their defensemen, however, raced back and got it before it went for icing.

Before we knew it, we were celebrating one of the greatest and most improbable victories of all time.

—*As told to Chuck O'Donnell*

After a long minor league apprenticeship served under the legendary but infamously eccentric Eddie Shore, **Bill White** got his break with the NHL expansion in 1967–68. The rangy defensive specialist joined the Los Angeles Kings, where he played until traded to Chicago in February 1970. White made the Second All-Star Team in 1972, 1973 and 1974. A neck injury forced him into retirement in 1976.

We made the Stanley Cup playoffs a few times in the dozen years I was with the New York Rangers, but we never got into

**MAY 1, 1965
MONTREAL FORUM, MONTREAL
MONTREAL 4, CHICAGO 0**

FIRST PERIOD
1. MON Beliveau (Duff, Rousseau) 0:14.
2. MON Duff (Beliveau, Rousseau) 5:03.
3. MON Cournoyer (Duff, Rousseau) 16:29.
4. MON Richard (Harris), 18:45 (PP).
Penalties: MON Harris (holding) 7:55; CHI Pilote (hooking) 16:08; CHI Esposito (hooking) 18:00; MON Harris (elbowing, misconduct) 19:56.

SECOND PERIOD
Penalties: CHI Nesterenko (hooking) 7:11; CHI Jarrett (charging) 17:42.

THIRD PERIOD
Penalties: CHI Vasko (high-sticking) 4:03; MON Richard (slashing) 4:03; CHI Mikita (slashing) 6:16; CHI Mohns (holding) 9:16; MON Provost (hooking) 14:23; MON Beliveau (tripping) 17:39; CHI Henry (high-sticking) 18:30; MON Provost (hooking) 19:27.

SHOTS ON GOAL:

MON	15	12	8	**35**
CHI	9	6	5	**20**

Goalies: MON Worsley: CHI Hall
Referee: John Ashley
Linesmen: Matt Pavelich, John D'Amico

the finals. Even when we did finish in second place, we got beat in the first round of the playoffs by the fourth-place team.

In 1963, the Rangers traded me to Montreal and I began to think, well maybe now we'll get into the finals. When you're with a club like Montreal, you always know that the chances of getting into the finals and winning the Stanley Cup are good.

It took a little bit of time, though. I even played quite a few games at Quebec of the American League the next couple of seasons before I got my chance in the Stanley Cup finals. That came in 1964–65, after we beat Toronto in the first round. We went up against Chicago in the finals and it was just one of those things, each team winning the games on its own ice until we got to the seventh game.

I was going pretty good until I got hurt. I shut out Chicago in the second game, but they beat me in the fourth game, and that's when I was injured. Stan Mikita ran into me and I twisted my knee. It was pretty bad and I thought I was through for the series.

We won the fifth game at Montreal and Chicago won the sixth game 2–1 on their ice to set up the seventh game for the Forum on Saturday, May 1, 1965. I'd skated a little during practice Friday but hadn't thought too much about it. Fact is, I didn't even expect to suit up for the game. I was sure [coach] Toe Blake would use Charlie Hodge. He had an extra goalie to suit up and take my place on the bench.

I was sitting in a restaurant having coffee with my wife that afternoon when one of our trainers came in and walked up to me. "Gump, Blake says he wants you to play tonight," he told me.

"You must be kidding," I said. "I've only been on skates once since I got hurt."

"No, Blake said to find you and tell you he wants you to play tonight."

Well, Blake had asked me how I felt after practice and I said, "Pretty good," because I

did feel good. He thought if I felt that way it was all right to play me.

Later he told people, "He practiced Friday and looked hot so I decided to take a chance with him. I figured Gump would be less nervous under pressure than Charlie Hodge."

I can tell you I was nervous enough. Just a couple of days earlier I couldn't even walk stairs and here I was getting ready to play the seventh game of the Stanley Cup finals with everything on the line. Luckily, I didn't have all that much time to think about it. Blake hadn't told me he was going to use me until just a few hours before the game. It didn't really hit me until I started getting dressed for the game.

But the way the game started out, I calmed down in a hurry. We got a great break right at the start and that took the pressure off me, although you couldn't really relax against Chicago, with guys like Bobby Hull, Mikita, Kenny Wharram and Doug Mohns coming at you. Right at the beginning, the puck skipped from the center zone over Chicago defenseman Pierre Pilote's stick toward their net. I think Dickie Duff for us was the first to get to the puck and he passed it to Jean Beliveau, coming in on to the left of Chicago goalie Glenn Hall. Beliveau got his stick on the puck and beat Hall for the first goal just 14 seconds into the game.

Something like that always takes the sting out of the other team. It must have had an effect on Chicago. They must have said to themselves "Oh-oh, here we go," and began to play a little down. Whatever it was, we got three more goals in the first period, by Duff, Yvan Cournoyer and Henri Richard to make it 4–0. Chicago just couldn't get untangled.

There was no way our guys were going to let them score so I had an easier game than I might have. I can remember only one big save and the reason I remember it is because it came when we were still ahead only 1–0. All of a sudden I looked up and I saw Camille Henry standing in front of me, with the puck right in front of the net. It wasn't an easy situation, no matter who was there, but Henry was tougher in front than most. I played with him in New York and knew how accurate and deadly he was at short range. He got the shot

off and I stopped it with my shoulder. The puck must have popped over the net. I don't know whether it helped me a bit having played with him or not, or whether I was just lucky. But that was the big save.

In a Cup game, when you get in front, stay in front. Those games are played tight and one goal can do it. The one goal was enough, too. Chicago had a hard time getting the puck into our end and in the third period, with five minutes to go, there was no way they could even get near me. We had five guys back, dumping the puck into center ice, more or less playing for me and the shutout. I got it, too, my second in that series. The score stayed 1–0 right to the end

and for the last five minutes of the game, you couldn't even hear yourself think, with everybody singing and yelling.

When the game ended, my teammates lifted both me and Toe Blake on their shoulders and carried us around the ice. Like I said, with the way our guys played, I didn't have to make that many big saves—or I don't remember making them. But even then, just winning that first Stanley Cup after 13 years of playing hockey has to be the biggest thrill I've ever had.

—As told to George Vass

Lorne "Gump" Worsley won the 1953 Calder Trophy with the New York Rangers. Although the team struggled perennially, Worsley earned respect for his reliable play under a decade of difficult circumstances. Traded to Montreal in June 1963, he won four Stanley Cup rings in the next six seasons. "The Gumper" joined the Minnesota North Stars in February 1970 and retired after the 1973–74 season, 44 years old. He entered the Hall of Fame in 1980.

INDEX

Numbers in *italics* refer to photographs and captions.

ACKNOWLEDGMENTS

Thanks to the team at Firefly Books for another great year. Lionel Koffler, Michael Worek and Brad Wilson shared my enthusiasm for the stories in *Hockey Digest* and made this book possible. Brad gently but persistently steered the project to a successful finish, with Lionel and Michael adding their invaluable insight at the critical junctures. Bob Wilcox got us excited with his design ideas and Christine Gilham helped realize them. I'm grateful to you all.

This book owes everything to the players who have shared their stories and to the *Hockey Digest* writers who transcribed them. You did a marvelous job. Special kudos to George Vass, the first to gather "The Game I'll Never Forget" reminiscences, and to Chuck O'Donnell, the magazine's current historian. Thank you also to Will Wagner, Editor in Chief at Century Publishing Co., for agreeing that such fine writing should be gathered into a beautiful book and arranging for permissions.

Michelle Good helped tremendously in gathering the statistical summaries for most of these games. Thank you to Dave McCarthy and Benny Ercolani of the National Hockey League for setting up Michelle's unfettered access to the league archives.

Bruce Bennett Studios provided the majority of the photos for the book. Glen Levy deserves special praise for his enthusiastic efforts in poring over thousands of images and providing me with great choices. Craig Campbell of the Hockey Hall of Fame was also, as usual, completely dependable in finding the great photos we needed to finish the book.

While completing this project took most of my attention at times, I've also been working for Ontario Energy Savings Corporation. To Kelly Krekel, Tammy Trotter, Hilda Walsh, Codey McCarthy and a large group of co-workers: thank you for your patience with me. I've learned a great deal from all of you about dreams, goals and focus. I am a better writer for this, as well as a better person. Your lessons will always be appreciated.

My family continues to be a blessing in my life. My parents, Alanson and Nora McDonell, have been as supportive with their interest and their time as a son could wish. Likewise, my sisters Anne, Carolyn, Marjorie, Barbara and Janet and my brother Kevin, along with their respective spouses, have been encouraging in every way. My brother-in-law Randy Gordon has given deeply of himself, and his wife Nancy and daughter Karen have also been a great support. Eric, Eileen and Mary Gordon have also been real boosters.

Above all, though, I owe my greatest debts to the good people I share daily life with. Sue Gordon has been the wind in my sails during the good times and my anchor in stormy seas. Sue had belief in me as a writer even before I did; I wouldn't be the person I am without her. Our children, Quinn, Tara and Isaac, have been patient about the little time I have had with them this year. These four people, the greatest treasure I have gathered in my lifetime, have worked hard to keep our household functioning smoothly, sacrificing their time to make my life easier. Thank you, with all my love.

—*Chris McDonell*